KETO
COOKBOOK
FOR BEGINNERS

Quick & Easy 800 Recipes
on a Budget

Barbara McCaulley

CONTENTS

POULTRY 62

BEEF 78

PORK 92

SEAFOOD 106

VEGAN & VEGETARIAN 112

SNACKS & SIDE DISHES 125

INTRODUCTION

Want to follow a ketogenic diet but not sure where to start? Struggling with finding delicious and tummy-filling recipes when going "against the grains"? Do not worry! This book will not only give you amazing keto recipes that will get you started in a jiffy, but it will also teach you the greatest tricks for adopting a keto lifestyle forever.

Mouth-watering delights for any occasion and any eater, you will not believe that these recipes will help you restore your health and slim down your body. Ditching carbs do not mean ditching yummy treats, and with these ingenious recipes, you will see that for yourself.

Successfully practiced for more than nine decades, the ketogenic diet has proven to be the ultimate long-term diet for any person. The restriction list may frighten many, but the truth is, this diet is super adaptable, and the food combinations and tasty meals are pretty endless.

KETOGENIC DIET — THE NEW LIFESTYLE

It is common knowledge that our body is designed to run on carbohydrates. We use them to provide our body with the energy that is required for normal functioning. However, what many people are clueless about, is that carbs are not the only source of fuel that our bodies can use. Just like they can run on carbs, our bodies can also use fats as an energy source. When we ditch the carbs and focus on providing our bodies with more fat, then we are embarking on the ketogenic train.

Despite what many people think, the ketogenic diet is not just another fad diet. It has been around since 1920 and has resulted in outstanding results and amazingly successful stories. If you are new to the keto world and have no idea what I am talking about, let me simplify this for you.

For you to truly understand what the ketogenic diet is all about and why you should choose to follow it, let me first explain what happens to your body after consuming a carb-loaded meal.

Imagine you have just swallowed a giant bowl of spaghetti. Your tummy is full, your taste buds are satisfied, and your body is provided with much more carbs than necessary. After consumption, your body immediately starts the process of digestion, during which your body will break down the consumed carbs into glucose, which is a source of energy that your body depends on. So one might ask," what is wrong with carbs?". There are some things. For starters, they raise the blood sugar, they make us fat, and in short, they hurt our overall health. So, how can ketogenic diet help?

A ketogenic diet skips this process by lowering the carbohydrate intake and providing high fat and moderate protein levels. Now, since there is no adequate amount of carbs to use as energy, your liver is forced to find the fuel elsewhere. And since your body is packed with lots of fat, the liver starts using these extra levels of fat as an energy source.

THE BENEFITS OF THE KETO DIET

Despite the fact that it is still considered to be 'controversial,' the keto diet is the best dietary choice that one can make. From weight loss to longevity, here are the benefits that following a ketogenic diet can bring to your life:

Loss of Appetite

Cannot tame your cravings? Do not worry. This diet will neither leave you exhausted nor with a rumbling gut. The ketogenic diet will help you say no to that second piece of cake. Once you train your body to run on fat and not on carbs, you will experience a drop in your appetite that will work magic for your figure.

Weight Loss

Since the body is forced to produce only a small amount of glucose, it will also be forced to lower the insulin production. When that happens, your kidneys will start getting rid of the extra sodium, which will lead to weight loss.

HDL Cholesterol Increase

While consuming a diet high in fat and staying clear of the harmful glucose, your body will experience a rise in the good HDL cholesterol levels, which will, in turn, reduce the risk for many cardiovascular problems.

Drop in Blood Pressure

Cutting back on carbs will also bring your blood pressure in check. The drop in the blood pressure can prevent many health problems such as strokes or heart diseases.

Lower Risk of Diabetes

Although this probably goes without saying, it is important to mention this one. When you ditch the carbs, your body is forced to lower the glucose productivity significantly, which naturally leads to a lower risk of diabetes.

Improved Brain Function

Many studies have shown that replacing carbohydrates with fat as an energy source leads to mental clarity and improved brain function. This is yet another reason why you should go keto.

Longevity

I am not saying that this diet will turn you into a 120-hundred-year-old monk; however, it has been scientifically proven that once the oxidative stress levels are lowered, the lifespan gets extended. And since this diet can result in a significant drop in the oxidative stress levels, the corresponding effect it could have on a person's lifespan is clear.

THE KETO PLATE

First, just because it is called a 'diet' doesn't mean that you are about to spend your days in starvation. The ketogenic diet will neither tell you not to eat five times a day if you want to nor will it leave your bellies empty.

The only rule that the keto diet has is to eat fewer carbohydrates, more foods that are high in fat, and consume a moderate protein intake. But how much is too much and what is the right amount? The general rule of a thumb is that your daily nutrition should consist of: **70-75% Fat; 20-25% Protein; 5-10% Carbohydrates**

To be more precise, it is not recommended that you consume more than 20 grams of carbs when on a ketogenic diet. This macronutrient percentage, however, can be achieved in whichever way you and your belly are comfortable with. For instance, if you crave a carb meal now, and want to eat, for example, 16 grams of carbs at once, you can do so, as long as your other meals do not contain more than 4 grams of carbs combined.

Some recipes in this book offer 0 grams of carbs, while others are packed with a few grams. By making a proper meal plan that works for you, you can easily skip the inconvenience cloaked around this diet, and start receiving the fantastic benefits.

KETO FLU

The term Keto flu describes a very common experience for new ketoers, but it often goes away in the first week. When starting with keto, you may have some slight discomfort or feel fatigue, headache, nausea, cramps, etc.

The reasons Keto flu occurs are two:

1. **Keto diet is diuretic**; therefore you visit the bathroom quite often, which leads to the loss of electrolytes and water. The solution is either drinking more water or bouillon cube, to replenish electrolytes reserves. I suggest that you also increase the consumption of potassium, magnesium. calcium, and phosphorus.

2. **Shifting to Keto is at first a big shock for the body**. The reason is that it's designed to process carbs and now there are almost none. You may feel increased fatigue, nausea, etc. The solution is to decrease carbs intake gradually.

WHAT TO EAT

Certain foods will help you up your fat intake and provide you with more longer-lasting energy: Meats, Eggs, Fish and Seafood, Bacon, Sausage, Cacao and sugar-free chocolate, Avocado and berries, Leafy Greens - all of them, Vegetables: cucumber, zucchini, asparagus, broccoli, onion, Brussel sprout, cabbage, tomato, eggplants, seaweed, peppers, squash, Full-Fat Dairy (heavy cream, yogurt, sour cream, cheese, etc.); Nuts — nuts are packed with healthy fats, chestnuts, and cashews, as they contain more carbs than the rest of the nuts. Macadamia nuts, walnuts pecans, and almonds are the best for the Keto diet.; Seeds - chia, flaxseeds, sunflower seeds; Sweeteners - stevia, erythritol, xylitol, monk fruit sugar. I use mostly stevia and erythritol. The latter is a sugar alcohol, but it doesn't spike blood sugar thanks to its zero glycemic indexes; Milk - consume full-fat coconut milk or almond milk; Flour - coconut or almond flour and almond meal; Oils - olive oil, avocado oil; Fats - butter or ghee;

WHAT TO AVOID

For you to stay on track with your Keto diet, there are certain foods that you need to say farewell to:

Sugar, honey, agave, soda and sugary drinks, and fruit juices. Starchy vegetables such as potatoes, beans, legumes, peas, yams, and corn are usually packed with tons of carbs, so they must be avoided. However, sneaking some starch when your daily carb limit allows, is not exactly a sin. Flours - all-purpose, wheat, and rice. Dried fruits and fruit in general, except for berries. Grains — rice, wheat, and everything made from grains such as pasta or traditional breads are not allowed. No margarine, milk, refined oils and fats such as corn oil, canola oil, vegetable oil, etc.

KETO SWAPS

Just because you are not allowed to eat rice or pasta, doesn't mean that you have to sacrifice eating risotto or spaghetti. Well, sort of. For every forbidden item on the keto diet, there is a healthier replacement that will not contradict your dietary goal and will still taste amazing.

Here are the last keto swaps that you need to know to overcome the cravings quicker, and become a Keto chef:

Bread and Buns → Bread made from nut flour, mushroom caps, cucumber slices

Wraps and Tortillas → Wraps and tortillas made from nut flour, lettuce leaves, kale leaves

Pasta and Spaghetti → Spiralized veggies such as zoodles, spaghetti squash, etc.

Lasagna Noodles → Zucchini or eggplant slices

Rice → Cauliflower rice (ground in a food processor)

Mashed Potatoes → Mashed Cauliflower or other veggies

Hash Browns → Cauliflower or Spaghetti squash

Flour → Coconut flour, Hazelnut flour, Almond Flour

Breadcrumbs → Almond flour

Pizza Crust → Crust made with almond flour or cauliflower crust

French Fries → Carrot sticks, Turnip fries, Zucchini fries

Potato Chips → Zucchini chips, Kale chips

Croutons → Bacon bits, nuts, sunflower seeds, flax crackers

Traditional High Carb Comfort Foods Made Keto

Bagel 1 plain 50g net carbs → **Low-Carb or FatHead Bagel** 1 plain 4.7g net carbs

Bread 1 slice 12g net carbs → **Keto Bread** - 1 slice 1.6g net carbs

Risotto 1 cup 40g net carbs → **Cauliflower Risotto** 1 cup 4.2g net carbs

Mashed Potatoes 1 cup 30g net carbs → **Mashed Cauliflower** 1 cup 5.3g net carbs

Roasted Potatoes 1 cup 20g net carbs → **Roasted Radishes** 1 cup 4.4g net carbs

Pasta 1 cup 40g net carbs → **Zoodles/Shirataki Noodles** 1 cup 3.6g/1.3g net carbs

Pepperoni Pizza 1 slice 23g net carbs → **Cheesy Bell Pepper Pizza** 3.5g net carbs

Waffle 1 waffle 17g → **Keto Waffle** 1 waffle 4.6g net carbs

GETTING STARTED IN 5 EASY STEPS

1. **Time to Revise The Pantry** - get rid of all pasta, rice, bread, potatoes, corn, wraps, sugary foods, drinks, legumes, fruits, etc. The less you see those foods, the less you will be tempted to drop on the Keto diet.

2. **Get the Basics** - now that you've cleaned out your pantry it's time to restock. Your journey toward a healthy and energetic lifestyle has started!

3. **Set Up Your Kitchen** - cooking delicious food requires additional help from some kitchen appliances. They will make your life easier and the cooking quick and efficient.

   My kitchen always has food scales, a blender/food processor, hand mixer, cast iron pans, baking dish, heatproof bowls, and a spiralizer. You will need most of these for the recipes in this cookbook, so I strongly suggest you acquire them to maximize results.

4. **Create a Meal Plan** - having a meal plan is a great start on the Keto diet. It improves your chances of success, and it's essential for beginners on a diet. That's why my team and I developed a complete 21-Day Meal Plan, which, if followed strictly, would make the transition to Keto diet smooth and delicious.

5. **Try to Exercise** - your body is designed to be in a constant move. Being on Keto diet isn't going to change that. Yeah, I know that it's difficult and you feel tired. You also have to think constantly about the macros and the food you are eating, but I guarantee you that the more you exercise, the easier you will stick to the diet. Any anaerobic activity would suffice - jogging, running, bicycling, even walking for at least 30 minutes a day will activate your body for optimal performance. I would also suggest some strength exercises but always consult previously on how to train, being on a diet, with your fitness instructor.

BREAKFAST & BRUNCH

Kale & Sausage Omelet

Ingredients for 2 servings

4 eggs
2 cups kale, chopped
4 oz sausages, chopped
4 tbsp ricotta cheese

6 ounces roasted squash
2 tbsp olive oil
Salt and black pepper to taste
Fresh parsley to garnish

Directions and Total Time: approx. 15 minutes

Beat eggs in a bowl, season with salt and pepper, and stir in kale and ricotta. In another bowl, mash the squash. Add the squash to the egg mixture. Heat ¼ tbsp of olive oil in a pan and cook sausage for 5 minutes. Drizzle the remaining olive oil. Pour the egg mixture over. Cook for 2 minutes per side. Run a spatula around the edges of the omelet, slide it onto a platter. Serve topped with parsley.

Per serving: Cal 258; Net Carbs 3.5g; Fat 22g; Protein 12g

Sausage Quiche with Tomatoes

Ingredients for 6 servings

6 eggs
12 ounces raw sausage rolls
10 cherry tomatoes, halved
2 tbsp heavy cream

2 tbsp Parmesan cheese
Salt and black pepper to taste
2 tbsp chopped parsley
5 eggplant slices

Directions and Total Time: approx. 55 minutes

Preheat oven to 370 F. Press the sausage roll at the bottom of a greased pie dish. Arrange the eggplants on top of the sausage. Top with cherry tomatoes. Whisk together the eggs along with the heavy cream, salt, Parmesan cheese, and pepper. Spoon the egg mixture over the sausage. Bake for about 40 minutes. Serve scattered with parsley.

Per serving: Cal 340; Net Carbs 3g; Fat 28g; Protein 1.7g

Bacon & Cream Cheese Mug Muffins

Ingredients for 2 servings

¼ cup flax meal
1 egg
2 tbsp heavy cream
2 tbsp pesto
¼ cup almond flour

¼ tsp baking soda
Salt and black pepper to taste
2 tbsp cream cheese
4 slices bacon
½ medium avocado, sliced

Directions and Total Time: approx. 10 minutes

Mix together flax meal, flour, and baking soda in a bowl. Add egg, heavy cream, and pesto, and whisk well. Season with salt and pepper. Divide the mixture between 2 ramekins. Microwave for 60-90 seconds. Let cool slightly before filling. In a nonstick skillet, cook bacon until crispy; set aside. Invert the muffins onto a plate and cut in half, crosswise. Assemble the sandwiches by spreading cream cheese and topping with bacon and avocado slices.

Per serving: Cal 511; Net Carbs 4.5g; Fat 38g; Protein 16g

Italian Omelet

Ingredients for 2 servings

4 eggs
4 oz mozzarella, grated
2 tbsp butter

8 thin slices chorizo
1 tomato, sliced
Salt and black pepper to taste

Directions and Total Time: approx. 15 minutes

Whisk the eggs with salt and pepper. Melt butter in a skillet and cook the eggs for 30 seconds. Spread the chorizo slices over. Arrange the sliced tomato and mozzarella over the chorizo. Cook for about 3 minutes. Cover the skillet and continue cooking for 3 more minutes until omelet is completely set. Run a spatula around the edges of the omelet and flip it onto a plate, folded side down. Serve.

Per serving: Cal 451; Net Carbs 3g; Fat 36.5g; Protein 30g

Broccoli & Red Bell Pepper Tart

Ingredients for 6 servings

12 eggs
1 ½ cups mozzarella, shredded
1 ½ cups almond milk
½ tsp dried thyme

Salt to taste
1 red bell pepper, sliced
½ cup broccoli, chopped
1 clove garlic, minced

For the Tart

¾ cup almond flour
2 oz cold butter

1 tbsp cold water
2 eggs

Directions and Total Time: approx. 60 minutes

Preheat oven to 400 F. Make breadcrumbs by rubbing the butter into the almond flour and a pinch of salt in a bowl. Add cold water and 2 eggs and mix everything until dough is formed. Press it into a greased baking dish and refrigerate for 25 minutes. Beat the 12 eggs with almond milk, thyme, and salt, then, stir in bell pepper, broccoli, and garlic; set aside. Remove dough from the fridge and prick it with a fork. Bake for 20 minutes. Spread mozzarella cheese on the pie crust and top with egg mixture. Bake for 30 minutes until the tart is set. Slice into pieces to serve.

Per serving: Cal 290; Net Carbs 7.3g; Fat 18g; Protein 22.6g

Breakfast Hash with Bacon & Zucchini

Ingredients for 1 serving

1 zucchini, diced
4 bacon slices
2 eggs

2 tbsp coconut oil
½ small onion, chopped
1 tbsp chopped parsley

Directions and Total Time: approx. 25 minutes

Cook bacon in a skillet for 5 minutes, until crispy; set aside. Warm coconut oil and cook the onion for 3 minutes. Add in zucchini and cook for 10 more minutes. Transfer to a plate and season with salt. Crack the eggs into the same skillet and fry. Top the zucchini mixture with bacon slices and fried eggs. Serve sprinkled with parsley.

Per serving: Cal 423; Net Carbs 6.6g; Fat 35g; Protein 17g

Ham & Egg Cups

Ingredients for 4 servings

1 cup chopped ham	4 eggs
2 tbsp grated Parmesan	⅓ cup mayonnaise
1 tbsp chopped parsley	¼ tsp garlic powder
2 tbsp almond flour	½ chopped onion

Directions and Total Time: approx. 35 minutes

Preheat oven to 375 F. Place onion, ham, and garlic in a food processor and pulse until ground. Stir in mayo, flour, and Parmesan. Press this mixture into greased muffin cups. Bake for 5 minutes. Crack an egg into each muffin cup. Return to the oven and bake for 20 minutes until the tops are firm and eggs are cooked. Let cool a bit and serve.

Per serving: Cal 267; Net Carbs 1g; Fat 18g; Protein 13.5g

Herbed Buttered Eggs

Ingredients for 2 servings

1 tbsp coconut oil	½ cup chopped parsley
2 tbsp butter	½ cup chopped cilantro
1 tsp fresh thyme	¼ tsp cumin
4 eggs	¼ tsp cayenne pepper
2 garlic cloves, minced	Salt and black pepper to taste

Directions and Total Time: approx. 15 minutes

Warm coconut oil and butter in a skillet and add garlic and thyme; cook for 30 seconds. Sprinkle with parsley and cilantro. Carefully crack the eggs into the skillet. Lower the heat and cook for 4-6 minutes. Adjust the seasoning. When the eggs are set, turn the heat off and serve.

Per serving: Cal 321; Net Carbs 2.5g; Fat 21g; Protein 12g

Tofu Scramble with Mushrooms & Spinach

Ingredients for 4 servings

1 tbsp butter	16 oz firm tofu, crumbled
1 cup sliced white mushrooms	½ cup spinach, sliced
2 cloves garlic, minced	6 fresh eggs

Directions and Total Time: approx. 30 minutes

Melt butter in a skillet over and sauté mushrooms and garlic for 5 minutes. Crumble tofu into the skillet, season with salt and pepper. Cook with continuous stirring for 6 minutes. Introduce the spinach and cook for 5 minutes. Crack the eggs into a bowl, whisk until well combined and creamy in color, and pour all over the kale. Use a spatula to immediately stir the eggs while cooking until scrambled and no more runny, about 5 minutes. Serve.

Per serving: Cal 469; Net Carbs 5g; Fat 39g; Protein 25g

Omelet Wrap with Avocado and Salmon

Ingredients for 2 servings

1 avocado, sliced	2 oz smoked salmon, sliced
2 tbsp chopped chives	1 spring onion, sliced
4 eggs, beaten	2 tbsp butter
3 tbsp cream cheese	Salt and black pepper to taste

Directions and Total Time: approx. 15 minutes

In a small bowl, combine the chives and cream cheese; set aside. Season the eggs with salt and pepper. Melt butter in a pan and add the eggs; cook for 3 minutes. Flip the omelet over and cook for another 2 minutes until golden. Remove to a plate and spread the chive mixture over. Top with salmon, avocado, and onion slices. Wrap and serve.

Per serving: Cal 514; Net Carbs 5.8g; Fat 47g; Protein 37g

Coconut Gruyere Biscuits

Ingredients for 4 servings

4 eggs	½ tsp xanthan gum
¼ cup butter melted	¼ tsp baking powder
¼ tsp salt	2 tsp garlic powder
1/3 cup coconut flour	¼ tsp onion powder
¼ cup coconut flakes	½ cup grated Gruyere cheese

Directions and Total Time: approx. 30 minutes

Preheat oven to 350 F; line a baking sheet with parchment paper. In a food processor, mix eggs, butter, and salt until smooth. Add coconut flour, coconut flakes, xanthan gum, baking, garlic, and onion powders, and Gruyere cheese. Combine smoothly. Mold 12 balls out of the mixture and arrange on the baking sheet at 2-inch intervals. Bake for 25 minutes or until the biscuits are golden brown.

Per serving: Cal 267; Net Carbs 5.1g, Fat 26g, Protein 12g

Feta & Spinach Frittata with Tomatoes

Ingredients for 4 servings

5 ounces spinach	10 eggs
8 oz crumbled feta cheese	3 tbsp olive oil
1 pint halved cherry tomatoes	4 scallions, diced

Directions and Total Time: approx. 35 minutes

Preheat oven to 350 F. Drizzle the oil in a casserole and place in the oven until heated. In a bowl, whisk eggs along with pepper and salt. Stir in spinach, feta cheese, and scallions. Pour the mixture into the casserole, top with the cherry tomatoes and place back in the oven. Bake for 25 minutes. Cut the frittata into wedges and serve with salad.

Per serving: Cal 461; Net Carbs 6g; Fat 35g; Protein 26g

Coconut Almond Muffins

Ingredients for 4 servings

2 cups almond flour	¼ cup melted butter
2 tsp baking powder	1 egg
8 oz ricotta cheese, softened	1 cup coconut milk

Directions and Total Time: approx. 30 minutes

Preheat oven to 400 F. Grease a muffin tray with cooking spray. Mix flour, baking powder, and salt in a bowl.

In a separate bowl, beat cream cheese and butter using a hand mixer and whisk in the egg and coconut milk. Fold in flour, and spoon the batter into the muffin cups two-thirds way up. Bake for 20 minutes, remove to a wire rack to cool slightly for 5 minutes before serving.

Per serving: Cal 320; Net Carbs 6g; Fat 30.6g; Protein 4g

Almond Butter Shake

Ingredients for 2 servings

3 cups almond milk	4 tbsp flax meal
3 tbsp almond butter	1 scoop collagen peptides
⅛ tsp almond extract	A pinch of salt
1 tsp cinnamon	15 drops stevia

Directions and Total Time: approx. 2 minutes

Add milk, butter, flax meal, almond extract, collagen, salt, and stevia to the blender. Blitz until uniform and smooth. Serve into smoothie glasses, sprinkled with cinnamon.

Per serving: Cal 326; Net Carbs 6g; Fat 27g; Protein 19g

Raspberry Mini Tarts

Ingredients for 4 servings

For the crust:

6 tbsp butter, melted	1/3 cup xylitol
2 cups almond flour	1 tsp cinnamon powder

For the filling:

3 cups raspberries, mashed	½ tsp cinnamon powder
½ tsp fresh lemon juice	¼ cup xylitol sweetener
¼ cup butter, melted	

Directions and Total Time: approx. 25 min + chilling time

Preheat oven to 350 F and lightly grease 4 (2x12-inch) mini tart tins with cooking spray. In a food processor, blend butter, flour, xylitol, and cinnamon. Divide and spread the dough in the tart tins and bake for 15 minutes. In a bowl, mix raspberries, lemon juice, butter, cinnamon, and xylitol. Pour filling into the crust, gently tap on a flat surface to release air bubbles and refrigerate for 1 hour.

Per serving: Cal 435; Net Carbs 4.8g, Fat 29g, Protein 2g

Morning Beef Stacks with Lemon

Ingredients for 6 servings

6 ground beef patties	2 tsp fresh lemon juice
4 tbsp olive oil	6 fresh eggs
2 ripe avocados, pitted	Red pepper flakes to garnish

Directions and Total Time: approx. 25 minutes

In a skillet, warm oil and fry patties for 8 minutes. Remove to a plate. Spoon avocado into a bowl, mash with the lemon juice, and season with salt and pepper. Spread the mash on the patties. Boil 3 cups of water in a pan over high heat, and reduce to simmer (don't boil). Crack each egg into a bowl and put the egg into the simmering water. Poach for 2-3 minutes. Remove to a plate. Top stack with eggs, sprinkle with chili flakes and chives.

Per serving: Cal 378; Net Carbs 5g; Fat 23g; Protein 16g

Coconut Blini with Berry Drizzle

Ingredients for 6 servings

Pancakes

1 cup cream cheese	1 tsp baking powder
1 cup coconut flour	1 ½ cups coconut milk
1 tsp salt	1 tsp vanilla extract
2 tsp xylitol	6 large eggs
1 tsp baking soda	¼ cup olive oil

Blackberry Sauce

3 cups fresh blackberries	½ tsp arrowroot starch
1 lemon, juiced	A pinch of salt
½ cup xylitol	

Directions and Total Time: approx. 40 minutes

Put coconut flour, salt, xylitol, baking soda and powder in a bowl and whisk to combine. Add in milk, cream cheese, vanilla, eggs, and olive oil and whisk until smooth. Set a pan and pour in a small ladle of batter. Cook on one side for 2 minutes, flip, and cook for 2 minutes. Transfer to a plate and repeat the cooking process until the batter is exhausted. Pour the berries and half cup of water into a saucepan and bring to a boil. Simmer for 12 minutes. Pour in xylitol, stir, and continue cooking for 5 minutes. Stir in salt and lemon juice. Mix arrowroot starch with 1 tbsp of water; pour the mixture into the berries. Stir and continue cooking the sauce to thicken to your desire. Serve.

Per serving: Cal 433; Net Carbs 4.9g; Fat 39g; Protein 8.2g

Pesto Bread Twists

Ingredients for 6 servings

1 tbsp flax seed powder + 3 tbsp water	
1½ cups grated mozzarella	1 tsp baking powder
4 tbsp coconut flour	5 tbsp butter
½ cup almond flour	2 oz pesto

Directions and Total Time: approx. 35 minutes

For flax egg, mix flax seed powder with water in a bowl, and let to soak for 5 minutes. Preheat oven to 350 F and line a baking sheet with parchment paper. In a bowl, combine coconut flour, almond flour, salt, and baking powder. Melt butter and cheese in a skillet and stir in the flax egg. Mix in flour mixture until a firm dough forms. Divide the mixture between 2 parchment papers, then use a rolling pin to flatten out the dough of about an inch's thickness. Remove the parchment paper on top and spread pesto all over the dough. Cut the dough into strips, twist each piece, and place on the baking sheet. Brush with olive oil and bake for 15-20 minutes until golden brown.

Per serving: Cal 206; Net Carbs 3g; Fat 17g; Protein 8g

Broccoli Hash Browns

Ingredients for 4 servings

3 tbsp flax seed powder + 9 tbsp water
1 head broccoli, rinse and cut into florets
½ white onion, grated   5 tbsp vegan butter

Directions and Total Time: approx. 35 minutes

In a bowl, mix flax seed powder with water, and allow soaking for 5 minutes. Pour broccoli into a food processor and pulse until smoothly grated. Transfer to a bowl, add in flax egg, onion, salt, and pepper. Mix and let sit for 10 minutes to firm up a bit. Melt butter in a skillet. Ladle scoops of the broccoli mixture into the skillet, flatten and fry until golden brown, 8 minutes, turning once. Transfer the hash browns to a plate and repeat the frying process for the remaining broccoli mixture. Serve warm.

Per serving: Cal 287; Net Carbs 4g; Fat 25g; Protein 8g

Spinach & Fontina Cheese Nest Bites

Ingredients for 4 servings

2 tbsp shredded Pecorino Romano cheese + some more
2 tbsp shredded fontina   ½ lb spinach, chopped
1 tbsp olive oil   4 eggs
1 clove garlic, grated

Directions and Total Time: approx. 40 minutes

Preheat oven to 350 F. Warm oil in a skillet; add garlic and sauté for 2 minutes. Add in spinach to wilt about 5 minutes and season with salt and pepper. Top with Pecorino Romano and fontina cheeses, sauté for 2 more minutes. Allow cooling. Mold 4 (firm separate) spinach nests on a greased sheet, and crack an egg into each nest. Season with salt and pepper, and sprinkle with Pecorino Romano cheese. Bake for 15 minutes. Serve right away.

Per serving: Cal 230; Net Carbs 4g; Fat 17.5g; Protein 12g

Mixed Seeds Bread

Ingredients for 6 servings

3 tbsp ground flax seeds   1 tsp hemp seeds
¾ cup coconut flour   ¼ cup psyllium husk powder
1 cup almond flour   1 tsp salt
3 tsp baking powder   1 cup vegan cream cheese
5 tbsp sesame seeds   ½ cup melted coconut oil
½ cup chia seeds   ¾ cup coconut cream
1 tsp ground caraway seeds   1 tbsp poppy seeds

Directions and Total Time: approx. 55 minutes

Preheat oven to 350 F and line a loaf pan with parchment paper. For flax egg, whisk flax seed powder with ½ cup water, and let the mixture soak for 5 minutes. In a bowl, combine coconut and almond flours, baking powder, sesame, chia, caraway and hemp seeds, psyllium husk powder, and salt. Whisk cream cheese, oil, cream, and flax egg in another bowl.

Pour the liquid ingredients into the dry ingredients, and continue whisking until a dough forms. Transfer to loaf pan, sprinkle with poppy seeds, and bake for 45 minutes. Remove parchment paper with the bread, and allow cooling on a rack. Slice and serve.

Per serving: Cal 230; Net Carbs 3g; Fat 19g; Protein 7g

Breakfast Egg Muffins with Bacon

Ingredients for 6 servings

12 eggs   1 cup Colby cheese, grated
¼ cup coconut milk   12 slices bacon
Salt and black pepper to taste 4 jalapeño peppers, minced

Directions and Total Time: approx. 30 minutes

Preheat oven to 370 F. Crack the eggs into a bowl and whisk with coconut milk until combined, season with salt and pepper, and evenly stir in the colby cheese. Line each hole of a muffin tin with a slice of bacon and fill each with the egg mixture two-thirds way up. Top with the jalapeños and bake in the oven for 18 to 20 minutes or until puffed and golden. Remove, let cool for a few minutes, and serve.

Per serving: Cal 302; Net Carbs 3.2g; Fat 23.7g; Protein 20g

Chorizo & Avocado Eggs

Ingredients for 4 servings

1 tsp ghee   1 cup chopped collard greens
1 yellow onion, sliced   1 avocado, chopped
4 oz chorizo, sliced   4 eggs

Directions and Total Time: approx. 25 minutes

Preheat oven to 370 F. Melt ghee in a pan and sauté onion for 2 minutes. Add in chorizo and cook for 2 minutes more, flipping once. Introduce the collard greens with a splash of water to wilt, season with salt, stir and cook for 3 minutes. Mix in avocado and turn the heat off. Create four holes in the mixture, crack the eggs into each hole, sprinkle with salt and pepper, and slide the pan into the preheated oven and bake for 6 minutes. Serve right away.

Per serving: Cal 274; Net Carbs 4g; Fat 23g; Protein 13g

Swiss Cheese Chorizo Waffles

Ingredients for 6 servings

3 chorizo sausages, cooked, chopped
1 cup Gruyere cheese, shredded
6 eggs   1 tsp Spanish spice mix
6 tbsp coconut milk   Salt and black pepper, to taste

Directions and Total Time: approx. 30 minutes

In a bowl, beat the eggs, Spanish spice mix, black pepper, salt, and coconut milk. Add in the cheese and chopped sausages. Use cooking spray to spray a waffle iron. Cook the egg mixture for 5 minutes. Serve with ketchup.

Per serving: Cal 316; Net Carbs: 1.5g; Fat: 25g; Protein: 20g

Quick Breakfast Porridge

Ingredients for 2 servings

½ tsp vanilla extract	4 tbsp almond meal
2 tbsp chia seeds	4 tbsp shredded coconut
4 tbsp hemp seeds	¼ tsp granulated stevia
2 tbsp flaxseed meal	2 tbsp walnuts, chopped

Directions and Total Time: approx. 10 minutes

Put chia seeds, hemp seeds, flaxseed meal, almond meal, granulated stevia, and shredded coconut in a nonstick saucepan and pour over ½ cup water. Simmer, stirring occasionally for about 3-4 minutes. Stir in vanilla. Sprinkle with chopped walnuts and serve warm.

Per serving: Cal 334; Net Carbs 1.5g; Fat 29g; Protein 15g

Mint Chocolate Protein Shake

Ingredients for 4 servings

3 cups flax milk, chilled	4 mint leaves
3 tsp cocoa powder	3 tbsp erythritol
1 avocado, sliced	1 scoop protein powder
1 cup coconut milk, chilled	Whipping cream for topping

Directions and Total Time: approx. 4 minutes:

Combine flax milk, cocoa powder, avocado, coconut milk, erythritol, and protein powder into the smoothie maker, and blend for 1 minute to smooth. Pour into serving cups, add some whipping cream on top, and garnish with mint.

Per serving: Cal 123; Net Carbs 4g; Fat 4.5g; Protein 15g

Zucchini Quiche with Pancetta Breakfast

Ingredients for 3 servings

3 medium zucchinis, diced	3 tbsp olive oil
6 pancetta slices	1 yellow onion, chopped
3 egg	1 tbsp cilantro, chopped

Directions and Total Time: approx. 25 minutes

Place pancetta in a skillet and cook for 5 minutes, until crispy; set aside. Warm olive oil and stir-fry onion for 3 minutes. Add zucchini, and cook for 10 more minutes. Transfer to a plate and season with salt. Crack the egg into the same skillet and fry over medium heat. Top the zucchini mixture with pancetta slices and a fried egg.

Per serving: Cal 423; Net Carbs: 6.6g; Fat: 35g; Protein: 17g

Bok Choy Pumpkin Omelet with Sausage

Ingredients for 2 servings

2 eggs	4 tbsp cotija cheese
1 cup bok choy, chopped	4 oz pumpkin puree
4 oz sausage, chopped	2 tbsp olive oil

Directions and Total Time: approx. 10 minutes

Whisk eggs in a bowl along with salt and pepper. Stir in bok choy, cotija cheese and pumpkin puree.

Heat olive oil in a pan and add sausage; cook for 5 minutes, turning often. Pour in egg mixture. Cook for 2 minutes per side until the eggs are cooked. Fold in half, and serve hot.

Per serving: Cal 558; Net Carbs 7.5g; Fat 52g; Protein 32g

Cauliflower & Ham Baked Eggs

Ingredients for 4 servings

2 heads cauliflower, cut into a small florets	
2 bell peppers, chopped	1 tsp dried oregano
¼ cup chopped ham	Salt and black pepper to taste
2 tsp ghee	8 fresh eggs

Directions and Total Time: approx. 25 minutes

Preheat oven to 425 F. Melt ghee in a pan over and brown the ham, stirring frequently, about 3 minutes. Arrange cauliflower, bell peppers, and ham on a foil-lined baking sheet; toss to combine. Season with salt, oregano, and pepper. Bake for 10 minutes. Remove, create 8 indentations with a spoon, and crack an egg into each. Return to the oven and continue baking for 7 more minutes. Serve.

Per serving: Cal 344; Net Carbs 4.2g; Fat 28g; Protein 11g

Butternut Squash & Zucchini Loaf Cake

Ingredients for 4 servings

5 large eggs	¾ tsp baking powder
½ cup sour cream	1 tbsp cinnamon powder
1 cup butternut squash, grated	½ tsp salt
1 cup zucchini, grated	1 tsp vinegar
⅓ cup coconut flour	½ tsp nutmeg powder
1 tbsp olive oil	

Directions and Total Time: approx. 70 minutes

Preheat oven to 360 F and line a loaf pan with baking parchment. In a bowl, put coconut flour, baking powder, cinnamon powder, salt, and nutmeg. In a separate bowl, whisk eggs, olive oil, sour cream, and vinegar until combined. Add butternut squash and zucchini. Fold the dry mixture into the wet mixture. Pour the batter into the loaf pan and bake for 55 minutes. Let cool before slicing.

Per serving: Cal 186; Net Carbs 7.5g; Fat 12g; Protein 9.5g

Creamy Avocado Drink

Ingredients for 4 servings

4 avocados, halved and pitted	1 tsp vanilla extract
4 tbsp swerve sugar	1 tbsp cold heavy cream
¼ cup cold almond milk	

Directions and Total Time: approx. 5 minutes

In a blender, add avocado pulp, swerve, milk, vanilla extract, and heavy cream. Process until smooth. Pour the mixture into 2 glasses, garnish with strawberries, and serve.

Per serving: Cal 388; Net Carbs 2.1g; Fat 32g, Protein 6.9g

Sausage & Grana Padano Egg Muffins

Ingredients for 3 servings

6 eggs, separated into yolks and whites
1 tsp butter, melted
½ tsp dried rosemary
1 cup Grana Padano, grated
3 beef sausages, chopped

Directions and Total Time: approx. 10 minutes

Set oven to 420 F. Lightly grease a muffin pan with the melted butter. Use an electric mixer to beat the egg whites until there is a formation of stiff peaks. Add in sausages, cheese, and seasonings. Add into muffin cups and bake for 4 minutes. Place in an egg to each of the cups. Bake for an additional of 4 minutes. Let cool before serving.

Per serving: Cal 423; Net Carbs: 2.2g; Fat: 34g; Protein: 26g

Frittata with Spinach and Ricotta

Ingredients for 4 servings

5 ounces spinach
8 oz crumbled ricotta cheese
1 pint halved cherry tomatoes
10 eggs
3 tbsp olive oil
4 green onions, diced

Directions and Total Time: approx. 40 minutes

Preheat oven to 350 F. In a bowl, whisk eggs with pepper and salt. Stir in spinach, ricotta cheese, and green onions. Pour the mixture into a greased casserole, top with cherry tomatoes and bake for 25 minutes. Cut in wedges to serve.

Per serving: Cal 461; Net Carbs: 6g; Fat: 35g; Protein: 26g

Herby Paprika Biscuits

Ingredients for 4 servings

1 cup almond flour
1/8 cup melted butter
1 egg
½ tsp salt
¼ tsp black pepper
¼ tsp garlic powder
½ tsp baking soda
½ tsp paprika powder
½ tbsp plain vinegar
½ cup mixed dried herbs

Directions and Total Time: approx. 30 minutes

Preheat oven to 350 F; line a baking sheet with parchment paper. In a food processor, mix flour, melted butter, egg, salt, pepper, garlic powder, baking soda, paprika, vinegar, and dried herbs until smoothly combined. Mold 12 balls out of the mixture and arrange on the baking sheet at 2-inch intervals. Bake for 25 minutes or until golden brown.

Per serving: Cal 73; Net Carbs 0.6g, Fat 7.2g, Protein 1.6g

Raspberry Almond Smoothie

Ingredients for 4 servings

1 ½ cups almond milk
½ cup raspberries
Juice from half lemon
½ tsp almond extract

Directions and Total Time: approx. 5 minutes

In a blender or smoothie maker, pour the almond milk, raspberries, lemon juice, and almond extract.

Puree the ingredients on high speed until the raspberries have blended almost entirely into the liquid. Serve immediately.

Per serving: Cal 406; Net Carbs 9g; Fat 38g; Protein 5g

Strawberry Donuts

Ingredients for 4 servings

For the donuts:

½ cup butter
2 oz cream cheese
¼ cup sour cream
1 ½ tsp vanilla extract
½ cup erythritol
10 fresh strawberries, mashed
2 tsp lemon juice
2 tsp water
2 egg whites
2 cups blanched almond flour
2 tbsp protein powder
2 tsp baking powder

For the glaze:

4 fresh strawberries, mashed
2 tbsp coconut cream
2 tbsp xylitol
2 tsp water

Directions and Total Time: approx. 25 minutes

Preheat oven to 350 F; lightly grease an 8-cup donut pan with cooking spray. In a bowl, whisk butter, cream cheese, sour cream, vanilla, erythritol, strawberries, lemon juice, water, and egg whites until smooth. In another bowl, mix almond flour, protein and baking powders. Combine both mixtures until smooth. Pour the batter into the donut cups and bake for 15 minutes or until set. Remove, flip the donut onto a wire rack and let cool. In a bowl, combine strawberries, cream, xylitol, and water until smooth. Swirl the glaze over the donut to serve.

Per serving: Cal 320; Net Carbs 5.9g, Fat 32g, Protein 4.2g

Coconut Waffles with Cranberries

Ingredients for 4 servings

6 tbsp unsalted butter, melted and cooled slightly
2/3 cup coconut flour
2 ½ tsp baking powder
A pinch of salt
2 eggs
1 ½ cups almond milk
Natural yogurt for topping
¼ cup fresh cranberries
2/3 cup erythritol
1 tsp lemon zest
1/2 tsp vanilla extract

Directions and Total Time: approx. 16 minutes

Add cranberries, erythritol, 3/4 cup water, and lemon zest in a saucepan. Bring to a boil and reduce the temperature to simmer for 15 minutes or until the cranberries break and a sauce forms; set aside. In a bowl, mix coconut flour, baking powder, and salt. In another bowl, whisk eggs, milk, and butter and pour the mixture into the flour mix. Combine until a smooth batter forms. Preheat a waffle iron and brush with butter. Pour some of the batter and cook until golden and crisp, 4 minutes. Repeat with the remaining batter. Plate the waffles, spoon a dollop of yogurt on top followed by the cranberry puree.

Per serving: Cal 247; Net Carbs 6.9g; Fat 21g; Protein 6.6g

Creamy Salmon Tortilla Wraps

Ingredients for 4 servings

3 tbsp cottage cheese	Salt and black pepper to taste
1 lime, zested and juiced	3 (7-inch) low carb tortillas
3 tsp chopped fresh dill	6 slices smoked salmon

Directions and Total Time: approx. 10 min + chilling time

In a bowl, mix cottage cheese, lime juice, zest, dill, salt, and black pepper. Lay each tortilla on a plastic wrap (just wide enough to cover the tortilla), spread with cottage cheese mixture, and top each (one) with two salmon slices. Roll up the tortillas and secure both ends by twisting. Refrigerate for 2 hours, remove plastic, cut off both ends of each wrap, and cut wraps into half-inch wheels.

Per serving: Cal 250; Net Carbs 7g; Fat 16g; Protein 18g

Spinach & Cheese Cups

Ingredients for 4 servings

1 cup mascarpone cheese	2 tsp baking soda
4 tbsp olive oil	1 egg
2 cups almond flour	1 cup almond milk

Directions and Total Time: approx. 30 minutes

Preheat oven to 380 F. Grease a muffin tray with cooking spray. Mix almond flour, baking soda, and a pinch of salt in a bowl. In a separate bowl, beat mascarpone cheese and olive oil and whisk in egg and almond milk. Fold in flour and spoon 2 tbsp of the batter into each muffin cup. Bake for 20 minutes, remove to a wire rack to cool. Serve.

Per serving: Cal 299; Net Carbs 3.2g; Fat 26g; Protein 11.5g

Croque Madame with Pesto

Ingredients for 4 servings

1 (7-oz) can sliced mushrooms, drained	
4 tbsp melted butter	¼ cup grated Parmesan
1 cup almond milk	1 garlic clove, peeled
2 tbsp almond flour	¼ cup + 1 tbsp olive oil
Salt and black pepper to taste	4 slices zero carb bread
½ tsp nutmeg powder	3 medium tomatoes, sliced
4 tbsp grated Monterey Jack	4 slices mozzarella cheese
½ cup basil leaves	4 large whole eggs
1/3 cup toasted pine nuts	Baby arugula for garnishing

Directions and Total Time: approx. 45 minutes

To make bechamel sauce, place half of the butter and half of the milk in a saucepan over medium heat. Whisk in the remaining milk with flour until smooth roux forms. Season with salt, pepper, and nutmeg. Reduce the heat and stir in Monterey Jack cheese until melted. Set aside the bechamel sauce. For the pesto, in a food processor, puree basil, pine nuts, Parmesan, garlic, and ¼ cup olive oil. Transfer the resulting pesto to a glass jar and refrigerate. Preheat grill to medium-high. Brush both sides of each bread slice with remaining butter.

Toast each on both sides. Remove onto a plate and spread béchamel sauce on one side of each bread, then pesto, and top with mushrooms, tomatoes, and mozzarella cheese. One after the other, return each sandwich to the grill and cook until the cheese melts. Transfer to plates. Heat the remaining olive oil in a skillet and crack in eggs. Cook until the whites set but the yolks still soft and runny. Place the eggs on the sandwiches. Garnish with arugula.

Per serving: Cal 630; Net Carbs 3.7g; Fat 55g; Protein 25g

Almond Flour English Cakes

Ingredients for 4 servings

2 tbsp flax seed powder + 6 tbsp water	
2 tbsp almond flour	1 pinch salt
½ tsp baking powder	3 tbsp vegan butter

Directions and Total Time: approx. 20 minutes

In a bowl, mix flax seed with water until evenly combined, and leave to soak for 5 minutes. In another bowl, combine almond flour, baking powder, and salt. Then, pour in the flax egg and whisk again. Let the batter sit for 5 minutes to set. Melt the vegan butter in a frying pan over medium heat, and add the mixture in four dollops. Fry until golden brown on one side, then, flip the bread with a spatula and fry further until golden brown. Serve with tea.

Per serving: Cal 161; Net Carbs 2g; Fat 13g; Protein 7g

Blueberry Smoothie

Ingredients for 4 servings

2 cups fresh blueberries	2 tbsp sesame seeds
1 cup almond milk	Chopped pistachio
½ cup heavy cream	1 tbsp chopped mint leaves
Sugar-free maple syrup to taste	

Directions and Total Time: approx. 5 minutes

Combine blueberries, milk, heavy cream, and syrup in a blender. Process until smooth and pour into glasses. Top with sesame seeds, pistachios, and mint leaves to serve.

Per serving: Cal 228, Net Carbs 1g, Fat 19g, Protein 5.8g

Strawberry, Walnut & Pecan Porridge

Ingredients for 2 servings

2 tbsp coconut flour	2 tbsp lemon juice
1 tsp psyllium husk powder	1 tsp cinnamon powder
6 tbsp heavy whipping cream	6 fresh strawberries, halved
2 oz butter	4 tbsp chopped walnuts
2 eggs	2 tbsp chopped pecans

Directions and Total Time: approx. 25 minutes

In a saucepan, combine flour, psyllium husk, whipping cream, butter, egg, lemon juice, and cinnamon. Cook over low heat, stirring constantly but do not allow boiling until thickened. Top with the strawberries, walnuts, and pecans.

Per serving: Cal 588; Net Carbs 6.1g; Fat 58g; Protein 11g

Coconut Smoothie with Berries

Ingredients for 4 servings

½ cup water	4 cup fresh blueberries
1 ½ cups coconut milk	¼ tsp vanilla extract
1 cup fresh blackberries	1 tbsp vegan protein powder

Directions and Total Time: approx. 5 minutes

In a blender, combine all ingredients and blend well until you attain a uniform and creamy consistency. Share in glasses and serve cold.

Per serving: Cal 335; Net Carbs: 3.5g; Fat: 22g; Protein: 4g

Bresaola & Mozzarella Scrambled Eggs

Ingredients for 3 servings

6 eggs	1 tbsp water
A bunch of chives, chopped	4 thin slices bresaola
2 ounces mozzarella cheese	Salt and black pepper, to taste
1 tbsp butter	

Directions and Total Time: approx. 15 minutes

Crack the eggs into a large bowl and whisk in water, salt and pepper. Melt the butter in a skillet and cook the eggs, stirring constantly for 30 seconds.

Spread bresaola slices over and top with mozzarella. Stir and cook for 3 minutes until omelet is set. Sprinkle with fresh chives and serve.

Per serving: Cal 224; Net Carbs 2.2g; Fat 15g; Protein 19g

Coconut Porridge with Strawberries

Ingredients for 2 servings

Flax egg: 1 tbsp flax seed powder + 3 tbsp water

1 oz olive oil	5 tbsp coconut cream
1 tbsp coconut flour	1 pinch salt
1 pinch ground chia seeds	Strawberries to serve

Directions and Total Time: approx. 12 minutes

For flax egg, in a bowl, mix flax seed powder with water, and let soak for 5 minutes. Place a saucepan over low heat and pour in olive oil, flax egg, flour, chia seeds, cream, and salt. Cook, while stirring continuously until the desired consistency is achieved. Top with strawberries and serve.

Per serving: Cal 521; Net Carbs 4g; Fat 49g; Protein 10g

Mexican Tofu Scramble

Ingredients for 4 servings

8 oz extra firm tofu	2 tbsp chopped scallions
2 tbsp vegan butter	Salt and black pepper to taste
1 green bell pepper, chopped	1 tsp Mexican chili powder
1 tomato, finely chopped	3 oz grated vegan Parmesan

Directions and Total Time: approx. 45 minutes

Melt vegan butter in a skillet. Fry tofu into until golden brown, stirring occasionally, about 5 minutes.

Stir in bell pepper, tomato, scallions, and cook until the vegetables are soft, 4 minutes. Season with salt, pepper, chili powder, and stir in Parmesan to melt cheese, about 2 minutes. Spoon the scramble into a serving platter and serve warm.

Per serving: Cal 254; Net Carbs 3g; Fat 19g; Protein 16g

No-Bread Avocado Sandwich

Ingredients for 2 servings

1 avocado, sliced	½ oz vegan butter, softened
1 large red tomato, sliced	1 oz tofu, sliced
2 oz little gem lettuce	Chopped parsley to garnish

Directions and Total Time: approx. 10 minutes

Arrange the lettuce on a flat serving plate. Smear each leave with vegan butter, and arrange tofu slices in the leaves. Then, share the avocado and tomato slices on each cheese. Garnish the sandwiches with parsley and serve.

Per serving: Cal 385; Net Carbs 4g; Fat 32g; Protein 12g

Blueberry Chia Pudding

Ingredients for 2 servings

¾ cup coconut milk	2 tbsp chia seeds
½ tsp vanilla extract	Chopped walnuts to garnish
½ cup blueberries	

Directions and Total Time: approx. 10 min + chilling time

In a blender, pour coconut milk, vanilla extract, and half of the blueberries. Process the ingredients in high speed until the blueberries have incorporated into the liquid. Mix in chia seeds. Share the mixture into 2 breakfast jars, cover, and refrigerate for 4 hours to allow it to gel. Garnish with the remaining blueberries and walnuts. Serve.

Per serving: Cal 301; Net Carbs 6g; Fat 23g; Protein 9g

Creamy Sesame Bread

Ingredients for 6 servings

4 tbsp flax seed powder	2 tbsp psyllium husk powder
1 cup dairy-free cream cheese	1 tsp salt
5 tbsp sesame oil	1 tsp baking powder
1 cup coconut flour	1 tbsp sesame seeds

Directions and Total Time: approx. 40 minutes

In a bowl, mix flax seed powder with 1 ½ cups water until smoothly combined and set aside to soak for 5 minutes. Preheat oven to 400 F. When the flax egg is ready, beat in cream cheese and 4 tbsp sesame oil until mixed. Whisk in coconut flour, psyllium husk powder, salt, and baking powder until adequately blended. Spread the dough in a greased baking tray. Allow to stand for 5 minutes and then brush with remaining sesame oil. Sprinkle with sesame seeds and bake the dough for 30 minutes. Slice and serve.

Per serving: Cal 285; Net Carbs 1g; Fat 26g; Protein 8g

Bulletproof Coffee

Ingredients for 2 servings

2 ½ heaping tbsp ground bulletproof coffee beans
1 tbsp coconut oil   2 tbsp unsalted vegan butter

Directions and Total Time: approx. 3 minutes

Using a coffee maker, brew one cup of coffee with the ground coffee beans and 1 cup of water. Transfer the coffee to a blender and add the coconut oil and vegan butter. Blend the mixture until frothy and smooth.

Per serving: Cal 336; Net Carbs 0g; Fat 36g; Protein 2g

Breakfast Naan Bread

Ingredients for 6 servings

¾ cup almond flour   ¼ cup olive oil
2 tbsp psyllium husk powder 2 cups boiling water
1 tsp salt + extra for sprinkling 8 oz vegan butter
½ tsp baking powder   2 garlic cloves, minced

Directions and Total Time: approx. 25 minutes

In a bowl, mix almond flour, psyllium husk powder, ½ teaspoon of salt, and baking powder. Mix in olive oil and boiling water to combine the ingredients, like a thick porridge. Stir and allow the dough rise for 5 minutes. Divide the dough into 6 to 8 pieces and mold into balls. Place the balls on a parchment paper and flatten. Melt half of the vegan butter in a frying pan and fry the naan on both sides to have a golden color. Transfer to a plate and keep warm. Add the remaining vegan butter to the pan and sauté garlic until fragrant, about 2 minutes. Pour the garlic butter into a bowl and serve a_s a dip along with the naan.

Per serving: Cal 224; Net Carbs 3g; Fat 19g; Protein 4g

Seeds Breakfast Loaf

Ingredients for 6 servings

¾ cup coconut flour   1 tsp ground caraway seeds
1 cup almond flour   1 tbsp poppy seeds
3 tbsp baking powder   1 tsp salt
2 tbsp psyllium husk powder 1 tsp mixed spice
2 tbsp desiccated coconut   6 eggs
5 tbsp sesame seeds   1 cup cream cheese, softened
¼ cup flaxseed   ¾ cup heavy cream
¼ cup hemp seeds   4 tbsp sesame oil

Directions and Total Time: approx. 55 minutes

Preheat oven to 350 F. In a bowl, mix coconut and almond flours, baking powder, psyllium husk, desiccated coconut, sesame seeds, flaxseed, hemp seeds, ground caraway, poppy seeds, salt, and mixed spice. In another bowl, whisk eggs, cream cheese, heavy cream, and sesame oil. Pour the mixture into the dry ingredients and combine both into a smooth dough. Pour the dough in a greased loaf pan. Bake for 45 minutes. Remove onto a rack, and let cool.

Per serving: Cal 584; Net Carbs 7.4g; Fat 50g; Protein 23g

Blackberry Chia Pudding

Ingredients for 4 servings

1 ½ cups coconut milk   7 tbsp chia seeds
½ cup Greek yogurt   1 cup fresh blackberries
4 tsp sugar-free maple syrup Chopped almonds to garnish
1 tsp vanilla extract   Mint leaves to garnish

Directions and Total Time: approx. 45 minutes

In a bowl, combine coconut milk, Greek yogurt, sugar-free maple syrup, and vanilla extract until evenly combined. Mix in the chia seeds. Puree half of blackberries in a bowl using a fork and stir in the yogurt mixture. Share the mixture into medium mason jars, cover the lids and refrigerate for 30 minutes to thicken the pudding. Remove the jars, take off the lid, and stir the mixture. Garnish with remaining blackberries, almonds, and some mint leaves.

Per serving: Cal 309; Net Carbs 6.8g; Fat 26g; Protein 7g

Blueberry Soufflé

Ingredients for 4 servings

1 cup frozen blueberries   3 egg whites
5 tbsp erythritol   1 tsp olive oil
4 egg yolks   ½ lemon, zested to garnish

Directions and Total Time: approx. 35 minutes

Pour blueberries, 2 tbsp erythritol and 1 tbsp water in a saucepan. Cook until the berries soften and become syrupy, 8-10 minutes. Stir in vanilla and set aside. Preheat oven to 350 F. In a bowl, beat egg yolks and 1 tbsp of erythritol until thick and pale. In another bowl, whisk egg whites until foamy. Add in remaining erythritol and whisk until soft peak forms, 3-4 minutes. Fold egg white mixture into egg yolk mix. Heat olive oil in a pan over low heat. Add in olive oil and pour in the egg mixture; swirl to spread. Cook for 3 minutes and transfer to the oven; bake for 2-3 minutes or until puffed and set. Plate omelet and spoon blueberry sauce all over. Garnish with lemon zest.

Per serving: Cal 99; Net Carbs 2.8g; Fat 5.9g; Protein 5.5g

Cheddar Biscuits

Ingredients for 4 servings

2 ½ cups almond flour   3 tbsp melted butter
2 tsp baking powder   ¾ cup grated cheddar cheese
2 eggs beaten

Directions and Total Time: approx. 30 minutes

Preheat oven to 350 F; line a baking sheet with parchment paper. In a bowl, mix flour, baking powder, and eggs until smooth. Whisk in the melted butter and cheddar cheese until well combined. Mold 12 balls out of the mixture and arrange on the sheet at 2-inch intervals. Bake for 25 minutes until golden brown. Remove, let cool and serve.

Per serving: Cal 355; Net Carbs 1.4g, Fat 28g, Protein 21g

Vanilla Buttermilk Pancakes

Ingredients for 4 servings

½ cup almond flour
½ tsp baking powder
1 tbsp swerve sugar
½ cup buttermilk
1 lemon, juiced
3 eggs

1 vanilla pod
2 tbsp unsalted butter
2 tbsp olive oil
3 tbsp sugar-free maple syrup
Greek yogurt to serve
Blueberries to serve

Directions and Total Time: approx. 25 minutes

Into a bowl, sift almond flour and baking powder and stir in swerve sugar. In a small bowl, whisk buttermilk, lemon juice, and eggs. Combine the mixture with the flour mix until smooth. Cut the vanilla pod open and scrape the beans into the flour mixture. Stir to incorporate evenly. In a skillet, melt a quarter each of the butter and olive oil and spoon in 1 ½ tablespoons of the pancake mixture into the pan. Cook for 4 minutes or until small bubbles appear. Flip and cook for 2 minutes or until set and golden. Repeat cooking until the batter finishes using the remaining butter and olive oil in the same proportions. Plate the pancakes, drizzle with maple syrup, top with a generous dollop of yogurt, and scatter some blueberries on top.

Per serving: Cal 168; Net Carbs 1.6g; Fat 11g; Protein 7g

Berry & Mascarpone Bowl

Ingredients for 4 servings

1 ½ cups blueberries and raspberries
4 cups Greek yogurt
liquid stevia to taste

1 ½ cups mascarpone cheese
1 cup raw pistachios

Directions and Total Time: approx. 10 minutes

Mix the yogurt, stevia, and mascarpone in a bowl until evenly combined. Divide the mixture into 4 bowls, share the berries and pistachios on top of the cream. Serve.

Per serving: Cal 480, Net Carbs 5g, Fat 40g, Protein 20g

Avocado Halloumi Scones

Ingredients for 4 servings

1 cup crumbled halloumi cheese
2 cups almond flour
3 tsp baking powder
½ cup butter, cold

1 avocado, pitted and mashed
1 large egg
1/3 cup buttermilk

Directions and Total Time: approx. 35 minutes

Preheat oven to 350 F and line a baking sheet with parchment paper. In a bowl, combine flour and baking powder. Add butter and mix. Top with halloumi cheese, avocado, and combine again. Whisk the egg with buttermilk and stir in the halloumi mix. Mold 8-10 scones out to the batter. Place on the baking sheet and bake for 25 minutes or until the scones turn a golden color. Let cool.

Per serving: Cal 432; Net Carbs 2.3g; Fat 42g; Protein 10g

Almond-Berry Pancakes with Sweet Syrup

Ingredients for 4 servings

1 handful of strawberries and raspberries, mashed
1 handful fresh strawberries and raspberries for topping
½ cup almond flour
1 tsp baking soda
A pinch of salt
1 tbsp swerve sugar
A pinch of cinnamon powder

1 egg
½ cup almond milk
2 tsp butter
1 cup Greek yogurt
Stevia for serving

Directions and Total Time: approx. 25 minutes

In a bowl, combine almond flour, baking soda, salt, swerve, and cinnamon. Whisk in mashed berries, and egg, and mix in the milk until smooth. Melt ½ tsp of butter in a skillet and pour in 1 tbsp of the mixture into the pan. Cook until small bubbles appear, flip, and cook until golden. Transfer to a plate and proceed using up the remaining batter for pancakes. Top pancakes with yogurt, berries, and stevia.

Per serving: Cal 234; Net Carbs 7.6g; Fat 17g; Protein 9g

Toast Sticks with Yogurt Berry Bowls

Ingredients for 2 servings

2 cups Greek yogurt
2 tbsp sugar-free maple syrup
½ cup strawberries, halved
½ cup blueberries
½ cup raspberries
2 eggs
¼ tsp cinnamon powder

¼ tsp nutmeg powder
2 tbsp almond milk
Salt and black pepper to taste
4 slices zero carb bread
1 ½ tbsp butter
1 tbsp olive oil

Directions and Total Time: approx. 15 minutes

In a bowl, mix yogurt, maple syrup, and berries. Chill the salad for about 1 hour. In another bowl, whisk eggs, cinnamon, nutmeg, milk, salt, and pepper. Set aside. Cut each slice into four strips. Heat butter and olive oil in a skillet. Dip each bread strip into the egg mixture and fry in the olive oil, flipping once until golden brown on both sides. Transfer to a serving plate and serve with the salad.

Per serving: Cal 207; Net Carbs 7.3g; Fat 14g; Protein 7.7g

Quick Protein Bars

Ingredients for 4 servings

1 cup almond butter
4 tbsp coconut oil
2 scoops vanilla protein
½ cup sugar-free maple syrup

4 tbsp unsweetened chocolate chips + extra for topping
1 tsp cinnamon powder
1 tbsp chopped toasted peanuts

Directions and Total Time: approx. 5 min + chilling time

Line a baking sheet with parchment paper. In a bowl, mix almond butter, coconut oil, vanilla protein, maple syrup, salt, chocolate chips, and cinnamon. Spread the mixture onto the sheet and scatter chocolate and peanuts on top. Refrigerate until firm, at least 1 hour. Cut into bars.

Per serving: Cal 326; Net Carbs 0.4g, Fat 29g, Protein 0.5g

Breakfast Ratatouille with Eggs & Avocado

Ingredients for 2 servings

1 tbsp olive oil	2 medium tomatoes, diced
1 zucchini, sliced	1 cup vegetable broth
1 medium red onion, sliced	4 eggs
1 red bell pepper, sliced	1 avocado, chopped
1 yellow bell pepper, sliced	2 tbsp chopped parsley

Directions and Total Time: approx. 50 minutes

Heat olive oil in a skillet and sauté the zucchini, onion, and bell peppers for 10 minutes. Pour in tomatoes, vegetable broth, and season with salt and pepper. Bring to a boil and then simmer until the sauce thickens slightly. Create four holes in the sauce and break an egg into each hole. Allow the eggs to cook through and turn the heat off. Plate the sauce, top with the avocado, and garnish with parsley.

Per serving: Cal 450; Net Carbs 5.6g; Fat 32g; Protein 18g

Ultra Flaxy Cookies

Ingredients for 4 servings

¼ cup golden flaxseed meal finely ground

1 ½ cups butter, melted	2 tsp xanthan gum
2 eggs	1 tbsp whey protein powder
2 cups sour cream	4 tsp baking powder
3 tbsp water	2 tsp baking soda
2 tbsp apple cider vinegar	½ tsp salt
2 tsp cream of tartar	3 tbsp coconut flour
3 cups almond flour	

Directions and Total Time: approx. 30 minutes

Preheat oven to 350 F; line a baking sheet with parchment paper. Using a food processor, mix butter, eggs, sour cream, water, vinegar, and cream of tartar until smooth. In a bowl, mix flours, xanthan gum, protein, baking powder, baking soda, salt, and flaxseed. Gradually, pour the mixture into the food processor and mix until smooth batter forms. Mold 12 balls out of the mixture and arrange on the baking sheet at 2-inch intervals. Bake for 25 minutes or until golden brown. Remove, let cool and serve.

Per serving: Cal 335; Net Carbs 5.2g, Fat 38g, Protein 5g

Shakshuka

Ingredients for 2 servings

1 tsp olive oil	Salt and black pepper to taste
1 garlic clove, minced	1 tsp cumin powder
1 small white onion, chopped	1/3 cup baby kale, chopped
1 red bell pepper, chopped	½ tsp dried basil
1 small green chili, minced	4 large eggs
1 cup diced tomatoes	¼ cup yogurt
½ cup tomato sauce	½ lemon, juiced

Directions and Total Time: approx. 40 minutes

Heat olive oil in a deep skillet and sauté garlic, onion, bell pepper, and green chili until softened, 5 minutes. Stir in tomatoes, tomato sauce, salt, pepper, and cumin.

Cover and cook for 10 minutes. Add kale to wilt and stir in basil. Create four holes in the sauce with a wooden spoon, crack an egg into each hole, and sprinkle with parsley. Cover with a lid and cook until the eggs are firm, 8-10 minutes. In a bowl, mix yogurt with lemon juice and set aside. Plate shakshuka, top with a dollop of yogurt mixture, and serve.

Per serving: Cal 320; Net Carbs 8g; Fat 16.9g; Protein 17g

Gruyere Breakfast Soufflés

Ingredients for 4 servings

2 ½ cup Gruyere cheese, grated + a little extra for topping	
2 egg whites, beaten until stiff	1 ½ tsp mustard powder
2 ½ tbsp butter, softened	½ cup almond milk
2 ½ tbsp almond flour	4 yolks, beaten

Directions and Total Time: approx. 20 minutes

Preheat oven to 370 F and brush the inner parts of 4 ramekins with butter. Melt the remaining butter in a pan over low heat and stir in flour for 1 minute. Remove from the heat, mix in mustard powder until evenly combined and slowly whisk in milk until no lumps form. Return to medium heat, while stirring until the sauce comes to a rolling boil. Stir in Gruyere cheese until melted. Into the egg yolks whisk ¼ cup of the warmed milk mixture, then combine with the remaining milk sauce. Fold in egg whites gradually until evenly combined. Spoon the mixture into the ramekins and top with the remaining cheese. Bake for 8 minutes, until the soufflés have a slight wobble, but soft at the center. Let cool and serve.

Per serving: Cal 488; Net Carbs 3.8g; Fat 39g; Protein 26g

Pumpkin Donuts

Ingredients for 4 servings

½ cup heavy cream	¼ cup sugar-free maple syrup
1 egg	1 cup almond flour
2 egg yolks	¼ cup coconut flour
½ tsp vanilla extract	1 tsp baking powder
2 tsp pumpkin pie spice	A pinch of salt
½ cup pumpkin puree	

For the glaze:

2 cups swerve confectioner's sugar
4 tbsp water

Directions and Total Time: approx. 25 minutes

Preheat oven to 350 F. In a bowl, mix heavy cream, egg, egg yolks, vanilla extract, pie spice, pumpkin pie puree, and maple syrup. One after another, smoothly mix in almond and coconut flours, baking powder, and salt. Pour the batter into greased donut cups and bake for 18 minutes or until set. Remove, flip onto a wire rack and let cool. In a bowl, whisk the swerve and water until smooth. Swirl the glaze over the donut and enjoy immediately.

Per serving: Cal 189; Net Carbs 4.3g, Fat 16g, Protein 7.7g

Chorizo, Goat Cheese & Eggs

Ingredients for 4 servings

2 green onions, thinly sliced diagonally
1 tsp olive oil   4 eggs
1 tsp smoked paprika   ½ cup crumbled goat cheese
3 oz chorizo, diced   2 tbsp fresh parsley, chopped

Directions and Total Time: approx. 15 minutes

Preheat oven to 350 F. In a pan, heat olive oil along with paprika for 30 seconds. Add the chorizo and cook until lightly browned; set aside. Crack the eggs into the pan, cook for 2 minutes, and then sprinkle with chorizo and crumble goat cheese all around the egg white, but not on the yolks. Transfer the pan to oven and bake for 2 more minutes, until the yolks are quite set, but still runny within. Garnish with green onions and parsley. Serve.

Per serving: Cal 257; Net Carbs 5.6g; Fat 18g; Protein 17g

Berries & Cream Bowl with Nuts

Ingredients for 6 servings

5 tbsp flax seed powder   4 tbsp lemon juice
1 cup dark chocolate   1 tsp vanilla extract
1 cup butter   2 cups coconut cream
1 pinch salt   4 oz walnuts, chopped
1 tsp vanilla extract   ½ cup roasted coconut chips
2 cups fresh blueberries

Directions and Total Time: approx. 10 minutes

Preheat oven to 320 F. Line a springform pan with parchment paper. In a bowl, mix the flax seed powder with 2/3 cup water and allow thickening for 5 minutes. Break chocolate and butter into a bowl and microwave for 2 minutes. Share the flax egg into 2 bowls; whisk the salt into one portion and then, 1 tsp of vanilla into the other. Pour the chocolate mixture into the vanilla mixture and combine well. Fold into the other flax egg mixture. Pour the batter into the springform pan and bake for 20 minutes. When ready, slice the cake into squares and share into serving bowls. Pour blueberries, lemon juice, and remaining vanilla into a small bowl. Break the blueberries and let sit for a few minutes. Whip coconut cream with a whisk until a soft peak forms. To serve, spoon the cream on the cakes, top with blueberry mixture, and sprinkle with walnuts and coconut flakes.

Per serving: Cal 345; Fat 31g; Net Carbs 7g; Protein 6g

Coffee-Flavored Muffins

Ingredients for 4 servings

For the batter:

2 tbsp butter, softened   ½ cup vanilla almond milk
2 oz cream cheese, softened   1 cup almond flour
1/3 cup sugar-free maple syrup   2 tsp instant coffee powder
4 eggs   ½ cup coconut flour
2 tsp vanilla extract   1 tsp baking powder

For the topping:

1 cup almond flour   ¼ cup butter softened
2 tbsp coconut flour   1 tsp cinnamon powder
¼ cup swerve sugar   ½ tsp sugar-free maple syrup

Directions and Total Time: approx. 35 minutes

Preheat oven to 350 F and line a 12-cup muffin pan with paper liners. In a bowl, whisk butter, cream cheese, maple syrup, eggs, vanilla, and almond milk until smooth. In another bowl, mix almond flour, coffee powder, coconut flour, baking powder, and a pinch of salt. Combine both mixtures and fill the muffin cups two-thirds way up. In a bowl, mix flours, swerve, butter, cinnamon powder, and maple syrup. Spoon the mixture onto the muffin batter and bake for 25 minutes or until a toothpick inserted comes out clean. Remove from the oven, and let cool to serve.

Per serving: Cal 294; Net Carbs 5g, Fat 23g, Protein 17g

Pecan Cookies

Ingredients for 8 servings

1 egg   ½ tsp baking soda
2 cups ground pecans   1 tbsp butter
¼ cup sweetener   20 pecan halves

Directions and Total Time: approx. 25 minutes

Preheat oven to 350 F. Mix the ingredients, except for the pecan halves, until combined. Make 20 balls out of the mixture and press them with your thumb onto a lined cookie sheet. Top each cookie with a pecan half. Bake for about 12 minutes. Serve warm or chilled.

Per serving: Cal 101; Net Carbs 0.6g; Fat 11g; Protein 2g

Cinnamon Faux Rice Pudding

Ingredients for 6 servings

1 ¼ cups coconut cream   1 cup mashed tofu
1 tsp vanilla extract   2 oz fresh strawberries
1 tsp cinnamon powder

Directions and Total Time: approx. 17 minutes

Pour coconut cream into a bowl and whisk until a soft peak forms. Mix in vanilla and cinnamon. Lightly fold in tofu and refrigerate for 10-15 minutes to set. Spoon into serving glasses, top with the strawberries and serve.

Per serving: Cal 225; Fat 20g; Net Carbs 3g; Protein 6g

Zucchini Muffins

Ingredients for 6 servings

½ cup almond flour   5 tbsp olive oil
1 tsp baking powder   ½ cup grated cheddar cheese
½ tsp baking soda   2 zucchinis, grated
1 ½ tsp mustard powder   6 green olives, sliced
Salt and black pepper to taste   1 spring onion, chopped
1/3 cup almond milk   1 red bell pepper, chopped
1 large egg   1 tbsp freshly chopped thyme

Directions and Total Time: approx. 10 minutes

Preheat oven to 325 F. In a bowl, combine flour, baking powder, baking soda, mustard powder, salt, pepper. In a smaller bowl, whisk milk, egg, and olive oil. Mix the wet ingredients into dry ingredients and add cheese, zucchini, olives, spring onion, bell pepper, and thyme; mix well. Spoon the batter into greased muffin cups, and bake for 30 minutes or until golden brown. Let the muffins to cool.

Per serving: Cal 172; Net Carbs 1.6g; Fat 16g; Protein 4g

Chia Pudding with Blackberries

Ingredients for 2 servings

1 cup full-fat natural yogurt	1 cup fresh blackberries
2 tsp swerve	1 tbsp lemon zest
2 tbsp chia seeds	Mint leaves, to serve

Directions and Total Time: approx. 35 minutes

Mix together the yogurt and swerve. Stir in chia seeds. Reserve 4 blackberries for garnish and mash the remaining with a fork until pureed. Stir in the yogurt mixture. Refrigerate for 30 minutes. Divide the mixture into 2 glasses. Serve topped with raspberries and mint leaves.

Per serving: Cal 169, Net Carbs 1.7g, Fat 10g, Protein 7g

Lemon Muffins

Ingredients for 4 servings

For the muffins:

½ cup butter, softened	2 tsp baking powder
¾ cup swerve sugar	¼ tsp arrowroot starch
3 large eggs	½ tsp vanilla extract
1 lemon, zested and juiced	1 cup sour cream
1 ½ cups almond flour	A pinch of salt
½ cup coconut flour	

For the topping:

3 tbsp butter, melted	1 tsp lemon zest
¾ cup almond flour	1 tbsp coconut flour
3 Tbsp swerve sugar	

For the lemon glaze:

½ cup swerve confectioner's sugar
3 tbsp lemon juice

Directions and Total Time: approx. 35 minutes

For the muffins:

Preheat oven to 350 F and line a 12-cup muffin pan with paper liners. In a bowl, mix butter, swerve, eggs, lemon zest, and lemon juice until smooth. In another bowl, combine flours, baking powder, and arrowroot. Combine both mixtures and mix in vanilla, sour cream, and salt until smooth. Fill the cups two-thirds way up; set aside.

For the topping:

In a bowl, mix butter, almond flour, swerve, lemon zest, and coconut flour until well combined.

Spoon the mixture onto the muffin batter and bake for 25 minutes or until a toothpick inserted comes out clean. Remove the muffins from the oven and cool while you prepare the glaze.

For the glaze:

In a bowl, whisk confectioner's sugar and lemon juice until smooth and semi-thick. Drizzle over the muffins.

Per serving: Cal 439; Net Carbs 7.6g; Fat 42g; Protein 8g

Yogurt Strawberry Pie with Basil

Ingredients for 4 servings

For the crust:

2 eggs	1 cup almond flour
1 tsp vanilla extract	½ cup cold butter, cubed
¼ cup erythritol	5 tbsp cold water
¼ tsp salt	1 tbsp olive oil

For the filling:

1 cup unsweetened strawberry jam	
¼ cup heavy cream	1 cup Greek yogurt
1/3 cup erythritol	1 tbsp chopped basil leaves

Directions and Total Time: approx. 90 min + chilling time

For the piecrust:

In a bowl, whisk eggs, olive oil, and vanilla until well combined. In another bowl, mix erythritol, salt, and flour. Combine both mixtures into a stand mixer and blend until smooth dough forms. Add butter and mix until breadcrumb-like mixture forms. Add one tbsp of water, mix further until the dough begins to come together. Keep adding water until it sticks together. Lightly flour a working surface, turn the dough onto it, knead a few times until formed into a ball, and comes together smoothly. Divide into half and flatten each piece into a disk. Wrap each dough in plastic and refrigerate for 1 hour. Preheat oven to 375 F and grease a 9-inch pie pan with olive oil. Remove the dough from the fridge, let it stand at room temperature and roll one piece into 12-inch round. Fit this piece into the bottom and walls to the rim of the pie pan while shaping to take the pan's form. Roll out the other dough into an 11-inch round and set aside.

For the filling:

Whip the heavy cream and erythritol in a stand mixer until creamy and smooth. Mix in the Greek yogurt, strawberry jam, basil and mix on low speed until well combined. Fill the pie dough in the pie pan with the filling and level well. Brush the overhanging pastry with water and attach the top pastry on top of the filling. Press the edges to merge the dough ends and trim the overhanging ends to 1-inch. Fold the edge under itself and then, decoratively crimp. Cut 2 slits on the top crust. Bake the pie for 75 minutes until the bottom crust is golden and the filling bubbly.

Per serving: Cal 341; Net Carbs 6.1g; Fat 33g; Protein 5.6g

STARTERS & SALADS

Chili Avocado with Cheese Sauce

Ingredients for 4 servings

5 tbsp melted butter	1 cup grated cheddar cheese
3 tbsp almond flour	4 oz cream cheese, softened
1 ½ cups almond milk	¼ cup grated Parmesan
¼ tsp mustard powder	2 avocados, sliced
¼ tsp garlic powder	2 tbsp sriracha sauce
Black pepper to taste	2 tbsp olive oil

Directions and Total Time: approx. 16 minutes

Mix 3 tbsps of butter with flour in a saucepan and cook until golden. Whisk in milk, mustard, garlic, and black pepper. Cook, whisking continuously until thickened, 2 minutes. Stir in cheddar, cream and Parmesan cheeses until melted; set aside. In a bowl, toss avocado in remaining butter and sriracha sauce. Heat olive oil in a pan and cook avocado until golden turning halfway, 4 minutes. Plate and pour the cheese sauce all over to serve.

Per serving: Cal 548; Net Carbs 3.2g; Fat 49g; Protein 10g

Chargrilled Broccoli in Tamarind Sauce

Ingredients for 6 servings

1 head broccoli, cut into florets	1 garlic clove, peeled
4 tbsp melted butter	1 inch ginger, peeled
1 white onion, finely chopped	½ lemon, juiced
3 garlic cloves, minced	½ cup peanut butter
1 tsp dried basil	2 tbsp tamarind sauce
Salt and black pepper to taste	1 tsp swerve brown sugar
A handful of chopped parsley	1 small red chili, chopped

Directions and Total Time: approx. 30 minutes

Simmer 2 cups of water in a pot and blanch broccoli for 2 minutes; drain. In a bowl, mix butter, onion, garlic, basil, salt, pepper. Toss broccoli in the mixture and marinate for 5 minutes. Heat a grill pan over high and cook broccoli until charred, turning once. Transfer to a plate. Place garlic and ginger in a blender and pulse until broken into pieces. Add in lemon juice, peanut butter, tamarind sauce, brown sugar, red chili, and 1/3 cup of water. Blend until smooth. Serve broccoli topped with peanut sauce and parsley.

Per serving: Cal 269; Net Carbs 5.2g; Fat 18g; Protein 7.6g

Caprese Salad with Bacon

Ingredients for 2 servings

1 tomato, sliced	2 tsp olive oil
4 basil leaves	3 ounces bacon, chopped
8 mozzarella cheese slices	1 tsp balsamic vinegar

Directions and Total Time: approx. 10 minutes

Place the bacon in a skillet over medium heat and cook until crispy. Divide the tomato slices between 2 serving plates. Arrange the mozzarella slices on top. Scatter basil leaves and add the bacon on top. Drizzle with olive oil and vinegar. Sprinkle with sea salt and serve.

Per serving: Cal 279; Net Carbs 1.5g; Fat 26g; Protein 21g

Tofu Skewers with Sesame Sauce

Ingredients for 4 servings

2 tbsp tahini	1 red onion, cut into wedges
1 (14 oz) firm tofu, cubed	1 tbsp soy sauce
1 zucchini, cut into wedges	1 tbsp olive oil
¼ cup cherry tomatoes, halved	Sesame seeds for garnishing

Directions and Total Time: approx. 15 minutes

In a bowl, mix tahini and soy sauce; mix toss tofu in the sauce. Let rest for 30 minutes. Thread tofu, zucchini, tomatoes and onion, alternately, on wooden skewers. Heat olive oil in a grill pan and cook tofu until golden brown, 8 minutes. Serve garnished with sesame seeds.

Per serving: Cal 266; Net Carbs 2.4g; Fat 19g; Protein 14g

Almond Cauliflower Cakes

Ingredients for 4 servings

½ cup grated Parmigiano Reggiano cheese	
2 cups cauliflower florets	1 tbsp chopped parsley
Salt and black pepper to taste	2 tbsp chopped almonds
1 large egg, beaten	1 cup golden flaxseed meal
2 green onions, chopped	1 cup olive oil

Directions and Total Time: approx. 25 minutes

Pour cauliflower and 1 cup of water into a pot and bring to a boil until soft; drain. Transfer to a food processor and puree until smooth. Pour into a bowl and mix in salt, pepper, egg, green onions, parsley, cheese, and almonds. Make 12 small cakes from the mixture and coat in the flaxseed meal. Heat olive oil a deep pan and cook patties on both sides until golden, 6-8 minutes. Serve warm.

Per serving: Cal 321; Net Carbs 5.5g; Fat 23g; Protein 14g

Roasted Jalapeño & Bell Pepper Soup

Ingredients for 4 servings

6 green bell peppers, halved	2 tbsp melted butter
1 jalapeño pepper, halved	½ cup heavy cream
1 bulb garlic, halved, not peeled	3 tbsp grated Parmesan
6 tomatoes, halved	Roughly chopped chives
3 cups vegetable broth	Salt and black pepper to taste

Directions and Total Time: approx. 40 minutes

Preheat oven to 350 F. Arrange bell peppers, jalapeño pepper, and garlic on a baking pan and roast for 15 minutes. Add tomatoes roast for 15 minutes. Let cool, peel of the skins, and place in a blender. Add salt, pepper, butter, and heavy cream; puree until completely smooth. Serve into bowls, sprinkle with Parmesan and chives.

Per serving: Cal 189; Net Carbs 8.7g; Fat 12g; Protein 5.3g

Goat Cheese & Raspberry Focaccia Squares

Ingredients for 6 servings

6 zero carb buns, cut into 4 squares each

1 cup fresh raspberries	1 cup mushrooms, sliced
2 cups erythritol	½ tsp dried thyme
1 lemon, juiced	2 oz goat cheese, crumbled
1 tbsp olive oil	1 green onion, chopped

Directions and Total Time: approx. 25 minutes

For the raspberry jam:

Pour raspberries into a saucepan, break into a puree using a potato masher, and stir in erythritol and lemon juice. Place the pot over low heat and cook with constant stirring until the sugar dissolves. Turn the heat up to medium and allow the mixture boil for 4 minutes, still with constant stirring to prevent the jam from burning; let cool. Preheat oven to 350 F. Arrange the squares on a baking tray and place in the oven for 6 minutes. Heat olive oil in a skillet and sauté mushrooms. Season with thyme, salt, and pepper; cook for 10 minutes. Remove the bread squares from the oven, cut each square into halves horizontally, and top with mushrooms. Scatter goat cheese on top, green onion, and raspberry jam. Cover with 6 pieces of focaccia, and serve.

Per serving: Cal 168; Net Carbs 5.7g; Fat 12g; Protein 7g

Walnut Roasted Asparagus

Ingredients for 4 servings

2 tbsp olive oil	1 ¼ lb asparagus, trimmed
1 garlic clove, crushed	3 tbsp tahini
1 tbsp tamarind sauce	2 tbsp balsamic vinegar
A handful of walnuts, chopped	½ tbsp chili pepper, chopped

Directions and Total Time: approx. 20 minutes

Preheat oven to 350 F. In a bowl, mix olive oil, garlic, tamarind sauce, and walnuts. Lay asparagus on a baking tray and drizzle tamarind mixture all over. Toss the veggies to coat and roast until tender and charred, 12 minutes. In a bowl, whisk tahini, vinegar, and chili pepper. Plate asparagus, drizzle with dressing, and serve with fried tofu.

Per serving: Cal 359; Net Carbs 8.4g; Fat 32g; Protein 9.6g

Crostini with Avocado

Ingredients for 4 servings

4 tbsp olive oil	1 lemon, zested and juiced
2 avocados, chopped	1 loaf zero carb bread, sliced
¼ tsp garlic powder	2 garlic cloves, halved
¼ tsp onion powder	3 tbsp grated Parmesan
1 tbsp chopped parsley	2 tbsp chopped toasted pecans

Directions and Total Time: approx. 25 minutes

In a bowl, using a fork, mix 2 tbsp of olive oil, avocado, garlic and onion powders, salt, pepper, parsley, zest, and juice until smooth; set aside. Heat a grill pan; rub both sides of the bread slices with garlic; brush with olive oil. Grill on both sides in the heated pan until crispy and golden. Transfer crostini to a plate and spread generously with avocado mixture. Sprinkle with Parmesan cheese and some pecans. Drizzle with some more olive oil and serve.

Per serving: Cal 327; Net Carbs 3.9g; Fat 31g; Protein 3.6g

Speedy Slaw with Pecans

Ingredients for 4 servings

½ cup toasted pecans, chopped	1 tbsp red wine vinegar
2 cups broccoli slaw	2 tbsp olive oil
1 red bell pepper, sliced	½ lemon, juiced
1 red onion, thinly sliced	1 tsp Dijon mustard
2 tbsp chopped cilantro	2 tbsp mayonnaise
2 tbsp flax seeds	Salt and black pepper to taste

Directions and Total Time: approx. 20 minutes

In a bowl, combine broccoli slaw, bell pepper, red onion, cilantro, and season with salt and pepper. Mix in pecans and flax seeds. In a bowl, whisk vinegar, olive oil, lemon juice, mayonnaise, and mustard. Drizzle the dressing over the slaw and mix. Serve.

Per serving: Cal 310; Net Carbs 3.2g; Fat 31g; Protein 4.8g

Chili Broccoli Rabe with Sesame Seeds

Ingredients for 4 servings

3 cups broccoli rabe, chopped	1 garlic clove, minced
1 cup water	1 orange bell pepper, sliced
1 tbsp melted butter	Salt and black pepper to taste
1 tbsp olive oil	Red chili flakes

Directions and Total Time: approx. 15 minutes

Cook broccoli in lightly salted water for 3 minutes or until softened; drain. Heat butter and olive oil in a skillet and sauté garlic and bell pepper until fragrant and softened. Toss in broccoli to heat up. Sprinkle with flakes and serve.

Per serving: Cal 68; Net Carbs 1.2g; Fat 6.4g; Protein 1.2g

Saffron Cauli Rice with Fried Garlic

Ingredients for 4 servings

A pinch of saffron soaked in ¼-cup almond milk

1 tbsp olive oil	2 cups cauli rice
6 garlic cloves, sliced	¼ cup vegetable broth
1 tbsp butter	Salt and black pepper to taste
1 yellow onion, thinly sliced	2 tbsp chopped parsley

Directions and Total Time: approx. 35 minutes

Heat olive oil in a skillet and fry garlic until golden brown but not burned. Set aside. Add butter to the oil and sauté onion for 3 minutes. Stir in cauli rice; remove the saffron from the milk and pour the milk and vegetable stock into the pot. Mix, cover the pot, and cook for 5 minutes. Season with salt, black pepper, and parsley. Fluff the rice and dish into serving plates. Garnish with fried garlic and serve.

Per serving: Cal 91; Net Carbs 5.9g; Fat 6.6g; Protein 2g

Cheesy Zucchini Bake

Ingredients for 4 servings

3 large zucchinis, sliced
3 tbsp salted butter, melted
2 tbsp olive oil
1 garlic clove, minced
1 tsp dried thyme
¼ cup grated mozzarella
2/3 cup grated Parmesan

Directions and Total Time: approx. 25 minutes

Preheat oven to 350 F. Pour zucchini in a bowl; add in butter, olive oil, garlic, and thyme; toss to coat. Spread onto a baking dish and sprinkle with the mozzarella and Parmesan cheeses. Bake for 15 minutes or until the cheese melts and is golden. Serve warm with garden green salad.

Per serving: Cal 194; Net Carbs 3g; Fat 17.2g; Protein 7.4g

Tofu & Mushroom Kebabs

Ingredients for 2 servings

1 cup white button mushrooms, quartered
1 (14 oz) block tofu, cubed
2 red onions, cut into wedges
2 tbsp olive oil
1 tsp Chinese five-spice
1 lemon, juiced
2 tbsp chopped parsley

Directions and Total Time: approx. 35 minutes

Thread tofu, mushrooms, and onions alternately on the skewers and set aside. In a bowl, mix olive oil, Chinese five-spice, and lemon juice. Brush the vegetable skewers with the sauce. Cook in a grill pan over high heat until the vegetables lightly char. Garnish with parsley and serve.

Per serving: Cal 372; Net Carbs 6.9g; Fat 27g; Protein 25g

Almond Bread & Bacon Pudding

Ingredients for 4 servings

1 tbsp olive oil
3 bacon slices, chopped
1 orange bell pepper, chopped
3 tbsp butter, softened
6 slices low carb bread
1 red onion, finely chopped
3 eggs
1 ½ cup almond milk
3 tbsp grated cheddar cheese
2 tbsp grated Parmesan

Directions and Total Time: approx. 35 minutes

Preheat oven to 300 F. Heat oil in a skillet t; add the bacon and bell pepper. Cook until the bacon browns. Brush a baking dish with the butter and apply some on both sides of each bread slice. Cut into cubes and arrange in the baking dish. Scatter with onions, bacon, and bell pepper. In a bowl, beat eggs with milk and pour the mixture over. Sprinkle with cheddar and Parmesan cheeses and bake for 20 minutes or until golden on top. Serve warm.

Per serving: Cal 362; Net Carbs 7.7g; Fat 27g; Protein 13g

One-Pan Mixed Garden Greens

Ingredients for 4 servings

1 red onion, finely sliced
A pinch swerve sugar
2 tbsp red wine vinegar
2 tbsp butter
1 tsp cumin powder
1 garlic clove, minced
1 cup asparagus, chopped
2 cups mixed garden greens
4 tbsp chopped parsley
Olive oil for drizzling
A handful pine nuts

Directions and Total Time: approx. 25 minutes

In a bowl, whisk onion, swerve and vinegar evenly and set aside. Melt butter in a skillet and stir in cumin and garlic; cook for 2 minutes. Add in asparagus to soften for 5 minutes. Mix in mixed the greens. Reduce the heat to low and steam the vegetables for 1 minute. Stir in parsley. Drizzle with olive oil, and garnish with pine nuts to serve.

Per serving: Cal 79; Net Carbs 3.5g; Fat 6.1g; Protein 1.9g

Walnut Broccoli Rice

Ingredients for 4 servings

2 tbsp butter
1 garlic clove, minced
2 heads large broccoli, riced
½ cup vegetable broth
Salt and black pepper to taste
¼ cup toasted walnuts, chopped
4 tbsp sesame seeds, toasted
3 tbsp chopped cilantro

Directions and Total Time: approx. 25 minutes

Melt butter in a pot and stir in garlic. Cook until fragrant, for 1 minute and stir in broccoli and vegetable broth. Allow steaming for 2 minutes. Season with salt and pepper and cook for 3-5 minutes. Open the lid; pour in walnuts, sesame seeds, and cilantro. Fluff the rice and serve.

Per serving: Cal 240; Net Carbs 3g; Fat 15g; Protein 11g

Mackerel and Green Beans Salad

Ingredients for 2 servings

2 mackerel fillets
2 hard-boiled eggs, sliced
1 tbsp coconut oil
2 cups green beans
1 avocado, sliced
4 cups mixed salad greens
2 tbsp olive oil
2 tbsp lemon juice
1 tsp Dijon mustard
Salt and black pepper to taste

Directions and Total Time: approx. 25 minutes

Fill a saucepan with water and add the beans and salt. Cook over medium heat for 3 minutes. Drain and set aside. Melt the coconut oil in a pan over medium heat. Add the mackerel fillets and cook for about 4 minutes per side, or until opaque and crispy. Divide the greens between two salad bowls. Top with mackerel, egg, and avocado slices. In a separate bowl, whisk together lemon juice, olive oil, mustard, salt, and pepper, and drizzle over the salad.

Per serving: Cal 525; Net Carbs 7.6g; Fat 42g; Protein 27g

Chicken Caesar Salad with Bok Choy

Ingredients for 4 servings

4 boneless and skinless chicken thighs
¼ cup lemon juice
4 tbsp olive oil
½ cup Caesar salad dressing,
12 bok choy, cut lengthwise
3 Parmesan crisps
Parmesan for garnishing

Directions and Total Time: approx. 1 hour 20 minutes

Combine the chicken, lemon juice, and 2 tbsp olive oil in a Ziploc bag. Seal the bag, shake to combine, and refrigerate for 1 hour. Preheat grill to medium heat and grill the chicken for about 4 minutes per side. Brush bok choy with the remaining olive oil and grill for 3 minutes. Place on a serving platter. Top with the chicken and drizzle the dressing over. Top with Parmesan crisps and sprinkle some grated Parmesan cheese over.

Per serving: Cal 529; Net Carbs 5g; Fat 39g; Protein 33g

Shrimp Salad with Cauliflower & Cucumber

Ingredients for 6 servings

1 cauliflower head, florets only	
1 pound medium shrimp	3 tbsp chopped dill
¼ cup plus 1 tbsp olive oil	¼ cup lemon juice
2 cucumber, chopped	2 tbsp lemon zest

Directions and Total Time: approx. 30 minutes

Heat 1 tbsp olive oil in a skillet and cook the shrimp until opaque, about 10 minutes. Microwave cauliflower florets for 5 minutes. Place shrimp, cauliflower, and cucumber in a large bowl. Whisk together the remaining olive oil, lemon zest, lemon juice, dill, salt, and pepper in another bowl. Pour the dressing over and toss to combine. Serve.

Per serving: Cal 214; Net Carbs 5g; Fat 17g; Protein 15g

Simple Italian Tricolore Salad

Ingredients for 4 servings

¼ pound buffalo mozzarella cheese, sliced	
3 tomatoes, sliced	2 tbsp pesto sauce
1 avocado, sliced	2 tbsp olive oil
8 kalamata olives	

Directions and Total Time: approx. 10 minutes

Arrange the tomato slices on a serving platter. Place the avocado slices in the middle. Arrange the olives around the avocado slices. Drop pieces of mozzarella on the platter. Drizzle pesto sauce and olive oil all over to serve.

Per serving: Cal 290; Net Carbs 4.3g; Fat 25g; Protein 9g

Low-Protein Artichoke Salad

Ingredients for 4 servings

6 baby artichokes	2 tsp balsamic vinegar
¼ cup cherry peppers, halved	1 tbsp chopped dill
¼ cup pitted olives, sliced	Salt and black pepper to taste
¼ cup olive oil	1 tbsp capers
¼ tsp lemon zest	¼ tsp caper brine

Directions and Total Time: approx. 35 minutes

Trim and halve the artichokes and put in a pot over medium heat and cover with salted water. Bring to a boil, lower the heat, and let simmer for 20 minutes until tender. Combine the rest of the ingredients, except for olives in a bowl.

Drain and plate the artichokes. Pour the prepared mixture over and toss to combine. Serve topped with olives.

Per serving: Cal 170; Net Carbs 5g; Fat 13g; Protein 1g

Cheddar & Chive Soufflés

Ingredients for 4 servings

½ cup almond flour	¾ cup heavy cream
A pinch of salt	2 cups grated cheddar cheese
1 tsp ground mustard	¼ cup chopped fresh chives
½ tsp black pepper	6 large eggs, separated
½ tsp arrowroot starch	¼ tsp cream of tartar
¼ tsp cayenne pepper	

Directions and Total Time: approx. 30 minutes

Preheat oven to 350 F and grease 8 ramekins with melted butter and arrange the ramekins on a large cookie sheet. In a bowl, whisk flour, salt, mustard, pepper, arrowroot starch and cayenne. Slowly whisk in heavy cream until well combined. Mix in cheddar cheese, chives, and egg yolks until well combined. In a large, clean bowl, beat the egg whites, cream of tartar and salt until stiff peaks form and glossy. Carefully fold this mixture into the cheese mix until well incorporated. Divide the mixture into the ramekins, place the cookie sheet in the oven and bake for 25 minutes or until the soufflés have risen by an inch or 2 above the rim and are golden brown. Remove and serve.

Per serving: Cal 460; Net Carbs 2g, Fat 38g, Protein 26g

Spinach Muffins

Ingredients for 4 servings

1 large egg, separated into egg white and yolk	
½ tsp salted butter	Salt and black pepper to taste
1/8 tsp cream of tartar	1/8 tsp onion powder
2 tbsp heavy cream	2 tbsp grated mozzarella
2 tbsp almond flour	¼ oz chopped spinach
1/8 tsp arrowroot starch	

Directions and Total Time: approx. 35 minutes

Preheat oven to 350 F, grease 8 ramekins with butter, and arrange the ramekins on a large cookie sheet. Remove to the fridge. Whip the egg white and cream of tartar using an electric mixer until stiff peaks forms. In another bowl, whisk the egg yolk and heavy cream until pale yellow and slightly thickened. Add almond flour, arrowroot starch, salt, pepper, and onion powder.

Mix smoothly and fold in mozzarella cheese and spinach. Mix one-third of the egg white mixture into the spinach mix until well incorporated. Add another third of the egg white mixture, mix again, and then add the last bit of the egg white mixture. Once well-mixed, divide the batter into the ramekins. Place the sheet in the oven and bake for 25 minutes or until golden brown on top, crisp around the edges, and tender inside.

Per serving: Cal 78; Net Carbs 2.4g, Fat 6.3g, Protein 3.4g

Cheese & Bacon Cups

Ingredients for 4 servings

4 eggs, separated into egg whites and egg yolks
2 tbsp butter
2 tbsp almond flour
1 cup heavy cream
1 ½ cups shredded Parmesan
4 oz bacon, chopped, cooked

Directions and Total Time: approx. 50 minutes

Preheat oven to 350 F and butter 4 ramekins with butter. Place the ramekins on a cookie sheet and set aside. Melt the butter over medium heat and mix in 1 tbsp of flour until well combined. Whisk in heavy cream, bring to a boil with frequent stirring and mix in almond flour until well combined. Turn the heat off and let cool for 3 minutes. Whisk in eggs yolks one after another until well combined and then, mix in Parmesan cheese. Beat the egg whites in a bowl using an electric hand mixer until stiff peaks form. Slowly fold this mixture into the egg yolk mix until with combined. Divide the mixture between the ramekins, top with bacon and bake for 35 minutes or until slight risen above the rim of the ramekins and golden brown.

Per serving: Cal 437; Net Carbs 4.8g, Fat 47g, Protein 21g

Lobster Roll Salad

Ingredients for 4 servings

5 cups cauliflower florets
⅓ cup diced celery
½ cup sliced black olives
2 cups cooked jumbo shrimp
1 tbsp dill, chopped
½ cup mayonnaise
1 tsp apple cider vinegar
¼ tsp celery seeds
2 tbsp lemon juice
2 tsp swerve sweetener

Directions and Total Time: approx. 1 hour 10 minutes

Combine cauliflower, celery, shrimp, olives, and dill in a large bowl. Whisk mayonnaise, vinegar, celery seeds, sweetener, and lemon juice in another bowl. Season with salt. Pour the dressing over the salad and toss to combine. Refrigerate for one hour. Serve cold topped with olives.

Per serving: Cal 182; Net Carbs 2g; Fat 15g; Protein 12g

Bacon & Avocado Salad

Ingredients for 4 servings

2 avocados, 1 chopped and 1 sliced
4 cooked bacon slices, crumbled
1 spring onion, sliced
2 cups spinach, chopped
1 lettuce head, chopped
2 hard-boiled eggs, chopped
3 tbsp olive oil
1 tsp Dijon mustard
1 tbsp apple cider vinegar
Salt and black pepper to taste

Directions and Total Time: approx. 20 minutes

Combine spinach, lettuce, eggs, chopped avocados, and spring onion in a large bowl. Whisk the olive oil, mustard, and vinegar in another bowl. Pour the dressing over. Toss to combine. Serve topped with sliced avocado and bacon.

Per serving: Cal 350; Net Carbs 3.4g; Fat 33g; Protein 7g

Quick and Easy Tuna Salad

Ingredients for 2 servings

1 cup shredded romaine lettuce
1 cup canned tuna, drained
1 tsp onion flakes
3 tbsp mayonnaise
1 tbsp lime juice
Sea salt to taste
6 black olives, sliced

Directions and Total Time: approx. 5 minutes

Combine tuna, mayo, lime juice, and salt in a small bowl. In a salad platter, arrange the lettuce and onion flakes. Spread tuna mixture, top with olives, and serve.

Per serving: Cal 248; Net Carbs 2g; Fat 20g; Protein 18.5g

Classic Greek Salad

Ingredients for 4 servings

5 tomatoes, chopped
1 cucumber, chopped
1 green bell pepper, chopped
1 small red onion, chopped
16 kalamata olives, chopped
4 tbsp capers
7 ounces feta cheese, chopped
1 tsp oregano, dried
4 tbsp olive oil
Salt to taste

Directions and Total Time: approx. 10 minutes

Place tomatoes, pepper, cucumber, onion, feta cheese, and olives in a bowl. Mix to combine well. Season with salt. Combine the capers, olive oil, and oregano in a small bowl. Drizzle the dressing over the salad.

Per serving: Cal 323; Net Carbs 8g; Fat 28g; Protein 9.3g

Mayo & Broccoli Slaw

Ingredients for 6 servings

2 tbsp swerve
1 tbsp Dijon mustard
1 tbsp olive oil
4 cups broccoli slaw
⅓ cup mayonnaise
1 tsp celery seeds
1 ½ tbsp apple cider vinegar
Salt and black pepper to taste

Directions and Total Time: approx. 10 minutes

Whisk together all ingredients, except for broccoli. Place broccoli in a large salad bowl. Pour the dressing over. Mix with your hands to combine well and serve.

Per serving: Cal 110; Net Carbs 2g; Fat 10g; Protein 3g

Roasted Mushrooms & Green Beans Salad

Ingredients for 4 servings

1 lb cremini mushrooms, sliced
½ cup green beans
3 tbsp melted vegan butter
Juice of 1 lemon
4 tbsp toasted hazelnuts

Directions and Total Time: approx. 25 minutes

Preheat oven to 450 F. Arrange mushrooms and green beans in a baking dish, drizzle butter, and sprinkle with salt and pepper. Roast for 20 minutes. Transfer to a bowl, drizzle with lemon juice and toss with hazelnuts. Serve.

Per serving: Cal 179; Net Carbs 7g; Fat 11g; Protein 5g

Squash Salad

Ingredients for 4 servings

3 oz fennel, sliced finely	1 cup vegan mayonnaise
2 lb green squash, cubed	2 tbsp chives, finely chopped
2 tbsp vegan butter	A pinch of mustard powder
2 oz chopped green onions	Chopped dill to garnish

Directions and Total Time: approx. 20 minutes

Put a pan over medium heat and melt butter. Fry squash until slightly softened, about 7 minutes; let cool. In a bowl, mix squash, fennel slices, green onions, vegan mayo, chives, and mustard powder. Garnish with dill and serve.

Per serving: Cal 317; Net Carbs 3g; Fat 31g; Protein 4g

Beet Tofu Salad

Ingredients for 4 servings

8 oz red beets, washed	1 cup mayonnaise
2 oz tofu, cubed	1 small romaine lettuce, torn
2 tbsp butter	Salt and black pepper to taste
½ red onion	Freshly chopped chives

Directions and Total Time: approx. 10 55

Put beets in a pot over medium heat, cover with salted water and bring to a boil for 40 minutes or until soft. Drain and allow cooling. Slip the skin off and slice the beets. Melt butter in a g pan over medium heat and fry tofu until browned, 3-4 minutes. Remove to a plate. In a salad bowl, combine beets, tofu, red onions, lettuce, salt, pepper, and mayonnaise. Garnish with chives and serve.

Per serving: Cal 415; Net Carbs 2g; Fat 40g; Protein 7g

Warm Collard Salad

Ingredients for 2 servings

¾ cup coconut cream	1 garlic clove, minced
2 tbsp vegan mayonnaise	2 oz vegan butter
A pinch of mustard powder	1 cup collards, rinsed
2 tbsp coconut oil	4 oz tofu cheese

Directions and Total Time: approx. 10 minutes

In a bowl, whisk whipping cream, vegan mayonnaise, mustard powder, coconut oil, garlic, salt, and pepper until well mixed; set aside. Melt vegan butter in a skillet over medium heat and sauté collards until wilted and brownish. Transfer to a salad bowl and pour the creamy dressing over. Mix the salad well and crumble the tofu cheese over.

Per serving: Cal 495; Net Carbs 5g; Fat 46g; Protein 11g

Cherry Tomato Salad with Chorizo

Ingredients for 4 servings

2 ½ cups cherry tomatoes	1 small red onion, chopped
2 ½ tbsp olive oil	2 tbsp chopped cilantro
4 chorizo sausages, chopped	Salt and black pepper to taste
2 tsp red wine vinegar	Sliced Kalamata olives

Directions and Total Time: approx. 10 minutes

Heat 1 tbsp of olive oil in a skillet and fry chorizo until golden. Cut in half tomatoes. In a salad bowl, whisk the remaining olive oil with vinegar and add onion, tomatoes, cilantro, and chorizo. Mix to coat in the dressing; season with salt and pepper. Garnish with olives to serve.

Per serving: Cal 138; Net Carbs 5.2g; Fat 8.9g; Protein 7g

Broccoli Salad with Tempeh & Cranberries

Ingredients for 4 servings

3 oz vegan butter	Salt and black pepper to taste
¾ lb tempeh slices, cubed	2 oz almonds
1 lb broccoli florets	½ cup frozen cranberries

Directions and Total Time: approx. 10 minutes

In a deep skillet, melt vegan butter over medium heat and fry tempeh cubes until brown on all sides. Add in broccoli and stir-fry for 6 minutes. Season with salt and pepper. Turn the heat off. Stir in almonds and cranberries to warm through. Share the salad into bowls and serve.

Per serving: Cal 740; Net Carbs 7g; Fat 72g; Protein 12g

Tangy Nutty Brussel Sprout Salad

Ingredients for 4 servings

1 lb Brussels sprouts, grated	1 tsp chili paste
1 lemon, juice and zest	2 oz pecans
½ cup olive oil	1 oz pumpkin seeds
Salt and black pepper to taste	1 oz sunflower seeds
1 tbsp vegan butter	½ tsp cumin powder

Directions and Total Time: approx. 20 minutes

Place Brussels sprouts in a salad bowl. In a bowl, mix lemon juice, zest, olive oil, salt, and pepper, and drizzle the dressing over Brussels sprouts. Toss and let marinate for 10 minutes. Melt vegan butter in a pan. Stir in chili paste, pecans, pumpkin and sunflower seeds, cumin powder, and salt. Cook on low heat for 4 minutes just to heat up; let cool. Mix nuts and seeds with Brussel sprouts to serve.

Per serving: Cal 420; Net Carbs 8g; Fat 35g; Protein 12g

Pesto Caprese Salad Stacks with Anchovies

Ingredients for 4 servings

4 red tomato slices	1 cup basil pesto
4 yellow tomato slices	4 anchovy fillets in oil
12 fresh mozzarella slices	

Directions and Total Time: approx. 10 minutes

On a serving platter, alternately stack a tomato slice, a mozzarella slice, an yellow tomato slice, another mozzarella slice, a red tomato slice, and then one a mozzarella slice. Repeat making 3 more stacks in the same way. Spoon pesto all over. Arrange anchovies on top to serve.

Per serving: Cal 178; Net Carbs 3.5g; Fat 6.1g; Protein 17g

Antipasti Skewers

Ingredients for 4 servings

4 zucchini lengthwise slices   8 cherry tomatoes
8 cubes cheddar cheese   8 fresh mint leaves
4 mini bamboo skewers

Directions and Total Time: approx. 45 minutes

Lay zucchini slices on a flat surface and place 2 cheddar cubes on one end of each slice. Wrap zucchini around the cheese cubes and insert a skewer each to secure. Alternately, thread the tomatoes and mint leaves onto the skewers and season with salt. Place the skewers on a plate, cover with plastic wrap, and chill for 30 minutes. Serve.

Per serving: Cal 93; Net Carbs 1.8g; Fat 3.9g; Protein 7g

Greek Salad

Ingredients for 2 servings

½ yellow bell pepper, sliced   10 Kalamata olives, pitted
3 tomatoes, sliced   ½ tbsp red wine vinegar
½ cucumber, sliced   4 tbsp olive oil
½ red onion, sliced thinly   Salt and ground black pepper
½ cup tofu cheese, cubed   2 tsp dried oregano

Directions and Total Time: approx. 10 minutes

Pour bell pepper, tomatoes, cucumber, red onion, and tofu cheese in a bowl. Drizzle red wine vinegar and olive oil all over and season with salt, pepper, and oregano; toss to coat. Transfer to a salad platter, top with olives, and serve.

Per serving: Cal 580; Net Carbs 13g; Fat 49g; Protein 15g

Buttered Greens with Almonds & Tofu Salad

Ingredients for 4 servings

2 tbsp olive oil   1 cup asparagus, halved
1 (7 oz) block tofu, cubed   Salt and black pepper to taste
2 tbsp butter   ½ lemon, juiced
1 cup green beans, trimmed   4 tbsp chopped almonds

Directions and Total Time: approx. 25 minutes

Heat olive oil in a skillet and fry the tofu until golden, 10 minutes; set aside. Add butter to the skillet and pour in green beans and asparagus; season with salt and pepper, toss and cook until softened. Mix in tofu and stir-fry further for 5 minutes. Drizzle with lemon juice and scatter almonds on top. Serve warm.

Per serving: Cal 237; Net Carbs 3.9g; Fat 15g; Protein 13g

Zucchini & Dill Bowls with Goat-Feta Cheese

Ingredients for 4 servings

4 zucchinis, spiralized   1 tbsp chopped dill leaves
Salt and black pepper to taste   ½ cup baby kale
½ lemon, zested and juiced   1/3 cup crumbled goat cheese
1 tbsp olive oil   1/3 cup crumbled feta cheese
¼ tsp Dijon mustard   2 tbsp toasted pine nuts

Directions and Total Time: approx. 35 minutes

Put the zucchinis in a bowl and season with salt and pepper. In a small bowl, mix the lemon juice, olive oil, and mustard. Pour the mixture over the zucchini and toss evenly. Add the dill, kale, goat cheese, feta cheese, and pine nuts. Toss to combine and serve.

Per serving: Cal 457; Net Carbs 9.5g; Fat 36g; Protein 26g

Roasted Bell Pepper Salad with Olives

Ingredients for 4 servings

8 large red bell peppers, deseeded and cut in wedges
½ tsp swerve sugar   3 tbsp toasted chopped walnuts
2 ½ tbsp olive oil   ½ tbsp balsamic vinegar
1/3 cup arugula   Crumbled goat cheese
1/3 cup pitted Kalamata olives   Toasted pine nuts for topping
1 tbsp mint leaves   Salt and black pepper to taste

Directions and Total Time: approx. 30 minutes

Preheat oven to 400 F. Pour bell peppers on a roasting pan; season with swerve sugar and drizzle with half of the olive oil. Roast for 20 minutes or until slightly charred; set aside to cool. Put arugula in a salad bowl and scatter with roasted bell peppers, olives, mint, walnuts, and drizzle with vinegar and olive oil. Season with salt and pepper. Toss, top with goat cheese and pine nuts and serve.

Per serving: Cal 163; Net Carbs 4.3g; Fat 13g; Protein 3.3g

Grandma's Cauliflower Salad with Peanuts

Ingredients for 4 servings

1 small head cauliflower, cut into florets
12 green olives, chopped   A handful of toasted peanuts
8 sun-dried tomatoes, drained   3 tbsp chopped parsley
3 tbsp chopped scallions   ½ cup watercress
1 lemon, zested and juiced   Salt and black pepper to taste
2 tbsp sesame oil   Lemon wedges to garnish

Directions and Total Time: approx. 20 minutes

Bring water to a boil in a pot. Pour cauliflower into a steamer basket and soften over the boiling water, 10 minutes. Transfer cauliflower to a salad bowl. Add in olives, tomatoes, scallions, lemon zest and juice, sesame oil, peanuts, parsley, and watercress. Season with salt, pepper, and mix using a spoon. Serve with lemon wedges.

Per serving: Cal 203; Net Carbs 6.4g; Fat 15g; Protein 6.6g

Bruschetta with Tomato & Basil

Ingredients for 4 servings

3 ripe tomatoes, chopped   Salt to taste
6 fresh basil leaves   4 slices zero carb bread, halved
5 tbsp olive oil   1 garlic clove, halved

Directions and Total Time: approx. 1 hour 15 minutes

In a bowl, mix tomatoes and basil until combined. Drizzle with 2 tbsp olive oil and salt; do not stir. Set aside.

Brush bread slices with the remaining olive oil, arrange on a baking sheet, and place under the broiler. Cook for 2 minutes per side or until lightly browned. Transfer to a plate and rub garlic on both sides. Cover with tomato topping. Drizzle a little more of olive oil on top and serve.

Per serving: Cal 212; Net Carbs 2.7g; Fat 19g; Protein 8g

Speedy Beef Carpaccio

Ingredients for 4 servings

1 tbsp olive oil	¼ lb rare roast beef, sliced
½ lemon, juiced	1 ½ cups baby arugula
Salt and black pepper to taste	¼ cup grated Parmesan cheese

Directions and Total Time: approx. 10 minutes

In a bowl, whisk olive oil, lemon juice, salt, and pepper until well combined. Spread the beef on a large serving plate, top with arugula and drizzle the olive oil mixture on top. Sprinkle with grated Parmesan cheese and serve.

Per serving: Cal 106; Net Carbs 4.1g; Fat 5g; Protein 10g

Roasted Asparagus with Goat Cheese

Ingredients for 4 servings

1 lb asparagus, halved	1 tbsp sugar-free maple syrup
2 tbsp olive oil	½ cup arugula
½ tsp dried tarragon	4 tbsp crumbled goat cheese
½ tsp dried oregano	2 tbsp hazelnuts
½ tsp sesame seeds	1 lemon, cut into wedges

Directions and Total Time: approx. 30 minutes

Preheat oven to 350 F. Pour asparagus on a baking tray, drizzle with olive oil, tarragon, oregano, salt, pepper, and sesame seeds. Toss and roast for 15 minutes; remove and drizzle the maple syrup, and continue cooking for 5 minutes or until slightly charred. Spread arugula in a salad bowl and spoon the asparagus on top. Scatter with the goat cheese, hazelnuts, and serve with the lemon wedges.

Per serving: Cal 146; Net Carbs 3.4g; Fat 13g; Protein 4.4g

Savory Gruyere & Bacon Cake

Ingredients for 4 servings

½ cup shredded Gruyere cheese	
4 eggs, eggs yolks and whites separated	
2 tbsp butter	1 cup heavy cream
2 tbsp almond flour	6 slices bacon, chopped

Directions and Total Time: approx. 50 minutes

Melt butter in a pan over medium heat and mix in 1 tbsp of almond flour until well combined. Whisk in heavy cream, bring to a boil and while stirring, mix in the remaining almond flour until smooth. Turn the heat off. Cool the mixture for 3 minutes and slowly mix the batter into the egg yolks until well combined without cooking. Stir in Gruyere cheese until evenly distributed. Beat the egg whites in a mixer until stiff peak forms.

Fold the egg whites into the egg yolk mixture until well combined. Divide the mixture between 4 ramekins, top with bacon and bake in the oven for 35 minutes at 320 F.

Per serving: Cal 495; Net Carbs 2g, Fat 46g, Protein 17.3g

Warm Mushroom & Yellow Pepper Salad

Ingredients for 4 servings

1 cup mixed mushrooms, chopped	
2 tbsp sesame oil	1 tsp sugar-free maple syrup
2 yellow bell peppers, sliced	½ tsp ginger paste
1 garlic clove, minced	Salt and black pepper to taste
2 tbsp tamarind sauce	Chopped toasted pecans
½ tsp hot sauce	Sesame seeds to garnish

Directions and Total Time: approx. 20 minutes

Heat half of the sesame oil in a skillet, sauté bell peppers and mushrooms for 8-10 minutes; season with salt and pepper. In a bowl, mix garlic, tamarind sauce, hot sauce, maple syrup, and ginger paste. Stir the mix into the vegetables and stir-fry for 2-3 minutes. Divide salad between 4 plates; drizzle with the remaining sesame oil and garnish with pecans and sesame seeds. Serve.

Per serving: Cal 289; Net Carbs 5.2g; Fat 27g; Protein 4.2g

Broccoli, Spinach & Feta Salad

Ingredients for 4 servings

2 tbsp olive oil	2 cups chopped spinach
1 tbsp white wine vinegar	1/3 cup chopped walnuts
2 tbsp poppy seeds	1/3 cup sunflower seeds
Salt and black pepper to taste	1/3 cup blueberries
2 cups broccoli slaw	2/3 cup chopped feta cheese

Directions and Total Time: approx. 15 minutes

In a bowl, whisk olive oil, vinegar, poppy seeds, salt, and pepper; set aside. In a salad bowl, combine the broccoli slaw, spinach, walnuts, sunflower seeds, blueberries, and feta cheese. Drizzle the dressing on top, toss, and serve.

Per serving: Cal 397; Net Carbs 4.9g; Fat 3.8g; Protein 9g

Tofu Pops

Ingredients for 4 servings

1 (14 oz) block tofu, cubed	12 slices bacon
1 bunch of chives, chopped	12 mini skewers
1 lemon, zested and juiced	1 tsp butter

Directions and Total Time: approx. 1 hour 17 minutes

Mix chives, lemon zest, and juice in a bowl and toss the tofu cubes in the mixture. Marinate for 1 hour. Remove the zest and chives off the cubes and wrap each tofu in a bacon slice; insert each skewer and the end of the bacon. Melt butter in a skillet and fry tofu skewers until the bacon browns and crisps. Serve with mayo dipping sauce.

Per serving: Cal 392; Net Carbs 9g, Fat 22g, Protein 18g

Blackberry Camembert Puffs

Ingredients for 4 servings

For the pastry cups:

¼ cup butter, cold and crumbled | 1/4 teaspoon cream of tartar
¼ cup almond flour | 3 whole eggs, unbeaten
3 tbsp coconut flour | 3 tbsp erythritol
½ tsp xanthan gum | 1 ½ tsp vanilla extract
½ tsp salt | 1 whole egg, beaten
4 tbsp cream cheese, softened

For the filling:

5 oz Camembert, sliced and cut into 16 cubes
1 tsp butter | 5 tbsp erythritol
1 yellow onion, chopped | ½ cup fresh blackberries
3 tbsp red wine | Freshly parsley to garnish
1 tbsp balsamic vinegar

Directions and Total Time: approx. 30 minutes

Preheat oven to 350 F, turn a muffin tray upside down and lightly grease with cooking spray. In a bowl, mix almond and coconut flours, xanthan gum, and salt. Add in cream cheese, cream of tartar, and butter; mix with an electric hand mixer until crumbly. Stir in erythritol and vanilla extract until mixed. Then, pour in three eggs, one after another while mixing until formed into a ball. Flatten the dough on a clean flat surface, cover in plastic wrap, and refrigerate for 1 hour. Dust a clean flat surface with almond flour, unwrap the dough, and roll out the dough into a large rectangle. Cut into 16 squares and press each onto each muffin mound on the tray to form a bowl shape. Brush with the remaining eggs and bake for 10 minutes.

To make the filling, melt butter in a skillet and sauté onion for 3 minutes. Stir in red wine, balsamic vinegar, erythritol, and blackberries. Cook until the berries become jammy and wine reduces, 10 minutes. Set aside. Take out the tray and place a cheese cubes in each pastry. Return to oven and bake for 3 minutes. Spoon a tsp each of the blackberry sauce on top. Garnish with parsley to serve.

Per serving: Cal 372; Net Carbs 4.4g, Fat 32g, Protein 14g

Mini Ricotta Cakes

Ingredients for 4 servings

2 tbsp olive oil | 2 scallions, chopped
2 tbsp butter | Salt and black pepper to taste
2 garlic cloves, minced | ¼ cup grated Parmesan
1 white onion, finely chopped | ½ cup ricotta cheese
1 cup cauli rice | 1 cup almond flour
¼ cup white wine | ½ cup golden flaxseed meal
¼ cup vegetable stock | 2 eggs

Directions and Total Time: approx. 40 minutes

Heat butter in a saucepan over medium heat. Stir in garlic and onion and cook until fragrant and soft, 3 minutes. Mix in cauli rice for 30 seconds; add in wine, stir, allow reduction and absorption into cauli rice.

Mix in stock, scallions, salt, pepper, remaining butter, Parmesan and ricotta cheeses. Cover the pot and cook until the liquid reduces and the rice thickens. Open the lid, stir well, and spoon the mixture into a bowl to cool. Mold the dough into mini patties, about 14 to 16 and set aside. Heat olive oil in a skillet over medium heat; meanwhile pour the almond flour onto a plate, the golden flaxseed meal in another, and beat the eggs in a medium bowl. Lightly dredge each patty in the flour, then in eggs, and then coated accurately in the flaxseed meal. Fry in the oil until compacted and golden brown, 2 minutes on each side. Transfer to a paper towel-lined plate, plate, and garnish with some scallions.

Per serving: Cal 362; Net Carbs 6.2g, Fat 29g, Protein 13g

Mediterranean Roasted Turnip Bites

Ingredients for 4 servings

1 lb turnips, sliced into rounds | 2 tbsp chopped fresh oregano
½ cup olive oil | 3 tbsp dried Italian seasoning
2 garlic cloves, minced | ¼ cup marinara sauce
1 tbsp chopped fresh parsley | ¼ cup grated mozzarella

Directions and Total Time: approx. 1 hour

Preheat oven to 400 F. Place turnip slices into a bowl and toss with olive oil. Add in garlic, parsley, oregano, and Italian seasoning and mix well. Arrange on a greased baking sheet and roast for 25 minutes, flipping halfway. Remove and brush the marinara sauce. Sprinkle with mozzarella cheese and bake in the oven until the cheese is golden, 15 minutes. Garnish with parsley and serve warm.

Per serving: Cal 326; Net Carbs 3.8g; Fat 28g; Protein 5g

Cream Cheese & Caramelized Onion Dip

Ingredients for 4 servings

2 tbsp butter | ¼ cup white wine
3 yellow onions, thinly sliced | 2 cups sour cream
1 tsp swerve sugar | 8 oz cream cheese, softened
Salt to taste | ½ tbsp Worcestershire sauce

Directions and Total Time: approx. 30 minutes

Melt butter in a skillet and add in onions, swerve sugar, and salt and cook with frequent stirring for 10-15 minutes. Add in white wine, stir and allow sizzling out, 10 minutes. In a serving bowl, mix sour cream and cream cheese until well combined. Add onions and Worcestershire sauce; stir well into the cream. Serve with celery sticks.

Per serving: Cal 383; Net Carbs 8.3g; Fat 34g; Protein 8g

Tofu Jalapeño Peppers

Ingredients for 4 servings

For the poppers:

1 tbsp olive oil | 1 garlic clove, minced
4 oz firm tofu, chopped in bits | ½ cup cream cheese

1 lemon, zested juiced	Salt and black pepper to taste
4 scallions, finely chopped	6 jalapeño peppers, halved
2 tbsp chopped cilantro	3 tbsp grated cheddar cheese

For the dip:

1 tsp lemon juice	1 tbsp chopped cilantro
1 cup sour cream	

Directions and Total Time: approx. 30 minutes

Preheat oven to 370 F. Heat olive oil in a skillet and fry tofu until golden. Transfer to a bowl. Mix in garlic, cream cheese, lemon zest, juice, scallions, cilantro, salt, and pepper. Arrange jalapeño peppers on a greased baking dish. Fill tofu mixture and sprinkle with cheddar cheese. Bake for 15 minutes or until the cheese is golden brown. In a bowl, mix lemon juice, sour cream, cilantro, and season with salt and pepper. Serve the dip with the poppers.

Per serving: Cal 247; Net Carbs 6.9g, Fat 21g, Protein 9g

Avocado Pate with Flaxseed Toasts

Ingredients for 4 servings

1/2 cup flaxseed meal	1 pinch salt

For the Avocado pate:

3 ripe avocado, chopped	1 lemon, zested and juiced
4 tbsp Greek yogurt	Black pepper to taste
2 tbsp chopped green onions	Smoked paprika to garnish

Directions and Total Time: approx. 5 minutes

For the flaxseed toasts:

Preheat oven to 350 F. Place a skillet over medium heat. Mix in flaxseed meal, 1/4 cup water, and salt and mix continually to form the dough into a ball. Place the dough between 2 parchment papers, put on a flat surface, and flatten thinly with a rolling pin. Remove the papers and cut the pastry into tortilla chips. Place on a baking sheet and bake for 8-12 minutes or until crispy. In a bowl, mix avocado, yogurt, green onions, lemon zest, juice, and black pepper until evenly combined. Spread the pate on the toasts and garnish with paprika. Serve immediately.

Per serving: Cal 364; Net Carbs 4g, Fat 31g, Protein 7.4g

Sweet Tahini Twists

Ingredients for 4 servings

For the puff pastry:

¼ cup almond flour	¼ cup butter, cold
3 tbsp coconut flour	3 whole eggs
½ tsp xanthan gum	3 tbsp erythritol
½ tsp salt	1 ½ tsp vanilla extract
4 tbsp cream cheese, softened	1 whole egg, beaten
¼ teaspoon cream of tartar	

For the filling:

2 tbsp sugar-free maple syrup	1 egg, beaten
3 tbsp tahini	2 tbsp poppy seeds
2 tbsp sesame seeds	

Directions and Total Time: approx. 15 min + cooling time

Preheat oven to 350 F and line a baking tray with parchment paper. In a bowl, mix almond and coconut flours, xanthan gum, and salt. Add in cream cheese, cream of tartar, and butter; mix with an electric mixer until crumbly. Add erythritol and vanilla extract until mixed. Then, pour in 3 eggs one after another while mixing until formed into a ball. Flatten the dough on a clean flat surface, cover in plastic wrap, and refrigerate for 1 hour.

Dust a clean flat surface with almond flour, unwrap the dough, and roll out the dough into a large rectangle. In a bowl, mix sugar-free maple syrup with tahini and spread the mixture over the pastry. Sprinkle with half of the sesame seeds and cut the dough into 16 thin strips. Fold each strip in half. Brush the top with the remaining egg, sprinkle with the remaining seeds, and poppy seeds. Twist the pastry three to four times into straws and place on the baking sheet. Bake until golden brown, 15 minutes. Serve with chocolate sauce.

Per serving: Cal 348; Net Carbs 3.1g, Fat 31g, Protein 11g

Feta Cheese Choux Buns

Ingredients for 4 servings

2 sprigs rosemary	2 white onions, thinly sliced
6 tbsp butter	2 tbsp red wine vinegar
2/3 cup almond flour	1 tsp swerve brown sugar
3 eggs, beaten	1 cup crumbled feta cheese
1 tbsp olive oil	½ cup heavy whipping cream

Directions and Total Time: approx. 40 minutes

Preheat oven to 350 F and line a baking tray with parchment paper. In a saucepan, warm 1 cup of water, salt, and butter melts. Bring to a boil and sift in flour, beating vigorously until ball forms. Turn the heat off; keep beating while adding the eggs, one at a time, until the dough is smooth and slightly thickened. Scoop mounds of the dough onto the baking dish. Press a hole in the center of each mound. Bake for 20 minutes until risen and golden. Remove from oven and pierce the sides of the buns with a toothpick. Return to oven and bake for 2 minutes until crispy. Set aside to cool.

Tear out the middle part of the bun (keep the torn out part) to create a hole in the bun for the cream filling. Set aside. Heat olive oil in a saucepan and sauté onions and rosemary for 2 minutes. Stir in swerve, vinegar, and cook to bubble for 3 minutes or until caramelized. In a bowl, beat whipping cream and feta together. Spoon the mixture into a piping bag and press a spoonful of the mixture into the buns. Cover with the torn out portion of pastry and top with onion relish to serve.

Per serving: Cal 384; Net Carbs 2.5g, Fat 37g, Protein 10g

SOUPS & STEWS

Cheddar & Broccoli Soup

Ingredients for 4 servings

¾ cup heavy cream	4 cups veggie broth
1 onion, diced	2 tbsp butter
1 tsp minced garlic	3 cups grated cheddar cheese
4 cups chopped broccoli	Salt and black pepper to taste

Directions and Total Time: approx. 20 minutes

Melt butter in a pot and sauté onion and garlic for 3 minutes. Season with salt and pepper. Add broth, broccoli and bring to a boil. Reduce the heat and simmer for 10 minutes. Blitz the soup with a hand blender until smooth. Add in 2 cups cheese and cook for 1 minute. Stir in heavy cream. Serve topped with remaining cheddar cheese.

Per serving: Cal 561; Net Carbs 7g; Fat 52g; Protein 24g

Slow Cooked Sausage Soup with Beer

Ingredients for 8 servings

1 cup heavy cream	1 tsp red pepper flakes
10 oz beef sausages, sliced	6 ounces beer
1 cup chopped celery	16 ounces beef stock
1 cup chopped carrots	1 onion, diced
4 garlic cloves, minced	1 cups cheddar cheese
8 ounces cream cheese	3 tbsp chopped cilantro

Directions and Total Time: approx. 8 hours

Add broth, beer, sausage, carrots, onion, celery, salt, red pepper flakes, salt, and pepper to a slow cooker and stir to combine. Add enough water to cover all ingredients by 2 inches. Close the lid and cook for 6 hours on Low. Stir in heavy cream, cheddar, and cream cheeses and cook for 2 hours. Ladle the soup into bowls and garnish with cilantro.

Per serving: Cal 244; Net Carbs 4g; Fat 17g, Protein 5g

Red Gazpacho

Ingredients for 6 servings

2 green peppers, roasted	1 cup olive oil
2 large red peppers, roasted	2 tbsp lemon juice
2 avocados, flesh scoped out	4 tomatoes, chopped
2 garlic cloves	7 ounces goat cheese
2 spring onions, chopped	1 red onion, coarsely chopped
1 cucumber, chopped	2 tbsp apple cider vinegar

Directions and Total Time: approx. 10 min + chilling time

Place peppers, tomatoes, avocado, spring onions, garlic, lemon juice, oil, vinegar, and salt in a food processor. Pulse until slightly chunky but smooth. Adjust the seasoning and transfer to a pot. Stir in cucumbers and red onion. Cover and chill in the fridge for 2 hours. Serve very cold, topped with goat cheese and a drizzle of olive oil.

Per serving: Cal 528; Net Carbs 8.5g; Fat 46g, Protein 7g

Superfood & Low-Protein Soup

Ingredients for 6 servings

1 broccoli head, chopped	4 cups veggie stock
7 ounces spinach	1 cup coconut milk
1 onion, chopped	1 tbsp ghee
2 garlic cloves, minced	1 bay leaf
5 ounces watercress	Salt and black pepper to taste

Directions and Total Time: approx. 20 minutes

Melt ghee in a pot over medium heat. Add onion and garlic and cook for 3 minutes. Stir in broccoli and cook for an additional 5 minutes. Pour in stock and bay leaf. Bring to a boil, reduce the heat and simmer for 3 minutes. Add spinach and watercress, and cook for 3 minutes. Stir in coconut cream and salt and pepper. Discard the bay leaf, and blend the soup with a hand blender. Serve cold.

Per serving: Cal 392; Net Carbs 5.8g; Fat 38g, Protein 5g

Chicken Enchilada Soup

Ingredients for 4 servings

½ cup salsa enchilada verde	4 ounces cream cheese
2 cups cooked shredded chicken	½ tsp chili powder
2 cups chicken broth	½ tsp ground cumin
1 cup grated cheddar cheese	½ tsp fresh cilantro, chopped

Directions and Total Time: approx. 15 minutes

Combine cream cheese, salsa verde, and broth in a food processor; pulse until smooth. Transfer to a pot. Cook until hot, but do not bring to a boil. Add chicken, chili powder, and cumin; cook for 5 minutes. Stir in cheddar cheese and season to taste. Serve sprinkled with cilantro.

Per serving: Cal 346; Net Carbs 3g; Fat 23g, Protein 25g

Creamy Chicken Soup

Ingredients for 4 servings

2 cups shredded cooked chicken	4 tbsp chopped cilantro
3 tbsp butter, melted	⅓ cup buffalo sauce
4 cups chicken broth	4 ounces cream cheese

Directions and Total Time: approx. 15 minutes

Blend butter, buffalo sauce, and cream cheese in a food processor until uniform and smooth. Transfer to a pot. Add the chicken to the pot, pour in the broth and cook until heated through. Serve garnished with cilantro.

Per serving: Cal 406; Net Carbs 5g; Fat 29.5g, Protein 26g

Coconut Cream Pumpkin Soup

Ingredients for 4 servings

2 red onions, cut into wedges	8 oz vegan butter
2 garlic cloves	Salt and black pepper to taste
10 oz pumpkin, cubed	Juice of 1 lime
10 oz butternut squash, cubed	¾ cup vegan mayonnaise
2 tbsp melted vegan butter	Toasted pumpkin seeds

Directions and Total Time: approx. 55 minutes

Preheat oven to 400 F. Place onions, pumpkin, and squash to a baking sheet and drizzle with melted butter. Season with salt and pepper. Roast for 30 minutes or until the veggies are golden brown and fragrant; transfer to a pot. Add in 2 cups water, bring to a boil and cook for 15 minutes. Break the remaining vegan butter in the pot and puree the vegetables until smooth. Stir in lime juice, and vegan mayo. Serve garnished with toasted pumpkin seeds.

Per serving: Cal 643; Fat 57g; Net Carbs 9g; Protein 10g

Keto Reuben Soup

Ingredients for 6 servings

1 onion, diced	2 cups heavy cream
7 cups beef stock	1 cup sauerkraut
1 tsp caraway seeds	1 pound corned beef, chopped
2 celery stalks, diced	3 tbsp butter
2 garlic cloves, minced	1 ½ cups Swiss cheese
¾ tsp black pepper	Salt and black pepper to taste

Directions and Total Time: approx. 30 minutes

Melt butter in a large pot. Add onions and celery, and fry for 3 minutes until tender. Add garlic, and cook for another minute. Pour the broth over and stir in sauerkraut, salt, caraway seeds, and add a pinch of pepper. Bring to a boil. Reduce the heat to low, and add the corned beef. Cook for about 15 minutes. Adjust the seasoning. Stir in heavy cream and Swiss cheese and cook for 1 minute. Serve.

Per serving: Cal 450; Net Carbs 8g; Fat 37g, Protein 23g

Chorizo & Cauliflower Soup

Ingredients for 4 servings

1 cauliflower head, chopped	2 cups chicken broth
1 turnip, chopped	1 small onion, chopped
3 tbsp butter	2 cups water
1 chorizo sausage, sliced	Salt and black pepper to taste

Directions and Total Time: approx. 40 minutes

Melt 2 tbsp of butter in a pot. Stir in onions and cook until soft and golden, 6 minutes. Add cauliflower and turnip, and cook for another 5 minutes. Pour in broth. Bring to a boil, simmer, and cook for 20 minutes. Melt the remaining butter in a skillet. Add in chorizo and cook for 5 minutes. Blitz the soup with a hand blender until smooth. Adjust the seasonings. Serve in deep bowls topped with chorizo.

Per serving: Cal 251; Net Carbs 5.7g; Fat 19g, Protein 10g

Ginger-Spinach Egg Benedict Soup

Ingredients for 4 servings

2 tbsp butter	2 cups baby spinach, chopped
1 tbsp sesame oil	2 cups chopped green beans
1 small onion, finely sliced	4 cups vegetable stock
3 garlic cloves, minced	3 tbsp chopped cilantro
2 tsp ginger paste	4 eggs

Directions and Total Time: approx. 35 minutes

Melt butter in a pot and sauté onions, garlic, and ginger for 4 minutes, stirring frequently. Stir in spinach, allowing wilting, and pour in green beans and stock. Bring to boil, reduce the heat, and simmer for 10 minutes. Transfer the soup to a blender and puree until smooth. Bring 3 cups of vinegared water to simmer and when hot, slide in an egg to poach for 3 minutes; remove with a perforated spoon. Repeat the process with the remaining eggs, one at time. Divide the soup between 4 bowls and place an egg on each one, drizzle with sesame oil and cilantro, and serve.

Per serving: Cal 463; Net Carbs 5.8g; Fat 30g, Protein 23g

Spinach & Poached Egg Soup

Ingredients for 4 servings

1 tbsp olive oil	4 cups vegetable stock
2 tbsp butter	6 sprigs parsley
1 red onion, thinly sliced	1 tbsp fresh dill for garnishing
3 garlic cloves, finely sliced	Salt and black pepper to taste
4 cups spinach, chopped	4 eggs
1 lettuce head, chopped	1 cup grated Parmesan cheese

Directions and Total Time: approx. 35 minutes

Warm oil and butter in a saucepan and sauté onion and garlic for 3 minutes. Stir in spinach and lettuce and cook for 5 minutes. Pour in vegetable stock; bring to a boil. Reduce the heat and simmer for 10 minutes. With an immersion blender, puree the soup until smooth. Season with salt and pepper. Bring 1 cup of water to a boil in another saucepan. Create a whirlpool in the center using a wooden spoon. Allow water to almost settle back to normal and crack in an egg. Poach for 3 minutes, remove, and set aside in a plate. Repeat poaching the remaining eggs. Divide the soup into serving bowls, top with poached eggs, garnish with dill, Parmesan cheese, and serve warm.

Per serving: Cal 515; Net Carbs 4.5g; Fat 33g, Protein 38g

Rosemary Onion Soup

Ingredients for 4 servings

2 tbsp butter	½ cup dry white wine
1 tbsp olive oil	2 sprigs chopped rosemary
3 cups sliced white onions	Salt and black pepper to taste
2 garlic cloves, thinly sliced	2 cups almond milk
2 tsp almond flour	1 cup grated Parmesan cheese

Directions and Total Time: approx. 35 minutes

Heat butter and oil in a pot and sauté onions and garlic for 6-7 minutes. Reduce the heat to low and cook further for 10 minutes. Stir in flour, wine, salt, pepper, and rosemary and pour in 2 cups water. Bring to a boil and simmer for 10 minutes. Pour in milk and half of the Parmesan cheese. Stir to melt the cheese and spoon into a serving bowl. Top with the remaining Parmesan cheese and serve.

Per serving: Cal 340; Net Carbs 5.6g; Fat 23g, Protein 15g

Wild Mushroom Soup

Ingredients for 4 servings

12 oz wild mushrooms, chopped
¼ cup butter — 2 garlic cloves, minced
5 ounces crème fraiche — 4 cups chicken broth
2 tsp thyme leaves — Salt and black pepper to taste

Directions and Total Time: approx. 30 minutes

Melt butter in a large pot over medium heat. Add and cook garlic for 1 minute until tender. Add mushrooms, season with salt and pepper, and cook for 9 minutes. Pour the broth over and bring to a boil. Reduce the heat and simmer for 10 minutes. Blitz with a hand blender until smooth. Stir in crème Fraiche. Serve garnished with thyme.

Per serving: Cal 281; Net Carbs 5.8g; Fat 25g, Protein 6g

Spinach & Kale Soup with Fried Collards

Ingredients for 4 servings

3 oz vegan butter — 3 tbsp chopped mint leaves
1 cup spinach, coarsely — Juice from 1 lime
1 cup kale, coarsely — 1 cup collard greens, chopped
1 large avocado — 3 garlic cloves, minced
3 ½ cups coconut cream — 3 tbsp green cardamom powder
1 cup vegetable broth — Toasted pistachios

Directions and Total Time: approx. 15 minutes

Set a saucepan and melt vegan butter. Put in spinach and kale and sauté for 5 minutes. Remove to a food processor. Add in avocado, coconut cream, broth, mint, lime juice, salt, and pepper and puree until smooth; reserve the soup. Reheat the saucepan with butter and add collard green, garlic, and cardamom and sauté for 4 minutes. Spoon into bowls and garnish with scoops of collards and pistachios.

Per serving: Cal 885; Fat 80g; Net Carbs 15g; Protein 14g

Tofu Goulash Soup

Ingredients for 4 servings

1 ½ cups tofu, crumbled — ¼ tsp red chili flakes
4 ¼ oz vegan butter — 1 tbsp dried basil
1 white onion — Salt and black pepper to taste
2 garlic cloves — 1 ½ cups crushed tomatoes
8 oz chopped butternut squash — 3 cups vegetable broth
1 red bell pepper — 1 ½ tsp red wine vinegar
1 tbsp paprika powder — Chopped cilantro to serve

Directions and Total Time: approx. 25 minutes

Melt vegan butter in a pot set over medium heat and sauté onion and garlic for 3 minutes until fragrant and soft. Stir in tofu and cook for 3 minutes; add squash, bell pepper, paprika, red chili flakes, basil, salt, and pepper. Cook for 2 minutes. Pour in tomatoes and broth. Cover the lid and bring to a boil, then reduce the heat to simmer for 10 minutes; mix in vinegar. Garnish with cilantro and serve.

Per serving: Cal 481; Fat 41.8g; Net Carbs 9g; Protein 12g

Celery Dill Soup

Ingredients for 4 servings

1 small head cauliflower, cut into florets
2 tbsp coconut oil — ¼ tsp nutmeg powder
½ lb celery root, chopped — 3 ½ cups vegetable stock
1 garlic clove — 5 oz butter
1 white onion, sliced — Juice from 1 lemon
¼ cup dill, roughly chopped — ¼ cup coconut cream
1 tsp cumin powder — Salt and black pepper to taste

Directions and Total Time: approx. 25 minutes

Warm coconut oil in a pot over medium heat and sauté celery root, garlic clove, and onion until fragrant and soft, about 5 minutes. Stir in dill, cumin, and nutmeg and fry further for 1 minute. Mix in cauli florets and stock. Bring the soup to a boil for 15 minutes. Turn the heat off. Add in butter and lemon juice. Puree the ingredients with an immersion blender until smooth. Mix in coconut cream and season to taste. Spoon into bowls and serve warm.

Per serving: Cal 410; Fat 37g; Net Carbs 9g; Protein 6g

Broccoli Fennel Soup

Ingredients for 4 servings

1 fennel bulb, chopped — 1 garlic clove
10 oz broccoli, cut into florets — 1 cup cream cheese
3 cups vegetable stock — 3 oz butter
Salt and black pepper to taste — ½ cup chopped fresh oregano

Directions and Total Time: approx. 25 minutes

Put fennel, broccoli, and garlic in a pot and cover with stock. Bring to a boil over medium heat and cook until the vegetables are soft, about 17 minutes. Season with salt and pepper. Pour in cream cheese, butter, and oregano; puree the ingredients with an immersion blender until smooth. Serve with vegan cheese crackers.

Per serving: Cal 510; Fat 44g; Net Carbs 7g; Protein 16g

Parsnip–Tomato Soup

Ingredients for 4 servings

1 tbsp butter — 2 parsnips, chopped
1 tbsp olive oil — 3 cups chopped tomatoes
1 large red onion, chopped — 4 cups vegetable stock
4 garlic cloves, minced — 3 cups coconut milk
6 red bell peppers, sliced — 2 cups toasted chopped walnuts
1 daikon radish, chopped — 1 cup grated Parmesan cheese

Directions and Total Time: approx. 40 minutes

Heat butter and olive oil in a pot and sauté onion and garlic for 3 minutes. Stir in bell peppers, daikon radish, and parsnips; cook for 10 minutes. Pour in tomatoes and stock; simmer for 20 minutes. Puree the soup with an immersion blender. Add in coconut milk and stir until mixed. Garnish with walnuts and Parmesan cheese to serve.

Per serving: Cal 955; Net Carbs 4g; Fat 86g, Protein 19.1g

Mixed Mushroom Soup

Ingredients for 4 servings

5 oz white button mushrooms, chopped
5 oz cremini mushrooms, chopped
5 oz shiitake mushrooms, chopped
4 oz unsalted butter   4 cups water
1 small onion, finely chopped   1 vegan stock cube, crushed
1 clove garlic, minced   1 tbsp plain vinegar
½ lb celery root, chopped   1 cup coconut cream
½ tsp dried rosemary   6 leaves basil, chopped

Directions and Total Time: approx. 35 minutes

Melt butter in a saucepan. Sauté onion, garlic, mushrooms, and celery root until golden brown and fragrant, about 6 minutes. Reserve some mushrooms for garnishing. Add in rosemary, water, stock cube, and vinegar. Stir and bring to a boil for 6 minutes. Reduce the heat and simmer for 15 minutes. Mix in coconut cream and puree. Spoon into bowls garnished with the reserved mushrooms and basil.

Per serving: Cal 506; Fat 46g; Net Carbs 12g; Protein 8g

Creamy Tofu Soup

Ingredients for 4 servings

1 cup cremini mushrooms, sliced and pre-cooked
1 tbsp olive oil   Salt and black pepper to taste
1 garlic clove, minced   2 (14 oz) silken tofu, drained
1 white onion, finely chopped   2 cups almond milk
1 tsp ginger puree   1 tbsp chopped basil
1 cup vegetable stock   Finely chopped parsley
2 turnips, peeled and chopped   Chopped walnuts for topping

Directions and Total Time: approx. 25 minutes

Heat olive oil in a saucepan and sauté garlic, onion, and ginger puree until fragrant and soft, about 3 minutes. Pour in stock, turnip, season with salt, and pepper; cook for 6 minutes. Add in silken tofu and use an immersion blender to puree the ingredients until smooth. Stir in mushrooms and simmer covered for 7 minutes. Add in milk and heat for 2 minutes. Stir in basil and parsley and serve.

Per serving: Cal 923; Net Carbs 7.4g; Fat 8.5g, Protein 23g

Spring Vegetable Soup

Ingredients for 4 servings

4 cups vegetable stock   2 cups baby spinach
1 cup pearl onions, halved   1 tbsp garlic powder
3 cups green beans, chopped   Salt and white pepper to taste
2 cups asparagus, chopped   2 cups grated Parmesan

Directions and Total Time: approx. 25 minutes

Pour vegetable broth into a pot; add pearl onions, green beans, and asparagus. Season with garlic powder, salt and white pepper and cook for 10 minutes. Stir in spinach and allow slight wilting. Top with Parmesan cheese to serve.

Per serving: Cal 196; Net Carbs 4.3g; Fat 12g, Protein 2.5g

Chilled Lemongrass & Avocado Soup

Ingredients for 4 servings

4 cups chopped avocado pulp   2 lemons, juiced
2 stalks lemongrass, chopped   3 tbsp chopped mint
4 cups vegetable broth   2 cups heavy cream

Directions and Total Time: approx. 20 min + chilling time

Bring avocado, lemongrass, and broth to a boil in a pot over low heat for 10 minutes. Remove from the heat, add in lemon juice, and puree the ingredients using an immersion blender. Stir in heavy cream. Spoon into bowls and chill for 1 hour. Garnish with mint to serve.

Per serving: Cal 339; Net Carbs 3.5g; Fat 33g, Protein 3.5g

Herby Cheese & Bacon Soup

Ingredients for 4 servings

1 tbsp olive oil   1 tbsp chopped fresh oregano
6 slices bacon, chopped   2 cups cubed parsnips
4 tbsp butter   3 ½ cups vegetable broth
1 small white onion, chopped   Salt and black pepper to taste
3 garlic cloves, minced   1 cup almond milk
2 tbsp finely chopped thyme   1 cup grated cheddar cheese
1 tbsp chopped fresh tarragon   2 tbsp chopped scallions

Directions and Total Time: approx. 25 minutes

Heat olive oil in a saucepan and fry bacon until browned and crunchy, 5 minutes; set aside. Melt butter and sauté onion, garlic, thyme, tarragon, and oregano for 3 minutes. Add the parsnips, season with salt and pepper, and cook for 12 minutes until the parsnips soften. Using an immersion blender, process the soup until smooth. Stir in milk and cheese and simmer with continuous stirring until the cheese melts. Top with bacon and scallions to serve.

Per serving: Cal 775; Net Carbs 6.5g; Fat 57g, Protein 18g

Pork & Pumpkin Stew

Ingredients for 6 servings

1 cup pumpkin puree   1 tbsp olive oil
2 lb chopped pork stew meat   1 tsp lemon juice
1 tbsp peanut butter   ¼ cup granulated sweetener
4 tbsp chopped peanuts   ¼ tsp cardamom powder
1 garlic clove, minced   ¼ tsp allspice
½ cup chopped onion   2 cups water
½ cup white wine   2 cups chicken stock

Directions and Total Time: approx. 45 minutes

Heat olive oil in a saucepan and sauté onion and garlic for 3 minutes. Add in pork and cook for 5-6 minutes. Pour in wine and cook for 1 minute. Add in the remaining ingredients, except for the lemon juice and peanuts. Bring to a boil and cook for 5 minutes. Reduce the heat to low and simmer for 30 minutes. Adjust seasonings and stir in the lemon. Serve topped with peanuts.

Per serving: Cal 451, Net Carbs: 4g, Fat: 33g, Protein: 27g

Asparagus & Shrimp Curry Soup

Ingredients for 4 servings

2 tbsp ghee	2 tbsp red curry paste
1 lb jumbo shrimp, deveined	6 oz coconut milk
2 tsp ginger-garlic puree	1 bunch asparagus

Directions and Total Time: approx. 20 minutes

Melt ghee in a saucepan and add shrimp. Season with salt and chili pepper and cook for 3 minutes; remove to a plate. Add ginger-garlic puree and red curry paste to the ghee and sauté for 2 minutes. Stir in coconut milk; add shrimp, and asparagus. Cook for 4 minutes. Reduce the heat and simmer for 3 more minutes. Serve with cauli rice.

Per serving: Cal 375; Net Carbs 2g; Fat 35.4g, Protein 9g

Thyme Tomato Soup

Ingredients for 6 servings

2 tbsp butter	1 tsp thyme
2 large red onions, diced	1 ½ cups water
½ cup raw cashew nuts, diced	Salt and black pepper to taste
2 (28-oz) cans tomatoes	1 cup half-and-half

Directions and Total Time: approx. 20 minutes

Melt butter in a pot and sautéthe onion for 4 minutes. Stir in tomatoes, thyme, water, cashews, and season with salt and pepper. Simmer for 10 minutes. Puree the ingredients with an immersion blender. Adjust the taste and stir in half-and-half. Spoon into soup bowls and serve.

Per serving: Cal 310; Net Carbs 3g; Fat 27g, Protein 11g

Cauliflower Soup with Kielbasa

Ingredients for 4 servings

1 cauliflower head, chopped	2 cups chicken broth
1 rutabaga, chopped	1 small onion, chopped
3 tbsp ghee	2 cups water
1 kielbasa sausage, sliced	Salt and black pepper, to taste

Directions and Total Time: approx. 40 minutes

Melt 2 tbsp of the ghee in a pot and cook onion for 3 minutes. Add cauliflower and rutabaga, and cook for another 5 minutes. Pour broth, water, salt. and pepper over. Bring to a boil and cook for 20 minutes. Melt remaining butter in a skillet. Add in kielbasa sausage and cook for 5 minutes. Puree the soup until smooth. Serve with kielbasa.

Per serving: Cal 251; Net Carbs: 5.7g; Fat: 19g, Protein: 10g

Tomato Soup with Parmesan Croutons

Ingredients for 6 servings

Parmesan Croutons:

3 tbsp flax seed powder	1¼ cups boiling water
1¼ cups almond flour	2 tsp plain vinegar
2 tsp baking powder	3 oz butter
5 tbsp psyllium husk powder	2 oz grated Parmesan

Tomato Soup

2 lb fresh ripe tomatoes	1 cup coconut cream
4 cloves garlic, peeled only	½ tsp dried rosemary
1 small white onion, diced	½ tsp dried oregano
1 red bell pepper, diced	2 tbsp chopped fresh basil
3 tbsp olive oil	Salt and black pepper to taste

Directions and Total Time: approx. 1 hour 25 minutes

For the parmesan croutons:

In a bowl, mix the flax seed powder with 2/3 cup of water and set aside for 5 minutes. Preheat oven to 350 F and line a baking sheet with parchment paper. In another bowl, combine almond flour, baking powder, psyllium husk powder. Mix the flax egg in the boiling water and plain vinegar. Add in flour mixture and whisk for 30 seconds until well combined but not overly mixed. Form 8 flat pieces out of the dough. Place on the baking sheet while leaving enough room between each to allow rising. Bake for 40 minutes. Remove croutons to cool and break into halves. Mix butter with Parmesan and spread the mixture in the inner parts of the croutons. Bake for 5 minutes.

For the tomato soup:

In a pan, add tomatoes, garlic, onion, bell pepper, and drizzle with olive oil. Roast vegetables in the oven for 25 minutes and after broil for 4 minutes. Transfer to a blender and add in coconut cream, rosemary, oregano, salt, and pepper. Puree until smooth. Serve, topped with croutons.

Per serving: Cal 434; Fat 38g; Net Carbs 6g; Protein 11g

Colby Cauliflower Soup with Pancetta Chips

Ingredients for 4 servings

2 heads cauliflower, cut into florets

2 tbsp ghee	3 cups almond milk
1 onion, chopped	1 cup Colby cheese, shredded
2 cups water	3 pancetta strips

Directions and Total Time: approx. 30 minutes

Melt ghee in a saucepan and sauté onion for 3 minutes. Include cauli florets, sauté for 3 minutes, add water, and season with salt and pepper. Bring to a boil, reduce the heat, and cook for 10 minutes. Puree cauliflower and stir in almond milk and cheese until the cheese melts. Adjust the taste. In a skillet, fry pancetta until crispy. Top the soup with crispy pancetta and serve.

Per serving: Cal 402; Net Carbs 6g; Fat 37g; Protein 8g

Coconut Turkey Chili

Ingredients for 4 servings

1 pound turkey breasts, cubed	2 garlic cloves, minced
1 cup broccoli, chopped	1 tbsp ground coriander
2 shallots, sliced	2 tbsp fresh ginger, grated
1 (14-ounce) can tomatoes	1 tbsp turmeric
2 tbsp coconut oil	1 tbsp cumin
2 tbsp coconut cream	2 tbsp chili powder

Directions and Total Time: approx. 30 minutes

Melt coconut oil in a pan over medium heat and stir-fry turkey, shallots, garlic, and ginger for 5 minutes. Stir in tomatoes, broccoli, turmeric, coriander, cumin, chili, salt and pepper. Pour in coconut cream and cook for 20-25 minutes. Transfer to a food processor to blend well. Serve.

Per serving: Cal 318; Net Carbs 6.6g; Fat 18.7g; Protein 27g

Effortless Chicken Chili

Ingredients for 4 servings

1 tbsp butter	8 oz diced tomatoes
1 tbsp sesame oil	2 oz tomato paste
¼ tsp ginger, ground	1 tbsp cumin
4 chicken tenders, cubed	1 red chili pepper, minced
1 onion, chopped	½ cup shredded cheddar
2 cups chicken broth	Salt and black pepper to taste

Directions and Total Time: approx. 30 minutes

Put a pan and add chicken. Cover with water and bring to a boil. Cook for 10 minutes. Transfer to a flat surface to shred with forks. In a pot, pour in butter and sesame oil and sauté onion and ginger for 5 minutes. Stir in chicken, tomatoes, cumin, red chili pepper, tomato paste, and broth. Bring the mixture to a boil. Reduce heat and simmer for 10 minutes. Top with the cheddar cheese to serve.

Per serving: Cal 396; Net Carbs 5.7g; Fat 22.9g; Protein 38g

Cauliflower Beef Curry

Ingredients for 4 servings

1 head cauliflower, cut into florets	
2 tbsp olive oil	¼ tsp allspice
1 ½ pounds ground beef	6 oz canned whole tomatoes
1 tbsp ginger-garlic paste	Salt and chili pepper to taste
½ tsp cumin	

Directions and Total Time: approx. 26 minutes

Cook beef in hot oil over medium heat for 5 minutes while breaking any lumps. Stir in cumin, allspice, salt, and chili pepper. Stir in tomatoes and cauliflower, and cook covered for 6 minutes. Add a ¼ cup of water and bring to a boil over medium heat for 10 minutes or until the water has reduced by half. Adjust the taste with salt. Serve warm.

Per serving: Cal 518; Net Carbs 3g; Fat 34.6g; Protein 44.6g

Chicken Stew with Spinach

Ingredients for 4 servings

28 oz chicken thighs, skinless, boneless	
2 oz sun-dried tomatoes, chopped	
2 carrots, chopped	½ tsp dried rosemary
2 tbsp olive oil	1 cup spinach
2 celery stalks, chopped	¼ tsp dried thyme
2 cups chicken stock	½ cup heavy cream
1 leek, chopped	Salt and black pepper to taste
3 garlic cloves, minced	A pinch of xanthan gum

Directions and Total Time: approx. 50 minutes

In a pot, heat olive oil and add garlic, carrots, celery, and leeek; season with salt and pepper and sauté for 5-6 minutes. Stir in chicken and cook for 5 minutes. Pour in stock, tomatoes, rosemary, and thyme and cook for 30 minutes covered. Add in xanthan gum, cream, and spinach; cook for 5 minutes. Serve.

Per serving: Cal 224, Net Carbs 6g, Fat 11g, Protein 23g

Bacon Stew with Cauliflower

Ingredients for 6 servings

1 head cauliflower, cut into florets	
8 oz grated mozzarella	Salt and black pepper, to taste
2 cups chicken broth	4 garlic cloves, minced
½ tsp garlic powder	¼ cup heavy cream
½ tsp onion powder	3 cups bacon, chopped

Directions and Total Time: approx. 40 minutes

In a pot, combine the bacon with broth, cauliflower, salt, heavy cream, black pepper, garlic powder, cheese, onion powder, and garlic, and cook for 35 minutes. Serve.

Per serving: Cal 380; Net Carbs 6g; Fat 25g; Protein 33g

Scottish Beef Stew

Ingredients for 4 servings

12 oz sweet potatoes, cut into quarters	
2 tbsp lard	1 clove garlic, minced
1 ¼ lb beef chuck roast, cubed	Salt and black pepper to taste
1 parsnip, chopped	1 ½ cups beef stock
1 onion, chopped	2 tsp rosemary, chopped

Directions and Total Time: approx. 60 minutes

Melt lard in a skillet over medium heat and cook onion and garlic for 4 minutes. Add in the beef, season with salt and pepper, and brown on all sides, for about 7-8 minutes. Add sweet potatoes, parsnip, rosemary, and beef stock. Stir and cook on low heat for 35-40 minutes, covered. Serve.

Per serving: Cal 445; Net Carbs 12.3g; Fat 18g; Protein 42g

Vegetable Stew

Ingredients for 4 servings

1 large head broccoli, cut into florets	
2 tbsp ghee	2 cups green beans, halved
1 tbsp onion-garlic puree	1 cup water
4 medium carrots, chopped	1 ½ cups heavy cream

Directions and Total Time: approx. 35 minutes

Melt ghee in a saucepan and sauté onion-garlic puree for 2 minutes. Stir in carrots, broccoli, and green beans, salt, and pepper, add water, stir again, and cook for 25 minutes. Mix in heavy cream, turn the heat off and adjust the taste. Serve the stew with almond flour bread.

Per serving: Cal 310; Net Carbs 6g; Fat 26.4g, Protein 8g

Chili Beef Stew with Cauliflower Grits

Ingredients for 4 servings

2 tbsp olive oil	2 tsp chili powder
2 lb chuck roast, cubed	2 cups beef broth
1 large yellow onion, chopped	2 tbsp butter
3 garlic cloves, minced	½ cup walnuts, chopped
2 large tomatoes, diced	2 cups cauliflower rice
1 tbsp rosemary	1 cup half and half
1 tbsp smoked paprika	1 cup shredded cheddar

Directions and Total Time: approx. 55 minutes

Heat olive oil in a pot. Season beef with salt and pepper and cook for 3 minutes. Stir in onion, garlic, and tomatoes, for 5 minutes. Mix in rosemary, paprika, chili and cook for 2 minutes. Pour in broth and bring to a boil, then simmer for 25 minutes; set aside. Melt butter in a pot, and cook walnuts for 3 minutes. Transfer to a cutting board, chop and plate. Pour cauli rice and ½ cup water into the pot and cook for 5 minutes. Stir in half and half for 3 minutes. Mix in cheddar cheese, fold in walnuts. Top with stewed beef.

Per serving: Cal 736; Net Carbs 7.8g; Fat 48g, Protein 63g

Rustic Lamb Stew with Root Veggies

Ingredients for 4 servings

2 tbsp olive oil	2 cups vegetable stock
1 pound lamb chops	2 carrots, chopped
1 garlic clove, minced	½ tbsp rosemary, chopped
1 parsnip, chopped	1 tbsp sweet paprika
1 onion, chopped	1 leek, chopped
1 celery stalk, chopped	1 tbsp tomato paste
Salt and black pepper to taste	½ fennel bulb, chopped

Directions and Total Time: approx. 1 hour 45 minutes

Warm olive oil in a pot over medium heat and cook celery, onion, leek, and garlic for 5 minutes. Add in lamb chops, and cook for 4 minutes. Add in paprika, carrots, parsnip, fennel, stock, tomato paste; let simmer for 1 hour. Adjust the seasoning, sprinkle with rosemary, and serve.

Per serving: Cal 472; Net Carbs 6.3g; Fat 37g; Protein 20.5g

Beef & Veggie Stew

Ingredients for 4 servings

1 pound ground beef	1 tbsp dried sage
2 tbsp olive oil	Salt and black pepper, to taste
1 onion, chopped	2 carrots, sliced
2 garlic cloves, minced	2 celery stalks, chopped
14 oz canned diced tomatoes	1 cup vegetable broth

Directions and Total Time: approx. 30 minutes

Warm olive oil in a pan and sauté onion, celery, and garlic for 5 minutes. Add in beef and cook for 6 minutes. Pour in tomatoes, carrots, broth, pepper, salt, and sage, lower the heat and simmer for 15 minutes.

Per serving: Cal 253, Net Carbs 5.2g, Fat 13g, Protein 30g

Veal Stew

Ingredients for 6 servings

3 lb veal shoulder, cubed	12 oz canned tomato sauce
2 tbsp olive oil	1 carrot, chopped
1 onion, chopped	1 cup mushrooms, chopped
1 garlic clove, minced	½ cup green beans
1 ½ cups red wine	2 tsp dried oregano

Directions and Total Time: approx. 120 minutes

Warm olive oil in a pot and brown the veal for 5-6 minutes. Stir in onion and garlic and cook for 3 minutes. Place in wine, oregano, carrot, pepper, salt, tomato sauce, 1 cup water, and mushrooms and bring to a boil. Reduce the heat to low and cook for 1 hour and 45 minutes, then add in green beans and cook for 5 minutes. Serve.

Per serving: Cal 415, Net Carbs 5.2g, Fat 21g, Protein 44g

Turkey Stew with Tomatillo Salsa

Ingredients for 6 servings

4 cups leftover turkey meat, chopped

2 cups green beans	1 tsp ground coriander
6 cups chicken stock	2 tsp cumin
Salt and black pepper to taste	¼ cup sour cream
1 chipotle pepper, chopped	1 tbsp fresh cilantro, chopped
½ cup tomatillo salsa	

Directions and Total Time: approx. 30 minutes

Set a pan over medium heat. Add in the stock and heat. Stir in green beans, and cook for 10 minutes. Place in turkey, ground coriander, salt, tomatillo salsa, chipotle pepper, cumin, and black pepper, and cook for 10 minutes. Stir in the sour cream, kill the heat, and separate into bowls. Top with chopped cilantro to serve.

Per serving: Cal 193, Net Carbs 2g, Fat 11g, Protein 27g

Pork & Pumpkin Stew with Peanuts

Ingredients for 6 servings

1 cup puree	1 tbsp olive oil
2 lb pork shoulder, cubed	1 tsp lemon juice
1 tbsp peanut butter	¼ cup granulated sweetener
4 tbsp chopped peanuts	¼ tsp cardamom
1 garlic clove, minced	¼ tsp allspice
½ cup chopped onion	3 cups chicken stock
½ cup white wine	Salt and black pepper to taste

Directions and Total Time: approx. 45 minutes

Heat olive oil in a pot. Add onions and garlic and sauté for 3 minutes. Add in pork and stir-fry for 5-6 minutes. Pour in wine and cook for 1 minute. Throw in the remaining ingredients, except lemon juice and peanuts. Bring the mixture to a boil, and cook for 5 minutes. Reduce the heat and let cook for 30 minutes. Adjust seasoning. Stir in lemon juice before serving. Serve topped with peanuts.

Per serving: Cal 451; Net Carbs 4g; Fat 33g, Protein 27.5g

Paprika Chicken & Bacon Stew

Ingredients for 3 servings

8 bacon strips, chopped   1 tbsp olive oil
¼ cup Dijon mustard   1 ½ cups chicken stock
Salt and black pepper to taste   3 chicken breasts
1 onion, chopped   ¼ tsp sweet paprika

Directions and Total Time: approx. 40 minutes

In a bowl, combine salt, pepper, and mustard. Massage onto chicken breasts. Set a pan over medium heat, stir in the bacon, cook until it browns, and remove to a plate. Heat oil in the same pan, add the breasts, cook each side for 2 minutes, set aside. Place in the stock and bring to a simmer. Stir in pancetta and onions. Return the chicken to the pan as well, stir gently, and simmer for 20 minutes over medium heat, turning halfway through. Serve.

Per serving: Cal 313; Net Carbs 3g; Fat 18g, Protein 26g

Parsley Sausage Stew

Ingredients for 6 servings

1 lb pork sausage, sliced   1 cup chicken stock
1 red bell pepper, chopped   2 garlic cloves, minced
1 onion, chopped   24 ounces canned tomatoes
Salt and black pepper, to taste   16 ounces okra, sliced
1 cup fresh parsley, chopped   6 ounces tomato sauce
6 green onions, chopped   2 tbsp coconut aminos
¼ cup avocado oil   1 tbsp hot sauce

Directions and Total Time: approx. 35 minutes

Set a pot over medium heat and warm oil. Place in sausages and cook for 2 minutes. Stir in onion, green onions, garlic, black pepper, bell pepper, and salt, and cook for 5 minutes. Add in hot sauce, stock, tomatoes, coconut aminos, okra, and tomato sauce, bring to a simmer and cook for 15 minutes. Sprinkle with fresh parsley to serve.

Per serving: Cal 314, Net Carbs 7g, Fat 25g, Protein 16g

Brazilian Moqueca (Shrimp Stew)

Ingredients for 6 servings

1 ½ pounds shrimp, peeled and deveined
1 cup coconut milk   14 ounces diced tomatoes
2 tbsp lime juice   2 tbsp harissa sauce
¼ cup diced roasted peppers   1 chopped onion
3 tbsp olive oil   ¼ cup chopped cilantro
1 garlic clove, minced   Salt and black pepper to taste

Directions and Total Time: approx. 25 minutes

Warm olive oil in a pot and sauté onion and garlic for 3 minutes. Add in tomatoes and shrimp. Cook for 3-4 minutes. Stir in harissa sauce, roasted peppers, and coconut milk and cook for 2 minutes. Add in lime juice and season with salt and pepper. Top with cilantro to serve.

Per serving: Cal 324; Net Carbs 5g; Fats 21g; Protein 23g

Yellow Squash Duck Breast Stew

Ingredients for 2 servings

1 pound duck breast, skin on and sliced
2 yellow squash, sliced   1 carrot, chopped
1 tbsp coconut oil   2 green bell peppers, chopped
1 green onion bunch, chopped   Salt and black pepper, to taste

Directions and Total Time: approx. 20 minutes

Set a pan over high heat and warm oil, stir in the green onions, and cook for 2 minutes. Place in the yellow squash, bell peppers, pepper, salt, and carrot, and cook for 10 minutes. Set another pan over high heat, add in duck slices and cook each side for 3 minutes. Pour the mixture into the vegetable pan. Cook for 3 minutes. Serve.

Per serving: Cal 433; Net Carbs 8g; Fat 21g, Protein 53g

Herby Chicken Stew

Ingredients for 6 servings

2 tbsp butter   1 celery, chopped
2 shallots, finely chopped   1 carrot, chopped
2 garlic cloves, minced   1 bay leaf
1 cup chicken broth   1 chili pepper, chopped
1 tsp dried rosemary   2 tomatoes, chopped
1 tsp dried thyme   Salt black pepper to taste
1 lb chicken breasts, cubed   ½ tsp paprika

Directions and Total Time: approx. 60 minutes

Melt butter in a pot over medium heat. Add in shallots, garlic, celery, carrot, salt, and pepper and sauté until tender, about 5 minutes. Pour in chicken broth, rosemary, thyme, chicken breasts, bay leaf, tomatoes, paprika, and chili pepper; bring to a boil. Reduce the heat to low. Simmer for 50 minutes. Discard the bay leaf and adjust the seasoning. Serve warm.

Per serving: Cal 240; Net Carbs 5g; Fat 9.6g, Protein 245

South-American Shrimp Stew

Ingredients for 6 servings

1 cup coconut milk   14 ounces diced tomatoes
2 tbsp lime juice   2 tbsp sriracha sauce
¼ cup diced roasted peppers   ¼ cup chopped onions
1 ½ lb shrimp, deveined   ¼ cup chopped cilantro
¼ cup olive oil   Fresh dill, chopped to garnish
1 garlic clove, minced   Salt and black pepper to taste

Directions and Total Time: approx. 25 minutes

Heat olive oil in a pot and add cook onions and garlic for 3 minutes. Add in tomatoes, shrimp, and cilantro. Cook for about 3-4 minutes. Stir in sriracha and coconut milk, and cook for 2 more minutes. Do not bring to a boil. Stir in lime juice and season with salt and pepper. Spoon the stew in bowls, garnish with fresh dill, and serve.

Per serving: Cal 324; Net Carbs 5g; Fat 21g, Protein 23g

LUNCH & DINNER

Primavera Spaghetti Squash

Ingredients for 4 servings

1 tbsp butter	3 tbsp scallions, chopped
1 cup cherry tomatoes	1 cup sugar snap peas
2 tbsp parsley	1 tsp lemon zest
4 bacon slices	2 cups cooked spaghetti squash
¼ cup Parmesan cheese	Salt and black pepper to taste

Directions and Total Time: approx. 15 minutes

Melt the butter in a saucepan and cook bacon until crispy. Add the tomatoes and peas, and cook for 5 more minutes. Stir in parsley, zest, and scallions, and remove the pan from heat. Stir in spaghetti and Parmesan cheese. Serve

Per serving: Cal 139; Net Carbs 6.8g; Fat 8g; Protein 6.9g

American Cobb Egg Salad in Lettuce Wraps

Ingredients for 4 servings

2 chicken breasts, cubed	2 tomatoes, seeded, chopped
1 tbsp olive oil	6 tbsp cream cheese
6 large eggs	1 head lettuce, leaves separated

Directions and Total Time: approx. 30 minutes

Preheat oven to 400 F. Put the chicken pieces in a bowl, drizzle with olive oil, and sprinkle with salt and pepper. Mix until the chicken is well coated. Put chicken on a greased baking sheet. Bake for 8 minutes, turning once. Bring eggs to boil in salted water for 10 minutes. Run the eggs in cold water, peel, and chop into small pieces. Transfer to a salad bowl. Remove the chicken from the oven and add to the salad bowl. Add tomatoes and cream cheese; mix evenly. Lay 2 lettuce leaves each as cups and fill with 2 tbsp of egg salad each. Serve.

Per serving: Cal 325; Net Carbs 4g; Fat 24.5g; Protein 21g

Feta Bacon Green Salad

Ingredients for 4 servings

2 (8 oz) pack mixed salad greens	
1 ½ cups feta cheese, crumbled	
8 strips bacon	3 tbsp extra virgin olive oil
1 tbsp white wine vinegar	Salt and black pepper to taste

Directions and Total Time: approx. 20 minutes

Pour the salad greens in a salad bowl; set aside. Fry bacon strips in a skillet for 6 minutes, until browned and crispy. Chop it and scatter over the salad. Add in half of the cheese, toss and set aside. In a small bowl, whisk white wine vinegar, olive oil, salt, and black pepper until well combined. Drizzle dressing over the salad, toss, and top with the remaining cheese. Serve.

Per serving: Cal 205; Net Carbs 2g; Fat 20g; Protein 4g

Minty Lamb with Butter Sauce

Ingredients for 4 servings

1 ¼ pounds rack of lamb	3 oz red wine
3 cloves garlic, minced	A handful of mint, chopped
3 oz butter, melted	Water for soaking

Butter Sauce

1 cup vegetable broth	2 cloves garlic, minced
2 tbsp olive oil	2 oz butter
1 zucchini, chopped	Salt and white pepper to taste

Directions and Total Time: approx. 25 min + cooling time

Put lamb in a large bowl and cover with water to soak for 30 minutes. Let sit on a rack to drain completely and rinse. Place in a bowl. Mix melted butter with red wine, salt, and 3 garlic cloves, and brush the mixture all over the lamb. Drop the chopped mint on, cover the bowl with plastic wrap, and refrigerate to marinate. Preheat grill to 435 F and cook the lamb for 6 minutes on both sides. Remove and let rest for 4 minutes. Heat olive oil in a pan and sauté 2 garlic and zucchini for 5 minutes. Pour in broth and continue cooking until the liquid reduces by half, 10 minutes. Add 2 oz of butter, salt and pepper. Stir to melt the butter and turn the heat off. Puree the ingredients in a food processor until very smooth and strain the sauce through a fine mesh into a bowl. Slice and serve.

Per serving: Cal 553; Net Carbs 2.3g; Fat 47g; Protein 30g

Pancetta Wrapped Chicken Rolls

Ingredients for 4 servings

1 tbsp fresh chives, chopped	12 pancetta slices
8 ounces blue cheese	2 tomatoes, chopped
2 lb chicken breasts, halved	Salt and black pepper, to taste

Directions and Total Time: approx. 50 minutes

Set a pan and cook in pancetta for 5 minutes. Remove to paper towels to drain the grease. In a bowl, stir blue cheese, chives, tomatoes, pepper, and salt. Use a meat tenderizer to flatten the chicken breasts well, season and spread the cream cheese mixture on top. Roll them up, and wrap each in pancetta slices. Transfer to a greased baking dish and roast in the oven at 370 F for 30 minutes. Serve.

Per serving: Cal 623; Net Carbs 5g; Fat 48g; Protein 38g

Tofu & Spinach Zucchini Lasagna

Ingredients for 4 servings

2 zucchinis, sliced	2 cups tofu cheese, shredded
Salt and black pepper to taste	3 cups tomato sauce
2 cups cream cheese	1 cup packed baby spinach

Directions and Total Time: approx. 60 minutes

Preheat oven to 370 F. Mix cream cheese, tofu, salt, and black pepper to evenly combine. Spread ¼ cup of the mixture in the bottom of a greased baking dish.

Lay a third of the zucchini slices on top, spread 1 cup of tomato sauce over, and scatter one-third cup of spinach on top. Repeat the layering process two more times to exhaust the ingredients while making sure to finish with the last ¼ of cheese mixture. Grease one end of foil with cooking spray and cover the baking dish with the foil. Bake for 35 minutes, remove foil, and bake further for 10 minute. Let sit for 5 minutes, make slices and serve.

Per serving: Cal 390; Net Carbs 2g; Fat 39g; Protein 7g

Roasted Stuffed Lamb Leg with Pine Nuts

Ingredients for 4 servings

1 lb rolled lamb leg, boneless	½ cup green olives, chopped
1 ½ cups rosemary, chopped	3 cloves garlic, minced
5 tbsp pine nuts, chopped	Salt and black pepper to taste

Directions and Total Time: approx. 1 hour 10 minutes

Preheat oven to 450 F. In a bowl, combine rosemary, pine nuts, olives, and garlic. Season with salt and pepper. Untie the lamb flat onto a chopping board, rub rosemary mixture all over the meat. Roll lamb over the spices and tie it together using 4 strings of butcher's twine. Place lamb into a baking dish bake for 10 minutes. Reduce the heat to 350 F and cook for 40 minutes. Transfer to a clean chopping board; let it rest for 10 minutes before slicing.

Per serving: Cal 547; Net Carbs 2.2g Fat 37.7g; Protein 43g

Kale & Mushroom Galette

Ingredients for 4 servings

1 tbsp flax seed powder	3 oz cream cheese,
1 cup grated mozzarella	1 garlic clove, finely minced
1 tbsp butter	Salt and black pepper to taste
½ cup almond flour	2/3 cup kale, chopped
¼ cup coconut flour	2 oz mushrooms, sliced
½ tsp onion powder	1 oz grated Parmesan
1 tsp baking powder	2 tbsp olive oil for brushing

Directions and Total Time: approx. 35 minutes

Preheat oven to 375 F, line a baking sheet with parchment paper. In a bowl, mix flax seed powder with 3 tbsp water and allow sitting for 5 minutes. Place a pot over low heat, add in ½ cup mozzarella and butter, and melt both. Turn the heat off. Stir in almond and coconut flour, onion powder, and baking powder. Pour in flax egg and combine until a quite sticky dough forms. Transfer the dough to the sheet, cover with another parchment paper and use a rolling pin to flatten into a circle. Remove parchment paper and spread cream cheese on the dough, leaving about 2-inch border around the edges. Sprinkle with garlic, salt, and pepper. Spread kale on top of the cheese, followed by mushrooms. Sprinkle the remaining mozzarella and Parmesan cheeses on top. Fold the ends of the crust over the filling and brush with olive oil. Bake for about 25-30 minutes.

Per serving: Cal 640; Net Carbs 2g; Fat 62g; Protein 16g

Bacon & Chicken Ranch Pizza

Ingredients for 4 servings

3 cups shredded mozzarella cheese	
3 tbsp cream cheese, softened	¼ cup half and half
¾ cup almond flour	1 tbsp dry Ranch seasoning
2 tbsp almond meal	3 bacon slices, chopped
1 tbsp butter	2 chicken breasts
2 garlic cloves, minced	6 fresh basil leaves

Directions and Total Time: approx. 45 minutes

Preheat oven to 390 F and line a pizza pan with parchment paper. Microwave 2 cups of mozzarella cheese and 2 tbsp of the cream cheese for 30 seconds. Mix in almond flour and almond meal. Spread the "dough" on the pan and bake for 15 minutes. In a bowl, mix butter, garlic, remaining cream cheese, half and half, and ranch mix; set aside. Heat a grill pan and cook the bacon for 5 minutes; set aside. Season the chicken with salt and pepper and grill in the pan on both sides for 10 minutes. Remove to a plate, allow cooling and cut into thin slices. Spread the ranch sauce on the pizza crust, followed by the chicken and bacon, and then, the remaining mozzarella cheese and basil. Bake for 5 minutes. Remove from the oven, slice and serve warm.

Per serving: Cal 528; Net Carbs 4.9g; Fats 28g; Protein 62g

Strawberry & Spinach Blue Cheese Salad

Ingredients for 2 servings

1 ½ cups gorgonzola cheese, grated	
4 cups spinach	½ cup flaked almonds
4 strawberries, sliced	4 tbsp raspberry vinaigrette

Directions and Total Time: approx. 20 minutes

Preheat oven to 400 F. Arrange gorgonzola cheese on 2 pieces of parchment paper. Bake for 10 minutes. In 2 identical bowls, set them upside down, and put 2 parchment papers on top to give the cheese a bowl-like shape. Cool for 15 minutes. Share spinach among the bowls and drizzle with vinaigrette. Top with almonds and strawberries.

Per serving: Cal 445; Net Carbs: 5.3g; Fat: 34g; Protein: 33g

Grana Padano Roasted Cabbage

Ingredients for 4 servings

1 head green cabbage	Salt and black pepper to taste
4 tbsp melted butter	1 cup grated Grana Padano
1 tsp garlic powder	1 tbsp parsley to garnish

Directions and Total Time: approx. 30 minutes

Preheat oven to 400 F. Line a baking sheet with foil. Cut cabbage into wedges. Mix butter, garlic, salt, and pepper in a bowl. Brush the mixture on all sides of the wedges and sprinkle with most of Grana Padano cheese. Bake for 20 minutes. Sprinkle with extra cheese and parsley.

Per serving: Cal 268; Net Carbs 4g; Fat 19.3g; Protein 17.5g

Pancetta Mashed Cauliflower

Ingredients for 6 servings

3 heads cauliflower, leaves removed
6 slices pancetta   ½ cup buttermilk
2 cups water   ¼ cup Colby cheese, grated
2 tbsp melted butter   2 tbsp chopped chives

Directions and Total Time: approx. 40 minutes

Preheat oven to 350 F. Fry pancetta in a heated skillet for 5 minutes. Let cool and crumble. Keep the pancetta fat. Boil cauli heads in water in a pot for 7 minutes. Drain and put in a bowl. Add butter, buttermilk, salt, pepper, and puree until smooth and creamy. Lightly grease a casserole dish with the pancetta fat and spread the mash inside it. Sprinkle with colby cheese and place under the broiler for 4 minutes. Top with pancetta and chopped chives. Serve.

Per serving: Cal 312; Net Carbs 6g; Fat 25g; Protein 14g

Fish Taco Green Bowl with Red Cabbage

Ingredients for 4 servings

2 cups broccoli, chopped   Salt and chili pepper to taste
2 tsp ghee   ¼ head red cabbage, shredded
4 tilapia fillets, cut into cubes 1 ripe avocado, chopped
¼ tsp taco seasoning   1 tsp dill

Directions and Total Time: approx. 20 minutes

Sprinkle broccoli in a bowl with a little bit of water and microwave for 3 minutes. Fluff with a fork and set aside. Melt ghee in a skillet, rub the tilapia with taco seasoning, salt, dill, and chili, and fry until brown on all sides, 8 minutes in total; set aside. In 4 serving bowls, share the broccoli, cabbage, fish, and avocado. Serve.

Per serving: Cal 269; Net Carbs 4g; Fat 23.4g; Protein 16.5g

Seitan Kabobs with BBQ Sauce

Ingredients for 4 servings

10 oz seitan, cut into chunks   1 yellow bell pepper, chopped
1 ½ cups water   2 tbsp olive oil
1 red onion, cut into chunks   1 cup barbecue sauce
1 red bell pepper, cut chunks   Salt and black pepper to taste

Directions and Total Time: approx. 2 hours 30 minutes

Bring water to a boil in a pot, turn the heat off, and add seitan. Cover the pot and let the tempeh steam for 5 minutes; drain. Pour barbecue sauce in a bowl, add in the seitan, and coat with the sauce. Cover the bowl and marinate in the fridge for 2 hours. Preheat grill to 350 F, and thread the seitan, yellow bell pepper, red bell pepper, and onion. Brush the grate of the grill with olive oil, place the skewers on it, and brush with barbecue sauce. Cook the kabobs for 3 minutes on each side while rotating and brushing with more barbecue sauce. Serve.

Per serving: Cal 228; Net Carbs 3.6g; Fat 15g; Protein 13.2g

Herbed Veal Rack

Ingredients for 4 servings

12 ounces veal rack   3 tbsp olive oil
2 fennel bulbs, sliced   ½ cup apple cider vinegar
Salt and black pepper to taste   1 tsp herbs de Provence

Directions and Total Time: approx. 50 minutes

In a bowl, mix the fennel with 2 tbsp of oil and vinegar, toss to coat well, and set to a baking dish. Season with herbs de Provence, pepper and salt, and cook in the oven at 400 F for 15 minutes.

Sprinkle pepper and salt on the veal, place into an oiled pan over medium-high heat, and cook for a couple of minutes. Place the veal in the baking dish with the fennel, and bake for 20 minutes. Serve.

Per serving: Cal 230; Net Carbs 5.2g; Fat 11.3g; Protein 19g

Cheese Scallops with Chorizo

Ingredients for 4 servings

2 tbsp ghee   1 red bell pepper, sliced
16 fresh scallops   1 cup red onions, chopped
8 ounces chorizo, chopped   1 cup Parmesan, grated

Directions and Total Time: approx. 15 minutes

Melt half of the ghee in a skillet and cook onion and bell pepper for 5 minutes. Add in chorizo and stir-fry for another 3 minutes; set aside. Season scallops with salt and pepper. Add the remaining ghee to the skillet and sear the scallops for 2 minutes on each side. Add the chorizo mixture back and warm through. Transfer to serving platter and top with Parmesan cheese to serve.

Per serving: Cal 491; Net Carbs 5g; Fat 32g; Protein 36g

Chicken Ham & Turnip Pasta

Ingredients for 4 servings

6 slices chicken ham, chopped
1 lb turnips, spiralized   Salt and black pepper to taste
1 tbsp smoked paprika   4 tbsp olive oil

Directions and Total Time: approx. 30 minutes

Preheat oven to 450 F. Pour turnips into a bowl; add in paprika, salt, and pepper; toss to coat. Spread the mixture on a greased baking sheet, scatter ham on top, and drizzle with olive oil. Bake for 10 minutes until golden brown.

Per serving: Cal 204; Net Carbs 1.6g; Fat 15g; Protein 10g

Grilled Lamb Chops with Minty Sauce

Ingredients for 4 servings

8 lamb chops   2 tbsp fresh mint
2 tbsp favorite spice mix   3 garlic cloves, pressed
¼ cup olive oil   2 tbsp lemon zest
1 tsp red pepper flakes   ¼ cup parsley
2 tbsp lemon juice   ½ tsp smoked paprika

Directions and Total Time: approx. 25 minutes

Preheat grill to medium heat. Rub the lamb with oil and sprinkle with spices. Grill for 3 minutes per side. Whisk together the remaining oil, lemon juice and zest, mint, garlic, parsley, and paprika. Serve the chops with sauce.

Per serving: Cal 392; Net Carbs 0g; Fat 31g; Protein 29g

Braised Sage-Flavored Lamb Chops

Ingredients for 6 servings

6 lamb chops	3 garlic cloves, minced
1 tbsp sage	2 tbsp olive oil
1 tsp thyme	½ cup white wine
1 onion, sliced	Salt and black pepper to taste

Directions and Total Time: approx. 1 hour 25 minutes

Heat the olive oil in a pan. Add onions and garlic and cook for a few minutes, until soft. Rub sage and thyme onto the chops. Cook the lamb for 3 minutes per side; set aside. Pour white wine and 1 cup of water into the pan, bring the mixture to a boil. Cook until the liquid reduces by half. Add the chops, lower the heat, and let simmer for 1 hour.

Per serving: Cal 397; Net Carbs 4.3g; Fat 30g; Protein 16g

Cheesy Stuffed Venison Tenderloin

Ingredients for 8 servings

2 pounds venison tenderloin	½ cup feta cheese
2 garlic cloves, minced	1 tsp chopped onion
2 tbsp chopped almonds	3 tbsp olive oil
½ cup Gorgonzola cheese	

Directions and Total Time: approx. 30 minutes

Preheat oven to 360 F. Slice the tenderloin lengthwise to make a pocket for the filling. In a skillet, heat the oil and brown the meat on all sides, 8-10 minutes in total. Combine the rest of the ingredients in a bowl. Stuff the tenderloin with the filling. Shut the meat with skewers. Transfer to a baking dish along with the oil and half cup of water, and cook for 25-30 minutes, until cooked through.

Per serving: Cal 194; Net Carbs 1.7g; Fat 12g; Protein 25g

Burritos with Avocado Greek Yogurt Filling

Ingredients for 4 servings

2 cups cauli rice	1 ½ cups tomato herb salsa
6 zero carb flatbread	2 avocados, sliced
2 cups Greek yogurt	

Directions and Total Time: approx. 5 minutes

Pour the cauli rice in a bowl, sprinkle with water, and soften in the microwave for 2 minutes. On flatbread, spread the Greek yogurt all over and distribute the salsa on top. Top with cauli rice and scatter the avocado evenly on top. Fold and tuck the burritos and cut into two.

Per serving: Cal 303; Net Carbs 6g; Fat 25g; Protein 8g

Cheesy Mushroom Pie

Ingredients for 4 servings

For the piecrust:

¼ cup butter, cold and crumbled	
¼ cup almond flour	3 tbsp erythritol
3 tbsp coconut flour	1 ½ tsp vanilla extract
½ tsp salt	4 whole eggs

For the filling:

2 cups mixed mushrooms, chopped	
1 cup green beans, cut into 3 pieces each	
2 tbsp butter	1/3 cup sour cream
1 medium yellow onion	½ cup almond milk
2 garlic cloves, minced	2 eggs, lightly beaten
1 green bell pepper, diced	¼ tsp nutmeg powder
Salt and black pepper to taste	1 tbsp chopped parsley
¼ cup heavy cream	1 cup grated Monterey Jack

Directions and Total Time: approx. 70 minutes

Preheat oven to 350 F. In a bowl, mix almond and coconut flours, and salt. Add in butter and mix until crumbly. Stir in erythritol and vanilla extract. Pour in the eggs one after another while mixing until formed into a ball. Flatten the dough on a clean flat surface, cover in plastic wrap, and refrigerate for 1 hour. Dust a clean flat surface with almond flour, unwrap the dough and roll out into a large rectangle. Fit into a greased pie pan and with a fork, prick the base of the crust. Bake for 15 minutes; let cool. Melt butter in a skillet and sauté onion and garlic for 3 minutes. Add in mushrooms, bell pepper, and green beans; cook for 5 minutes. In a bowl, beat heavy cream, sour cream, milk, and eggs. Season with salt and nutmeg. Stir in parsley and cheese. Spread the mushroom mixture on the baked pastry and spread the cheese filling on top. Place the pie in the oven and bake for 35 minutes. Slice and serve.

Per serving: Cal 527; Net Carbs 6.5g; Fat 43g; Protein 21g

Cheesy Muffins with Ajillo Mushrooms

Ingredients for 6 servings

1 ½ cups heavy cream	1 tbsp butter, softened
5 ounces mascarpone cheese	2 cups mushrooms, chopped
3 eggs, beaten	2 garlic cloves, minced

Directions and Total Time: approx. 45 minutes

Preheat oven to 320 F. Insert 6 ramekins into a large pan. Add in boiling water up to 1-inch depth. In a pan, over, warm heavy cream. Set heat low and stir in mascarpone cheese; cook until melted. Set beaten eggs in a bowl and place in 3 tbsp of the hot cream mixture; mix well. Place the mixture back to the pan with hot cream/cheese mixture. Sprinkle with pepper and salt. Ladle the mixture into ramekins. Bake for 40 minutes. Melt butter in a pan and add garlic and mushrooms; sauté for 5-6 minutes. Spread the ajillo mushrooms on top of each cooled muffin.

Per serving: Cal 263; Net Carbs: 6g; Fat: 22g; Protein: 10g

Easy Lamb Kebabs

Ingredients for 4 servings

1 pound ground lamb	1 grated onion
¼ tsp cinnamon	Salt and black pepper to taste
1 egg	2 tbsp mint, chopped

Directions and Total Time: approx. 20 minutes

Place all ingredients in a bowl; mix to combine. Divide the meat into 4 pieces. Shape all of the meat portions around previously-soaked skewers. Preheat grill to medium heat. Grill the kebabs for 5 minutes per side.

Per serving: Cal 467; Net Carbs 3.2g; Fat 37g; Protein 27g

Cheese Brussels Sprouts Salad

Ingredients for 6 servings

2 lb Brussels sprouts, halved	¼ red cabbage, shredded
3 tbsp olive oil	1 tbsp Dijon mustard
Salt and black pepper to taste	1 cup Parmesan, grated
2 ½ tbsp balsamic vinegar	2 tbsp pumpkin seeds, toasted

Directions and Total Time: approx. 35 minutes

Preheat oven to 400 F and line a baking sheet with foil. Toss brussels sprouts with olive oil, salt, pepper, and balsamic vinegar, in a bowl, and spread on the baking sheet. Bake for 20-25 minutes. Transfer to a salad bowl and add red cabbage, mustard and half of the cheese. Sprinkle with the remaining cheese and pumpkin seeds, and serve.

Per serving: Cal 210; Net Carbs 6g; Fat 18g; Protein 4g

Baked Cheese & Cauliflower

Ingredients for 4 servings

2 heads cauliflower, cut into florets	
¼ cup butter, cubed	¼ almond milk
2 tbsp melted butter	½ cup almond flour
1 white onion, chopped	1 ½ cups grated Colby cheese

Directions and Total Time: approx. 30 minutes

Preheat oven to 350 F. Microwave the cauli florets for 4-5 minutes. Melt the ¼ cup of butter in a saucepan and sauté onions for 3 minutes. Add in cauliflower, season with salt and pepper and mix in almond milk. Simmer for 3 minutes. Mix the remaining melted butter with almond flour. Stir into the cauliflower as well as half of the cheese. Sprinkle the top with the remaining cheese and bake for 10 minutes. Plate the bake and serve with arugula salad.

Per serving: Cal 215; Net Carbs 4g; Fat 15g; Protein 12g

Broccoli Gratin with Gorgonzola Cheese

Ingredients for 4 servings

1 ½ pounds broccoli, broken into florets	
2 cups gorgonzola cheese, crumbled	
2 tbsp olive oil, divided	1 rosemary sprig, chopped
1 tsp crushed garlic	1 thyme sprig, chopped

Directions and Total Time: approx. 15 minutes

Add broccoli to boil in salted water for 8 minutes. Remove to a casserole dish. In a food processor, pulse ½ of the broccoli. Place in 1 tbsp of oil and 1 cup of the cooking liquid. Repeat with the remaining water, broccoli, and 1 tbsp of olive oil. Stir in remaining ingredients to serve.

Per serving: Cal 230; Net Carbs: 7.2g; Fat: 17g; Protein: 12g

Prosciutto-Wrapped Chicken with Asparagus

Ingredients for 4 servings

6 chicken breasts	1 lb asparagus spears
8 prosciutto slices	2 tbsp fresh lemon juice
4 tbsp olive oil	Manchego cheese for topping

Directions and Total Time: approx. 50 minutes

Preheat oven to 400 F. Season chicken with salt and pepper, and wrap 2 prosciutto slices around each chicken breast. Arrange on a lined with parchment paper baking sheet, drizzle with oil and bake for 25-30 minutes. Preheat grill. Brush asparagus spears with olive oil and season with salt. Grill for 8-10 minutes, frequently turning until slightly charred. Remove to a plate and drizzle with lemon juice. Grate over Manchego cheese to serve.

Per serving: Cal 468; Net Carbs 2g; Fat 38g; Protein 26g

Smothered Chicken Breasts with Bacon

Ingredients for 6 servings

7 strips bacon, chopped	5 sprigs fresh thyme
3 chicken breasts, halved	¼ cup chicken broth
Salt and black pepper to taste	½ cup heavy cream

Directions and Total Time: approx. 25 minutes

Cook bacon in a skillet for 5 minutes; remove to a plate. Season chicken breasts with salt and pepper and brown in the bacon fat for 4 minutes on each side. Remove to the bacon plate. Stir in thyme, broth, and heavy cream and simmer for 5 minutes. Return the chicken and bacon, and cook for 2 minutes. Serve with the sauce and cauli mash.

Per serving: Cal 435; Net Carbs 3g; Fat 37g; Protein 22g

Spinach with Garlic & Thyme

Ingredients for 4 servings

½ tsp red pepper flakes, crushed	
2 pound spinach, chopped	1 tsp garlic, minced
2 tbsp almond oil	½ tsp thyme

Directions and Total Time: approx. 25 minutes

Add spinach in a pot with salted water and cook for 10 minutes. Drain and set aside. Place a sauté pan over medium-high heat and warm the oil. Add in garlic and cook until soft. Stir in the spinach, red pepper, and thyme and ensure they are heated through. Serve warm.

Per serving: Cal 118; Net Carbs: 13.4g; Fat: 7g; Protein: 3g

Spinach & Cheese Stuffed Flank Steak Rolls

Ingredients for 6 servings

1 ½ lb flank steak	½ loose cup baby spinach
Salt and black pepper to taste	1 jalapeño pepper, chopped
1 cup ricotta cheese, crumbled	¼ cup chopped basil leaves

Directions and Total Time: approx. 45 minutes

Preheat oven to 400 F. Wrap steak in plastic wrap, place on a flat surface, and run a rolling pin over to flatten. Take off the wraps. Sprinkle with half of the ricotta cheese, top with spinach, jalapeño, basil leaves, and remaining cheese.

Roll the steak over on the stuffing and secure with toothpicks. Place in a greased baking sheet and cook for 30 minutes, flipping once. Let cool for 3 minutes, slice into pinwheels and serve with sautéed veggies.

Per serving: Cal 490; Net Carbs 2g; Fat 41g; Protein 28g

Spinach, Kale & Mushroom Biryani

Ingredients for 4 servings

1 cup sliced cremini mushrooms	
6 cups cauli rice	1 habanero pepper, minced
2 tbsp water	1 tbsp tomato puree
Salt and black pepper to taste	1 cup diced paneer cheese
3 tbsp ghee	½ cup spinach, chopped
3 white onions, chopped	½ cup kale, chopped
6 garlic cloves, minced	1/3 cup water
1 tsp ginger puree	¼ cup chopped parsley
1 tbsp turmeric powder	1 cup Greek yogurt
2 cups chopped tomatoes	Olive oil for drizzling

Directions and Total Time: approx. 1 hour 20 minutes

Preheat oven to 400 F. Microwave cauli rice for 1 minute. Remove and season with salt and black pepper; set aside. Melt ghee in a pan and sauté onion, garlic, ginger puree, and turmeric. Cook for 15 minutes, stirring regularly. Add in tomatoes, habanero pepper, and tomato puree; cook for 5 minutes. Stir in mushrooms, paneer cheese, spinach, kale, and water; season with salt and pepper and simmer for 15 minutes or until the mushrooms soften.

Turn the heat off and stir in yogurt. Spoon half of the stew into a bowl. Sprinkle half of the parsley over the stew in the pan, half of the cauli rice, and dust with turmeric. Repeat the layering a second time including the reserved stew. Drizzle with olive oil and bake for 25 minutes.

Per serving: Cal 346; Net Carbs 2g; Fat 21.4g; Protein 16g

Turnip Chips with Avocado Dip

Ingredients for 6 servings

2 avocados, mashed	2 garlic cloves, minced
2 tsp lime juice	2 tbsp olive oil

For turnip chips

1 ½ pounds turnips, sliced	½ tsp onion powder
1 tbsp olive oil	½ tsp garlic powder

Directions and Total Time: approx. 20 minutes

Stir avocado in lime juice, 2 tbsp of olive oil, garlic, and salt and pepper until well combined. Remove to a bowl and set oven to 300 F. Set turnip slices on a greased baking sheet; toss with garlic powder, 1 tbsp of olive oil, and salt. Bake for 15 minutes. Serve with chilled avocado dip.

Per serving: Cal 269; Net Carbs: 9.4g; Fat: 27g; Protein: 3g

Prosciutto Eggplant Boats

Ingredients for 3 servings

3 eggplants, cut into halves	6 eggs
1 tbsp deli mustard	Salt and black pepper to taste
2 prosciutto slices, chopped	¼ tsp dried parsley

Directions and Total Time: approx. 35 minutes

Scoop flesh from eggplant halves to make shells; set the eggplant boats on a greased baking pan. Spread mustard on the bottom of every eggplant half. Split the prosciutto among eggplant boats. Crack an egg in each half, sprinkle with parsley, pepper, and salt. Set oven at 400 F and bake for 30 minutes or until boats become tender.

Per serving: Cal 506; Net Carbs 4.5g; Fat 41g; Protein 27.5g

Basic Keto Pizza Dough

Ingredients for 8 servings

3 cups almond flour	¼ tsp salt
3 tbsp ghee	3 large eggs

Directions and Total Time: approx. 10 minutes

Preheat oven to 350 F. In a bowl, mix almond flour, ghee, salt, and eggs until a dough forms. Mold the dough into a ball and place in between 2 wide pieces of parchment paper on a flat surface. Use a pin roll it out into a circle of a quarter-inch thickness. Slide the dough into the pizza pan and remove the parchment papers. Bake the dough for 20 minutes. Decorate and bake further.

Per serving: Cal 151; Net Carbs: 2.7g; Fat: 11g; Protein: 7g

Hazelnut Tofu Stir-Fry

Ingredients for 4 servings

1 tbsp tomato paste with garlic and onion	
1 tbsp olive oil	Salt and black pepper to taste
1 (8 oz) firm tofu, cubed	½ tsp mixed dried herbs
1 tbsp balsamic vinegar	1 cup chopped raw hazelnuts

Directions and Total Time: approx. 15 minutes

Heat oil in a skillet and cook tofu for 3 minutes. Mix in tomato paste with the vinegar and add to the tofu. Stir, season with salt and black pepper, and cook for another 4 minutes. Add the herbs and hazelnuts. Stir and cook on low heat for 3 minutes to be fragrant. Spoon to a side of squash mash and a sweet berry sauce to serve.

Per serving: Cal 320; Net Carbs 4g; Fat 24g; Protein 18g

Avocado Carbonara

Ingredients for 4 servings

8 tbsp flax seed powder	1 teaspoon onion powder
1 ½ cups cream cheese	½ teaspoon garlic powder
1 tsp salt	¼ cup olive oil
5 ½ tbsp psyllium husk	¾ teaspoon sea salt
1 avocado, peeled and pitted	¼ teaspoon black pepper
1 ¾ cups coconut cream	¼ cup grated Parmesan
Juice of ½ lemon	4 tbsp toasted pecans

Directions and Total Time: approx. 30 minutes

Preheat oven to 300 F. In a bowl, mix flax seed powder with 1 ½ cups water and let sit to thicken for 5 minutes. Add cream cheese, salt, and psyllium husk. Whisk until smooth batter forms. Line a baking sheet with parchment paper, pour in the batter and cover with another parchment paper. Use a rolling pin to flatten the dough into the sheet. Bake for 12 minutes. Remove, take off the parchment papers and slice the "pasta" into thin strips lengthwise. Cut each piece into halves, pour into a bowl, and set aside. In a blender, combine avocado, coconut cream, lemon juice, onion and garlic powders and puree until smooth. Pour olive oil over the pasta and stir to coat. Pour avocado sauce on top and mix. Sprinkle with salt, pepper, and Parmesan. Plate the pasta, garnish with pecans, and serve.

Per serving: Cal 870; Net Carbs 8g; Fat 69g; Protein 35g

Tomato Pizza with Strawberries

Ingredients for 4 servings

3 cups shredded mozzarella	1 tomato, chopped
2 tbsp cream cheese, softened	1 tbsp olive oil
¾ cup almond flour	2 tbsp balsamic vinegar
2 tbsp almond meal	1 cup strawberries, halved
2 celery stalks, chopped	1 tbsp chopped mint leaves

Directions and Total Time: approx. 35 minutes

Preheat oven to 390 F and line a pizza pan with parchment paper. Microwave 2 cups of mozzarella cheese and cream cheese in the microwave for 1 minute. Remove and mix in almond flour and almond meal. Spread the mixture on the pizza pan and bake for 10 minutes. Spread remaining mozzarella cheese on the crust. In a bowl, toss celery, tomato, olive oil and balsamic vinegar. Spoon the mixture onto the mozzarella cheese and arrange the strawberries on top. Top with mint leaves. Bake for 15 minutes.

Per serving: Cal 306; Net Carbs 4.1g; Fats 11g; Protein 28g

Tomato Bites with Vegan Cheese Topping

Ingredients for 6 servings

2 spring onions, chopped	¼ cup olive oil
5 tomatoes, sliced	1 tbsp seasoning mix

For vegan cheese

½ cup pepitas seeds	Salt and black pepper, to taste
1 tbsp nutritional yeast	1 tsp garlic puree

Directions and Total Time: approx. 15 minutes

Drizzle tomatoes with olive oil. Preheat oven to 400 F. In a food processor, add all vegan cheese ingredients and pulse until the desired consistency is attained. Combine vegan cheese and seasoning mixture. Toss in seasoned tomato slices to coat. Set tomato slices on a baking pan and bake for 10 minutes. Top with spring onions to serve.

Per serving: Cal 161; Net Carbs: 7.2g; Fat: 14g; Protein: 5g

Margherita Pizza with Broccoli Crust

Ingredients for 2 servings

1 small head broccoli, riced	
2 ½ oz cremini mushrooms, sliced	
4 eggs	6 tbsp tomato sauce
¼ cup shredded cheddar	1 small red onion, sliced
¼ cup Parmesan cheese	½ cup cottage cheese
Salt and black pepper to taste	½ tbsp olive oil
½ tsp Italian seasoning mix	A handful of fresh basil

Directions and Total Time: approx. 40 minutes

Preheat oven 400 F and line a baking sheet with parchment paper. Microwave broccoli for 2 minutes; let cool. Crack in the eggs, add cheeses, salt, pepper, and Italian seasoning; whisk until evenly combined. Spread the mixture on the baking sheet and bake for 15 minutes. Allow cooling the crust for 2 minutes. Spread tomato sauce on the crust, scatter with mushrooms, onion, and cottage cheese; drizzle with olive oil. Place the pan in the oven to bake for 15 minutes. Scatter with basil leaves, slice, and serve.

Per serving: Cal 290; Net Carbs 0.8g; Fat 22g; Protein 13g

Herby Mushrooms Stroganoff

Ingredients for 4 servings

½ cup grated Pecorino Romano cheese	
3 tbsp butter	½ cup heavy cream
1 white onion, chopped	1 ½ tbsp dried mixed herbs
4 cups mushrooms, chopped	Salt and black pepper to taste

Directions and Total Time: approx. 15 minutes

Melt butter in a saucepan and sauté onion for 3 minutes. Stir in mushrooms and cook for 3 minutes. Add 2 cups water and bring to boil for 4 minutes. Pour in heavy cream and Pecorino Romano cheese. Stir to melt the cheese. Also, mix in dried herbs. Season with salt and pepper. Ladle stroganoff over spaghetti squash and serve.

Per serving: Cal 284; Net Carbs 1.5g; Fat 28g; Protein 8g

Meatless Florentine Pizza

Ingredients for 2 servings

1 cup shredded provolone cheese	
1 (7 oz) can sliced mushrooms, drained	
10 eggs	2 cups chopped kale, wilted
1 tsp Italian seasoning	½ cup grated mozzarella
2/3 cup tomato sauce	4 eggs

Directions and Total Time: approx. 35 minutes

Preheat oven to 400 F and line a pizza-baking pan with parchment paper. Whisk 6 eggs with provolone cheese and Italian seasoning. Spread the mixture on a pizza-baking pan, bake for 15 minutes; let cool for 2 minutes. Increase the oven's temperature to 450 F. Spread tomato sauce on the crust, top with kale, mozzarella cheese, and mushrooms. Bake for 8 minutes. Crack remaining eggs on top and continue baking until the eggs are set, 3 minutes.

Per serving: Cal 646; Net Carbs 4.9g; Fat 39g; Protein 36g

Hazelnut & Cheese Stuffed Zucchinis

Ingredients for 4 servings

2 tbsp olive oil	¼ cup hazelnuts
1 cup cauliflower rice	4 tbsp chopped cilantro
¼ cup vegetable broth	1 tbsp balsamic vinegar
1 ¼ cup diced tomatoes	1 tbsp smoked paprika
1 medium red onion, chopped	4 medium zucchinis, halved
¼ cup pine nuts	1 cup grated Monterey Jack

Directions and Total Time: approx. 35 minutes

Preheat oven to 350 F. Pour cauli rice and broth in a pot and cook for 5 minutes. Fluff the cauli rice and allow cooling. Scoop the flesh out of the zucchini halves using a spoon and chop the pulp. Brush the inner parts of the vegetable with olive oil. In a bowl, mix cauli rice, tomatoes, red onion, pine nuts, hazelnuts, cilantro, vinegar, paprika, and zucchini pulp. Spoon the mixture into the zucchini halves, drizzle with more olive oil, and sprinkle the cheese on top. Bake for 20 minutes until the cheese melts. Serve.

Per serving: Cal 330; Net Carbs 5.2g; Fat 28g; Protein 12g

Smoked Tempeh with Broccoli Fritters

Ingredients for 4 servings

2 eggs	1 head Broccoli, grated
1 tbsp soy sauce	8 oz halloumi cheese
3 tbsp olive oil	3 tbsp almond flour
1 tbsp grated ginger	½ tsp onion powder
3 tbsp fresh lime juice	Salt and black pepper to taste
Salt and cayenne pepper to taste	4¼ oz butter
10 oz tempeh slices	

Directions and Total Time: approx. 40 minutes

In a bowl, combine soy sauce, olive oil, grated ginger, lime juice, salt, and cayenne pepper. Brush the tempeh slices with the mixture. Heat a grill pan and grill tempeh on both sides until golden brown; remove to a plate. Put broccoli in a bowl and grate halloumi cheese on top. Add in eggs, almond flour, onion powder, salt, and pepper. Mix and form 12 patties out of the mixture. Melt butter in a skillet and fry the patties until golden brown. Plate the grilled tempeh with the broccoli fritters and serve.

Per serving: Cal 850; Net Carbs 7g; Fat 71g; Protein 35g

Sesame Cauliflower Dip

Ingredients for 4 servings

¾ lb cauliflower, cut into florets

¼ cup olive oil	1 tbsp sesame paste
Salt and black pepper, to taste	1 tbsp fresh lemon juice
1 garlic clove, smashed	½ tsp garam masala

Directions and Total Time: approx. 15 minutes

Steam cauliflower until tender for 7 minutes. Transfer to a blender and pulse until you attain a rice-like consistency. Place in garam masala, oil, black paper, fresh lemon juice, garlic, salt, and sesame paste. Blend the mixture until well combined. Decorate with some additional olive oil and serve. Otherwise, refrigerate until ready to use.

Per serving: Cal 103; Net Carbs: 4.7g; Fat: 8.2g; Protein: 4g

Spanish Paella "Keto-Style"

Ingredients for 4 servings

½ pound rabbit, cut into pieces

½ pound chicken drumsticks	2 tbsp tomato puree
1 white onion, chopped	½ cup white wine
2 garlic cloves, minced	1 cup chicken broth
1 red bell pepper, chopped	2 cups cauli rice
2 tbsp olive oil	1 cup green beans, chopped
½ cup thyme, chopped	A pinch of saffron
1 tsp smoked paprika	

Directions and Total Time: approx. 70 minutes

Preheat oven to 350 F. Warm oil in a pan. Season chicken and rabbit with salt and pepper. Fry on all sides for 8 minutes; remove to a plate. Add in onion and garlic and sauté for 3 minutes. Include in tomato puree, bell pepper, and paprika, and let simmer for 2 minutes. Pour in broth, and bring to a boil for 6 minutes. Stir in cauli rice, white wine, green beans, saffron, and thyme, and lay the meat on top. Transfer the pan to the oven and cook for 20 minutes.

Per serving: Cal 378; Net Carbs 7.6g; Fat 21g; Protein 37.2g

Baked Spicy Cauliflower & Peppers

Ingredients for 4 servings

1 lb cauliflower, cut into florets

1 yellow bell pepper, halved	Salt and black pepper, to taste
1 red bell pepper, halved	½ tsp cayenne pepper
¼ cup olive oil	1 tsp curry powder

Directions and Total Time: approx. 35 minutes

Set oven to 425 F. Line a parchment paper to a large baking sheet. Sprinkle olive oil to the peppers and cauliflower alongside curry powder, pepper, salt, and cayenne pepper. Set the vegetables on the baking sheet. Roast for 30 minutes as you toss in intervals until they start to brown. Serve alongside mushroom pate or homemade tomato dip.

Per serving: Cal 166; Net Carbs: 7.4g; Fat: 14g; Protein: 3g

Salami Cauliflower Pizza

Ingredients for 4 servings

2 cups grated mozzarella ¼ cup tomato sauce
4 cups cauliflower rice 4 oz salami slices
1 tbsp dried thyme

Directions and Total Time: approx. 40 minutes

Preheat oven to 390 F. Microwave cauliflower rice mixed with 1 tbsp of water for 1 minute. Remove and mix in 1 cup of the mozzarella cheese and thyme. Pour the mixture into a greased baking dish, spread out and bake for 5 minutes. Remove the dish and spread the tomato sauce on top. Scatter remaining mozzarella cheese on the sauce and then arrange salami slices on top. Bake for 15 minutes.

Per serving: Cal 276; Net Carbs 1.7g; Fats 15g; Protein 20g

Tofu & Bok Choy Stir-Fry

Ingredients for 4 servings

2 ½ cups baby bok choy, quartered lengthwise
5 oz butter
2 cups extra firm tofu, cubed 1 tbsp plain vinegar
2 garlic cloves, minced
Salt and black pepper to taste 1 tsp chili flakes
1 tsp garlic powder 1 tbsp fresh ginger, grated
1 tsp onion powder 3 green onions, sliced

Directions and Total Time: approx. 45 minutes

Melt half of butter in a wok over medium heat, add bok choy, and stir-fry until softened. Season with salt, pepper, garlic and onion powders, and plain vinegar. Sauté for 2 minutes and set aside. Melt the remaining butter in the wok, and sauté garlic, chili flakes, and ginger until fragrant. Put in tofu and cook until browned. Add in green onions and bok choy, for 2 minutes and serve.

Per serving: Cal 686; Net Carbs 8g; Fat 64g; Protein 35g

Tofu Loaf with Walnuts

Ingredients for 4 servings

3 tbsp olive oil 1 tbsp Italian mixed herbs
2 white onions, chopped ½ tsp swerve sugar
4 garlic cloves, minced ¼ cup golden flaxseed meal
1 lb tofu, pressed and cubed 1 tbsp sesame seeds
2 tbsp soy sauce 1 green bell pepper, chopped
¾ cup chopped walnuts 1 red bell pepper, chopped
Salt and black pepper ½ cup tomato sauce

Directions and Total Time: approx. 70 minutes

Preheat oven to 350 F. In a bowl, combine olive oil, onion, garlic, tofu, soy sauce, walnuts, salt, pepper, Italian herbs, swerve sugar, golden flaxseed meal and mix with your hands. Pour the mixture into a bowl and stir in sesame seeds and bell peppers. Transfer the loaf into a greased and spoon tomato sauce on top. Bake for 45 minutes. Turn onto a chopping board, slice, and serve.

Per serving: Cal 432; Net Carbs 2.5g; Fat 31g; Protein 24g

Tofu & Spinach Lasagna with Red Sauce

Ingredients for 4 servings

2 tbsp butter 8 tbsp flax seed powder
1 white onion, chopped 1 ½ cups cream cheese
1 garlic clove, minced 5 tbsp psyllium husk powder
2 ½ cups crumbled tofu 2 cups coconut cream
3 tbsp tomato paste 5 oz grated mozzarella
½ tbsp dried oregano 2 oz grated Parmesan cheese
1 cup baby spinach ½ cup fresh parsley, chopped

Directions and Total Time: approx. 65 minutes

Melt butter in a pot and sauté onion and garlic for 3 minutes. Stir in tofu and cook until brown. Mix in tomato paste, oregano, salt, and pepper. Pour ½ cup water into the pot, stir, and simmer until most of the liquid has evaporated. Preheat oven to 300 F and mix the flax seed powder with 1 ½ cups water in a bowl to make flax egg. Let thicken for 5 minutes. Combine the flax egg with cream cheese and salt. Whisk in psyllium husk a bit at a time and let the mixture sit for 5 more minutes. Line a baking sheet with parchment paper and spread the mixture. Cover with another parchment paper and use a rolling pin to flatten the dough into the sheet. Bake for 12 minutes, remove, take off the parchment papers, and slice the pasta into sheets. In a bowl, combine coconut cream and two-thirds of mozzarella cheese. Fetch out 2 tbsp of the mixture and reserve. Mix in Parmesan, salt, pepper, and parsley; set aside. Grease a baking dish, lay a single line of pasta, spread with some tomato sauce, 1/3 of the spinach, and ¼ of the coconut cream mixture. Repeat the layering twice in the same manner making sure to top the final layer with the coconut cream mixture and the reserved cream cheese. Bake for 30 minutes at 400 F.

Per serving: Cal 775; Net Carbs 8g; Fat 64g; Protein 40g

Mushroom Pizza Bowls with Avocado

Ingredients for 4 servings

1 ½ cups cauli rice 2 large tomatoes, chopped
2 tbsp water 1 small red onion, chopped
Olive oil for brushing 1 tsp dried oregano
2 cups pizza sauce 2 jalapeño peppers, chopped
1 cup grated Monterey Jack Salt and black pepper to taste
1 cup grated mozzarella 1 avocado, chopped
½ cup sliced mushrooms ¼ cup chopped cilantro

Directions and Total Time: approx. 40 minutes

Preheat oven to 400 F. Microwave cauli rice for 2 minutes. Fluff with a fork and set aside. Brush 4 ramekins with olive oil and spread half of pizza sauce at the bottom. Top with half of cauli rice and half of the cheeses. In a bowl, mix mushrooms, tomatoes, onions, oregano, jalapeños, salt, and pepper. Spoon half of the mixture into the ramekin and repeat the layering process, finishing off with cheese. Bake for 20 minutes. Top with avocados and cilantro.

Per serving: Cal 378; Net Carbs 3.4g; Fat 22g; Protein 21g

Pesto Tofu Zoodles

Ingredients for 4 servings

2/3 cup grated Pecorino Romano cheese
2 tbsp olive oil
1 white onion, chopped
1 garlic clove, minced
28 oz tofu, pressed and cubed
1 red bell pepper, sliced
6 zucchinis, spiralized
Salt and black pepper to taste
¼ cup basil pesto
½ cup shredded mozzarella
Toasted pine nuts to garnish

Directions and Total Time: approx. 20 minutes

Heat olive oil in a pot and sauté onion and garlic for 3 minutes. Add in tofu and cook until golden on all sides, then pour in the bell pepper and cook for 4 minutes. Mix in zucchinis, pour pesto on top, and season with salt and pepper. Cook for 3-4 minutes. Stir in the Pecorino cheese. Top with mozzarella, garnish with pine nuts, and serve.

Per serving: Cal 477; Net Carbs 5.4g; Fat 32g; Protein 20g

Veal Chops with Raspberry Sauce

Ingredients for 4 servings

3 tbsp olive oil
2 Ib veal chops
Salt and black pepper to taste
2 cups raspberries
¼ cup water
1 ½ tbsp Italian Herb mix
3 tbsp balsamic vinegar
2 tsp Worcestershire sauce

Directions and Total Time: approx. 20 minutes

Heat oil in a skillet, season veal with salt and pepper and cook for 5 minutes on each side. Put on serving plates and reserve the pork drippings. Mash the raspberries in a bowl until jam-like. Pour into a saucepan, add water, and herb mix. Bring to boil on low heat for 4 minutes. Stir in veal drippings, vinegar, and Worcestershire sauce. Simmer for 1 minute. Spoon sauce over the veal chops and serve.

Per serving: Cal 413; Net Carbs 1.1g; Fat 32.5g; Protein 26g

Kale & Mushroom Pierogis

Ingredients for 4 servings

7 tbsp butter
2 garlic cloves, chopped
1 small red onion, chopped
3 oz bella mushrooms, sliced
2 oz fresh kale
Salt and black pepper to taste
½ cup cream cheese
2 cups Parmesan, grated
1 tbsp flax seed powder
½ cup almond flour
4 tbsp coconut flour
1 tsp baking powder

Directions and Total Time: approx. 45 minutes

Melt 2 tbsp of butter in a skillet and sauté garlic, red onion, mushrooms, and kale for 5 minutes. Season with salt and pepper and reduce the heat to low. Stir in cream cheese and ½ cup Parmesan; simmer for 1 minute. Set aside to cool. In a bowl, mix flax seed powder with 3 tbsp water and allow sitting for 5 minutes. In a another bowl, combine almond and coconut flours, salt, and baking powder. Put a pan over low heat and melt the remaining Parmesan and butter. Turn the heat off.

Pour the flax egg into the cream mixture, continue stirring, while adding the flour mixture until a firm dough forms. Mold the dough into four balls, place on a chopping board, and use a rolling pin to flatten each into ½ inch thin round pieces. Spread a generous amount of stuffing on one-half of each dough, then fold over the filling, and seal the dough with fingers. Brush with olive oil and bake for 20 minutes at 380 F. Serve.

Per serving: Cal 540; Net Carbs 6g; Fat 47g; Protein 18g

Cashew Quesadillas with Leafy Greens

Ingredients for 4 servings

3 tbsp flax seed powder
½ cup cream cheese
1½ tsp psyllium husk powder
1 tbsp coconut flour
½ tsp salt
2 tbsp cashew butter
5 oz grated cheddar cheese
1 oz leafy greens

Directions and Total Time: approx. 30 minutes

Preheat oven to 400 F. In a bowl, mix flax seed powder with ½ cup water and allow sitting to thicken for 5 minutes. Whisk the cream cheese into the flax egg until the batter is smooth. In another bowl, combine psyllium husk, coconut flour, and salt. Add flour mixture to the flax egg batter and fold in until fully incorporated. Let sit for a few minutes. Line a baking sheet with parchment paper and pour in the mixture. Bake for 7 minutes until brown around the edges. Remove and slice into 8 pieces; set aside. Warm some cashew butter in a skillet and place a tortilla in the pan. Sprinkle with cheddar, leafy greens, and cover with another tortilla. Brown each side for 1 minute until the cheese melts. Repeat with the remaining cashew butter.

Per serving: Cal 470; Net Carbs 4g; Fat 40g; Protein 19g

BBQ Tofu Skewers with Squash Mash

Ingredients for 4 servings

7 tbsp fresh cilantro, chopped
4 tbsp fresh basil, chopped
2 garlic cloves
Juice of ½ a lemon
4 tbsp capers
2/3 cup olive oil
Salt and black pepper to taste
1 lb tofu, cubed
½ tbsp sugar-free BBQ sauce
½ cup butter
3 cups butternut squash, cubed
2 oz grated Parmesan

Directions and Total Time: approx. 30 minutes

In a blender, add cilantro, basil, garlic, lemon juice, capers, olive oil, salt, and pepper and process until smooth. Set aside the salsa verde. Thread tofu cubes on wooden skewers. Season with salt and brush with BBQ sauce. Melt 1 tbsp butter in a grill pan and fry tofu until browned on both sides; remove to a plate. Pour squash into a pot, add some salted water, and bring to a boil for 15 minutes. Drain and pour the squash into a bowl. Add remaining butter, Parmesan cheese, salt, and pepper; mash vegetable. Serve tofu skewers with mashed squash and salsa verde.

Per serving: Cal 850; Net Carbs 5g; Fat 78g; Protein 26g

Roasted Chorizo & Mixed Greens

Ingredients for 4 servings

1 lb chorizo, cubed
1 lb asparagus, halved
2 mixed bell peppers, diced
1 cup green beans, trimmed
2 red onions, cut into wedges
1 head broccoli, cut into florets
Salt and black pepper to taste
4 tbsp olive oil
1 tbsp sugar-free maple syrup
1 lemon, juiced

Directions and Total Time: approx. 30 minutes

Preheat oven to 400 F. On a baking tray, add chorizo, asparagus, bell peppers, green beans, onions, and broccoli; season with salt, pepper, and drizzle with olive oil and maple syrup. Rub the seasoning onto the vegetables. Bake for 15 minutes. Drizzle with lemon juice and serve warm.

Per serving: Cal 300; Net Carbs 3.3g; Fat 18g; Protein 15g

Spicy Veggie Steaks with Green Salad

Ingredients for 2 servings

1/3 eggplant, sliced
½ zucchini, sliced
¼ cup coconut oil
Juice of ½ lemon
5 oz cheddar cheese, cubed
10 Kalamata olives
2 tbsp pecans
1 oz mixed salad greens
½ cup mayonnaise
½ tsp Cayenne pepper to taste

Directions and Total Time: approx. 35 minutes

Set the oven to broil and line a baking sheet with parchment paper. Arrange zucchini and eggplant slices on the sheet. Brush with coconut oil and sprinkle with salt and cayenne pepper. Broil until golden brown, about 18 minutes. Remove to a serving platter and drizzle with lemon juice. Arrange cheddar, olives, pecans, and mixed greens next to grilled veggies. Top with mayonnaise and serve.

Per serving: Cal 512g; Net Carbs 8g; Fat 31g; Protein 22g

Grilled Zucchini with Spinach Avocado Pesto

Ingredients for 4 servings

3 oz spinach, chopped
1 ripe avocado, chopped
Juice of 1 lemon
1 garlic clove, minced
2 oz pecans
Salt and black pepper to taste
¾ cup olive oil
2 zucchini, sliced
2 tbsp melted butter
1 ½ lb tempeh slices

Directions and Total Time: approx. 20 minutes

Place spinach in a food processor along with avocado, half of lemon juice, garlic, and pecans and blend until smooth; season with salt and pepper. Add in olive oil and process a little more. Pour the pesto into a bowl and set aside. Season zucchini with the remaining lemon juice, salt, pepper, and butter. Brush tempeh with some olive oil. Preheat a grill pan and cook both the tempeh and zucchini slices until browned. Plate the tempeh and zucchini, spoon some pesto to the side, and serve.

Per serving: Cal 550; Net Carbs 6g; Fat 46g; Protein 25g

Seitan Cakes with Broccoli Mash

Ingredients for 4 servings

1 tbsp flax seed powder
1½ lbs crumbled seitan
½ white onion, chopped
2 oz olive oil
1 lb broccoli
5 tbsp butter
2 oz grated Parmesan
2 tbsp lemon juice

Directions and Total Time: approx. 30 minutes

Preheat oven to 220 F. In a bowl, mix flax seed powder with 3 tbsp water and let sit for 5 minutes. When the flax egg is ready, add crumbled seitan, onion, salt, and pepper. Mix and mold out 6-8 cakes out of the mixture. Warm olive oil in a skillet and fry the patties on both sides. Remove onto a wire rack to cool slightly. Pour lightly salted water into a pot, bring to a boil over medium heat, and add broccoli. Cook until tender but not too soft. Drain and transfer to a bowl. Add in 2 tbsp of butter, and Parmesan. Use an immersion blender to puree the ingredients until smooth and creamy; set aside. To make the lemon butter, mix soft butter with lemon juice, salt, and pepper in a bowl. Serve seitan cakes with broccoli mash and lemon butter.

Per serving: Cal 860; Net Carbs 6g; Fat 76g; Protein 35g

Greek-Style Pizza

Ingredients for 4 servings

½ cup almond flour
¼ tsp salt
2 tbsp ground psyllium husk
1 tbsp olive oil
¼ tsp red chili flakes
¼ tsp dried Greek seasoning
1 cup crumbled feta cheese
3 sliced plum tomatoes
6 Kalamata olives, chopped
5 basil leaves, chopped

Directions and Total Time: approx. 30 minutes

Preheat oven to 390 F and line a baking sheet with parchment paper. In a bowl, mix almond flour, salt, psyllium powder, olive oil, and 1 cup of lukewarm water until dough forms. Spread the mixture on the pizza pan and bake for 10 minutes. Sprinkle the red chili flakes and Greek seasoning on the crust and top with the feta cheese. Arrange the tomatoes and olives on top. Bake for 10 minutes. Garnish pizza with basil, slice and serve warm.

Per serving: Cal 276; Net Carbs 4.5g; Fats 12g; Protein 8g

Baked Stuffed Avocados

Ingredients for 4 servings

3 avocados, halved and pitted, skin on
½ cup mozzarella, shredded
½ cup Swiss cheese, grated
2 eggs, beaten
1 tbsp fresh basil, chopped

Directions and Total Time: approx. 20 minutes

Set oven to 360 F. Lay avocado halves in an ovenproof dish. In a bowl, mix both types of cheeses, pepper, eggs, and salt. Split the mixture into the avocado halves. Bake for 15 to 17 minutes. Decorate with basil before serving.

Per serving: Cal 342; Net Carbs: 7.5g; Fat: 30g; Protein: 11g

Curried Tofu with Buttery Cabbage

Ingredients for 4 servings

2 cups extra firm tofu, cubed	½ tsp onion powder
3 tbsp coconut oil	2 cups Napa cabbage
½ cup grated coconut	4 oz butter
1 tsp yellow curry powder	Lemon wedges for serving

Directions and Total Time: approx. 55 minutes

In a bowl, mix shredded coconut, curry powder, salt, and onion powder. Toss in tofu. Heat coconut oil in a skillet and fry tofu until golden brown; transfer to a plate. In the same skillet, melt half of butter, add, and sauté the cabbage until slightly caramelized. Season with salt and pepper. Place the cabbage into plates with tofu and lemon wedges. Melt the remaining butter in the skillet and drizzle over the cabbage and tofu. Serve immediately.

Per serving: Cal 733; Net Carbs 4g; Fat 61g; Protein 36g

Avocado Coconut Pie

Ingredients for 4 servings

1 egg	2 ripe avocados, chopped
4 tbsp coconut flour	1 cup mayonnaise
4 tbsp chia seeds	2 tbsp fresh parsley, chopped
¾ cup almond flour	1 jalapeño pepper, chopped
1 tbsp psyllium husk powder	½ tsp onion powder
1 tsp baking powder	½ cup cream cheese
3 tbsp coconut oil	1¼ cups grated Parmesan

Directions and Total Time: approx. 80 minutes

Preheat oven to 350 F. In a food processor, add coconut flour, chia seeds, almond flour, psyllium husk, baking powder, pinch of salt, coconut oil, and 4 tbsp water. Blend until the resulting dough forms into a ball. Line a springform pan with parchment paper and spread the dough. Bake for 15 minutes. In a bowl, put avocado, mayonnaise, egg, parsley, jalapeño, onion, salt, cream cheese, and Parmesan; mix well. Remove the piecrust when ready and fill with creamy mixture. Continue baking for 35 minutes until lightly golden brown.

Per serving: Cal 876; Net Carbs 10g; Fat 67g; Protein 24g

Asparagus with Creamy Puree

Ingredients for 4 servings

4 tbsp flax seed powder	1 tbsp olive oil
5 oz butter, melted	½ lb asparagus, stalks removed
3 oz grated cashew cheese	Juice of ½ lemon
½ cup coconut cream	½ tsp chili pepper

Directions and Total Time: approx. 15 minutes

In a microwave bowl, mix flax seed powder with ½ cup water and set aside for 5 minutes. Warm the flax egg in the microwave for 2 minutes, then, pour into a blender. Add in 2 oz butter, coconut cream, salt, and chili pepper; puree until smooth. Heat olive oil in a saucepan.

Roast the asparagus until lightly charred. Season with salt and pepper; set aside. Warm the remaining butter in a frying pan until nutty and golden brown. Stir in lemon juice and pour the mixture into a sauce cup. Spoon the creamy blend into four plates and spread out lightly. Top with asparagus and drizzle the lemon butter on top. Serve.

Per serving: Cal 520g; Net Carbs 6g; Fat 53g; Protein 6.3g

Caprese Casserole

Ingredients for 4 servings

1 cup mozzarella cheese, cut into pieces	
1 cup cherry tomatoes, halved	2 oz Parmesan cheese
2 tbsp basil pesto	1 cup arugula
1 cup mayonnaise	4 tbsp olive oil

Directions and Total Time: approx. 25 minutes

Preheat oven to 350 F. In a baking dish, mix cherry tomatoes, mozzarella cheese, basil pesto, mayonnaise, and half of the Parmesan cheese. Level the ingredients with a spatula and sprinkle the remaining Parmesan on top. Bake for 20 minutes until the top is golden brown; let cool. Slice, top with arugula and olive oil, and serve.

Per serving: Cal 450; Net Carbs 5g; Fat 41g; Protein 12g

Mushroom Lettuce Wraps

Ingredients for 4 servings

4 oz baby bella mushrooms, sliced	
1 iceberg lettuce, leaves extracted	
1 cup grated cheddar cheese	Salt and black pepper to taste
2 tbsp butter	1 large tomato, sliced
1½ lbs tofu, crumbled	

Directions and Total Time: approx. 20 minutes

Melt butter in a skillet over medium heat. Add mushrooms and sauté until browned and tender, 6 minutes; set aside. Add in tofu, season with salt and pepper, and cook until brown, about 10 minutes. Spoon the tofu and mushrooms into the lettuce leaves, sprinkle with cheddar, and share tomato slices on top. Serve the burger immediately.

Per serving: Cal 620; Net Carbs 3g; Fat 52g; Protein 32g

Buttered Carrot Noodles with Kale

Ingredients for 4 servings

2 carrots, spiralized	1 garlic clove, minced
¼ cup vegetable broth	1 cup chopped kale
4 tbsp butter	Salt and black pepper to serve

Directions and Total Time: approx. 15 minutes

Pour broth into a saucepan over low heat and add in carrot noodles to simmer for 3 minutes; strain and set aside. Melt butter a skillet and sauté garlic and kale until the kale is wilted. Pour in carrots, season with to taste, and stir-fry for 4 minutes. Serve with grilled tofu.

Per serving: Cal 335; Net Carbs 8g; Fat 28g; Protein 6g

Eggplant Fries with Chili Aioli & Beet Salad

Ingredients for 4 servings

1 egg, beaten in a bowl	1 cup olive oil
2 eggplants, sliced	½ tsp red chili flakes
2 cups almond flour	2 tbsp lemon juice
Salt and black pepper to taste	3 tbsp yogurt
2 tbsp melted butter	3½ oz cooked beets, shredded
2 egg yolks	3½ oz red cabbage, grated
2 garlic cloves, minced	2 tbsp fresh cilantro

Directions and Total Time: approx. 25 minutes

Preheat oven to 400 F. In a deep plate, mix flour, salt, and pepper. Dip eggplants into the egg, then in the flour mixture. Place on a greased baking sheet and brush with butter. Bake for 15 minutes. To make aioli whisk egg yolks with garlic, gradually pouring ¾ cup olive oil. Stir in chili flakes, salt, pepper, 1 tbsp of lemon juice, and yogurt. In a salad bowl, mix beets, cabbage, cilantro, remaining oil, remaining lemon juice, salt, and pepper; toss to coat. Serve the fries with the chili aioli and beet salad.

Per serving: Cal 850; Net Carbs 8g; Fat 77g; Protein 26g

Baked Cheesy Spaghetti Squash

Ingredients for 4 servings

2 lb spaghetti squash	1 cup coconut cream
1 tbsp coconut oil	2 oz cream cheese
Salt and black pepper to taste	1 cup grated mozzarella
2 tbsp melted butter	2 oz grated Parmesan
½ tbsp garlic powder	2 tbsp fresh cilantro, chopped
1/5 tsp chili powder	Olive oil for drizzling

Directions and Total Time: approx. 40 minutes

Preheat oven to 350 F. Cut squash in halves lengthwise and spoon out the seeds and fiber. Place the halves on a baking dish, brush each with coconut oil, and season with salt and pepper. Bake for 30 minutes. Remove and use two forks to shred the flesh into strands. Empty the spaghetti strands into a bowl and mix with butter, garlic powder, chili powder, coconut cream, cream cheese, half of mozzarella cheese, and Parmesan. Spoon the mixture into the squash cups and sprinkle with the remaining mozzarella. Bake further for 5 minutes or until the cheese is golden brown. Season with black pepper, cilantro; drizzle with olive oil.

Per serving: Cal 515; Net Carbs 7g; Fat 45g; Protein 18g

Tempeh Garam Masala Bake

Ingredients for 4 servings

3 tbsp butter	1 green bell pepper, diced
3 cups tempeh slices	1 ¼ cups coconut cream
2 tbsp garam masala	1 tbsp fresh cilantro, chopped

Directions and Total Time: approx. 30 minutes

Preheat oven to 400 F. Melt butter in a skillet and fry tempeh until browned, about 4 minutes. Stir in half of garam masala; turn the heat off.

Transfer the tempeh to a baking dish. In a bowl, mix bell pepper, coconut cream, cilantro, and the remaining garam masala. Pour over tempeh and bake for 20 minutes. Garnish with cilantro to serve.

Per serving: Cal 610; Net Carbs 5g; Fat 47g; Protein 35g

Cheesy Cauliflower Casserole

Ingredients for 4 servings

2 oz butter, melted	1 head cauliflower, chopped
1 white onion, finely chopped	1 cup mayonnaise
½ cup celery stalks, chopped	4 oz grated Parmesan
1 green bell pepper, chopped	1 tsp red chili flakes

Directions and Total Time: approx. 35 minutes

Preheat oven to 400 F. Season onion, celery, and bell pepper with salt and pepper. In a bowl, mix cauliflower, mayo, butter, Parmesan, and chili flakes. Pour the mixture into a greased baking dish, add and distribute the veggies evenly. Bake until golden, 20 minutes. Serve with spinach.

Per serving: Cal 464; Net Carbs 4g; Fat 37g; Protein 36g

Tempeh Coconut Curry Bake

Ingredients for 4 servings

15 oz cauliflower, cut into florets	
Salt and black pepper to taste	2 tbsp red curry paste
2 ½ cups chopped tempeh	1 ½ cups coconut cream
4 tbsp butter	½ cup fresh parsley, chopped

Directions and Total Time: approx. 30 minutes

Preheat oven to 400 F. Arrange tempeh on a greased baking dish, sprinkle with salt and pepper, and top each tempeh with a slice of butter. In a bowl, mix curry paste with coconut cream and parsley. Pour the mixture over the tempeh. Bake for 20 minutes. Season cauliflower with salt and microwave for 3 minutes until soft and tender within. Remove the curry bake and serve with the cauliflower.

Per serving: Cal 860; Net Carbs 10g; Fat 56g; Protein 73g

Creamy Brussels Sprouts Bake

Ingredients for 4 servings

3 tbsp butter	1¼ cups coconut cream
1 cup tempeh, cubed	2 cups grated cheddar
1½ lb halved Brussels sprouts	¼ cup grated Parmesan
5 garlic cloves, minced	Salt and black pepper to taste

Directions and Total Time: approx. 40 minutes

Preheat oven to 400 F. Melt butter in a skillet and fry tempeh cubes for 6 minutes; remove to a plate. Pour the Brussels sprouts and garlic into the skillet and sauté until nice color forms. Mix in coconut cream and simmer for 4 minutes. Mix in tempeh cubes. Pour the sauté into a baking dish, sprinkle with cheddar and Parmesan cheeses. Bake for 10 minutes. Serve with tomato salad.

Per serving: Cal 420; Net Carbs 7g; Fat 34g; Protein 13g

Zoodle Bolognese

Ingredients for 4 servings

3 oz olive oil	1 ½ cups crushed tomatoes
1 white onion, chopped	Salt and black pepper to taste
1 garlic clove, minced	1 tbsp dried basil
3 oz carrots, chopped	1 tbsp Worcestershire sauce
3 cups crumbled tofu	2 lbs zucchini, spiralized
2 tbsp tomato paste	2 tbsp butter

Directions and Total Time: approx. 45 minutes

Heat olive oil in a saucepan and sauté onion, garlic, and carrots for 3 minutes. Pour in tofu, tomato paste, tomatoes, salt, pepper, basil, some water, and Worcestershire sauce. Stir and cook for 15 minutes. Melt butter in a skillet and toss in zoodles quickly, about 1 minute. Season with salt and pepper. Serve zoodles topped with the sauce.

Per serving: Cal 425; Net Carbs 6g; Fat 33g; Protein 20g

Baked Tofu with Roasted Peppers

Ingredients for 4 servings

3 oz dairy-free cream cheese	2 tsp dried parsley
¾ cup mayonnaise	4 orange bell peppers
2 oz cucumber, diced	2 ½ cups cubed tofu
1 large tomato, chopped	1 tbsp melted butter
Salt and black pepper to taste	1 tsp dried basil

Directions and Total Time: approx. 20 minutes

Preheat a broiler to 450 F and line a baking sheet with parchment paper. In a salad bowl, combine cream cheese, mayonnaise, cucumber, tomato, salt, pepper, and parsley; refrigerate. Arrange bell peppers and tofu on the paper-lined baking sheet, drizzle with melted butter, and season with basil, salt, and pepper. Use hands to rub the ingredients until evenly coated. Bake for 15 minutes until the peppers have charred lightly and the tofu browned.

Per serving: Cal 840; Net Carbs 8g; Fat 76g; Protein 28g

Spicy Cheese with Tofu Balls

Ingredients for 4 servings

1/3 cup mayonnaise	4 oz grated cheddar
¼ cup pickled jalapenos	1 tbsp flax seed powder
1 tsp paprika powder	2 ½ cup crumbled tofu
1 tbsp mustard powder	Salt and black pepper to taste
1 pinch cayenne pepper	2 tbsp butter, for frying

Directions and Total Time: approx. 40 minutes

In a bowl, mix mayonnaise, jalapenos, paprika, mustard, cayenne, and cheddar; set aside. In another bowl, combine flax seed powder with 3 tbsp water and allow absorbing for 5 minutes. Add the flax egg to the cheese mixture, crumbled tofu, salt, and pepper; mix well. Form meatballs out of the mix. Melt butter in a skillet over medium heat and fry balls until cooked and browned on the outside.

Per serving: Cal 650; Net Carbs 2g; Fat 52g; Protein 43g

Zucchini Boats with Vegan Cheese

Ingredients for 2 servings

1 zucchini, halved	Salt and black pepper to taste
4 tbsp vegan butter	2 tbsp tomato sauce
2 garlic cloves, minced	1 cup vegan cheddar cheese
1½ oz baby kale	1 tbsp olive oil

Directions and Total Time: approx. 40 minutes

Preheat oven to 375 F. Scoop out zucchini pulp with a spoon. Keep the flesh. Grease a baking sheet with cooking spray and place the zucchini boats on top. Melt butter in a skillet and sauté garlic until fragrant and slightly browned, 4 minutes. Add in kale and zucchini pulp. Cook until the kale wilts; season with salt and pepper. Spoon tomato sauce into the boats and spread to coat evenly. Spoon kale mixture into the zucchinis and sprinkle with vegan cheese. Bake for 25 minutes. Drizzle with olive oil.

Per serving: Cal 620; Net Carbs 4g; Fat 57g; Protein 20g

Sweet & Spicy Brussel Sprout Stir-Fry

Ingredients for 4 servings

4 tbsp butter	Salt and black pepper to taste
4 shallots, chopped	2 cups Brussels sprouts, halved
1 tbsp apple cider vinegar	Hot chili sauce

Directions and Total Time: approx. 15 minutes

Melt half of butter in a saucepan over medium heat and sauté shallots for 2 minutes until slightly soften. Add in apple cider vinegar, salt, and pepper. Stir and reduce the heat to cook the shallots further with continuous stirring, about 5 minutes. Transfer to a plate. Pour Brussel sprouts into the saucepan and stir-fry with remaining butter until softened. Season with salt and pepper, stir in the shallots and hot chili sauce, and heat for a few seconds.

Per serving: Cal 260; Net Carbs 7g; Fat 23g; Protein 3g

Roasted Butternut Squash with Chimichurri

Ingredients for 4 servings

Zest and juice of 1 lemon	2 garlic cloves, minced
½ red bell pepper, chopped	Salt and black pepper to taste
1 jalapeño pepper, chopped	1 lb butternut squash
1 cup olive oil	1 tbsp butter, melted
½ cup chopped fresh parsley	3 tbsp toasted pine nuts

Directions and Total Time: approx. 15 minutes

In a bowl, add lemon zest and juice, bell pepper, jalapeño, olive oil, parsley, garlic, salt, and pepper. Use an immersion blender to grind the ingredients until desired consistency is achieved; set chimichurri aside. Slice the squash into rounds and remove the seeds. Drizzle with butter and season with salt and pepper. Preheat grill pan over medium heat and cook the squash for 2 minutes on each side. Scatter pine nuts on top and serve with chimichurri.

Per serving: Cal 650; Net Carbs 6g; Fat 44g; Protein 55g

Tofu Eggplant Pizza

Ingredients for 4 servings

2 eggplants, sliced
1/3 cup melted butter
2 garlic cloves, minced
1 red onion
12 oz crumbled tofu

7 oz tomato sauce
Salt and black pepper to taste
½ tsp cinnamon powder
1 cup grated Parmesan
¼ cup chopped fresh oregano

Directions and Total Time: approx. 45 minutes

Preheat oven to 400 F and line a baking sheet with parchment paper. Brush eggplants with butter. Bake until lightly browned, 20 minutes. Heat the remaining butter in a skillet and sauté garlic and onion until fragrant and soft, about 3 minutes. Stir in tofu and cook for 3 minutes. Add tomato sauce and season with salt and pepper. Simmer for 10 minutes. Remove eggplants from the oven and spread the tofu sauce on top. Sprinkle with Parmesan cheese and oregano. Bake further for 10 minutes.

Per serving: Cal 600; Net Carbs 12g; Fat 46g; Protein 26g

Tomato Artichoke Pizza

Ingredients for 4 servings

2 oz canned artichokes, cut into wedges
2 tbsp flax seed powder
4¼ oz grated broccoli
6¼ oz grated Parmesan
½ tsp salt
2 tbsp tomato sauce

2 oz smozzarella, grated
1 garlic clove, thinly sliced
1 tbsp dried oregano
Green olives for garnish

Directions and Total Time: approx. 40 minutes

Preheat oven to 350 F and line a baking sheet with parchment paper. In a bowl, mix flax seed powder and 6 tbsp water and allow thickening for 5 minutes. When the flax egg is ready, add broccoli, 4 ½ ounces of Parmesan, salt, and stir to combine. Pour the mixture into the baking sheet and bake until the crust is lightly browned, 20 minutes. Remove from oven and spread tomato sauce on top, sprinkle with the remaining Parmesan and mozzarella cheeses, add artichokes and garlic. Spread oregano on top. Bake pizza for 10 minutes at 420 F. Garnish with olives.

Per serving: Cal 860; Net Carbs 10g; Fat 63g; Protein 55g

White Pizza with Mixed Mushrooms

Ingredients for 4 servings

2 tbsp flax seed powder
½ cup mayonnaise
¾ cup almond flour
1 tbsp psyllium husk powder
1 tsp baking powder

2 oz mixed mushrooms, sliced
1 tbsp basil pesto
2 tbsp olive oil
½ cup coconut cream
¾ cup grated Parmesan

Directions and Total Time: approx. 35 minutes

Preheat oven to 350 F. Combine flax seed powder with 6 tbsp water and allow sitting for 5 minutes. Whisk in mayonnaise, flour, psyllium husk, baking powder, and ½ tsp salt; let rest. Pour batter into a baking sheet.

Bake for 10 minutes. In a bowl, mix mushrooms with pesto, olive oil, salt, and pepper. Remove crust from the oven and spread coconut cream on top. Add the mushroom mixture and Parmesan. Bake the pizza further until the cheese melts, about 5-10 minutes. Slice and serve.

Per serving: Cal 750; Net Carbs 6g; Fat 69g; Protein 22g

Pepperoni Fat Head Pizza

Ingredients for 4 servings

3 ½ cups grated mozzarella
2 tbsp cream cheese, softened
2 eggs, beaten

1/3 cup almond flour
1 tsp dried oregano
½ cup sliced pepperoni

Directions and Total Time: approx. 35 minutes

Preheat oven to 420 F and line a round pizza pan with parchment paper. Microwave 2 cups of the mozzarella cheese and cream cheese for 1 minute. Mix in eggs and almond flour. Transfer the pizza "dough" onto a flat surface and knead until smooth. Spread it on the pizza pan. Bake for 6 minutes. Top with remaining mozzarella, oregano, and pepperoni. Bake for 15 minutes.

Per serving: Cal 229; Net Carbs 0.4g; Fats 7g; Protein 36.4g

Tofu Cordon Bleu Casserole

Ingredients for 4 servings

2 cups grilled tofu, cubed
1 cup smoked seitan, cubed
1 cup cream cheese
1 tbsp mustard powder

1 tbsp plain vinegar
1 ¼ cup grated cheddar
½ cup baby spinach
4 tbsp olive oil

Directions and Total Time: approx. 30 minutes

Preheat oven to 400 F. Mix cream cheese, mustard powder, plain vinegar, and cheddar in a baking dish. Top with tofu and seitan. Bake until the casserole is golden brown, about 20 minutes. Drizzle with olive oil.

Per serving: Cal 980; Net Carbs 6g; Fat 92g; Protein 30g

Parmesan Meatballs

Ingredients for 4 servings

½ lb ground beef
½ lb ground Italian sausage
¾ cup pork rinds
½ cup grated Parmesan cheese
2 eggs
1 tsp onion powder

1 tsp garlic powder
1 tbsp chopped fresh basil
Salt and black pepper to taste
2 tsp dried Italian seasoning
3 tbsp olive oil
2 ½ cups marinara sauce

Directions and Total Time: approx. 1 hour

In a bowl, add beef, Italian sausage, pork rinds, Parmesan cheese, eggs, onion powder, garlic powder, basil, salt, pepper, and Italian seasoning. Form meatballs out of the mixture. Heat the remaining olive oil in a skillet and brown the meatballs for 10 minutes. Pour in marinara sauce and submerge the meatballs in the sauce; cook for 45 minutes.

Per serving: Cal 513; Net Carbs 8.2g; Fat 24g; Protein 35g

Seitan Cauliflower Gratin

Ingredients for 4 servings

2 oz butter	2 cups crumbled seitan
1 leek, coarsely chopped	1 cup coconut cream
1 onion, coarsely chopped	2 tbsp mustard powder
2 cups broccoli florets	5 oz grated Parmesan
1 cup cauliflower florets	4 tbsp fresh rosemary

Directions and Total Time: approx. 40 minutes

Preheat oven to 450 F. Put half of butter in a pot, set over medium heat to melt. Add leek, onion, broccoli, and cauliflower and cook until the vegetables have softened, about 6 minutes. Transfer them to a baking dish. Melt the remaining butter in a skillet over medium heat, and cook seitan until browned.

Mix coconut cream and mustard powder in a bowl. Pour mixture over the veggies. Scatter seitan and Parmesan on top and sprinkle with rosemary. Bake for 15 minutes.

Per serving: Cal 480; Net Carbs 9.8g; Fat 40g; Protein 16g

Walnut Stuffed Mushrooms

Ingredients for 4 servings

½ cup grated Pecorino Romano cheese
12 button mushrooms, stemmed

¼ cup pork rinds	Salt and black pepper to taste
2 garlic cloves, minced	¼ cup ground walnuts
2 tbsp chopped fresh parsley	¼ cup olive oil

Directions and Total Time: approx. 30 minutes

Preheat oven to 400 F. In a bowl, mix pork rinds, Pecorino Romano cheese, garlic, parsley, salt, and pepper. Brush a baking sheet with 2 tablespoons of the olive oil. Spoon the cheese mixture into the mushrooms and arrange on the baking sheet.

Top with the ground walnuts and drizzle the remaining olive oil on the mushrooms. Bake for 20 minutes or until golden. Transfer to a platter and serve.

Per serving: Cal 292; Net Carbs 7.1g; Fat 25g; Protein 8g

Kentucky Cauliflower with Mashed Parsnips

Ingredients for 6 servings

½ cup almond milk	1 lb parsnips, quartered
¼ cup coconut flour	3 tbsp melted butter
¼ tsp cayenne pepper	A pinch nutmeg
½ cup almond breadcrumbs	1 tsp cumin powder
½ cup grated cheddar cheese	1 cup coconut cream
30 oz cauliflower florets	2 tbsp sesame oil

Directions and Total Time: approx. 35 minutes

Preheat oven to 425 F and line a baking sheet with parchment paper. In a bowl, combine almond milk, coconut flour, and cayenne. In another bowl, mix breadcrumbs and cheddar cheese. Dip each cauliflower floret into the milk mixture, and then into the cheese mixture.

Place breaded cauliflower on the baking sheet and bake for 30 minutes, turning once. Pour 4 cups of slightly salted water in a pot and add in parsnips. Bring to boil for 15 minutes. Drain and transfer to a bowl.

Add in melted butter, cumin, nutmeg, and coconut cream. Mash the ingredients using a potato mash. Spoon the mash into plates and drizzle with some sesame oil. Serve with baked cauliflower.

Per serving: Cal 385; Net Carbs 8g; Fat 35g; Protein 6g

Arugula & Pecan Pizza

Ingredients for 4 servings

½ cup almond flour	1 tomato, thinly sliced
2 tbsp ground psyllium husk	1 zucchini, cut into half-moons
1 tbsp olive oil	1 cup baby arugula
1 cup basil pesto	2 tbsp chopped pecans
1 cup grated mozzarella	¼ tsp red chili flakes

Directions and Total Time: approx. 30 minutes

Preheat oven to 390 F and line a baking sheet with parchment paper. In a bowl, mix almond flour, a pinch of salt, psyllium powder, olive oil, and 1 cup of lukewarm water until dough forms. Spread the mixture on the pizza pan and bake for 10 minutes.

Spread pesto on the crust and top with mozzarella cheese, tomato, and zucchini. Bake until the cheese melts, 15 minutes. Top with arugula, pecans, and red chili flakes. Slice and serve.

Per serving: Cal 186; Net Carbs 3.4g; Fats 14g; Protein 11g

Curry Cauli Rice with Mushrooms

Ingredients for 4 servings

8 oz baby bella mushrooms, stemmed and sliced

2 heads cauliflower, chopped	Salt and black pepper to taste
2 tbsp toasted sesame oil	½ tsp curry powder
1 onion, chopped	1 tsp freshly chopped parsley
3 garlic cloves, minced	2 scallions, thinly sliced

Directions and Total Time: approx. 15 minutes

Place cauliflower in a food processor and pulse until rice-like consistency. Heat sesame oil in a skillet over medium heat, and sauté onion, garlic, and mushrooms for 5 minutes until the mushrooms are soft.

Pour in cauli rice and cook for 6 minutes. Season with salt, pepper, and curry powder. Remove from heat. Stir in parsley and scallions, and serve.

Per serving: Cal 305; Net Carbs 7g; Fat 25g; Protein 6g

POULTRY

Spinach & Cheese Stuffed Chicken Breasts

Ingredients for 4 servings

4 chicken breasts	½ tsp minced garlic
½ cup mozzarella, shredded	2 eggs, beaten in a bowl
1 cup Parmesan cheese	⅓ cup almond flour
6 ounces cream cheese	4 tbsp olive oil
2 cups spinach, chopped	½ tsp parsley
A pinch of nutmeg	A pinch of onion powder

Directions and Total Time: approx. 50 minutes

Pound the chicken until it doubles in size. Mix the cream cheese, spinach, mozzarella cheese, nutmeg, salt, pepper, and half of Parmesan cheese in a bowl. Divide the mixture between the chicken breasts and spread it out evenly. Wrap the chicken in a plastic wrap. Refrigerate for 15 minutes. Combine 2 tbsp olive oil, parsley, the remaining Parmesan, and onion powder in a bowl. Dip the chicken in egg first, then in the breading mixture. Heat the remaining olive oil in a pan over medium heat. Cook the chicken until browned. Place on a lined baking sheet and bake in the oven at 370 F for 20 minutes. Serve immediately.

Per serving: Cal 491; Net Carbs 3.5g; Fat 36g; Protein 38g

Chicken in Peanut Sauce

Ingredients for 6 servings

1 tbsp wheat-free soy sauce	1 tbsp olive oil
1 tbsp sugar-free fish sauce	1 tbsp rice wine vinegar
1 tbsp lime juice	1 tsp cayenne pepper
1 tsp coriander	1 tbsp erythritol
1 tsp minced garlic	6 chicken thighs
1 tsp minced ginger	

Peanut Sauce:

½ cup peanut butter	1 tbsp chopped Jalapeno
1 tsp minced garlic	2 tbsp rice wine vinegar
1 tbsp lime juice	2 tbsp erythritol
1 tsp minced ginger	1 tbsp fish sauce

Directions and Total Time: approx. 1 hour 30 minutes

Combine all chicken ingredients in a large Ziploc bag. Seal the bag and shake to combine. Refrigerate for 1 hour. Remove from fridge 15 minutes before cooking. Preheat the grill to medium, and grill the chicken for 7 minutes per side. Whisk together all sauce ingredients with 2 tbsp water in a bowl. Serve chicken drizzled with peanut sauce.

Per serving: Cal 492; Net Carbs 3g; Fat 36g; Protein 35g

Chicken & Mushrooms in Skillet

Ingredients for 6 servings

2 cups sliced mushrooms	1 tsp Dijon mustard
½ tsp onion powder	1 tbsp tarragon, chopped
½ tsp garlic powder	4 chicken thighs
¼ cup butter	Salt and black pepper to taste

Directions and Total Time: approx. 35 minutes

Season the thighs with salt, pepper, garlic, and onion powder. Melt butter in a skillet and cook the chicken until browned. Set aside. Add in mushrooms and cook for 5 minutes. Stir in mustard and ½ cup of water. Return the chicken. Season with salt and pepper. Reduce the heat and cover, and let simmer for 15 minutes. Stir in tarragon.

Per serving: Cal 447; Net Carbs 1g; Fat 37g; Protein 31g

Citrus Chicken Wings

Ingredients for 4 servings

1 cup omission IPA	2 tbsp butter
A pinch of garlic powder	¼ tsp xanthan gum
1 tsp grapefruit zest	3 tbsp swerve sweetener
3 tbsp lemon juice	12 chicken wings
1 tbsp fish sauce	Salt and black pepper to taste

Directions and Total Time: approx. 30 minutes

Combine lemon juice and zest, fish sauce, omission IPA, sweetener, and garlic powder in a saucepan. Bring to a boil, cover, lower the heat, and let simmer for 10 minutes. Stir in butter and xanthan gum; set aside. Season the wings with salt and pepper. Preheat the grill and cook for 5 minutes per side. Serve topped with the sauce.

Per serving: Cal 365; Net Carbs 4g; Fat 25g; Protein 21g

Spicy Chicken Skewers

Ingredients for 6 servings

2 lb chicken breasts, cubed	2 tbsp five-spice powder
1 tsp sesame oil	2 tbsp granulated sweetener
1 cup red bell pepper pieces	1 tbsp fish sauce
1 tbsp olive oil	Salt and black pepper to taste

Directions and Total Time: approx. 1 hour 20 minutes

Combine all the ingredients, except chicken, in a bowl. Add in chicken, and let marinate for 1 hour in the fridge. Preheat the grill. Take 12 skewers and thread the chicken and bell peppers. Grill for about 3 minutes per side.

Per serving: Cal 198; Net Carbs 1g; Fat 13.5g; Protein 35g

Simple Dijon Chicken Thighs

Ingredients for 4 servings

½ cup chicken stock	¼ cup heavy cream
1 tbsp olive oil	2 tbsp Dijon mustard
½ cup chopped onion	1 tsp thyme
4 chicken thighs	1 tsp garlic powder

Directions and Total Time: approx. 30 minutes

Heat olive oil in a pan. Cook the chicken for about 4 minutes per side. Set aside. Sauté the onions in the same pan for 3 minutes, add the stock, and simmer for 5 minutes. Stir in mustard and heavy cream, along with thyme and garlic powder. Pour the sauce over the chicken and serve.

Per serving: Cal 528; Net Carbs 4g; Fat 42g; Protein 33g

Italian Chicken Linguine

Ingredients for 4 servings

For the keto linguine:

1 cup shredded mozzarella cheese
¾ cup grated Pecorino Romano cheese
1 cup sun-dried tomatoes in oil, drained and chopped

1 egg yolk	5 garlic cloves, minced
2 tbsp olive oil	1 tsp dried oregano
4 chicken breasts	¾ cup chicken broth
1 white onion, chopped	1 ½ cup heavy cream
1 red bell pepper, chopped	1 cup baby kale, chopped

Directions and Total Time: approx. 35 min + chilling time

Microwave mozzarella cheese for 2 minutes. Take out the bowl and allow cooling for 1 minute. Mix in egg yolk until well-combined. Lay a parchment paper on a flat surface, pour the cheese mixture on top and cover with another parchment paper. Flatten the dough into 1/8-inch thickness. Take off the parchment paper and cut the dough into linguine-like strands. Place in a bowl and refrigerate overnight. Bring 2 cups water to a boil and add the keto linguine. Cook for 1 minute and drain; set aside. Heat olive oil in a skillet, season the chicken with salt and pepper and cook for 7-8 minutes. Transfer to a plate and cut into 4 slices each; set aside. Add onion, sundried tomatoes, bell pepper, garlic, and oregano to the skillet and sauté for 5 minutes. Deglaze the skillet with chicken broth and mix in heavy cream. Simmer for 2 minutes and stir in Pecorino Romano cheese for 2 minutes. Stir in kale to wilt. Mix in linguine and chicken. Dish the food and serve warm.

Per serving: Cal 941; Net Carbs 9.7g; Fats 60g; Protein 79g

Hasselback Chicken

Ingredients for 6 servings

4 ounces cream cheese	1 tbsp olive oil
3 oz mozzarella cheese slices	⅔ cup tomato basil sauce
10 ounces spinach	3 whole chicken breasts
⅓ cup shredded mozzarella	

Directions and Total Time: approx. 45 minutes

Preheat oven to 400 F. Combine cream cheese, shredded mozzarella, and spinach in the microwave, until the cheese melts. Cut the chicken a couple of times horizontally. Stuff with the filling. Brush the top with olive oil. Place on a lined baking dish and in the oven. Bake for 25 minutes. Pour the sauce over and top with mozzarella. Return to oven and cook for 5 minutes.

Per serving: Cal 338; Net Carbs 2.5g; Fat 28g; Protein 37g

Spicy Chicken & Cheddar Pasta

Ingredients for 4 servings

2 (8 oz) packs shirataki fettuccine

4 chicken breasts	3 garlic cloves, minced
1 yellow onion, minced	1 tsp Italian seasoning
½ tsp garlic powder	1 cup grated mozzarella cheese
¼ tsp red chili flakes	½ cup grated cheddar cheese
¼ tsp cayenne pepper	Salt and black pepper to taste
1 cup marinara sauce	2 tbsp chopped parsley

Directions and Total Time: approx. 35 minutes

Boil 2 cups water in a pot over medium heat. Strain the shirataki pasta and rinse well under hot running water. Allow proper draining and pour the shirataki pasta into the boiling water. Cook for 3 minutes and strain again. Place a dry skillet and stir-fry the pasta until visibly dry, 1 to 2 minutes; set aside. Heat olive oil in a pot, season the chicken with salt and pepper, and cook for 10 minutes. Cut into cubes and set aside. Add onion and garlic to the pan and cook for 3 minutes. Season with Italian seasoning, garlic powder, red chili flakes, and cayenne pepper. Stir in marinara sauce and simmer for 5 minutes. Return the chicken and shirataki fettuccine, mozzarella and cheddar cheeses. Stir until the cheeses melt. Garnish with parsley.

Per serving: Cal 763; Net Carbs 17.9g; Fat 34g; Protein 83g

Roasted Chicken with Brussel Sprouts

Ingredients for 8 servings

5 pounds whole chicken	1 tbsp olive oil
1 bunch oregano	2 pounds Brussels sprouts
1 bunch thyme	1 lemon
1 tbsp parsley	4 tbsp butter

Directions and Total Time: approx. 2 hours

Preheat oven to 450 F. Stuff the chicken with oregano, thyme, and lemon. Make sure the wings are tucked over and behind. Roast for 15 minutes. Reduce the heat to 325 F and cook for 40 minutes. Spread the butter over the chicken and sprinkle with parsley. Add the Brussels sprouts. Return to oven and bake for 40 more minutes. Let sit for 10 minutes before carving.

Per serving: Cal 430; Net Carbs 5.1g; Fat 32g; Protein 30g

Mustard Chicken Casserole with Pancetta

Ingredients for 4 servings

3 oz smoked pancetta, chopped	2 tbsp olive oil
5 tbsp Dijon mustard	1 cup chicken stock
1 fennel bulb, sliced	1 pound chicken breasts
1 onion, chopped	¼ tsp sweet paprika

Directions and Total Time: approx. 40 minutes

Put mustard in a bowl and add in paprika, salt, and pepper; stir to combine. Massage the mixture onto all sides. Warm 1 tbsp olive oil in a casserole over medium heat and cook the chicken for 3 minutes per side or until golden. Set aside. To the same casserole, add the remaining olive oil and cook pancetta, onion, and fennel for 5 minutes. Return chicken, pour in stock and simmer for 20 minutes.

Per serving: Cal 368; Net Carbs 2.5g; Fat 24g; Protein 28.4g

Creamy Greens & Chicken in a Skillet

Ingredients for 4 servings

1 pound chicken thighs	1 tsp oregano
2 tbsp coconut oil	1 cup cream
2 tbsp coconut flour	1 cup chicken broth
2 carp dark leafy greens	2 tbsp butter, melted

Directions and Total Time: approx. 20 minutes

Melt coconut oil in a skillet and brown the chicken on all sides; set aside. Melt butter and whisk in the coconut flour over medium heat. Whisk in the cream and bring to a boil. Stir in oregano. Add the greens to the skillet and cook until wilted. Pour the sauce over, and cook for a minute. Add the thighs in the skillet and cook for an additional minute.

Per serving: Cal 446; Net Carbs 2.6g; Fat 38g; Protein 18g

Crispy Lemon & Thyme Chicken

Ingredients for 4 servings

8 chicken thighs	2 tbsp olive oil
1 tsp salt	1 tbsp chopped thyme
2 tbsp lemon juice	¼ tsp black pepper
1 tsp lemon zest	1 garlic cloves, minced

Directions and Total Time: approx. 1 hour 20 minutes

Combine all ingredients in a bowl. Place in the fridge for 1 hour. Heat a skillet over medium heat. Add the chicken and the juices and cook until crispy, 7 minutes per side.

Per serving: Cal 477; Net Carbs 1.2g; Fat 32g; Protein 31g

Braised Chicken with Tomatoes & Eggplants

Ingredients for 4 servings

2 cups canned tomatoes	1 lb chicken thighs
2 green onions, chopped	Salt and black pepper to taste
2 cloves garlic, minced	1 cup eggplants, cubed
2 tbsp butter	2 tbsp fresh basil, chopped

Directions and Total Time: approx. 45 minutes

Season chicken with salt and pepper. Melt butter in a saucepan and fry chicken, skin side down for 4 minutes. Flip and cook for another 2 minutes; remove to a plate. In the same saucepan, sauté garlic and onions for 3 minutes, add in eggplants and cook for 5 minutes. Chop tomatoes and stir them in; cook for 10 minutes. Season the sauce with salt and pepper, stir and add chicken. Coat with sauce and simmer for 15 minutes. Garnish with basil and serve.

Per serving: Cal 366; Net Carbs 6.9g; Fat 25g; Protein 21.5g

Punjabi-Style Chicken & Spinach Bake

Ingredients for 4 servings

3 tbsp ghee	1 cup baby spinach, pressed
4 chicken breasts, cubed	1 ¼ cups coconut cream
2 ½ tbsp garam masala	1 tbsp cilantro, finely chopped

Directions and Total Time: approx. 40 minutes

Preheat oven to 350 F. Heat ghee in a skillet, season the chicken with salt and pepper, and cook until golden, 6 minutes. Mix in half of garam masala and transfer the chicken with juices into a greased baking dish. Add spinach and spread coconut cream on top. Bake for 20 minutes or until the cream is bubbly. Remove the dish, garnish with cilantro, and serve with cauli rice.

Per serving: Cal 778; Net Carbs 3.3g; Fat 42g; Protein 86g

Chicken & Bacon Pie

Ingredients for 4 servings

¾ cup Greek yogurt	3 garlic cloves, minced
1 sweet onion, chopped	Salt and black pepper, to taste
3 oz bacon, chopped	½ cup chicken stock
3 tbsp butter	½ lb chicken breasts, cubed
1 carrot, chopped	¾ cup mozzarella, shredded

For the dough

¾ cup almond flour	1 egg
2 tbsp cottage cheese	1 tsp onion powder
2 cups mozzarella, shredded	1 tsp garlic powder

Directions and Total Time: approx. 55 minutes

Preheat oven to 370 F. Sauté onion, garlic, pepper, bacon, salt, and carrot for 5 minutes in warm butter. Add in chicken and cook for 3 minutes. Stir in Greek yogurt and stock and cook for 7 minutes. Add in ¾ cup mozzarella cheese and set aside. Microwave mozzarella and cottage cheeses from the dough ingredients for 1 minute. Stir in garlic powder, almond flour, onion powder, and egg. Knead the dough well, split into 4 pieces, and flatten each into a circle. Set the chicken mixture into 4 ramekins, top each with a dough circle, and bake for 25 minutes. Serve.

Per serving: Cal 503; Net Carbs 5.6g; Fat 31g; Protein 40.9g

Kale & Tomato Chicken with Linguine

Ingredients for 4 servings

1 cup grated Parmigiano-Reggiano cheese for serving	
4 chicken thighs, cut into 1-inch pieces	
1 cup cherry tomatoes, halved	1 yellow onion, chopped
1 cup shredded mozzarella	4 garlic cloves, minced
1 egg yolk	½ cup chicken broth
3 tbsp olive oil	2 cups baby kale, chopped
Salt and black pepper to taste	2 tbsp pine nuts for topping

Directions and Total Time: approx. 30 min + chilling time

Microwave mozzarella cheese for 2 minutes. Take out the bowl and allow cooling for 1 minute. Mix in egg yolk until well-combined. Lay a parchment paper on a flat surface, pour the cheese mixture on top and cover with another parchment paper. Flatten the dough into 1/8-inch thickness. Take off the parchment paper and cut the dough into linguine strands. Place in a bowl and refrigerate overnight. Bring 2 cups water to a boil and add in keto linguine. Cook for 1 minute and drain; set aside.

Heat olive oil in a pot, season the chicken with salt and pepper and sear for 6-8 minutes; set aside. Add onion and garlic and cook for 3 minutes. Mix in tomatoes and chicken broth and cook until the liquid reduces by half. Return the chicken and stir in kale for 2 minutes. Divide linguine between serving plates, top with kale sauce, and Parmigianino-Reggiano cheese. Garnish with pine nuts.

Per serving: Cal 740; Net Carbs 6.1g; Fats 52g; Protein 51g

Chicken & Vegetable Bake

Ingredients for 4 servings

1 lb chicken breasts, sliced	1 zucchini, sliced
1 tbsp butter	2 garlic cloves, minced
2 green bell peppers, sliced	2 tsp Italian seasoning
1 turnip, chopped	Salt and black pepper to taste
1 onion, chopped	8 oz mozzarella, sliced

Directions and Total Time: approx. 45 minutes

Grease a baking dish with cooking spray and place in the chicken slices. Melt butter in a pan over medium heat and sauté onion, zucchini, garlic, bell peppers, turnip, salt, pepper, and Italian seasonings. Cook until tender, 8 minutes. Spread the vegetables over the chicken and cover with cheese slices. Set into the oven and cook until browned for 30 minutes at 370 F. Serve.

Per serving: Cal 341; Net Carbs 8.3g; Fat 13.5g; Protein 43g

Chicken Thighs with Greens

Ingredients for 4 servings

4 chicken thighs	1 tsp parsley
1 cup spinach, chopped	1 cup half-and-half
½ cup celery leaves, chopped	1 cup vegetable broth
½ cup Swiss chard, chopped	4 tbsp butter

Directions and Total Time: approx. 25 minutes

Melt half of the butter in a skillet and brown the chicken on all sides, about 8 minutes; set aside. Add the remaining butter. Whisk in half-and-half, bring to a boil, and stir in parsley. Add spinach, Swiss chard, and celery and cook until wilted. Add the thighs and cook for 6 minutes. Serve.

Per serving: Cal 558; Net Carbs 5.7g; Fat 43.7g; Protein 35g

Chargrilled Chili Chicken

Ingredients for 4 servings

3 tbsp chili powder	2 tbsp olive oil
2 tsp garlic powder	1 ½ pounds chicken breasts

Directions and Total Time: approx. 17 minutes

Grease grill grate with cooking spray and preheat to 400 F. Combine chili, salt, black pepper, and garlic in a bowl. Brush chicken with olive oil, sprinkle with the spice mixture and massage with your hands. Grill for 7 minutes per side until well done or to your preference. Serve hot.

Per serving: Cal 253; Net Carbs 1.8g; Fat 15g; Protein 24.5g

Cheese-Crusted Chicken Breasts

Ingredients for 4 servings

3 tbsp olive oil	½ cup pork rinds, crushed
3 cups Monterey Jack, grated	1 lb chicken breasts, boneless
2 eggs	Salt to taste

Directions and Total Time: approx. 40 minutes

Line a baking sheet with parchment paper. Whisk the eggs with the olive oil in one bowl, and mix the cheese and pork rinds in another bowl. Season the chicken with salt, dip in egg mixture, and coat generously in the cheese mixture. Place on a baking sheet, cover with aluminium foil and bake in the oven for 25 minutes at 350 F. Remove foil and bake further for 12 minutes until golden brown. Serve.

Per serving: Cal 622; Net Carbs 1.2g; Fat 53.8; Protein 45g

Shiitake Chicken in a Skillet

Ingredients for 4 servings

1 cup shiitake mushrooms, sliced	
4 green onions, sliced	1 tsp Dijon mustard
2 garlic cloves, minced	1 tbsp fresh cilantro, chopped
4 tbsp coconut oil	1 pound chicken thighs

Directions and Total Time: approx. 35 minutes

Season the thighs with salt and pepper. Melt coconut oil in a pan and cook chicken until browned, for 4 minutes per side; set aside. Add mushrooms, garlic, and green onions and cook for 5 minutes. Stir in mustard and a ½ cup water. Return chicken to the pan, reduce the heat, cover, and simmer for 15 minutes. Sprinkle with cilantro and serve.

Per serving: Cal 383; Net Carbs 2.9g; Fat 32.6g; Protein 19g

Creamy Chicken Thighs with Capers

Ingredients for 4 servings

2 tbsp butter	8 oz cream cheese
1 ½ lb chicken thighs	1/3 cup capers
2 cups crème fraîche	1 tbsp tamari sauce

Directions and Total Time: approx. 30 minutes

Heat oven to 350 F and grease a baking sheet. Melt butter in a skillet, season the chicken with salt and pepper, and fry until golden brown, 8 minutes. Transfer chicken to the baking sheet, cover with aluminum foil, and bake for 8 minutes. Reserve the butter used to sear the chicken. Remove chicken from the oven, take off the foil, and pour the drippings into a pan along with the butter from frying. Set the chicken aside in a warmer for serving. Place the saucepan over low heat and mix in crème fraiche and cream cheese. Simmer until the sauce thickens. Mix in capers and tamari sauce; cook further for 1 minute, and season with salt and pepper. Dish the chicken into plates and drizzle the sauce all over. Serve with buttered broccoli.

Per serving: Cal 834; Net Carbs 0.9g; Fat 73g; Protein 36g

Creamy Chicken with Mushrooms

Ingredients for 4 servings

2 tbsp olive oil	1 cup chicken stock
2 garlic cloves, minced	¼ cup dry white wine
1 onion, sliced into half-moons	1 cup heavy cream
1 cup mushrooms, chopped	4 chicken breasts, sliced
1 tbsp sweet paprika	2 tbsp fresh parsley, chopped

Directions and Total Time: approx. 40 minutes

Heat olive oil in a saucepan and sauté onion and garlic for 3 minutes. Remove to a plate. Add in chicken and fry for 5 minutes. Pour in white wine, mushrooms, paprika, salt, and pepper, and cook for 3-4 minutes until the liquid is reduced by half. Return onion and garlic, and add in the stock. Cook for 20 minutes, then stir in heavy cream and cook for 2 more minutes. Scatter the parsley and serve.

Per serving: Cal 485; Net Carbs 3.4g; Fat 26g; Protein 56.7g

Rosemary Chicken & Pumpkin Bake

Ingredients for 4 servings

1 pound chicken thighs	¼ tsp ground nutmeg
1 pound pumpkin, cubed	4 tbsp olive oil
½ cup black olives, pitted	5 garlic cloves, sliced
3 onion springs, sliced	1 tbsp dried rosemary
½ tsp ground cinnamon	Salt and black pepper, to taste

Directions and Total Time: approx. 60 minutes

Set oven to 400 F and grease a baking dish with cooking spray. Place in the chicken, skin down. Arrange garlic, olives, onions, and pumpkin around the chicken. Drizzle with olive oil. Season with pepper, salt, cinnamon, nutmeg and rosemary, and bake in the oven for 45 minutes. Serve.

Per serving: Cal 431; Net Carbs 6.1g; Fat 34g; Protein 20.5g

Celery & Radish Chicken Casserole

Ingredients for 4 servings

½ lemon, juiced	2 lb chicken breasts, cubed
3 tbsp basil pesto	1 celery, chopped
¾ cup heavy cream	¼ cup chopped tomatoes
½ cup cream cheese, softened	1 lb radishes, sliced
3 tbsp butter	½ cup shredded Pepper Jack

Directions and Total Time: approx. 50 minutes

Preheat oven to 400 F. In a bowl, combine lemon juice, pesto, heavy cream, cream cheese, salt, and pepper; set aside. Melt butter in a skillet, season the chicken with salt and pepper, and cook in the fat until no longer pink. 8 minutes. Transfer to a greased casserole dish and spread the pesto mixture on top. Top with celery, tomatoes, and radishes. Sprinkle cheese on top and bake for 30 minutes or until the cheese melts and golden brown on top. Remove from the oven, dish, and serve with braised green beans.

Per serving: Cal 667; Net Carbs 0.8g; Fat 47g; Protein 51g

Lettuce Chicken Fajita Bowl with Cilantro

Ingredients for 4 servings

1½ lb boneless chicken breasts, cut into strips	
½ cup shredded Mexican cheese blend	
2 tbsp olive oil	2 avocados, chopped
Salt and black pepper to taste	1 green bell pepper, sliced
2 tbsp Tex-Mex seasoning	1 yellow onion, thinly sliced
1 iceberg lettuce, chopped	4 tbsp fresh cilantro leaves
2 tomatoes, and chopped	1 cup crème fraiche

Directions and Total Time: approx. 20 minutes

Heat olive oil in a skillet, season the chicken with salt, pepper, and Tex-Mex seasoning. Fry until golden, 10 minutes; transfer to a plate. Divide lettuce into 4 bowls, share the chicken on top, and add tomatoes, avocados, bell pepper, onion, cilantro, and Mexican cheese. Top with dollops of crème fraiche and serve with low carb tortillas.

Per serving: Cal 626; Net Carbs 4.5g; Fat 42g; Protein 47g

Melt-In-The-Middle Chicken Meatballs

Ingredients for 4 servings

2 tbsp olive oil	2 garlic cloves, minced
1 large egg	2 shallots, chopped
1 pound ground chicken	1 tbsp dried oregano
1 cup celery, chopped	2 tbsp fresh parsley, chopped
2 tbsp pork rinds, crushed	1 cup pecorino cheese, grated

Directions and Total Time: approx. 20 minutes

Put ground chicken, egg, shallots, garlic, celery, oregano, parsley, black pepper, and salt in a bowl and mix to combine. Form meatballs from the mixture. Lay the pork rinds on a large plate and roll the meatballs in them. Fry the meatballs in warm olive oil over medium heat on all sides until lightly golden, about 5-6 minutes and transfer to a baking dish. Scatter the grated cheese over and bake for 5 minutes, until the cheese melts. Serve.

Per serving: Cal 466; Net Carbs 2.7g; Fat 35g; Protein 32.4g

Sweet Onion Chicken with Coconut Sauce

Ingredients for 6 servings

1 tbsp coconut oil	1 lime, juiced
3 chicken breasts, halved	2 oz coconut cream
1 cup vegetable stock	1 tsp red pepper flakes
2 sweet onions, sliced	1 tbsp fresh cilantro, chopped

Directions and Total Time: approx. 35 minutes

Cook the chicken in hot coconut oil, in a pan over medium heat, for about 4-5 minutes; set aside. Place the sweet onions in the pan and cook for 4 minutes. Stir in black pepper, stock, pepper flakes, salt, coconut cream, and lime juice. Return the chicken to the pan, and cook covered for 15 minutes. Sprinkle with fresh cilantro and serve.

Per serving: Cal 481; Net Carbs 5.2g; Fat 27g; Protein 39g

Greek-Style Chicken Drumsticks

Ingredients for 4 servings

5 kaffir lime leaves	2 lb chicken drumsticks
1 tbsp cumin powder	Salt and black pepper to taste
1 tbsp ginger powder	1 tbsp olive oil
1 cup Greek yogurt	2 limes, juiced

Directions and Total Time: approx. 90 minutes

In a bowl, combine kaffir leaves, cumin, ginger, and yogurt. Add chicken, salt, and pepper, and mix to coat. Cover the bowl with plastic wrap and marinate in the fridge for 3 hours. Preheat oven to 350 F. Arrange chicken on a greased baking sheet. Drizzle with olive oil, lime juice, cover with aluminum foil, and bake for 60-80 minutes. Remove foil, turn broiler on, and brown the chicken for 10 minutes. Serve with red cabbage slaw.

Per serving: Cal 463; Net Carbs 6.1g; Fat 27g; Protein 44g

One-Pot Chicken Alfredo Zoodles

Ingredients for 4 servings

1 cup grated Pecorino Romano cheese	
4 tbsp butter	3 garlic cloves, minced
4 chicken breasts, cubed	¾ cup heavy cream
4 large turnips, spiralized	2 tbsp chopped fresh parsley

Directions and Total Time: approx. 25 minutes

Melt butter in a skillet, season the chicken with salt and pepper, and cook until golden brown, 10 minutes. Transfer to a plate. In the same skillet sauté turnips and garlic until softened, 6 minutes. Stir in the heavy cream and Pecorino Romano cheese until melted. Season with salt, black pepper. Stir in the chicken, garnish with parsley and serve.

Per serving: Cal 771; Net Carbs 2.3g; Fats 49g; Protein 69g

Worcestershire Chicken Peanut Puffs

Ingredients for 4 servings

1 ½ cups chopped chicken thighs, boneless and skinless	
1/3 cup peanuts, crushed	Salt and black pepper to taste
1 cup chicken broth	1 tsp celery seeds
½ cup olive oil	¼ tsp cayenne pepper
2 tsp Worcestershire sauce	1 cup almond flour
1 tbsp dried parsley flakes	4 eggs

Directions and Total Time: approx. 30 minutes

In a bowl, combine chicken and peanuts; set aside. In a saucepan, mix broth, olive oil, Worcestershire sauce, parsley, salt, pepper, celery seeds, and cayenne. Bring to a boil over medium heat and stir in almond flour until smooth ball forms. Allow resting for 5 minutes. Add eggs into the batter one after the other and beat until smooth. Mix in chicken and peanuts until well combined. Drop tbsp heaps of the mixture onto a greased baking sheet and bake in the oven at 450 F, 12-14 minutes. Serve warm.

Per serving: Cal 514; Net Carbs 1.6g; Fat 47g; Protein 20g

Broccoli & Cheese Chicken Sausage

Ingredients for 4 servings

2 tbsp salted butter	¼ cup red wine
4 links chicken sausages, sliced	½ tsp red pepper flakes
3 cups broccoli florets	3 cups chopped kale
4 garlic cloves, minced	½ cup Pecorino Romano
½ cup tomato sauce	Salt and black pepper to taste

Directions and Total Time: approx. 30 minutes

Melt 1 tbsp of butter in a wok and fry the sausages until brown, 5 minutes; set aside. Melt the remaining butter and sauté broccoli for 5 minutes. Mix in garlic and cook for 3 minutes, then pour in tomato sauce, wine, red flakes, and season with salt and pepper. Cover the lid and cook for 10 minutes or until the tomato sauce reduces by one-third. Return the sausages to the pan and heat for 1 minute. Stir in kale to wilt. Spoon onto a platter and sprinkle with Pecorino cheese. Serve warm with cauliflower rice.

Per serving: Cal 263; Net Carbs 7.1g; Fat 17g; Protein 15g

Parmesan Chicken & Broccoli Casserole

Ingredients for 4 servings

5 tbsp butter	1 lb ground chicken
1 small white onion, chopped	1 lb broccoli rabe, chopped
2 garlic cloves, minced	1 cup grated Parmesan cheese

Directions and Total Time: approx. 40 minutes

Preheat oven to 350 F. Melt butter in a skillet and sauté onion and garlic for 3 minutes. Put in chicken and cook until no longer pink, 8 minutes. Add chicken and broccoli rabe to a greased baking dish and mix evenly. Top with butter from the skillet and sprinkle Parmesan on top. Bake for 20 minutes until the cheese melts. Serve.

Per serving: Cal 429; Net Carbs 4.3g; Fat 31g; Protein 31g

Smoked Chicken Tart with Baby Kale

Ingredients for 4 servings

1 cup shredded provolone cheese	
1 lb ground chicken	½ cup tomato sauce
2 cups powdered Parmesan	1 tsp white vinegar
¼ tsp onion powder	½ tsp liquid smoke
¼ tsp garlic powder	¼ cup baby kale, chopped

Directions and Total Time: approx. 30 minutes

Preheat oven to 400 F and line a pizza pan with parchment paper and grease with cooking spray. In a bowl, combine chicken, salt, pepper, and Parmesan. Spread the mixture on the pan to fit. Bake for 15 minutes until the meat cooks. In a bowl, mix onion and garlic powder, tomato sauce, vinegar, and liquid smoke. Remove the meat crust from the oven and spread tomato mixture on top. Add kale and sprinkle with provolone cheese. Bake for 7 minutes or until the cheese melts. Slice and serve warm.

Per serving: Cal 517; Net Carbs 16.2g; Fat 28g; Protein 46g

Baked Cheese Chicken with Acorn Squash

Ingredients for 6 servings

6 chicken breasts
1 lb acorn squash, sliced

Salt and black pepper to taste
1 cup blue cheese, crumbled

Directions and Total Time: approx. 1 hour 15 minutes

Grease a baking dish, add in chicken breasts, salt, pepper, squash, and drizzle with olive oil. Transfer to the oven set at 420 F, and bake for 1 hour. Scatter blue cheese, and bake for 15 minutes. Remove to a plate and serve.

Per serving: Cal 235, Net Carbs 5g, Fat 16g, Protein 12g

Cheesy Chicken Tenders

Ingredients for 4 servings

2 eggs
3 tbsp butter, melted
3 cups Monterey Jack, crushed

½ cup pork rinds, crushed
1 lb chicken tenders
Salt to taste

Directions and Total Time: approx. 45 minutes

Preheat oven to 350 F and line a baking sheet with parchment paper. Whisk the eggs with the butter in one bowl and mix the cheese and pork rinds in another bowl. Season chicken with salt, dip in egg mixture, and coat in cheddar mixture. Place on baking sheet, cover with aluminium foil and bake for 25 minutes. Remove foil and bake further for 12 minutes to golden brown. Serve.

Per serving: Cal 507, Net Carbs 1.3g, Fat 54g, Protein 42g

Thyme Zucchini & Chicken Chunks Skillet

Ingredients for 4 servings

2 tbsp olive oil
1 tbsp unsalted butter
1 (4.6 oz) chicken chunks
¼ cup finely chopped onion

¼ cup chopped fresh parsley
3 zucchinis, cut into 1-inch dices
1 tsp dried thyme
Salt and black pepper to taste

Directions and Total Time: approx. 30 minutes

Heat olive oil and butter in a skillet and sauté chicken for 5 minutes. Add in onion and parsley and cook further for 3 minutes. Stir in zucchini and thyme, season with salt, pepper, cover, and cook for 8-10 minutes or until the vegetables soften. Serve immediately.

Per serving: Cal 157; Net Carbs 0.2g; Fat 12g; Protein 8g

Roasted Chicken with Yogurt Scallions Sauce

Ingredients for 4 servings

2 tbsp butter
4 scallions, chopped
4 chicken breasts

Salt and black pepper, to taste
6 ounces plain yogurt
2 tbsp fresh dill, chopped

Directions and Total Time: approx. 35 minutes

Heat a pan with butter, add in chicken, season with pepper and salt, and fry for 2-3 per side. Transfer to a baking dish and bake for 15 minutes at 390 F.

To the pan, add scallions and cook for 2 minutes. Pour in plain yogurt, warm through without boil. Slice the chicken and serve.

Per serving: Cal 236, Net Carbs 2.3g, Fat 9g, Protein 18g

Cheesy Chicken with Cauliflower Steaks

Ingredients for 4 servings

4 slices chicken luncheon meat
1 large head cauliflower
½ tsp smoked paprika
2 tbsp olive oil

½ cup grated cheddar cheese
4 tbsp ranch dressing
2 tbsp chopped parsley

Directions and Total Time: approx. 30 minutes

Stand cauliflower on a flat surface and into 4 steaks from top to bottom. Season with paprika, salt, and pepper. Heat olive oil in a grill pan over medium heat and cook cauliflower on both sides until softened, 4 minutes. Top one side with chicken and sprinkle with cheddar cheese. Heat to melt the cheese. Transfer to serving plates, drizzle with ranch dressing, and garnish with parsley. Serve.

Per serving: Cal 253; Net Carbs 1g; Fat 22g; Protein 9g

Savory Cheesy Chicken

Ingredients for 4 servings

1 ½ lb chicken breasts, halved lengthwise
½ cup sliced Pecorino Romano cheese
Salt and black pepper to taste
2 eggs
2 tbsp Italian seasoning
1 pinch red chili flakes
¼ cup fresh parsley, chopped

4 tbsp butter
2 garlic cloves, minced
2 cups crushed tomatoes
1 tbsp dried basil
½ lb sliced mozzarella cheese

Directions and Total Time: approx. 45 minutes

Preheat oven to 400 F. Season chicken with salt and pepper; set aside. In a bowl, whisk eggs with Italian seasoning and chili flakes. On a plate, combine Pecorino cheese with parsley. Melt butter in a skillet. Dip the chicken in the egg mixture and then dredge in the cheese mixture. Place in the butter and fry on both sides until the cheese melts and is golden brown, 10 minutes; set aside. Sauté garlic in the same pan and mix in tomatoes. Top with basil, salt, and pepper, and cook for 10 minutes. Pour the sauce into a greased baking dish. Lay the chicken pieces in the sauce and top with mozzarella. Bake for 15 minutes or until the cheese melts. Remove and serve with leafy green salad.

Per serving: Cal 674; Net Carbs 5.3g; Fat 43g; Protein 59g

Delicious Veggies & Chicken Casserole

Ingredients for 4 servings

¾ lb Brussels sprouts, halved
2 large zucchinis, chopped
2 red bell peppers, quartered
2 chicken breasts, cubed
¼ cup olive oil

1 tbsp balsamic vinegar
1 tsp chopped thyme leaves
1 tsp chopped rosemary
½ cup toasted walnuts

Directions and Total Time: approx. 30 minutes

Preheat oven to 400 F. Scatter Brussels sprouts, zucchinis, bell peppers, and chicken on a baking sheet. Season with salt and pepper, and drizzle with olive oil. Add balsamic vinegar and toss. Scatter thyme and rosemary on top. Bake for 25 minutes, shaking once. Top with walnuts and serve.

Per serving: Cal 485; Net Carbs 3.7g; Fat 34g; Protein 35g

Parsley Chicken & Cauliflower Stir-Fry

Ingredients for 4 servings

1 large head cauliflower, cut into florets
2 tbsp olive oil	1 yellow bell pepper, diced
2 chicken breasts, sliced	3 tbsp chicken broth
1 red bell pepper, diced	2 tbsp chopped parsley

Directions and Total Time: approx. 30 minutes

Heat olive oil in a skillet and season chicken with salt and pepper; cook until brown on all sides, 8 minutes. Transfer to a plate. Pour bell peppers into the pan and sauté until softened, 5 minutes. Add in cauliflower, broth, season to taste, and mix. Cover the pan and cook for 5 minutes or until cauliflower is tender. Mix in chicken, parsley. Serve.

Per serving: Cal 345; Net Carbs 3.5g; Fat 21g; Protein 32g

Baked Cheese Chicken

Ingredients for 6 servings

2 tbsp olive oil	1 cup buffalo sauce
8 oz cottage cheese, grated	1 cup ranch dressing
1 lb ground chicken	3 cups Monterey Jack, grated

Directions and Total Time: approx. 30 minutes

Preheat oven to 350 F. Warm oil in a skillet and brown chicken for a couple of minutes; set aside. Spread cottage cheese on a greased sheet, top with chicken, pour buffalo sauce, add ranch dressing, and sprinkle with Monterey cheese. Bake for 23 minutes. Serve with veggie sticks.

Per serving: Cal 216; Net Carbs 3g; Fat 16g; Protein 14g

Parsnip & Bacon Chicken Bake

Ingredients for 4 servings

6 bacon slices, chopped	2 tbsp butter
2 tbsp butter	1 cup heavy cream
½ lb parsnips, diced	2 oz cream cheese, softened
2 tbsp olive oil	1 ¼ cups grated Pepper Jack
1 lb ground chicken	¼ cup chopped scallions

Directions and Total Time: approx. 50 minutes

Preheat oven to 300 F. Put the bacon in a pot and fry on until brown and crispy, 7 minutes; set aside. Melt butter in a skillet and sauté parsnips until softened and lightly browned. Transfer to a greased baking sheet. Heat olive oil in the same pan and cook the chicken until no longer pink, 8 minutes. Spoon onto a plate and set aside too.

Add heavy cream, cream cheese, two-thirds of the Pepper Jack cheese, salt, and pepper to the pot. Melt the ingredients over medium heat, frequently stirring, 7 minutes. Spread the parsnips on the baking dish, top with chicken, pour the heavy cream mixture over, and scatter bacon and scallions. Sprinkle the remaining cheese on top and bake until the cheese melts and is golden, 30 minutes.

Per serving: Cal 757; Net Carbs 5.5g; Fat 66g; Protein 29g

Baked Chicken with Kale & Feta

Ingredients for 4 servings

4 chicken breasts, cut into strips
¼ cup shredded Monterey Jack cheese
2 tbsp olive oil	2 tbsp tomato paste
Salt and black pepper to taste	1 tsp Italian mixed herbs
1 small onion, chopped	2 medium zucchinis, chopped
2 garlic cloves, minced	1 cup baby kale
½ tbsp red wine vinegar	¼ cup crumbled feta cheese
1 ½ crushed tomatoes	½ cup grated Parmesan

Directions and Total Time: approx. 45 minutes

Preheat oven to 400 F. Heat olive oil in a skillet, season the chicken with salt and pepper, and cook for 8 minutes; set aside. Add in and sauté onion and garlic for 3 minutes. Mix in vinegar, tomatoes, tomato paste. Cook for 8 minutes. Season with salt, pepper, and mixed herbs. Stir in chicken, zucchinis, kale, and feta cheese. Pour the mixture into a baking dish and top with Monterey Jack cheese. Bake for 15 minutes or until the cheese melts and is golden. Garnish with Parmesan cheese and serve.

Per serving: Cal 681; Net Carbs 6.6g; Fat 39g; Protein 69g

Yummy Chicken Squash Lasagna

Ingredients for 4 servings

2 tbsp butter	2 cups crumbled ricotta
1 ½ lb ground chicken	1 large egg, beaten
1 tsp garlic powder	2 cups marinara sauce
1 tsp onion powder	1 tbsp Italian mixed herbs
2 tbsp coconut flour	¼ tsp red chili flakes
1 ½ cups grated mozzarella	4 large yellow squash, sliced
1/3 cup Parmesan cheese	¼ cup fresh basil leaves

Directions and Total Time: approx. 55 minutes

Preheat oven to 375 F. Melt butter in a skillet and cook chicken for 10 minutes; set aside. In a bowl, mix garlic and onion powders, coconut flour, salt, pepper, mozzarella, half of Parmesan, ricotta cheese, and egg. In another bowl, combine marinara sauce, mixed herbs, and chili flakes; set aside. Make a single layer of the squash slices in a greased baking dish; spread a quarter of the egg mixture on top, a layer of the chicken, then a quarter of the marinara sauce. Repeat the layering process in the same proportions and sprinkle with the remaining Parmesan. Bake for 30 minutes. Garnish with basil leaves, slice, and serve.

Per serving: Cal 664; Net Carbs 7g; Fat 39g; Protein 62g

Mustard Chicken Cordon Blue Casserole

Ingredients for 4 servings

1 rotisserie chicken, shredded	1 tbsp Dijon mustard
7 oz smoked deli ham, chopped	1 tbsp plain vinegar
8 oz cream cheese	10 oz shredded Gruyere

Directions and Total Time: approx. 30 minutes

Preheat oven to 350 F. Spread the chicken and ham on a greased baking dish. In a bowl, mix cream cheese, mustard, vinegar, and two-thirds of Gruyere cheese. Spread the mixture on top of chicken and ham, season with salt and pepper, and cover with the remaining cheese. Bake for 20 minutes or until the cheese melts and is golden brown.

Per serving: Cal 692; Net Carbs 3.6g; Fat 48g; Protein 60g

Tasty Chicken Pot Pie with Vegetables

Ingredients for 4 servings

1/3 cup cremini mushrooms, sliced	
3 tbsp butter	½ cup coconut cream
1 lb ground chicken	½ tsp dried rosemary
Salt and black pepper to taste	¼ tsp poultry seasoning
1 large yellow onion, chopped	10 egg whites
2 baby zucchinis, chopped	4 tbsp coconut flour
1 cup green beans, chopped	2½ cups fine almond flour
½ cup chopped broccoli rabe	2 tsp baking powder
2 celery stalks, chopped	½ cup shredded cheddar
4 oz cream cheese	6 tbsp butter

Directions and Total Time: approx. 60 minutes

Preheat oven to 350 F. Melt 1 tbsp of butter in a skillet, add chicken, season with salt and pepper, and cook for 8 minutes or until the chicken is no longer pink; set aside. Melt the remaining butter in the same skillet and sauté onion, zucchini, green beans, broccoli rabe, celery, and mushrooms. Cook until the vegetables soften, 5 minutes. Stir in chicken, cream cheese, and coconut cream. Simmer until the sauce thickens, 5 minutes. Season with rosemary and poultry seasoning and cook for 2 minutes. Turn the heat off and pour the mixture into a baking dish. Pour the egg whites into a bowl and using a hand mixer, beat the whites until frothy, but not stiff. Mix in coconut flour, almond flour, baking powder, cheddar, and salt until evenly combined. Beat the batter until smooth. Spoon the content in the baking dish and bake for 30 minutes or until the top browns. Remove from the oven and serve.

Per serving: Cal 808; Net Carbs 4.7g; Fat 68g; Protein 39g

Chili Pulled Chicken with Avocado

Ingredients for 4 servings

1 white onion, finely chopped	1 tbsp red wine vinegar
¼ cup chicken stock	Salt and black pepper to taste
3 tbsp coconut oil	2 lb boneless chicken thighs
3 tbsp tamari sauce	1 avocado, halved and pitted
3 tbsp chili pepper	½ lemon, juiced

Directions and Total Time: approx. 2 hours 30 minutes

In a pot, combine onion, stock, coconut oil, tamari sauce, chili, vinegar, salt, pepper. Add thighs, close the lid, and cook over low heat for 2 hours. Scoop avocado pulp into a bowl, add lemon juice, and mash the avocado into a puree; set aside. When the chicken is ready, open the lid and use two forks to shred it. Cook further for 15 minutes. Turn the heat off and mix in avocado. Serve with low carb tortillas.

Per serving: Cal 710; Net Carbs 4g; Fat 56g; Protein 40g

Savory Chicken Wings with Chimichurri

Ingredients for 4 servings

16 chicken wings, halved	1 cup fresh parsley leaves
Salt and black pepper to taste	¼ cup fresh cilantro leaves
½ cup butter, melted	2 tbsp red wine vinegar
3 garlic cloves, peeled	½ cup olive oil

Directions and Total Time: approx. 50 minutes

Preheat oven to 350 F. Put chicken in a bowl, season with salt and pepper, and pour butter all over. Toss to coat and transfer to a greased baking sheet. Bake for 40-45 minutes or until light brown and cooked within. Transfer to the same bowl. In a food processor, blend garlic, parsley, cilantro, salt, and pepper until smooth. Add in vinegar and gradually pour in olive oil while blending further. Pour the mixture (chimichurri) over the chicken; toss well to serve.

Per serving: Cal 603; Net Carbs 1.4g; Fat 54g; Protein 27g

Scallion & Saffron Chicken with Pasta

Ingredients for 4 servings

1 cup shredded mozzarella cheese	
4 chicken breasts, cut into strips	
1 egg yolk	1 pinch cardamom powder
3 tbsp butter	1 pinch cinnamon powder
½ tsp ground saffron threads	1 cup heavy cream
1 yellow onion, chopped	1 cup chicken stock
2 garlic cloves, minced	¼ cup chopped scallions
1 tbsp almond flour	3 tbsp chopped parsley

Directions and Total Time: approx. 35 min + chilling time

Microwave mozzarella cheese for 2 minutes. Take out the bowl and allow cooling for 1 minute. Mix in egg yolk until well-combined. Lay a parchment paper on a flat surface, pour the cheese mixture on top and cover with another parchment paper. Flatten the dough into 1/8-inch thickness. Take off the parchment paper and cut the dough into thick fettuccine strands. Place in a bowl and refrigerate overnight. Bring 2 cups of water to a boil and add the keto fettuccine. Cook for 1 minute and drain; set aside. Melt butter in a skillet, season the chicken with salt and pepper, and cook for 5 minutes. Stir in saffron, onion, and garlic and cook until the onion softens, 3 minutes. Stir in almond flour, cardamom powder, and cinnamon powder and cook for 1 minute.

Add in heavy cream and chicken stock and cook for 2-3 minutes. Mix in fettuccine and scallions. Garnish with parsley and serve warm.

Per serving: Cal 775; Net Carbs 3.1g; Fats 48g; Protein 73g

Spiralized Zucchini with Chicken & Pine Nuts

Ingredients for 4 servings

2 ½ lb chicken breast, cut into strips
5 garlic cloves, minced
¼ tsp pureed onion
Salt and black pepper to taste
2 tbsp avocado oil
3 large eggs, lightly beaten
¼ cup chicken broth

2 tbsp coconut aminos
1 tbsp white vinegar
½ cup chopped scallions
1 tsp red chili flakes
4 zucchinis, spiralized
½ cup toasted pine nuts

Directions and Total Time: approx. 30 minutes

In a bowl, combine half of garlic, onion, salt, and pepper. Add chicken and mix well. Heat avocado oil in a deep skillet over medium heat and add the chicken. Cook for 8 minutes until no longer pink with a slight brown crust. Transfer to a plate. Pour the eggs into the pan and scramble for 1 minute. Spoon the eggs to the side of the chicken and set aside. Reduce the heat to low and in a bowl, mix broth, coconut aminos, vinegar, scallions, remaining garlic, and chili flakes; simmer for 3 minutes. Stir in chicken, zucchini, and eggs. Cook for 1 minute and turn the heat off. Spoon into plates, top with pine nuts and serve warm.

Per serving: Cal 766; Net Carbs 3.3g; Fat 50g; Protein 71g

Lovely Pulled Chicken Egg Bites

Ingredients for 4 servings

2 tbsp butter
1 chicken breast
2 tbsp chopped green onions

½ tsp red chili flakes
12 eggs
¼ cup grated Monterey Jack

Directions and Total Time: approx. 30 minutes

Preheat oven to 400 F and line a 12-hole muffin tin with cupcake liners. Melt butter in a skillet, season chicken with salt and pepper, and cook it until brown on each side, 10 minutes. Transfer to a plate and shred with 2 forks. Divide between muffin holes along with green onions and chili flakes. Crack an egg into each muffin hole and scatter the cheese on top. Bake for 15 minutes until eggs set.

Per serving: Cal 393; Net Carbs 0.5g; Fat 27g; Protein 34g

Buffalo Spinach Chicken Sliders

Ingredients for 4 servings

4 zero carb hamburger buns, halved
3 lb chicken thighs, boneless and skinless
1 tsp onion powder
2 tsp garlic powder
Salt and black pepper to taste
2 tbsp ranch dressing mix
¼ cup white vinegar

2 tbsp hot sauce
½ cup chicken broth
¼ cup melted butter
¼ cup baby spinach
4 slices cheddar cheese

Directions and Total Time: approx. 3 hours 30 minutes

In a bowl, combine onion and garlic powders, salt, pepper, and ranch dressing mix. Rub the mixture onto chicken and place into a pot. In another bowl, mix vinegar, hot sauce, broth, and butter. Pour the mixture all over the chicken and cook on low heat for 3 hours. Using two forks, shred the chicken into small strands. Mix and adjust the taste. Divide the spinach in the bottom half of each low carb bun, spoon the chicken on top, and add a slice of cheddar cheese. Cover with the remaining bun halves and serve.

Per serving: Cal 774; Net Carbs 15.7g; Fat 37g; Protein 87g

Creamy Mustard Chicken with Shirataki

Ingredients for 4 servings

2 (8 oz) packs angel hair shirataki
4 chicken breasts, cut into strips
1 cup chopped mustard greens
1 yellow bell pepper, sliced
1 tbsp olive oil
1 yellow onion, finely sliced

1 garlic clove, minced
1 tbsp wholegrain mustard
5 tbsp heavy cream
1 tbsp chopped parsley

Directions and Total Time: approx. 30 minutes

Boil 2 cups of water in a medium pot. Strain the shirataki pasta and rinse well under hot running water. Allow proper draining and pour the shirataki pasta into the boiling water. Cook for 3 minutes and strain again. Place a dry skillet and stir-fry the shirataki pasta until visibly dry, 1-2 minutes; set aside. Heat olive oil in a skillet, season the chicken with salt and pepper and cook for 8-10 minutes; set aside. Stir in onion, bell pepper, and garlic and cook until softened, 5 minutes. Mix in mustard and heavy cream; simmer for 2 minutes and mix in the chicken and mustard greens for 2 minutes. Stir in shirataki pasta, garnish with parsley and serve.

Per serving: Cal 692; Net Carbs 15g; Fats 38g; Protein 65g

Creamy Chicken with Broccoli & Prosciutto

Ingredients for 4 servings

6 slices prosciutto, chopped
2 tbsp butter
4 chicken breasts, cubed
4 garlic cloves, minced

1 cup baby kale, chopped
1 ½ cups heavy cream
1 head broccoli, cut into florets
¼ cup shredded Parmesan

Directions and Total Time: approx. 30 minutes

Put prosciutto in a skillet and fry it until crispy and brown, 5 minutes; set aside. Melt butter in the same skillet and cook chicken until no longer pink. Add garlic to sauté for 1 minute. Mix in heavy cream, prosciutto, and kale and let simmer for 5 minutes until the sauce thickens. Pour broccoli into a safe-microwave bowl, sprinkle with some water, season with salt and pepper, and microwave for 2 minutes until broccoli softens. Spoon into the sauce, top with Parmesan, stir, and cook until the cheese melts.

Per serving: Cal 805; Net Carbs 4.5g; Fat 53g; Protein 71g

Chicken Bake with Onion & Parsnip

Ingredients for 6 servings

3 parsnips, sliced	2 lb chicken breasts
1 onion, sliced	½ cup chicken broth
4 garlic cloves, crushed	¼ cup white wine
2 tbsp olive oil	Salt and black pepper to taste

Directions and Total Time: approx. 30 minutes

Preheat oven to 360 F. Warm oil in a skillet over medium heat and brown chicken for a couple of minutes, and transfer to a baking dish. Arrange the vegetables around the chicken, add in wine and broth; season with salt and pepper. Bake for 25 minutes, stirring once. Serve.

Per serving: Cal 278; Net Carbs 5.1g; Fat 8.7g; Protein 35g

Cheddar Taco Chicken Bake

Ingredients for 4 servings

1 rotisserie chicken, shredded	1 yellow bell pepper, chopped
1/3 cup mayonnaise	2 tbsp taco seasoning
8 oz cream cheese	½ cup shredded cheddar
1 yellow onion, sliced	Salt and black pepper to taste

Directions and Total Time: approx. 30 minutes

Preheat oven to 400 F. Into a greased baking dish, add chicken, mayo, cream cheese, onion, bell pepper, taco seasoning, and two-thirds of cheese. Mix the ingredients and top with the remaining cheese. Bake for 20 minutes.

Per serving: Cal 477; Net Carbs 6.7g; Fat 33g; Protein 34g

Buttered Roast Chicken

Ingredients for 6 servings

3 lb chicken, whole bird	1 large lemon, juiced
8 tbsp butter, melted	2 large lemons, thinly sliced

Directions and Total Time: approx. 1 hour 30 minutes

Preheat oven to 400 F. Season the chicken with salt and pepper. Put the chicken, breast side up in a baking dish. In a bowl, combine butter and lemon juice. Allow to cool a little and spread the mixture all over the chicken. Arrange lemon slices at the bottom of the dish and bake for 1 to 1½ hours. Baste the chicken with the juice every 20 minutes. Remove the chicken and serve with mashed turnips.

Per serving: Cal 393; Net Carbs 1g; Fat 22g; Protein 46g

Baked Chicken Skewers with Rutabaga Fries

Ingredients for 4 servings

2 chicken breasts	2 tbsp olive oil
½ tsp salt	¼ cup chicken broth
¼ tsp ground black pepper	

For the fries

1 lb rutabaga	½ tsp salt
2 tbsp olive oil	¼ tsp ground black pepper

Directions and Total Time: approx. 60 minutes

Set oven to 400 F. Grease and line a baking sheet. In a bowl, mix oil, spices and chicken; set in the fridge for 10 minutes. Peel and chop rutabaga to form fry shapes and place into a separate bowl. Apply oil to coat and season with pepper and salt. Arrange on the baking tray and bake for 10 minutes. Take the chicken from the refrigerator and thread onto the skewers. Place over the rutabaga, pour in the chicken broth, and bake for 30 minutes. Serve.

Per serving: Cal: 579, Net Carbs: 6g, Fat: 53g, Protein: 39g

Chicken Wraps in Bacon with Spinach

Ingredients for 4 servings

4 chicken breasts	For the buttered spinach:
8 slices bacon	2 tbsp butter
Salt and black pepper to taste	1 lb spinach
2 tbsp olive oil	4 garlic cloves

Directions and Total Time: approx. 30 minutes

Preheat oven to 450 F. Wrap each chicken breast with 2 bacon slices, season with salt and pepper; place on a baking sheet. Drizzle with olive oil and bake for 15 minutes until the bacon browns and chicken cooks within. Melt butter in a skillet, and sauté spinach and garlic until the leaves wilt, 5 minutes. Season with salt and pepper. Remove from the oven and serve with buttered spinach.

Per serving: Cal 856; Net Carbs 2.4g; Fat 60g; Protein 71g

Louisiana Chicken Fettuccine

Ingredients for 4 servings

1 medium red bell pepper, deseeded and thinly sliced	
1 medium green bell pepper, deseeded and thinly sliced	
2 cups grated mozzarella	1 yellow onion, thinly sliced
½ cup grated Parmesan	4 garlic cloves, minced
1 cup shredded mozzarella	4 tsp Cajun seasoning
1 egg yolk	1 cup Alfredo sauce
2 tbsp olive oil	½ cup marinara sauce
4 chicken breasts, cubed	2 tbsp chopped fresh parsley

Directions and Total Time: approx. 45 min + chilling time

Microwave mozzarella cheese for 2 minutes. Take out the bowl and allow cooling for 1 minute. Mix in egg yolk until well-combined. Lay a parchment paper on a flat surface, pour the cheese mixture on top and cover with another parchment paper. Flatten the dough into 1/8-inch thickness. Take off the parchment paper and cut the dough into thick fettuccine strands. Place in a bowl and refrigerate overnight. Bring 2 cups water to a boil and add fettuccine. Cook for 1 minute and drain; set aside. Preheat oven to 350 F. Heat olive oil in a skillet, season the chicken with salt and pepper, and cook for 6 minutes. Transfer to a plate. Add in onion, garlic and bell peppers and cook for 5 minutes. Return the chicken to the pot and stir in Cajun seasoning, Alfredo sauce, and marinara sauce.

Cook for 3 minutes. Stir in fettuccine and transfer to a greased baking dish. Cover with the mozzarella and Parmesan cheeses and bake for 15 minutes. Garnish with parsley and serve warm.

Per serving: Cal 777; Net Carbs 4.6g; Fats 38g; Protein 93g

Mushroom Chicken Cheeseburgers

Ingredients for 4 servings

4 large Portobello caps, destemmed
1 ½ lb ground chicken   6 slices Gruyere cheese
Salt and black pepper to taste   4 lettuce leaves
1 tbsp tomato sauce   4 large tomato slices
1 tbsp olive oil   ¼ cup mayonnaise

Directions and Total Time: approx. 30 minutes

In a bowl, combine chicken, salt, pepper, and tomato sauce. Mold into 4 patties and set aside. Heat olive oil in a skillet; place in Portobello caps and cook until softened, 3 minutes; set aside. Put the patties in the skillet and fry until brown and compacted, 8 minutes. Place Gruyere slices on the patties, allow melting for 1 minute and lift each patty onto each mushroom cap. Divide the lettuce on top, then tomato slices, and top with some mayonnaise.

Per serving: Cal 510; Net Carbs 2.2g; Fat 34g; Protein 45g

Stuffed Peppers with Chicken & Broccoli

Ingredients for 6 servings

6 yellow bell peppers, halved 2 lb ground chicken
1 ½ tbsp olive oil   3 tsp taco seasoning
3 tbsp butter   1 cup riced broccoli
3 garlic cloves, minced   ¼ cup grated cheddar cheese
½ white onion, chopped   Crème fraiche for serving

Directions and Total Time: approx. 2 hours

Preheat oven to 400 F. Drizzle bell peppers with olive oil and season with salt; set aside. Melt butter in a skillet and sauté garlic and onion for 3 minutes. Stir in chicken and taco seasoning. Cook for 8 minutes. Mix in broccoli. Spoon the mixture into the peppers, top with cheddar cheese, and place in a greased baking dish. Bake until the cheese melts and is bubbly, 30 minutes. Plate the peppers. Top with the crème fraiche and serve.

Per serving: Cal 386; Net Carbs 11.5g; Fat 24g; Protein 30g

Grilled Chicken Kebabs with Curry & Yogurt

Ingredients for 4 servings4

1 ½ lb boneless chicken thighs, cut into 1-inch pieces
½ cup Greek yogurt   2 tbsp curry powder
Salt and black pepper to taste   1 tbsp olive oil

Directions and Total Time: approx. 30 minutes

Preheat oven to 400 F. In a bowl, combine Greek yogurt, salt, pepper, curry, and olive oil. Mix in chicken, cover the bowl with a plastic wrap and marinate for 20 minutes.

Remove the wrap and thread the chicken onto skewers. Grill in the middle rack of the oven for 4 minutes on each side or until fully cooked. Remove the chicken skewers and serve with cauliflower rice or steamed green beans.

Per serving: Cal 440; Net Carbs 0.5g; Fat 29g; Protein 41g

Herby Chicken Meatloaf

Ingredients for 6 servings

2 ½ lb ground chicken   ¼ cup chopped parsley
3 tbsp flaxseed meal   ¼ cup chopped oregano
2 large eggs   4 garlic cloves, minced
2 tbsp olive oil   Lemon slices to garnish
1 lemon,1 tbsp juiced

Directions and Total Time: approx. 50 minutes

Preheat oven to 400 F. In a bowl, combine chicken, salt, pepper, and flaxseed meal; set aside. In a small bowl, whisk the eggs with olive oil, lemon juice, parsley, oregano, and garlic. Pour the mixture onto the chicken mixture and mix well. Spoon into a greased loaf pan and press to fit. Bake for 40 minutes. Remove the pan, drain the liquid, and let cool a bit. Slice, garnish with lemon slices and serve.

Per serving: Cal 362; Net Carbs 1.3g; Fat 24g; Protein 35g

Eggplant Chicken Gratin With Swiss Cheese

Ingredients for 4 servings

3 tbsp butter   Salt and black pepper, to taste
1 eggplant, chopped   2 garlic cloves, minced
2 tbsp Swiss cheese, grated 6 chicken thighs

Directions and Total Time: approx. 55 minutes

Warm butter in a pan and cook chicken for 3 minutes per side. Transfer to a baking dish and season with salt and pepper. In the same pan, cook garlic, eggplant, pepper, and salt for 10 minutes. Ladle this mixture over the chicken, spread with the cheese, set in oven at 350 F, and bake for 30 minutes. Turn on the broiler, and broil for 2 minutes.

Per serving: Cal 412, Net Carbs 5g, Fat 37g, Protein 34g

Chicken with Tomato and Zucchini

Ingredients for 4 servings

2 tbsp ghee   1 (14 oz) can whole tomatoes
1 lb chicken thighs   1 zucchini, diced
2 cloves garlic, minced   10 fresh basil leaves, chopped

Directions and Total Time: approx. 45 minutes

Melt ghee in a saucepan, season the chicken with salt and pepper, and fry for 4 minutes on each side. Remove to a plate. Sauté garlic in the ghee for 2 minutes, pour in tomatoes, and cook for 8 minutes. Add in zucchini and cook for 4 minutes. Season the sauce with salt and pepper, stir, and add the chicken. Coat with sauce and simmer for 3 minutes. Serve chicken with sauce garnished with basil.

Per serving: Cal 468, Net Carbs 2g, Fat 39g, Protein 26g

Cauli Rice & Chicken Collard Wraps

Ingredients for 4 servings

2 tbsp avocado oil	1 ½ lb chicken breasts, cubed
1 large yellow onion, chopped	1 cup cauliflower rice
2 garlic cloves, minced	2 tsp hot sauce
Salt and black pepper to taste	8 collard leaves
1 jalapeño pepper, chopped	¼ cup crème fraiche

Directions and Total Time: approx. 30 minutes

Heat avocado oil in a deep skillet and sauté onion and garlic until softened, 3 minutes. Stir in jalapeño pepper salt, and pepper. Mix in chicken and cook until no longer pink on all sides, 10 minutes. Add in cauliflower rice and hot sauce. Sauté until the cauliflower slightly softens, 3 minutes. Lay out the collards on a clean flat surface and spoon the curried mixture onto the middle part of the leaves, about 3 tbsp per leaf. Spoon crème fraiche on top, wrap the leaves, and serve immediately.

Per serving: Cal 437; Net Carbs 1.8g; Fat 28g; Protein 38g

Almond Crusted Chicken Zucchini Stacks

Ingredients for 4 servings

1 ½ lb chicken thighs, skinless and boneless, cut into strips	
3 tbsp almond flour	4 tbsp olive oil
Salt and black pepper to taste	2 tsp Italian mixed herb blend
2 large zucchinis, sliced	½ cup chicken broth

Directions and Total Time: approx. 30 minutes

Preheat oven to 400 F. In a zipper bag, add almond flour, salt, and pepper. Mix and add the chicken slices. Seal the bag and shake to coat. Arrange the zucchinis on a greased baking sheet. Season with salt and pepper, and drizzle with 2 tbsp of olive oil. Remove the chicken from the almond flour mixture, shake off, and put 2-3 chicken strips on each zucchini. Season with herb blend and drizzle again with olive oil. Bake for 8 minutes; remove the sheet and pour in broth. Bake further for 10 minutes. Serve warm.

Per serving: Cal 512; Net Carbs 1.2g; Fat 42g; Protein 29g

Paleo Coconut Flour Chicken Nuggets

Ingredients for 2 servings

½ cup coconut flour	2 chicken breasts, cubed
1 egg	Salt and black pepper, to taste
2 tbsp garlic powder	½ cup butter

Directions and Total Time: approx. 30 minutes

In a bowl, combine salt, garlic powder, flour, and pepper, and stir. In a separate bowl, beat the egg. Add the chicken in egg mixture, then in the flour mixture. Set a pan over medium heat and warm butter. Add in chicken nuggets, and cook for 6 minutes on each side. Remove to paper towels, drain the excess grease and serve.

Per serving: Cal 417, Net Carbs 4.3g, Fat 37g, Protein 35g

Bacon Chicken Skillet with Bok Choy

Ingredients for 4 servings

2 lb ground chicken, cubed	1 orange bell pepper, chopped
Salt and black pepper to taste	2 cups baby bok choy
4 bacon slices, chopped	2 tbsp chopped oregano
1 tbsp coconut oil	2 garlic cloves, pressed

Directions and Total Time: approx. 30 minutes

Season the chicken with salt and pepper; set aside. Heat a skillet over medium heat and fry bacon until brown and crispy. Transfer to a plate. Melt coconut oil in the skillet and cook chicken until no longer pink, 10 minutes. Remove to the bacon plate. Add bell pepper and bok choy and sauté until softened, 5 minutes. Stir in bacon, chicken, oregano, and garlic, for 3 minutes. Serve with cauli rice.

Per serving: Cal 639; Net Carbs 1.2g; Fat 48g; Protein 46g

Celery Chicken Sausage Frittata

Ingredients for 4 servings

12 whole eggs	1 celery stalk, chopped
1 cup crème fraiche	12 oz ground chicken sausages
2 tbsp butter	¼ cup shredded Swiss cheese

Directions and Total Time: approx. 45 minutes

Preheat oven to 350 F. In a bowl, whisk eggs, crème fraiche, salt, and pepper. Melt butter in a safe oven skillet over medium heat. Sauté celery until soft, 5 minutes; set aside. Add the sausages to the skillet and cook until brown with frequent stirring to break the lumps that form, 8 minutes. Scatter celery on top, pour the egg mixture all over, and sprinkle with Swiss cheese. Put the skillet in the oven and bake until the eggs set and cheese melts, 20 minutes. Slice the frittata, and serve warm.

Per serving: Cal 529; Net Carbs 3g; Fat 44g; Protein 28g

Rosemary Turkey Brussels Sprouts Cakes

Ingredients for 4 servings

For the burgers

1 pound ground turkey	1 garlic clove, minced
1 egg	1 tsp fresh rosemary, chopped
1 onion, chopped	4 tbsp olive oil

For the fried Brussels sprouts

1 ½ lb Brussels sprouts	2 tbsp balsamic vinegar
4 tbsp olive oil	Salt to taste

Directions and Total Time: approx. 35 minutes

Preheat oven to 320 F and arrange Brussels sprouts in a baking dish. Toss to coat with olive oil and season with salt. Bake for 20 minutes, stirring once. Pour vinegar over and cook for 5 minutes. Combine burger ingredients in a bowl. Form patties out of the mixture. Set a pan, warm olive oil, and fry patties until cooked through. Serve.

Per serving: Cal 535; Net Carbs 6.7g; Fat 38g; Protein 31g

Jerk Chicken Drumsticks

Ingredients for 4 servings

½ cup Greek yogurt
2 tbsp melted butter
2 tbsp Jamaican seasoning
2 lb chicken drumsticks
3 tbsp pork rinds
¼ cup almond meal

Directions and Total Time: approx. 45 minutes

Preheat oven to 350 F. In a bowl, combine Greek yogurt, butter, Jamaican seasoning, salt, and pepper. Add the chicken and toss to coat evenly. Marinate for 15 minutes. In a food processor, blend the pork rinds with almond meal until well combined. Pour the mixture onto a wide plate. Remove chicken from the marinade, shake off any excess liquid, and coat generously in the pork rind mixture. Place on a greased baking sheet and bake for 30 minutes until golden brown and crispy, turning once. Serve warm.

Per serving: Cal 453; Net Carbs 1.8g; Fat 27g; Protein 45g

Creamy Chicken Thighs

Ingredients for 4 servings

1 pound chicken thighs
Salt and black pepper, to taste
1 tsp onion powder
¼ cup half-and-half
2 tbsp butter
2 tbsp sweet paprika

Directions and Total Time: approx. 50 minutes

In a bowl, combine paprika with onion, pepper, and salt. Season chicken pieces with this mixture and lay on a lined baking sheet; bake for 40 minutes in the oven at 400 F. Split the chicken in serving plates. Add the cooking juices to a skillet over medium heat, and mix with the half-and-half and butter. Cook for 6 minutes until the sauce thickens. Drizzle the sauce over the chicken and serve.

Per serving: Cal 381, Net Carbs 2.6g, Fat 33g, Protein 31g

Chicken Breasts with Jarred Pickle Juice

Ingredients for 4 servings

2 chicken breasts, cut into strips
4 oz chicken crisps, crushed
2 cups coconut oil
16 ounces jarred pickle juice
2 eggs, whisked

Directions and Total Time: approx. 30 min + chilling time

In a bowl, combine chicken with pickle juice; refrigerate for 12 hours. Place eggs in a bowl, and chicken crisps in a separate one. Dip the chicken pieces in the eggs, and then in chicken crisps until well coated. Set a pan and warm oil. Fry chicken for 3 minutes per side, remove to paper towels, drain the excess grease, and serve.

Per serving: Cal 387, Net Carbs 2.5g, Fat 16g, Protein 23g

Cream Cheese & Turkey Tortilla Rolls

Ingredients for 4 servings

10 canned pepperoncini peppers, sliced and drained
8 oz softened cream cheese   10 oz turkey pastrami, sliced

Directions and Total Time: approx. 2 hours 40 minutes

Lay a plastic wrap on a flat surface and arrange the pastrami all over, slightly overlapping each other. Spread the cheese on top of the salami layers and arrange the pepperoncini on top. Hold 2 opposite ends of the plastic wrap and roll the pastrami. Twist both ends to tighten and refrigerate for 2 hours. Slice into 2-inch pinwheels. Serve.

Per serving: Cal 266; Net Carbs 1g; Fat 24g; Protein 13g

Cucumber-Turkey Canapes

Ingredients for 6 servings

2 cucumbers, sliced
2 cups dices leftover turkey
¼ jalapeño pepper, minced
1 tbsp Dijon mustard
¼ cup mayonnaise
Salt and black pepper to taste

Directions and Total Time: approx. 5 minutes

Cut mid-level holes in cucumber slices with a knife and set aside. Combine turkey, jalapeno, mustard, mayonnaise, salt, and black pepper to be evenly mixed. Fill cucumber holes with turkey mixture and serve.

Per serving: Cal 170; Net Carbs 1.3g; Fat 14g; Protein 10g

Provolone Chicken Spinach Bake

Ingredients for 6 servings

1 ¼ cups provolone cheese, shredded
6 chicken breasts
1 tsp mixed spice seasoning
Salt and black pepper to taste
2 loose cups baby spinach
3 tsp olive oil
4 oz cream cheese, cubed

Directions and Total Time: approx. 45 minutes

Preheat oven to 370 F. Season chicken with spice mix, salt, and pepper. Put in a greased casserole dish and layer spinach over the chicken. Mix oil with cream cheese, provolone cheese, salt, and pepper and stir in 4 tbsp of water, one tbsp at a time. Pour the mixture over the chicken and cover the pot with aluminium foil. Bake for 20 minutes, remove foil and cook for 15 minutes. Serve.

Per serving: Cal 340, Net Carbs 3.1g, Fat 30g, Protein 15g

Italian Chicken-Basil Pizza

Ingredients for 4 servings

1 ½ cups grated mozzarella cheese
1 lb ground chicken
1 tsp Italian seasoning
1 cup tomato sauce
½ cup fresh basil leaves

Directions and Total Time: approx. 40 minutes

Preheat oven to 390 F and line a round pizza pan with parchment paper. In a bowl, mix ground chicken, Italian seasoning, and 1 cup of mozzarella cheese. Spread the pizza "dough" on the pizza pan and bake for 18 minutes. Spread tomato sauce on top. Scatter the mozzarella cheese and basil all over and bake for 15 minutes. Slice and serve.

Per serving: Cal 316; Net Carbs 0.4g; Fats 17g; Protein 35g

Tomato Basil Stuffed Chicken Breasts

Ingredients for 6 servings

4 ounces cream cheese
3 oz provolone cheese slices
10 ounces spinach
½ cup mozzarella, shredded

1 tbsp olive oil
1 cup tomato basil sauce
3 whole chicken breasts

Directions and Total Time: approx. 45 minutes

Preheat oven to 400 F. Microwave cream cheese, provolone cheese slices, and spinach for 2 minutes. Cut the chicken with the knife a couple of times horizontally. Stuff with the cheese filling. Brush the top with olive oil. Place on a lined baking dish and bake for 25 minutes. Pour the sauce over and top with mozzarella cheese. Return to oven and cook for 5 minutes. Serve.

Per serving: Cal 338, Net Carbs: 2.5g, Fat: 28g, Protein: 37g

Cranberry Glazed Chicken with Onions

Ingredients for 6 servings

4 green onions, chopped diagonally
4 tbsp unsweetened cranberry puree
2 lb chicken wings
2 tbsp olive oil

Chili sauce to taste
Juice from 1 lime

Directions and Total Time: approx. 50 minutes

Preheat the oven (broiler side) to 400 F. Then, in a bowl, mix the cranberry puree, olive oil, salt, sweet chili sauce, and lime juice. After, add in the wings and toss to coat. Place the chicken under the broiler, and cook for 45 minutes, turning once halfway. Remove the chicken after and serve warm with a cranberry puree and cheese dipping sauce. Top with green onions to serve.

Per serving: Cal 152, Net Carbs 1.6g, Fat 8.5g, Protein 17g

Acorn Squash Chicken Traybake

Ingredients for 4 servings

2 lb chicken thighs
1 lb acorn squash, cubed
½ cup black olives, pitted

¼ cup olive oil
5 garlic cloves, sliced
1 tbsp dried oregano

Directions and Total Time: approx. 60 minutes

Set oven to 400 F. Place the chicken with the skin down in a greased baking dish. Set garlic, olives and acorn squash around the chicken then drizzle with oil. Spread pepper, salt, and thyme over the mixture. Bake for 45 minutes.

Per serving: Cal: 411, Net Carbs: 5g, Fat: 15g, Protein: 31g

Turkey Bolognese Veggie Pasta

Ingredients for 6 servings

2 cups sliced mushrooms
2 tsp olive oil
1 pound ground turkey
3 tbsp pesto sauce

1 cup diced onion
2 cups sliced zucchini
6 cups veggie pasta, spiralized
Salt and black pepper to taste

Directions and Total Time: approx. 30 minutes

Heat oil in a skillet. Add turkey and cook until browned. Transfer to a plate. Add onions to the skillet, and cook until translucent, about 3 minutes. Add zucchini and mushrooms and cook for 7 more minutes. Return the turkey to skillet and stir in pesto sauce. Cover the pan, lower the heat, and simmer for 5 minutes. Serve immediately.

Per serving: Cal 273; Net Carbs 3.8g Fat 16g; Protein 19g

Grilled Garlic Chicken with Cauliflower

Ingredients for 6 servings

1 head cauliflower, cut into florets
3 tbsp smoked paprika
2 tsp garlic powder

1 tbsp olive oil
6 chicken breasts

Directions and Total Time: approx. 30 minutes

Place the cauliflower florets onto the steamer basket over boiling water and steam for approximately 8 minutes or until crisp-tender; set aside. Grease grill grate with cooking spray and preheat to 400 F. Combine paprika, salt, black pepper, and garlic powder in a bowl. Brush chicken with olive oil and sprinkle spice mixture over and massage with hands. Grill chicken for 7 minutes per side until well-cooked, and plate. Serve warm.

Per serving: Cal 422, Net Carbs 2g, Fat 35g, Protein 26g

Cucumber Salsa Topped Turkey Patties

Ingredients for 4 servings

2 spring onions, thinly sliced
1 pound ground turkey
1 egg
4 garlic cloves, minced
1 tbsp chopped herbs
2 tbsp ghee

1 tbsp apple cider vinegar
1 tbsp chopped dill
2 cucumbers, grated
1 cup sour cream
1 jalapeño pepper, minced
2 tbsp olive oil

Directions and Total Time: approx. 30 minutes

In a bowl, place spring onions, turkey, egg, two garlic cloves, and herbs; mix to combine. Make patties out of the mixture. Melt ghee in a skillet over medium heat. Cook the patties for 3 minutes per side. In a bowl, combine vinegar, dill, remaining garlic, cucumber, sour cream, jalapeño, and olive oil; toss well. Serve patties topped with salsa.

Per serving: Cal 475; Net Carbs 5g; Fat 38g; Protein 26g

Turkey with Avocado Sauce

Ingredients for 4 servings

1 avocado, pitted
½ cup mayonnaise
3 tbsp ghee

1 pound turkey breasts
1 cup chopped cilantro leaves
½ cup chicken broth

Directions and Total Time: approx. 25 minutes

Spoon avocado, mayo, and salt into a food processor and puree until smooth. Season with salt. Pour sauce into a jar and refrigerate.

Melt ghee in a skillet, fry turkey for 4 minutes on each side. Remove to a plate. Pour broth in the same skillet and add cilantro. Bring to a simmer for 15 minutes and add the turkey. Cook on low heat for 5 minutes until liquid reduces by half. Dish and spoon mayo-avocado sauce over.

Per serving: Cal 398, Net Carbs 4g, Fat 32g, Protein 24g

Bell Pepper Turkey Keto Carnitas

Ingredients for 4 servings

1 lb turkey breasts, sliced	1 tsp sweet paprika
1 garlic clove, minced	2 tbsp olive oil
1 red onion, sliced	1 tsp ground coriander
1 green chili, minced	1 green bell pepper, sliced
2 tsp ground cumin	1 red bell pepper, sliced
2 tbsp lime juice	1 tbsp fresh cilantro, chopped

Directions and Total Time: approx. 25 minutes

In a bowl, combine lime juice, cumin, garlic, coriander, paprika, salt, green chili, and pepper. Toss in the turkey pieces to coat well. Place a pan over medium heat and warm oil. Cook in turkey on each side, for 3 minutes; set aside. In the same pan, sauté bell peppers, cilantro, and onion for 6 minutes. Serve keto carnitas in lettuce leaves.

Per serving: Cal 262; Net Carbs 4.2g; Fat 15.2g; Protein 26g

Caprese Turkey Meatballs

Ingredients for 4 servings

2 tbsp chopped sun-dried tomatoes

1 pound ground turkey	¼ cup almond flour
2 tbsp chopped basil	2 tbsp olive oil
½ tsp garlic powder	½ cup shredded mozzarella
1 egg	Salt and black pepper to taste

Directions and Total Time: approx. 15 minutes

Place everything except for the oil in a bowl; mix well. Form 16 meatballs out of the mixture. Heat the olive oil in a skillet. Cook the meatballs for about 6 minutes. Serve.

Per serving: Cal 310; Net Carbs 2g; Fat 26g; Protein 22g

Tasty Curried Chicken Meatballs

Ingredients for 4 servings

3 lb ground chicken	1 tsp dried parsley
1 yellow onion, chopped	2 tbsp hot sauce
2 green bell peppers, chopped	Salt and black pepper to taste
3 garlic cloves, minced	1 tbsp red curry powder
2 tbsp melted butter	3 tbsp olive oil

Directions and Total Time: approx. 30 minutes

Preheat oven to 400 F. In a bowl, combine chicken, onion, bell peppers, garlic, butter, parsley, hot sauce, salt, pepper, and curry. Form meatballs and place on a greased baking sheet. Drizzle with olive oil and bake until the meatballs brown on the outside and cook within, 25 minutes. Serve.

Per serving: Cal 908; Net Carbs 2.7g; Fat 67g; Protein 65g

Hot Chicken Meatball Tray

Ingredients for 4 servings

1 egg	¼ cup Pecorino, grated
1 pound ground chicken	1 tbsp dry Italian seasoning
Salt and black pepper, to taste	2 tbsp olive oil
1 red pepper, chopped	¼ cup hot sauce
2 spring onions, chopped	2 tbsp parsley, chopped

Directions and Total Time: approx. 25 minutes

Preheat oven to 480 F. In a bowl, combine ground chicken, red pepper, onions, Italian seasoning, Pecorino cheese, salt, black pepper, parsley, and egg, and mix well with hands. Form into meatballs, arrange them on a greased with olive oil baking tray and bake for 16 minutes. Remove from the oven to a bowl and cover with hot sauce. Serve.

Per serving: Cal 383; Net Carbs 4.4g; Fat 28.1g; Protein 26g

Creamy Turkey & Broccoli Bake

Ingredients for 4 servings

1 lb turkey breasts, cooked	½ cup heavy cream
2 tbsp butter, melted	1 cup cheddar cheese, grated
1 head broccoli, cut into florets	4 tbsp pork rinds, crushed
½ cup buttermilk	Salt and black pepper, to taste
1 carrot, sliced	1 tsp oregano

Directions and Total Time: approx. 40 minutes

Cook broccoli in salted water for 4 minutes. Shred the turkey and place into a bowl together with buttermilk, butter, oregano, carrot, and broccoli; mix to combine. Season with salt and pepper, and transfer the mixture to a greased pan. Pour in heavy cream and top with cheese. Cover with pork rinds. Bake for 25 minutes at 450 F.

Per serving: Cal 469; Net Carbs 6.2g; Fat 3g; Protein 38.4g

Cheesy Turkey Sausage Egg Cups

Ingredients for 4 servings

1 cup Pecorino Romano cheese, grated

1 tsp butter	½ tsp dried thyme
6 eggs	3 turkey sausages, chopped

Salt and black pepper, to taste

Directions and Total Time: approx. 15 minutes

Preheat oven to 400 F and grease muffin cups with cooking spray.

In a skillet over medium heat add the butter and cook the turkey sausages for 4-5 minutes.

Beat 3 eggs with a fork. Add in sausages, cheese, and seasonings. Divide between the ups and bake for 4 minutes. Crack in an egg to each of the cups. Bake for an additional 4 minutes. Allow cooling before serving.

Per serving: Cal 423; Net Carbs 2.2g; Fat 34g; Protein 26.4g

BEEF

Bell Pepper & Beef Sausage Frittata

Ingredients for 4 servings

12 whole eggs	2 red bell peppers, chopped
1 cup sour cream	12 oz ground beef sausage
1 tbsp butter	¼ cup shredded cheddar

Directions and Total Time: approx. 60 minutes

Preheat the oven to 350 F. Crack the eggs into a blender; add the sour cream, salt, and pepper. Process over low speed to mix the ingredients; set aside. Melt butter in a large skillet over medium heat. Add bell peppers and sauté until soft, 6 minutes; set aside. Add the beef sausage and cook until brown, continuously stirring and breaking the lumps into small bits, 10 minutes. Flatten the beef on the bottom of skillet, scatter bell peppers on top, pour the egg mixture all over, and scatter the top with cheddar cheese. Put the skillet in the oven and bake for 30 minutes or until the eggs set and the cheddar cheese melts. Remove, slice the frittata, and serve warm with a nutty spinach salad.

Per serving: Cal 617; Net Carbs 5g; Fat 50g; Protein 33g

Chili Zucchini Beef Lasagna

Ingredients for 4 servings

½ cup Pecorino Romano cheese	
4 yellow zucchini, sliced	1 ½ cups grated mozzarella
Salt and black pepper to taste	2 cups crumbled goat cheese
1 tbsp lard	1 large egg
½ lb ground beef	2 cups marinara sauce
1 tsp garlic powder	1 tbsp Italian herb seasoning
1 tsp onion powder	¼ tsp red chili flakes
2 tbsp coconut flour	¼ cup fresh basil leaves

Directions and Total Time: approx. 55 minutes

Preheat oven to 375 F. Melt the lard in a skillet t and cook beef for 10 minutes; set aside. In a bowl, combine garlic powder, onion powder, coconut flour, salt, pepper, mozzarella cheese, half of Pecorino cheese, goat cheese, and egg. Mix Italian herb seasoning and chili flakes with marinara sauce. Make a single layer of the zucchini in a greased baking dish, spread ¼ of the egg mixture on top, and ¼ of the marinara sauce. Repeat the process and top with the remaining Pecorino cheese. Bake in the oven for 20 minutes. Garnish with basil, slice, and serve.

Per serving: Cal 608; Net Carbs 5.5g; Fat 37g; Protein 52g

Tarragon Beef Meatloaf

Ingredients for 4 servings

2 lb ground beef	1 lemon, zested
3 tbsp flaxseed meal	¼ cup chopped tarragon
2 large eggs	¼ cup chopped oregano
2 tbsp olive oil	4 garlic cloves, minced

Directions and Total Time: approx. 70 minutes

Preheat the oven to 400 F and grease a loaf pan with cooking spray. In a bowl, combine beef, salt, pepper, and flaxseed meal; set aside. In another bowl, whisk the eggs with olive oil, lemon zest, tarragon, oregano, and garlic. Pour the mixture onto the beef mix and evenly combine. Spoon the meat mixture into the pan and press to fit in. Bake in oven for 1 hour. Remove the pan, tilt to drain the meat's liquid, and let cool for 5 minutes. Slice, garnish with some lemon slices and serve with curried cauli rice.

Per serving: Cal 631; Net Carbs 2.8g; Fat 38g; Protein 64g

Broccoli Beef Bake with Pancetta

Ingredients for 4 servings

1 large broccoli head, cut into florets	
6 slices pancetta, chopped	1 cup coconut cream
2 tbsp olive oil	2 oz cream cheese, softened
1 lb ground beef	1 ¼ cups grated cheddar
2 tbsp butter	¼ cup chopped scallions

Directions and Total Time: approx. 55 minutes

Preheat the oven to 300 F. Fill a pot with water and bring to a boil. Pour in broccoli and blanch for 2 minutes. Drain and set aside. Place pancetta in the pot and fry on both sides for 7 minutes. Remove to a plate. Heat olive oil in the pot and cook the beef until browned; set aside. Add butter, coconut cream, cream cheese, two-thirds of cheddar cheese, salt, and pepper to the pot and stir for 7 minutes. Arrange the broccoli florets in a baking dish, pour the cream mixture over, and scatter the top with pancetta and scallions. Top with the remaining cheddar, and bake in the oven until the cheese is bubbly and golden, 30 minutes.

Per serving: Cal 854; Net Carbs 7.3g; Fat 69g; Protein 51g

Slow-Cooked BBQ Beef Sliders

Ingredients for 4 servings

4 zero carb hamburger buns, halved	
3 lb chuck roast, boneless	2 tbsp tamari sauce
1 tsp onion powder	½ cup bone broth
2 tsp garlic powder	¼ cup melted butter
1 tbsp smoked paprika	Salt and black pepper to taste
2 tbsp tomato paste	¼ cup baby spinach
¼ cup white vinegar	4 slices cheddar cheese

Directions and Total Time: approx. 12 hours 25 minutes

Cut the beef into two pieces. In a small bowl, combine salt, pepper, onion and garlic powders, and paprika. Rub the mixture onto beef and place in a slow cooker. In another bowl, mix tomato paste, vinegar, tamari sauce, broth, and melted butter. Pour over the beef and cook for 6 hours on High. When the beef cooks, shred it using two forks. Divide the spinach on each bun, spoon the meat on top, and add a cheese slice. Cover and serve immediately.

Per serving: Cal 648; Net Carbs 17.6g; Fat 27g; Protein 72g

Roasted Beef Stacks with Cabbage

Ingredients for 6 servings

1 head canon cabbage, shredded
1 lb chuck steak, sliced thinly   ¼ cup olive oil
across the grain   2 tsp Italian mixed herb blend
3 tbsp coconut flour   ½ cup bone broth

Directions and Total Time: approx. 55 minutes

Preheat the oven to 400 F. In a zipper bag, add coconut flour, salt, and pepper. Mix and add the beef slices. Seal the bag and shake to coat. Grease a baking sheet with 2 tbsp olive oil and make in little mounds of cabbage. Sprinkle with salt and pepper, and drizzle with 2 tbsp of olive oil. Remove the beef strips from the coconut flour mixture, shake off the excess flour, and place 2-3 beef strips on each cabbage mound. Sprinkle the Italian herb blend and drizzle again with olive oil. Roast for 30 minutes; remove the pan, and carefully pour in the broth. Return to oven and roast further for 10 minutes, until beef cooks through.

Per serving: Cal 222; Net Carbs 1.5g; Fat 14g; Protein 18g

Savory Portobello Beef Burgers

Ingredients for 6 servings

6 large Portobello caps, destemmed and rinsed
1 lb ground beef   6 slices Monterey Jack
Salt and black pepper to taste   6 lettuce leaves
1 tbsp Worcestershire sauce   6 large tomato slices
1 tbsp coconut oil   ¼ cup mayonnaise

Directions and Total Time: approx. 30 minutes

In a bowl, combine beef, salt, pepper, and Worcestershire sauce. Using your hands, mold the meat into 6 patties, and set aside. Heat the coconut oil in a medium skillet; place in the Portobello caps and cook until softened, 3 to 4 minutes. Remove to serving plates. Cook the beef patties in the skillet until brown, 10 minutes in total. Place the cheese slices on the beef, allow melting for 1 minute and lift each beef patty onto each mushroom cap. Divide the lettuce on top, tomato slices, and top with mayo to serve.

Per serving: Cal 332; Net Carbs 0.7g; Fat 22g; Protein 29g

Spicy Enchilada Beef Stuffed Peppers

Ingredients for 6 servings

6 bell peppers, deseeded   2 ½ lb ground beef
1 ½ tbsp olive oil   3 tsp enchilada seasoning
3 tbsp butter, softened   1 cup cauliflower rice
½ white onion, chopped   ¼ cup grated cheddar cheese
3 cloves garlic, minced   Sour cream for serving

Directions and Total Time: approx. 70 minutes

Preheat oven to 400 F. Melt butter in a skillet and sauté onion and garlic for 3 minutes. Stir in beef, enchilada seasoning, salt, and pepper. Cook for 10 minutes. Mix in the cauli rice until incorporated.

Spoon the mixture into the peppers, divide the cheddar cheese on top, and put the stuffed peppers in a greased baking dish. Bake for 40 minutes. Drop generous dollops of sour cream on the peppers to serve.

Per serving: Cal 409; Net Carbs 4g; Fat 21g; Protein 45g

Spicy Beef Lettuce Wraps

Ingredients for 4 servings

1 lb chuck steak, sliced thinly against the grain
3 tbsp ghee, divided   2 tsp red curry powder
1 large white onion, chopped   1 cup cauliflower rice
2 garlic cloves, minced   8 small lettuce leaves
1 jalapeño pepper, chopped   ¼ cup sour cream for topping

Directions and Total Time: approx. 20 minutes

Melt 2 tbsp of ghee in a large deep skillet; season the beef and cook until brown and cooked within, 10 minutes; set aside. Sauté the onion for 3 minutes. Pour in garlic, salt, pepper, and jalapeño; cook for 1 minute. Add the remaining ghee, curry powder, and beef. Cook for 5 minutes and stir in the cauliflower rice. Sauté until adequately mixed and the cauliflower slightly softened, 2 to 3 minutes. Adjust the taste with salt and black pepper.

Lay out the lettuce leaves on a lean flat surface and spoon the beef mixture onto the middle part of the leaves, about 3 tbsp per leaf. Divide sour cream on top, wrap the leaves, and serve.

Per serving: Cal 298; Net Carbs 3.3g; Fat 18g; Protein 27g

Sunday Beef Fathead Pizza

Ingredients for 4 servings

2 tbsp cream cheese, softened   2 tbsp butter
6 oz shredded cheese   8 oz ground beef sausage
¾ cup almond flour   ¼ cup tomato sauce
1 egg   ½ tsp dried basil
1 tsp plain vinegar   4 ½ oz shredded mozzarella

Directions and Total Time: approx. 45 minutes

Preheat oven to 400 F. Line a pizza pan with parchment paper. Melt cream and mozzarella cheeses in a skillet while stirring until evenly combined. Turn the heat off and mix in almond flour, egg, ½ tsp of salt, and vinegar. Let cool slightly. Flatten the mixture onto the pizza pan. Cover with another parchment paper and using a rolling pin, smoothen the dough into a circle. Take off the parchment paper on top, prick the dough all over with a fork, and bake for 10 to 15 minutes until golden brown.

While the crust bakes, melt butter in a skillet over and fry sausage until brown, 8 minutes. Turn the heat off. Spread the tomato sauce on the crust, top with basil, meat, and mozzarella cheese, and return to the oven. Bake for 12 minutes. Remove the pizza, slice, and serve warm.

Per serving: Cal 361; Net Carbs 0.8g; Fat 21g; Protein 37g

Lemon & Spinach Cheeseburgers

Ingredients for 4 servings

1 large tomato, sliced into 4 pieces and deseeded
1 lb ground beef   16 large spinach leaves
½ cup chopped cilantro   4 tbsp mayonnaise
1 lemon, zested and juiced   1 medium red onion, sliced
Salt and black pepper to taste   ¼ cup grated Parmesan
1 tsp garlic powder   1 avocado, halved, sliced
2 tbsp hot chili puree

Directions and Total Time: approx. 15 minutes

Preheat the grill on high heat. In a bowl, add beef, cilantro, lemon zest, juice, salt, pepper, garlic powder, and chili puree. Wearing a set of gloves on your hands, mix the ingredients until evenly combined. Make 4 patties from the mixture. Grill for 3 minutes on each side. Transfer to a serving plate. Lay 2 spinach leaves side to side in 4 portions on a clean flat surface. Place a beef patty on each, spread a tbsp of mayo on top of the meat, add a slice of tomato and onion, sprinkle with some Parmesan cheese, and divide avocado on top. Cover with 2 pieces of spinach leaves each. Serve the burgers with cream cheese sauce.

Per serving: Cal 310; Net Carbs 6.5g; Fat 16g; Protein 29g

Herby Beef Meatballs

Ingredients for 4 servings

3 lb ground beef   1 tsp dried basil
1 red onion, finely chopped   2 tbsp tamari sauce
2 red bell peppers, chopped   Salt and black pepper to taste
3 garlic cloves, minced   1 tbsp dried rosemary
2 tbsp melted butter   3 tbsp olive oil

Directions and Total Time: approx. 30 minutes

Preheat the oven to 400 F and grease a baking sheet with cooking spray. In a bowl, mix beef, onion, bell peppers, garlic, butter, basil, tamari sauce, salt, pepper, and rosemary. Using hands to form 1-inch meatballs from the mixture and place on the greased baking sheet. Drizzle olive oil over the beef and bake in the oven for 20 minutes or until the meatballs brown on the outside. Serve, garnished with scallions, and topped with ranch dressing.

Per serving: Cal 618; Net Carbs 2.5g; Fat 33g; Protein 74g

Peanut Zucchini & Beef Pad Thai

Ingredients for 4 servings

2 ½ lb chuck steak, sliced thinly against the grain
1 tsp crushed red pepper flakes
¼ tsp freshly pureed garlic   2 tbsp tamari sauce
¼ tsp freshly ground ginger   1 tbsp white vinegar
Salt and black pepper to taste   ½ cup chopped green onions
2 tbsp peanut oil   2 garlic cloves, minced
3 large eggs, lightly beaten   4 zucchinis, spiralized
1/3 cup beef broth   ½ cup bean sprouts
3 ¼ tbsp peanut butter   ½ cup crushed peanuts

Directions and Total Time: approx. 35 minutes

In a bowl, combine garlic, ginger, salt, and pepper. Add in beef and toss to coat. Heat peanut oil in a deep skillet and cook the beef for 12 minutes; transfer to a plate. Pour the eggs to the skillet and scramble for 1 minute; set aside. Reduce the heat and combine broth, peanut butter, tamari sauce, vinegar, green onions, minced garlic, and red pepper flakes. Mix until adequately combined and simmer for 3 minutes. Stir in beef, zucchini, bean sprouts, and eggs. Cook for 1 minute. Garnish with peanuts to serve.

Per serving: Cal 425; Net Carbs 3.3g; Fat 40g; Protein 70g

Beef Taco pizza

Ingredients for 4 servings

2 cups shredded mozzarella   ½ cup cheese sauce
2 tbsp cream cheese, softened   1 cup grated cheddar cheese
1 egg   1 cup chopped lettuce
¾ cup almond flour   1 tomato, diced
1 lb ground beef   ¼ cup sliced black olives
2 tsp taco seasoning   1 cup sour cream for topping

Directions and Total Time: approx. 45 minutes

Preheat oven to 390 F and line a pizza pan with parchment paper. Microwave the mozzarella and cream cheeses for 1 minute. Remove and mix in egg and almond flour. Spread the mixture on the pan and bake for 15 minutes. Put the beef in a pot and cook for 5 minutes. Stir in taco seasoning; salt and pepper. Spread the cheese sauce on the crust and top with the meat. Add cheddar cheese, lettuce, tomato, and black olives. Bake until the cheese melts, 5 minutes. Remove the pizza, drizzle sour cream on top, and serve.

Per serving: Cal 590; Net Carbs 7.9g; Fat 29g; Protein 64g

Mushroom & Bell Pepper Beef Skewers

Ingredients for 4 servings

2 cups cremini mushrooms, halved
2 yellow bell peppers, deseeded and cut into squares
2 lb tri-tip steak, cubed   3 limes, juiced
2 tbsp coconut oil   1 tbsp ginger powder
1 tbsp tamari sauce   ½ tsp ground cumin

Directions and Total Time: approx. 1 hour 25 minutes

In a bowl, mix coconut oil, tamari sauce, lime juice, ginger, salt, pepper, and cumin powder. Add the beef, mushrooms, and bell peppers; toss to coat. Cover the bowl with a plastic wrap and marinate for 1 hour. Preheat the grill to high heat. Take off the plastic wrap and thread the mushrooms, beef, and bell peppers in this order on each skewer until the ingredients are exhausted. Grill the skewers for 5 minutes on each side. Remove to serving plates, garnish with sesame seeds, parsley, and serve warm with steamed cauliflower rice or braised asparagus.

Per serving: Cal 383; Net Carbs 3.2g; Fat 17g; Protein 51g

Beef & Shiitake Mushroom Stir-Fry

Ingredients for 4 servings

2 cups shiitake mushrooms, halved
2 sprigs rosemary, leaves extracted
1 green bell pepper, chopped   1 tbsp coconut oil
1 lb chuck steak   1 tbsp freshly pureed garlic
4 slices prosciutto, chopped

Directions and Total Time: approx. 30 minutes

Using a sharp knife, slice the chuck steak thinly against the grain and cut into smaller pieces. Season with salt and black pepper. Heat a skillet over medium heat; and fry prosciutto until brown and crispy; set aside. Melt coconut oil in the skillet and cook the beef until brown, 12 minutes. Remove to the prosciutto plate. Add mushrooms and bell pepper and sauté until softened, 5 minutes. Stir in prosciutto, beef, rosemary, and garlic. Season to taste and cook for 4 minutes. Serve with buttered green beans.

Per serving: Cal 231; Net Carbs 2.1g; Fat 12g; Protein 27g

Hot Beef & Cauli Rice with Cashew Nuts

Ingredients for 4 servings

3 tbsp olive oil   ½ cup green beans, chopped
1 ½ lb chuck steak   3 garlic cloves, minced
2 large eggs, beaten   4 cups cauliflower rice
1 tbsp avocado oil   ¼ cup coconut aminos
1 red onion, finely chopped 1 cup toasted cashew nuts
½ cup chopped bell peppers 1 tbsp toasted sesame seeds

Directions and Total Time: approx. 25 minutes

Heat 2 tbsp olive oil in a wok over medium heat; season the beef with salt and pepper, and cook in the oil on both sides until tender; set aside. Pour in the eggs and scramble for 1 minute; set aside. Add the remaining olive oil and avocado oil to heat. Stir in onion, bell peppers, green beans, and garlic. Sauté until soft, 3 minutes. Pour in cauli rice, coconut aminos, and stir until evenly combined. Mix in the beef, eggs, and cashew nuts and cook for 3 minutes. Turn the heat off; dish into 4 serving plates and garnish with sesame seeds. Serve warm with hot sauce.

Per serving: Cal 500; Net Carbs 3.2g; Fat 32; Protein 44g

Coconut Beef with Mushroom & Olive Sauce

Ingredients for 4 servings

¼ cup button mushrooms, sliced
3 tbsp unsalted butter   2 tbsp coconut cream
1 yellow onion, chopped   1/2 tsp dried thyme
4 rib-eye steaks   2 tbsp chopped parsley
1/3 cup coconut milk   3 tbsp black olives, sliced

Directions and Total Time: approx. 30 minutes

Melt 2 tbsp butter in a large, deep skillet over medium heat; add and sauté the mushrooms, 4 minutes. Stir in onion and cook further for 3 minutes; set aside.

Season the beef with salt and pepper. Melt the remaining butter in the skillet and cook the beef on both sides for 10 minutes. Pour mushrooms and onion back to the skillet and add milk, coconut cream, thyme and 1 tbsp of parsley. Stir and simmer for 2 minutes. Mix in olives and turn the heat off. Serve garnished with the remaining parsley.

Per serving: Cal 639; Net Carbs 1.9g; Fat 39g; Protein 69g

Maple BBQ Rib Steak

Ingredients for 4 servings

2 lb rib steak, membrane removed
2 tbsp avocado oil   3 tbsp barbecue dry rub
3 tbsp maple syrup, sugar-free

Directions and Total Time: approx. 2 hours 40 minutes

Preheat the oven to 300 F and line a baking sheet with aluminum foil. In a bowl, mix avocado oil, maple syrup and brush the mixture onto meat. Sprinkle and pat BBQ rub all over the meat. Put the ribs in the baking sheet and bake until the meat is tender and crispy on the top, 2 ½ hours. Serve with buttered broccoli and green beans.

Per serving: Cal 490; Net Carbs 1.8g; Fat 26g; Protein 49g

Keto Burgers

Ingredients for 4 servings

1 pound ground beef   4 zero carb burger buns
½ tsp onion powder   ¼ cup mayonnaise
½ tsp garlic powder   1 tsp Sriracha sauce
2 tbsp ghee   4 tbsp slaw
1 tsp Dijon mustard   Salt and black pepper to taste

Directions and Total Time: approx. 15 minutes

Mix together beef, onion powder, garlic powder, mustard, salt, and pepper. Create 4 burgers. Melt ghee in a skillet and cook the burgers for 3 minutes per side. Serve on a bun topped with mayonnaise, sriracha sauce, and slaw.

Per serving: Cal 664; Net Carbs 7.9g; Fat 55g; Protein 39g

Beef Steak Fajitas

Ingredients for 4 servings

2 lb flank steak, cut in halves 2 large white onion, chopped
2 tbsp Adobo seasoning   1 cup sliced bell peppers
2 tbsp olive oil   12 zero carb tortillas

Directions and Total Time: approx. 10 minutes

Season steak with adobo and marinate in the fridge for 1 hour. Preheat grill and cook steak for 6 minutes on each side, flipping once. Remove from heat and wrap in foil and let sit for 10 minutes. Heat olive oil in a skillet and sauté onion and bell peppers for 5 minutes. Cut steak against the grain into strips and share on the tortillas. Top with vegetables and serve.

Per serving: Cal 348, Net Carbs 5g, Fat 25g, Protein 18g

Garlicky Beef with Creamy Curry Sauce

Ingredients for 4 servings

2 tbsp ghee	2 long red chilies, sliced
4 large rib-eye steak	1 cup beef stock
2 garlic cloves, minced	1 cup coconut milk
½ cup chopped brown onion	1 tbsp Thai green curry paste
1 green bell pepper, sliced	1 lime, juiced
1 red bell pepper, sliced	3 tbsp chopped cilantro

Directions and Total Time: approx. 40 minutes

Melt the 1 tbsp of ghee in a pan over medium heat, season beef with salt and pepper, and cook for 3 minutes on each side. Remove to a plate. Add the remaining ghee to the skillet and sauté garlic and onion for 3 minutes. Stir-fry in bell peppers and red chili until softened, 5 minutes. Pour in beef stock, coconut milk, curry paste, and lime juice. Let simmer for 4 minutes. Put the beef back into the sauce, cook for 10 minutes, and transfer the pan to the oven. Cook further under the broiler for 5 minutes. Garnish with cilantro and serve with cauliflower rice.

Per serving: Cal 644; Net Carbs 2.6g; Fat 35g; Protein 72g

Walnut Beef Skillet with Brussel Sprouts

Ingredients for 4 servings

¼ cup toasted walnuts, chopped
1 ½ cups Brussel sprouts, halved

2 tbsp avocado oil	1 lb ground beef
1 garlic clove, minced	1 bok choy, quartered
½ white onion, chopped	2 tbsp chopped scallions
Salt and black pepper to taste	1 tbsp black sesame seeds

Directions and Total Time: approx. 30 minutes

Heat 1 tbsp of avocado oil in a skillet; add and sauté garlic and onion for 3 minutes. Stir in ground beef and cook until brown while breaking the lumps, 7 minutes. Pour in Brussel sprouts, bok choy, walnuts, scallions, and season with salt and black pepper. Sauté for 5 minutes. Dish into 4 serving plates and serve with low carb bread.

Per serving: Cal 302; Net Carbs 3.1g; Fat 18g; Protein 29g

Easy Pressure-Cooked Shredded Beef

Ingredients for 4 servings

3 tbsp coconut oil	1 tsp dried Italian herb blend
1 large white onion, chopped	1 ½ tbsp balsamic vinegar
3 garlic cloves, minced	½ cup beef broth
1 cup shredded red cabbage	2 lb chuck steak
1 lemon, zested and juiced	Salt and black pepper to taste

Directions and Total Time: approx. 45 minutes

Select Sauté mode on your pressure cooker. Heat coconut oil and sauté onion, garlic, and cabbage for 3 minutes. Stir in lemon zest, lemon juice, Italian herb blend, balsamic vinegar, salt, and pepper, for 2 minutes; mix in the broth. Season the meat with salt and pepper. Place in the cooker.

Close the lid, secure the pressure valve, and select Manual mode on High for 25 minutes. Once the timer is done, perform a natural pressure release, then a quick pressure release to let out any remaining steam, and open the lid. Using two forks, shred the meat. Select Sauté to reduce the sauce, 5 minutes, and then spoon the pulled beef with sauce over on a bed of zucchini noodles. Serve.

Per serving: Cal 652; Net Carbs 5.8g; Fat 49g; Protein 44g

Easy Beef Burger Bake

Ingredients for 4 servings

¼ cup shredded Monterey Jack cheese

1 tbsp butter	1 tbsp dried basil
1 lb ground beef	Salt and black pepper to taste
1 garlic clove, minced	2 eggs
1 medium red onion, chopped	2 tbsp tomato paste
2 tomatoes	1 cup coconut cream

Directions and Total Time: approx. 35 minutes

Preheat oven to 400 F. Melt the butter in a large skillet and add the beef. Cook for 10 minutes. Stir in garlic and onion and cook for another 3 minutes. Mix in tomatoes, basil, salt, and pepper until the tomatoes soften. Add 2/3 of Monterey Jack cheese and stir to melt. In a bowl, crack the eggs and whisk with tomato paste, salt, and coconut cream. Spoon the beef mixture into a greased baking sheet and spread the egg mixture on top. Sprinkle with the remaining cheese and bake for 20 minutes. Serve.

Per serving: Cal 469; Net Carbs 4.5g; Fat 34g; Protein 33g

Awesome Zucchini Boats Stuffed with Beef

Ingredients for 4 servings4

2 zucchinis	1 shallot, finely chopped
2 tbsp butter	2 tbsp taco seasoning
1 lb ground beef	½ cup finely chopped parsley
1 red bell pepper, chopped	1 tbsp olive oil
2 garlic cloves, minced	1¼ cups shredded cheddar

Directions and Total Time: approx. 50 minutes

Preheat oven to 400 F and grease a baking sheet with cooking spray. Using a knife, cut zucchinis into halves and scoop out the pulp using to form 4 vegetable boats. Set aside and chop the flesh. Melt the butter in a skillet over medium heat and cook the beef until brown, frequently stirring and breaking the lumps, 10 minutes. Stir in bell pepper, pulp, garlic, shallot, taco seasoning, and cook until softened, 5 minutes. Turn the heat off. Place the boats on the baking sheet with the open side up. Spoon in the beef mixture, divide the parsley on top, drizzle with olive oil, and top with cheddar cheese. Bake for 20 minutes until the cheese melts and is golden brown on top. Plate the boats, and serve warm with tangy lettuce salad.

Per serving: Cal 423; Net Carbs 2.9g; Fat 29g; Protein 35g

Sage Beef Meatloaf with Pecans

Ingredients for 4 servings

2 tbsp olive oil	1 egg, lightly beaten
1 white onion, finely chopped	1 tbsp dried sage
1 ½ lb ground beef	4 tbsp toasted pecans, chopped
½ cup coconut cream	Salt and black pepper to taste
½ cup shredded Parmesan	6 bacon slices

Directions and Total Time: approx. 45 minutes

Preheat oven to 400 F. Heat olive oil in a skillet and sauté the onion for 3 minutes. In a bowl, mix ground beef, onion, coconut cream, Parmesan cheese, eggs, sage, pecans, salt, and pepper. Form into a loaf, wrap it with bacon slices, secure with toothpicks, and place on a greased baking sheet. Bake for 30 minutes. Serve sliced.

Per serving: Cal 617; Net Carbs 6.6g; Fat 43g; Protein 48g

Tangy Cabbage & Beef Bowl with Creamy Blue Cheese

Ingredients for 4 servings

3 tbsp butter	1 tbsp red wine vinegar
1 canon cabbage, shredded	1 ½ lb ground beef
1 tsp onion powder	1 cup coconut cream
1 tsp garlic powder	¼ cup blue cheese
2 tsp dried oregano	½ cup fresh parsley, chopped

Directions and Total Time: approx. 25 minutes

Melt 1 tbsp of butter in a deep skillet, and sauté cabbage, onion and garlic powders, oregano, salt, pepper, and vinegar, for 5 minutes; set aside. Melt the 2 tbsp butter in the skillet and cook the beef until browned, frequently stirring and breaking the lumps, 10 minutes. Stir in coconut cream and blue cheese until the cheese melts, 3 minutes. Return the cabbage mixture, and add parsley. Stir-fry for 2 minutes. Dish into serving bowls with low carb bread.

Per serving: Cal 542; Net Carbs 4.2g; Fat 41g; Protein 41g

Cheesy Tomato Beef Tart

Ingredients for 4 servings

2 tbsp olive oil	¾ cup almond flour
1 small brown onion, chopped	4 tbsp flaxseeds
1 garlic clove, finely chopped	1 tsp baking powder
2 lb ground beef	3 tbsp coconut oil, melted
1 tbsp Italian mixed herbs	1 egg
4 tbsp tomato paste	¼ cup ricotta, crumbled
4 tbsp coconut flour	¼ cup shredded cheddar

Directions and Total Time: approx. 1 hour 30 minutes

Preheat oven to 350 F. Line a pie dish with parchment paper and grease with cooking spray; set aside. Heat olive oil in a large skillet over medium heat; and sauté onion and garlic until softened. Add in beef and cook until brown. Season with herbs, salt, and pepper. Stir in tomato paste and ½ cup water, reduce the heat to low.

Simmer for 20 minutes; set aside. In a food processor, add the flours, flaxseeds, baking powder, a pinch of salt, coconut oil, egg, and 4 tbsp water. Mix starting on low speed to medium until evenly combined and dough is formed. Spread the dough in the pie pan and bake for 12 minutes. Remove and spread the meat filling on top. In a small bowl, mix ricotta and cheddar cheeses, and scatter on top. Bake until the cheeses melt and are golden brown on top, 35 minutes. Remove the pie, let cool for 3 minutes, slice, and serve with green salad and garlic vinaigrette.

Per serving: Cal 603; Net Carbs 2.3g; Fat 39g; Protein 57g

Olive & Pesto Beef Casserole with Goat Cheese

Ingredients for 4 servings

2 tbsp ghee	5 oz goat cheese, crumbled
1 ½ lb ground beef	1 garlic clove, minced
Salt and black pepper to taste	3 oz basil pesto
3 oz pitted green olives	1¼ cups coconut cream

Directions and Total Time: approx. 45 minutes

Preheat oven to 400 F and grease a casserole dish with cooking spray. Melt ghee in a deep, medium skillet, and cook the beef until brown; season to taste. Stir frequently. Spoon and spread the beef at the bottom of the casserole dish. Top with olives, goat cheese, and garlic. In a bowl, mix pesto and coconut cream and pour the mixture all over the beef. Bake until lightly brown around the edges and bubbly, 25 minutes. Serve with a leafy green salad.

Per serving: Cal 656; Net Carbs 4g; Fat 51g; Protein 47g

Maple Jalapeño Beef Plate

Ingredients for 4 servings

1 lb ribeye steak, sliced into ¼-inch strips	
2 tsp sugar-free maple syrup	4 tbsp tamari sauce
Salt and black pepper to taste	1 tsp sesame oil
1 tbsp coconut flour	1 tsp fish sauce
1/2 tsp xanthan gum	2 tbsp white wine vinegar
½ cup olive oil, for frying	1 tsp hot sauce
1 tbsp coconut oil	1 small bok choy, quartered
1 tsp freshly pureed ginger	½ jalapeño, sliced into rings
1 clove garlic, minced	1 tbsp toasted sesame seeds
1 red chili, minced	1 scallion, chopped

Directions and Total Time: approx. 40 minutes

Season the beef with salt and pepper, and rub with coconut flour and xanthan gum; set aside. Heat olive oil in a skillet and fry the beef until brown on all sides. Heat coconut oil in a wok and sauté ginger, garlic, red chili, and bok choy for 5 minutes. Mix in tamari sauce, sesame oil, fish sauce, vinegar, hot sauce, and maple syrup; cook for 2 minutes. Add the beef and cook for 2 minutes. Spoon into bowls, top with jalapeños, scallion and sesame seeds. Serve.

Per serving: Cal 507; Net Carbs 2.9g; Fat 43g; Protein 25g

Cheese & Beef Avocado Boats

Ingredients for 4 servings

4 tbsp avocado oil	1 cup raw pecans, chopped
1 lb ground beef	1 tbsp hemp seeds, hulled
Salt and black pepper to taste	7 tbsp shredded Monterey Jack
1 tsp onion powder	2 avocados, halved and pitted
1 tsp cumin powder	1 medium tomato, sliced
1 tsp garlic powder	¼ cup shredded iceberg lettuce
2 tsp taco seasoning	4 tbsp sour cream
2 tsp smoked paprika	4 tbsp shredded Monterey Jack

Directions and Total Time: approx. 30 minutes

Heat half of avocado oil in a skillet and cook beef for 10 minutes. Season with salt, pepper, onion powder, cumin, garlic, taco seasoning, and paprika. Add the pecans and hemp seeds; stir-fry for 10 minutes. Fold in 3 tbsp Monterey Jack cheese to melt. Spoon the filling into avocado holes, top with 1-2 slices of tomatoes, some lettuce, a tbsp each of sour cream, and the remaining Monterey Jack cheese, and serve immediately.

Per serving: Cal 840; Net Carbs 4g; Fat 70g; Protein 42g

Morning Beef Bowl

Ingredients for 4 servings

1 lb beef sirloin, cut into strips	
¼ cup tamari sauce	6 garlic cloves, minced
2 tbsp lemon juice	1 lb cauliflower rice
3 tsp garlic powder	2 tbsp olive oil
1 tbsp swerve sugar	4 large eggs
1 cup coconut oil	2 tbsp chopped scallions

Directions and Total Time: approx. 35 min + chilling time

In a bowl, mix tamari sauce, lemon juice, garlic powder, and swerve. Pour beef into a zipper bag and add in seasoning. Massage the meat to coat well. Refrigerate overnight. The next day, heat coconut oil in a wok, and fry the beef until the liquid evaporates and the meat cooks through, 12 minutes; set aside. Sauté garlic for 2 minutes. Mix in cauli rice until softened, 5 minutes. Season with salt and pepper; spoon into 4 serving bowls and set aside. Wipe the pan clean and heat 1 tbsp of olive oil. Crack in two eggs and fry sunshine-style, 1 minute. Place an egg on each cauliflower rice bowl and fry the other 2 eggs with the remaining olive oil. Serve garnished with scallions.

Per serving: Cal 908; Net Carbs 5.1g; Fat 83g; Protein 34g

Rosemary Beef Meatza

Ingredients for 4 servings

1 ½ lb ground beef	1 tsp basil
Salt and black pepper to taste	½ tbsp oregano
1 large egg	¾ cup low-carb tomato sauce
1 tsp rosemary	¼ cup shredded Parmesan
1 tsp thyme	1 cup shredded Pepper Jack
3 garlic cloves, minced	1 cup shredded mozzarella

Directions and Total Time: approx. 30 minutes

Preheat oven to 350 F and grease a pizza pan with cooking spray. In a bowl, combine beef, salt, pepper, egg, rosemary, thyme, garlic, basil, and oregano. Transfer the mixture into pan and using hands, flatten to a two-inch thickness. Bake for 15 minutes until the beef has a lightly brown crust. Remove and spread tomato sauce on top. Sprinkle with Parmesan, Pepper Jack, and mozzarella cheeses. Return to oven to bake until the cheeses melt, 5 minutes.

Per serving: Cal 319; Net Carbs 3.6g; Fat 10g; Protein 49g

Homemade Philly Cheesesteak in Omelet

Ingredients for 2 servings

4 large eggs	½ green bell pepper, sliced
2 tbsp almond milk	¼ lb beef ribeye shaved steak
2 tbsp olive oil	Salt and black pepper to taste
1 yellow onion, sliced	2 oz provolone cheese, sliced

Directions and Total Time: approx. 35 minutes

In a bowl, beat the eggs with milk. Heat half of the oil in a skillet and pour in half of the eggs. Fry until cooked on one side, flip, and cook until well done. Slide into a plate and fry the remaining eggs. Place them into another plate. Heat the remaining olive oil in the same skillet and sauté the onion and bell pepper for 5 minutes; set aside. Season beef with salt and pepper, and cook in the skillet until brown with no crust. Add onion and pepper back to the pan and cook for 1 minute. Lay provolone cheese in the omelet and top with the hot meat mixture. Roll the eggs and place back to the skillet to melt the cheese. Serve.

Per serving: Cal 497; Net Carbs 3.6g; Fat 36g; Protein 34g

Celery & Beef Stuffed Mushrooms

Ingredients for 4 servings

½ cup shredded Pecorino Romano cheese	
2 tbsp olive oil	½ tsp garlic powder
½ celery stalk, chopped	2 large eggs
1 shallot, finely chopped	4 caps Portobello mushrooms
1 lb ground beef	1 tbsp flaxseed meal
2 tbsp mayonnaise	2 tbsp shredded Parmesan
1 tsp Old Bay seasoning	1 tbsp chopped parsley

Directions and Total Time: approx. 55 minutes

Preheat oven to 350 F. Heat olive oil in a skillet and sauté celery and shallot for 3 minutes. Transfer to a bowl. Add beef to the skillet and cook for 10 minutes; transfer to the bowl. Pour in mayo, Old Bay seasoning, garlic powder, Pecorino cheese, and crack in the eggs. Combine the mixture evenly. Arrange the mushrooms on a greased baking sheet and fill with the meat mixture. Combine flaxseed meal and Parmesan in a bowl, and sprinkle over the mushroom filling. Bake until the cheese melts, 30 minutes. Garnish with parsley to serve.

Per serving: Cal 375; Net Carbs 3.5g; Fat 22g; Protein 37g

Korean Braised Beef with Kelp Noodles

Ingredients for 4 servings

1 ½ lb sirloin steak, cut into strips
2 (16- oz) packs kelp noodles, thoroughly rinsed
1 tbsp coconut oil
2 pieces star anise
1 cinnamon stick
1 garlic clove, minced
1-inch ginger, grated
3 tbsp coconut aminos
2 tbsp swerve brown sugar
¼ cup red wine
4 cups beef broth
1 head napa cabbage, steamed
Scallions, thinly sliced

Directions and Total Time: approx. 2 hours 15 minutes

Heat oil in a pot over and sauté anise, cinnamon, garlic, and ginger until fragrant, 5 minutes. Add in beef, season with salt and pepper, and sear on both sides, 10 minutes. In a bowl, combine aminos, sugar, wine, and ¼ cup water. Pour the mixture into the pot, close the lid, and bring to a boil. Reduce the heat and simmer for 1 to 1 ½ hours or until the meat is tender. Strain the pot's content through a colander into a bowl and pour the braising liquid back into the pot. Discard cinnamon and anise and set aside. Add broth and simmer until hot, 10 minutes. Put kelp noodles in the broth and cook until softened and separated, 6 minutes. Spoon the noodles and some broth into bowls, add beef strips, and top with cabbage and scallions.

Per serving: Cal 548; Net Carbs 26.6g; Fat 27g; Protein 44g

Homemade Pasta with Meatballs

Ingredients for 4 servings

1 cup shredded mozzarella
1 egg yolk
½ cup olive oil
2 yellow onions, chopped
6 garlic cloves, minced
2 tbsp tomato paste
2 large tomatoes, chopped
¼ tsp saffron powder
2 cinnamon sticks
4 ½ cups chicken broth
Salt and black pepper to taste
2 cups pork rinds
1 lb ground beef
1 egg
¼ cup almond milk
¼ tsp nutmeg powder
1 tbsp smoked paprika
1 ½ tsp fresh ginger paste
1 tsp cumin powder
½ tsp cayenne pepper
½ tsp cloves powder
4 tbsp chopped cilantro
4 tbsp chopped scallions
4 tbsp chopped parsley
¼ cup almond flour
1 cup crumbled feta cheese

Directions and Total Time: approx. 1 hour + chilling time

Microwave mozzarella cheese for 2 minutes. Mix in egg yolk until combined. Lay parchment paper on a flat surface, pour the cheese mixture on top and cover with another piece of parchment paper. Flatten the dough into 1/8-inch thickness. Take off the parchment paper and cut the dough into spaghetti strands; refrigerate overnight. When ready, bring 2 cups of water to a boil in a saucepan and add the pasta. Cook for 1 minute, drain, and let cool. In a pot, heat 3 tbsp of olive oil and sauté onions and half of the garlic for 3 minutes. Stir in tomato paste, tomatoes, saffron, and cinnamon sticks; cook for 2 minutes. Mix in chicken broth, salt, and pepper. Simmer for 25 minutes.

In a bowl, mix pork rinds, beef, egg, almond milk, remaining garlic, salt, pepper, nutmeg, paprika, ginger, cumin, cayenne, cloves powder, cilantro, parsley, 3 tbsp of scallions, and almond flour. Form balls out of the mixture. Heat the remaining olive oil in a skillet and fry the meatballs for 10 minutes. Place them into the sauce and continue cooking for 5-10 minutes. Divide the pasta onto serving plates and spoon the meatballs with sauce on top. Garnish with feta cheese and scallions and serve.

Per serving: Cal 783; Net Carbs 6.3g; Fats 56g; Protein 55g

Mustard Beef Collard Rolls

Ingredients for 4 servings

2 lb corned beef
1 tbsp butter
Salt and black pepper to taste
2 tsp Worcestershire sauce
1 tsp Dijon mustard
1 tsp whole peppercorns
¼ tsp cloves
¼ tsp allspice
½ tsp red pepper flakes
1 large bay leaf
1 lemon, zested and juiced
¼ cup white wine
¼ cup freshly brewed coffee
2/3 tbsp swerve sugar
8 large Swiss collard leaves
1 medium red onion, sliced

Directions and Total Time: approx. 70 minutes

In a pot, add beef, butter, salt, pepper, Worcestershire sauce, mustard, peppercorns, cloves, allspice, flakes, bay leaf, lemon zest, lemon juice, wine, coffee, and swerve. Close the lid and cook over low heat for 1 hour. Ten minutes before the end, bring a pot of water to a boil, add collards with one slice of onion for 30 seconds and transfer to ice bath to blanch for 2-3 minutes. Remove, pat dry, and lay on a flat surface. Remove the meat from the pot, place on a cutting board, and slice. Divide meat onto the collards, top with onion slices, and roll the leaves. Serve with tomato gravy and pickled cabbages.

Per serving: Cal 349; Net Carbs 1.5g; Fat 16g; Protein 47g

Parsley Steak Bites with Shirataki Fettucine

Ingredients for 4 servings

2 (8 oz) packs shirataki fettuccine
1 lb thick-cut New York strip steaks, cut into 1-inch cubes
1 cup freshly grated Pecorino Romano cheese
4 tbsp butter   4 garlic cloves, minced
Salt and black pepper to taste   2 tbsp chopped fresh parsley

Directions and Total Time: approx. 30 minutes

Boil 2 cups of water in a pot. Strain the shirataki pasta and rinse well under hot running water. Allow proper draining and pour into the boiling water. Cook for 3 minutes and strain again. Place a dry skillet and stir-fry the shirataki pasta until visibly dry, 1-2 minutes; set aside. Melt butter in a skillet, season the steaks with salt and pepper, and cook for 10 minutes. Stir in garlic and cook for 1 minute. Mix in parsley and shirataki; toss and season with salt and pepper. Top with the Pecorino Romano cheese and serve.

Per serving: Cal 422; Net Carbs 7.3g; Fats 22g; Protein 36g

Cheddar Zucchini & Beef Mugs

Ingredients for 2 servings

4 oz roast beef deli slices, torn apart
3 tbsp sour cream | 2 tbsp chopped green chilies
1 small zucchini, chopped | 3 oz shredded cheddar cheese

Directions and Total Time: approx. 10 minutes

Divide the beef slices at the bottom of 2 wide mugs and spread 1 tbsp of sour cream. Top with 2 zucchini slices, season with salt and pepper, add green chilies, top with the remaining sour cream and then cheddar cheese. Place the mugs in the microwave for 1-2 minutes until the cheese melts. Remove the mugs, let cool for 1 minute, and serve.

Per serving: Cal 188; Net Carbs 3.7g; Fat 9g; Protein 18g

Balsamic Meatloaf

Ingredients for 8 servings

3 pounds ground beef | 3 eggs
½ cup chopped onion | 2 tbsp chopped parsley
½ cup almond flour | ¼ cup chopped bell peppers
2 garlic cloves, minced | ⅓ cup grated Parmesan
1 cup sliced mushrooms | 1 tsp balsamic vinegar

Glaze:

2 cups balsamic vinegar | 2 tbsp sugar-free ketchup
1 tbsp sweetener

Directions and Total Time: approx. 1 hour 15 minutes

Combine all meatloaf ingredients in a large bowl. Press this mixture into 2 greased loaf pans. Bake at 370 F for about 30 minutes. Combining all glaze ingredients in a saucepan over medium heat. Simmer for 20 minutes, until the glaze is thickened. Pour ¼ cup of the glaze over the meatloaf. Save the extra for future use. Put the meatloaf back in the oven and cook for 20 more minutes.

Per serving: Cal 264; Net Carbs 6g; Fat 19g; Protein 23g

Sautéed Thai Beef Shirataki

Ingredients for 4 servings

2 (8 oz) packs angel hair shirataki
1 cup sliced shiitake mushrooms
2 tbsp olive oil, divided | 2 tbsp toasted sesame seeds
1 ¼ lb flank steak, sliced | 1 tbsp chopped peanuts
1 white onion, thinly sliced | 1 tbsp chopped scallions
1 red bell pepper, sliced | 3 tbsp coconut aminos
4 garlic cloves, minced | 2 tbsp fish sauce
1 ½ cups Thai basil leaves | 1 tbsp hot sauce

Directions and Total Time: approx. 35 minutes

Boil 2 cups of water. Strain the shirataki pasta and rinse very well under hot running water. Allow proper draining and pour the shirataki pasta into the boiling water. Cook for 3 minutes and strain again. Place a dry skillet and stir-fry the shirataki pasta until visibly dry, 1-2 minutes; set aside.

Heat olive oil in a skillet, season the meat with salt and pepper and sear on both sides until brown, 5 minutes; set aside. Add onion, bell pepper, garlic, and mushrooms to the skillet; cook for 5 minutes. Return the beef to the skillet and add the pasta. Combine aminos, fish sauce, and hot sauce in a bowl. Pour the mixture over the beef. Top with Thai basil and toss to coat. Cook for 1-2 minutes. Serve garnished with sesame seeds, peanuts, and scallions.

Per serving: Cal 358; Net Carbs 7.5g; Fats 16g; Protein 30g

Bacon-Wrapped Beef Hot Dogs

Ingredients for 4 servings

8 large beef hot dogs | 1 tsp onion powder
½ cup grated Gruyere cheese | 1 tsp garlic powder
16 slices bacon | Salt and black pepper to taste

Directions and Total Time: approx. 45 minutes

Preheat oven to 400 F. Cut a slit in the middle of each hot dog and stuff evenly with the cheese. Wrap each hot dog with 2 bacon slices each and secure with toothpicks. Season with onion and garlic powders, salt, and pepper. Place the hot dogs in the middle rack of the oven and slide in the cookie sheet beneath the rack to catch dripping grease. Grill for 40 minutes until the bacon browns and crisps. Serve with creamy spinach puree.

Per serving: Cal 958; Net Carbs 4.1g; Fat 86g; Protein 37g

Parsley Beef Carbonara

Ingredients for 4 servings

1 cup shredded mozzarella | ¼ cup mayonnaise
1 ¼ cups grated Parmesan | 4 egg yolks
4 bacon slices, chopped | 2 tbsp parsley, chopped
1 ¼ cups heavy cream | Salt and black pepper to taste

Directions and Total Time: approx. 30 minutes

Microwave mozzarella cheese for 2 minutes. Remove and let cool for 1 minute. Mix in 1 egg yolk until combined. Lay a parchment paper on a flat surface, pour the cheese mixture on top and cover with another parchment paper. Flatten the dough into 1/8-inch thickness. Take off the parchment paper and cut the dough into thin spaghetti strands. Place in a bowl and refrigerate overnight. When ready, bring 2 cups water to a boil in saucepan and add pasta. Cook for 1 minute and drain; divide between serving bowls. Add bacon to a skillet and cook until crispy, 5 minutes; set aside. Pour heavy cream into a pot and let simmer for 5 minutes. Whisk in mayo and season with salt and pepper. Cook for 1 minute. Spoon 2 tbsp of the mixture into a bowl and mix in remaining egg yolks. Pour the mixture in the pot and mix. Stir in 1 cup of Parmesan cheese and fold in the pasta. Spoon into pasta bowls and top with Parmesan cheese and parsley to serve.

Per serving: Cal 470; Net Carbs 8.9g; Fats 35g; Protein 25g

Salisbury Steak

Ingredients for 6 servings

2 pounds ground beef | ¼ cup beef broth
1 tbsp onion flakes | 1 tbsp chopped parsley
¾ almond flour | 1 tbsp Worcestershire sauce

Directions and Total Time: approx. 25 minutes

Combine all ingredients in a bowl. Mix well and make 6 patties out of the mixture. Arrange on a lined baking sheet. Bake at 375 F for about 18 minutes. Serve.

Per serving: Cal 354; Net Carbs 2.5g; Fat 28g; Protein 27g

Beef Alfredo Squash Spaghetti

Ingredients for 4 servings

2 medium spaghetti squashes, halved
2 tbsp olive oil | 1 tsp arrowroot starch
2 tbsp butter | 1 ½ cups heavy cream
1 lb ground beef | A pinch of nutmeg
½ tsp garlic powder | 1/3 cup grated Parmesan
Salt and black pepper to taste | 1/3 cup grated mozzarella

Directions and Total Time: approx. 1 hour 20 minutes

Preheat oven to 375 F. Season the squash with olive oil, salt, and pepper. Place on a lined with foil baking dish and roast for 45 minutes. Let cool and shred the inner part of the noodles; set aside. Melt butter in a pot, add in beef, garlic powder, salt, and pepper, and cook for 10 minutes. Stir in arrowroot starch, heavy cream, and nutmeg.

Cook until the sauce thickens, 2-3 minutes. Spoon the sauce into the squashes and cover with Parmesan and mozzarella cheeses. Cook under the broiler for 3 minutes.

Per serving: Cal 563; Net Carbs 4g; Fats 42g; Protein 36g

Cheesy Beef-Asparagus Shirataki Mix

Ingredients for 4 servings

2 (8 oz) packs angel hair shirataki
1 lb fresh asparagus, cut into 1-inch pieces
1 lb ground beef | 3 garlic cloves, minced
3 tbsp olive oil | Salt and black pepper to taste
2 shallots, finely chopped | 1 cup grated Parmesan cheese

Directions and Total Time: approx. 40 minutes

Bring 2 cups of water to a boil. Strain the shirataki pasta and rinse well under hot running water. Drain and transfer to the boiling water. Cook for 3 minutes and strain again. Place a dry skillet and stir-fry the shirataki pasta until visibly dry, 1 to 2 minutes; set aside. Heat olive oil in a skillet and add the beef. Cook for 10 minutes. Transfer to a plate. In the same skillet sauté for 7 minutes. Stir in shallots and garlic and cook until fragrant, 2 minutes. Season with salt and pepper. Stir in beef and shirataki and toss until combined. Top with Parmesan cheese and serve.

Per serving: Cal 513; Net Carbs 7.2g; Fat 25g; Protein 44g

Classic Beef Ragu with Veggie Pasta

Ingredients for 4 servings

8 mixed bell peppers, spiralized
2 tbsp butter | ¼ cup tomato sauce
1 lb ground beef | 1 small red onion, spiralized
Salt and black pepper to taste | 1 cup grated Parmesan cheese

Directions and Total Time: approx. 20 minutes

Heat the butter in a skillet and cook the beef until brown, 5 minutes. Season with salt and pepper. Stir in tomato sauce and cook for 10 minutes, until the sauce reduces by a quarter. Stir in bell peppers and onion noodles; cook for 1 minute. Top with Parmesan cheese and serve.

Per serving: Cal 451; Net Carbs 7.2g; Fats 25g; Protein 40g

Barbecued Beef Pizza

Ingredients for 4 servings

1 cup grated mozzarella cheese
1 ½ cups grated Gruyere cheese
1 lb ground beef | ¼ cup sliced red onion
2 eggs, beaten | 2 bacon slices, chopped
¼ cup sugar-free BBQ sauce | 2 tbsp chopped parsley

Directions and Total Time: approx. 40 minutes

Preheat oven to 390 F and line a round pizza pan with parchment paper. Mix beef, mozzarella cheese and eggs, and salt. Spread the pizza "dough" on the pan and bake for 20 minutes. Spread BBQ sauce on top, scatter Gruyere cheese all over, followed by the red onion, and bacon slices. Bake for 15 minutes or until the cheese has melted and the back is crispy. Serve warm sprinkled with parsley.

Per serving: Cal 538; Net Carbs 0.4g; Fats 32g; Protein 56g

Beef with Parsnip Noodles

Ingredients for 4 servings

1 lb beef stew meat, cut into strips
1 cup sun-dried tomatoes in oil, chopped
1 cup shaved Parmesan cheese
3 tbsp butter | 1 ¼ cups heavy cream
Salt and black pepper to taste | ¼ tsp dried basil
4 large parsnips, spiralized | ¼ tsp red chili flakes
4 garlic cloves, minced | 2 tbsp chopped parsley

Directions and Total Time: approx. 35 minutes

Melt butter in a skillet and sauté the parsnips until softened, 5-7 minutes. Set aside. Season the beef with salt and pepper and add to the same skillet; cook until brown, and cooked within, 8-10 minutes. Stir in sun-dried tomatoes and garlic and cook until fragrant, 1 minute. Reduce the heat to low and stir in heavy cream and Parmesan cheese. Simmer until the cheese melts. Season with basil and red chili flakes. Fold in the parsnips until well coated and cook for 2 more minutes. Garnish with parsley and serve.

Per serving: Cal 596; Net Carbs 6.5g; Fats 35g; Protein 37g

Assorted Grilled Veggies & Beef Steaks

Ingredients for 4 servings

1 red and 1 green bell peppers, cut into strips
4 tbsp olive oil   ½ lb asparagus, trimmed
1 ¼ pounds sirloin steaks   1 eggplant, sliced
Salt and black pepper to taste   2 zucchinis, sliced
3 tbsp balsamic vinegar   1 red onion, sliced

Directions and Total Time: approx. 30 minutes

Divide the meat and vegetables between 2 bowls. Mix salt, pepper, olive oil, and balsamic vinegar in a 2 bowl. Rub the beef all over with half of this mixture. Pour the remaining mixture over the vegetables. Preheat a grill pan. Drain the steaks and reserve the marinade. Sear the steaks on both sides for 10 minutes, flipping once halfway through; set aside. Pour the vegetables and marinade in the pan; and cook for 5 minutes, turning once. Serve.

Per serving: Cal 459; Net Carbs 4.5g; Fat 31g; Protein 32.8g

Classic Swedish Coconut Meatballs

Ingredients for 4 servings

1 ½ lb ground beef   2 tbsp almond flour
2 tsp garlic powder   1 cup beef broth
1 tsp onion powder   ½ cup coconut cream
Salt and black pepper to taste   ¼ freshly chopped dill
2 tbsp olive oil   ¼ cup chopped parsley
2 tbsp butter

Directions and Total Time: approx. 30 minutes

Preheat oven to 400 F. In a bowl, combine beef, garlic powder, onion powder, salt, and pepper. Form meatballs from the mixture and place on a greased baking sheet. Drizzle with olive oil and bake until the meat cooks, 10-15 minutes. Remove the baking sheet. Melt butter in a saucepan and stir in almond flour until smooth. Gradually mix in broth, while stirring until thickened, 2 minutes. Stir in coconut cream and dill, simmer for 1 minute and stir in meatballs. Spoon the meatballs with sauce onto a serving platter and garnish with parsley. Serve immediately.

Per serving: Cal 459; Net Carbs 3.2g; Fat 32g; Protein 40g

Herbed Bolognese Sauce

Ingredients for 5 servings

1 pound ground beef   1 tsp marjoram
2 garlic cloves   1 tsp rosemary
1 onion, chopped   7 oz canned chopped tomatoes
1 tsp oregano   1 tbsp olive oil

Directions and Total Time: approx. 35 minutes

Heat olive oil in a saucepan. Cook onions and garlic for 3 minutes. Add beef and cook until browned, about 5 minutes. Stir in herbs and tomatoes. Cook for 15 minutes.

Per serving: Cal 318; Net Carbs 9g; Fat 20g; Protein 26g

Cheese & Beef Bake

Ingredients for 6 servings

2 lb ground beef   2 cups chopped cabbage
Salt and black pepper to taste   14 oz can diced tomatoes
1 cup cauli rice   1 cup shredded Gouda cheese

Directions and Total Time: approx. 30 minutes

Preheat oven to 370 F. Put beef in a pot, season with salt and pepper, and cook for 6 minutes. Add cauli rice, cabbage, tomatoes, and ¼ cup water. Stir and bring to boil for 5 minutes to thicken the sauce. Spoon the beef mixture into a greased baking dish. Sprinkle with cheese and bake for 15 minutes. Cool for 4 minutes and serve.

Per serving: Cal 385, Net Carbs 5g, Fat 25g, Protein 20g

Beef Burgers with Roasted Brussels Sprouts

Ingredients for 4 servings

1 ½ lb Brussels sprouts, halved
1 pound ground beef   1 tsp dried thyme
1 egg   4 oz butter
½ onion, chopped   Salt and black pepper to taste

Directions and Total Time: approx. 30 minutes

Combine beef, egg, onion, thyme, salt, and pepper in a mixing bowl. Create patties out of the mixture. Set a pan over medium heat, warm half of the butter, and fry the patties until browned. Remove to a plate and cover with aluminium foil. Fry Brussels sprouts in the remaining butter, season to taste, then set into a bowl. Plate the burgers and Brussels sprouts and serve.

Per serving: Cal: 443, Net Carbs: 5g, Fat: 25g, Protein: 31g

Easy Rump Steak Salad

Ingredients for 4 servings

1 pound flank steak   1 cucumber, sliced
½ pound Brussels sprouts   1 cup green beans, sliced
3 green onions, sliced   9 oz mixed salad greens
Salad Dressing
2 tsp Dijon mustard   3 tbsp extra virgin olive oil
1 tsp xylitol   1 tbsp red wine vinegar

Directions and Total Time: approx. 40 minutes

Preheat a grill pan, season the meat with salt and pepper, and brown the steak for 5 minutes per side. Remove to a chopping board and slice thinly. Put Brussels sprouts on a baking sheet, drizzle with olive oil and bake for 25 minutes at 400 F; set aside. In a bowl, mix mustard, xylitol, salt, pepper, vinegar, and olive oil. Set aside. In a shallow salad bowl, add green onions, cucumber, green beans, cooled Brussels sprouts, salad greens, and steak slices. Serve.

Per serving: Cal 244; Net Carbs 3.3g; Fat 11g; Protein 27.4g

Garlicky Roast Rib of Beef

Ingredients for 6 servings

4 tbsp olive oil	A pinch of mustard powder
3 pounds beef ribs	3 tbsp xylitol
3 heads garlic, cut in half	Salt and black pepper to taste
3 onions, halved	3 tbsp fresh sage leaves
2 lemons, zested	¼ cup red wine

Directions and Total Time: approx. 55 minutes

Score shallow crisscrosses patterns on the meat. Mix xylitol, mustard powder, sage, salt, pepper, and lemon zest to make a rub; and apply it all over the beef with your hands, particularly into the cuts. Place garlic heads and onion halves in a baking dish, toss with olive oil, and bake for 15 minutes at 410 F. Place beef on top of the onion and garlic. Pour in ¼ cup water and red wine, cover the dish with foil and bake for 15 minutes. Remove the foil and bake for 10 minutes. Let cool and slice. Serve warm.

Per serving: Cal 749; Net Carbs 5.5g; Fat 65.6g; Protein 53g

Spicy Cheese & Kale Pinwheel

Ingredients for 4 servings

2 tbsp olive oil	1 cup kale
1 pound flank steak	1 habanero pepper, chopped
1 cup cotija cheese, crumbled	2 tbsp cilantro, chopped

Directions and Total Time: approx. 42 minutes

Cover the meat with plastic wrap on a flat surface and flatten with a mallet. Take off the wraps. Sprinkle with half of the cheese, top with kale, habanero pepper, cilantro, and the remaining cheese. Roll the steak over on the stuffing and secure with toothpicks. Place in a greased baking sheet and cook for 30 minutes at 400 F, flipping once. Cool for 3 minutes and slice into pinwheels to serve.

Per serving: Cal 349; Net Carbs 2.2g; Fat 22.5g; Protein 33g

Beef Stuffed Zucchini Boats

Ingredients for 4 servings

4 zucchinis	1 medium red onion, chopped
2 tbsp olive oil	2 tbsp chopped pimiento
1 ½ lb ground beef	1 cup Colby cheese, grated

Directions and Total Time: approx. 45 minutes

Preheat oven to 350 F. Lay the zucchinis on a flat surface, trim off the ends and cut in half lengthwise. Scoop out pulp from each half with a spoon to make shells. Chop the pulp. Heat oil in a skillet; add the ground beef, red onion, pimiento, and zucchini pulp, and season with salt and black pepper. Cook for 6 minutes. Spoon the beef into the boats and sprinkle with colby cheese. Place on a greased baking sheet and cook for 15 minutes. Serve warm.

Per serving: Cal 335, Net Carbs 7g, Fat 24g, Protein 18g

Pickled Peppers & Beef Salad with Feta

Ingredients for 4 servings

1 lb skirt steak, sliced	1 ½ cups mixed salad greens
Salt and black pepper to taste	3 chopped pickled peppers
1 taste olive oil	2 tbsp red wine vinaigrette
4 radishes, sliced	½ cup feta cheese, crumbled

Directions and Total Time: approx. 15 minutes

Brush steaks with olive oil and season with salt and pepper. Heat a pan and cook steaks for about 5-6 minutes. Remove to a bowl, cover and leave to rest while you make the salad. Mix the salad greens, radishes, pickled peppers, and vinaigrette in a salad bowl. Add the beef and sprinkle with cheese. Serve the salad with roasted parsnips.

Per serving: Cal 315, Net Carbs 2g, Fat 26g, Protein 18g

Beef Stir-Fry with Peanut Sauce

Ingredients for 4 servings

2 cups mixed vegetables	2 tsp ginger-garlic paste
1 ½ tbsp ghee	¼ cup chicken broth
2 lb beef loin, cut into strips	5 tbsp peanut butter
Salt and chili pepper to taste	

Directions and Total Time: approx. 30 minutes

Melt ghee in a wok. Season the beef with salt, chili pepper, and ginger-garlic paste. Pour the beef into the wok and cook for 6 minutes until no longer pink. In a small bowl, mix the peanut butter with some broth, add to the beef and stir; cook for 2 minutes. Pour in the remaining broth, cook for 4 minutes, and add the mixed veggies. Simmer for 5 minutes. Adjust the taste with salt and pepper and serve.

Per serving: Cal 571, Net Carbs 1g, Fat 49g, Protein 22.5g

Rosemary Creamy Beef

Ingredients for 4 servings

1 tbsp olive oil	½ cup half-and-half
3 tbsp butter	½ cup beef stock
2 tbsp rosemary, chopped	1 tbsp mustard
1 tbsp garlic powder	2 tsp lemon juice
4 beef steaks	A sprig of sage
1 red onion, chopped	A sprig of thyme

Directions and Total Time: approx. 25 minutes

Rub olive oil, garlic powder, and chopped rosemary all over the steaks slices and season with salt and pepper. Heat butter in a pan, place in beef steaks, and cook for 6 minutes, flipping once; set aside. In the same pan, add red onion and cook for 3 minutes; stir in beef stock, thyme sprig, half-and-half, mustard, and sage sprig, and cook for 8 minutes. Stir in lemon juice, pepper, and salt. Remove sage and thyme sprigs. Sprinkle with rosemary to serve.

Per serving: Cal 481; Net Carbs 7.8g; Fat 25g; Protein 51.7g

Steak Carnitas

Ingredients for 4 servings

2 lb sirloin steak, cut into strips   2 tbsp olive oil
2 tbsp Cajun seasoning   2 shallots, sliced
4 oz guacamole   1 red bell pepper, sliced
Salt to taste   8 low carb tortillas

Directions and Total Time: approx. 35 minutes

Preheat grill to 425 F. Rub the steaks all over with Cajun seasoning and place in the fridge for 1 hour. Grill the steaks for 6 minutes per side, flipping once. Wrap in foil and let sit for 10 minutes. Heat olive oil in a skillet and sauté shallots and bell pepper for 5 minutes. Share the strips in the tortillas and top with veggies and guacamole.

Per serving: Cal 381; Net Carbs 5g; Fat 16.7g; Protein 47g

Tasty Beef Cheeseburgers

Ingredients for 4 servings

1 lb ground beef   Salt and black pepper to taste
1 tsp dried parsley   1 cup feta cheese, shredded
½ tsp Worcestershire sauce   4 zero carb buns, halved

Directions and Total Time: approx. 20 minutes

Preheat grill to 400 F and grease the grate with cooking spray. Mix beef, parsley, Worcestershire sauce, salt, and pepper with until evenly combined. Make patties out of the mixture. Cook on the grill for 7 minutes one side. Flip the patties and top with cheese. Cook for another 7 minutes. Remove the patties and sandwich into 2 halves of a bun each. Serve with a tomato dipping sauce.

Per serving: Cal 386, Net Carbs 2g, Fat 32g, Protein 21g

Beef & Pesto Filled Tomatoes

Ingredients for 6 servings

1 tbsp olive oil   4 medium tomatoes, halved
¼ lb ground beef   4 tsp basil pesto
Salt and black pepper to taste   5 tbsp shredded Parmesan

Directions and Total Time: approx. 30 minutes

Preheat oven to 400 F. Heat olive oil in a skillet, add in beef, season with salt and pepper, and cook until brown while breaking the lumps that form, 8 minutes. Remove the seeds of tomatoes to create a cavity and spoon the beef inside them. Top with pesto and Parmesan. Place the filled tomatoes on a greased baking sheet and bake until the cheese melts and the tomatoes slightly brown, 20 minutes.

Per serving: Cal 122; Net Carbs 2.9g; Fat 4.4g; Protein 7.3g

Habanero Beef Cauliflower Pilaf

Ingredients for 4 servings

3 tbsp olive oil   1 yellow onion, chopped
½ lb ground beef   3 garlic cloves, minced
Salt and black pepper to taste   1 habanero pepper, minced
½ tsp Italian seasoning   ½ cup beef broth
2 ½ cups cauliflower rice   ¼ cup chopped parsley
2 tbsp tomato paste   1 lemon, sliced

Directions and Total Time: approx. 30 minutes

Heat olive oil in a skillet over medium heat and cook the beef until no longer brown, 8 minutes. Season with salt and pepper and spoon into a serving plate. In the same skillet, sauté onion, garlic, and habanero pepper, 2 minutes. Mix in Italian seasoning. Stir in cauli rice, tomato paste, and broth. Season to taste, and cook covered for 10 minutes. Mix in beef for 3 minutes. Garnish with parsley to serve.

Per serving: Cal 216; Net Carbs 3.8g; Fat 14g; Protein 15g

Beef Patties with Cherry Tomatoes

Ingredients for 4 servings

2 slices cheddar cheese, cut into 4 pieces each
2 pearl onions, thinly sliced into 8 pieces
½ lb ground beef   8 slices zero carb bread
1 tsp garlic powder   2 tbsp ranch dressing
1 tsp onion powder   4 cherry tomatoes, halved

Directions and Total Time: approx. 30 minutes

Preheat oven to 400 F. In a bowl, combine beef, salt, pepper, garlic and onion powders. Form 8 patties and place them on a greased baking sheet. Bake until brown and cooked, 10 minutes. Let cool for 3 minutes. Cut out 16 circles from the bread slices. Lay half of the bread circles on clean, flat surface and brush with the ranch dressing. Place the meat patties on the bread slices, divide cheese slices on top, onions, and tomatoes. Cover with the remaining bread slices and secure with a toothpick. Serve.

Per serving: Cal 281; Net Carbs 2.8g; Fat 12g; Protein 20g

Mexican Pizza

Ingredients for 4 servings

2 cups shredded mozzarella   2 tsp taco seasoning mix
2 tbsp cream cheese, softened   Salt and black pepper to taste
¾ cup almond flour   ½ cup chicken broth
2 eggs, beaten   1 ½ cups salsa
¾ lb ground beef   2 cups Mexican 4 cheese blend

Directions and Total Time: approx. 50 minutes

Preheat oven to 390 F and line a pizza pan with parchment paper. Microwave 2 cups of mozzarella cheese and cream cheese for 30 seconds. Remove and mix in almond flour and eggs. Spread the mixture on the pizza pan and bake for 15 minutes. Add the beef to a pot and cook for 5 minutes. Stir in taco seasoning, salt, pepper, and chicken broth. Cook for 3 minutes. Stir in salsa. Spread the beef mixture onto the crust and scatter the cheese blend on top. Bake until the cheese melts, 15 minutes. Slice and serve hot.

Per serving: Cal 556; Net Carbs 4.2g; Fats 30g; Protein 59g

Beef with Broccoli Rice & Eggs

Ingredients for 4 servings

2 cups cauli rice	1 lb sirloin steak, sliced
3 cups mixed vegetables	4 fresh eggs
3 tbsp butter	Hot sauce for topping

Directions and Total Time: approx. 25 minutes

Mix cauli rice and mixed vegetables in a bowl, sprinkle with a little water, and steam in the microwave for 1 minute. Share into 4 serving bowls. Melt butter in a skillet, season beef with salt and pepper, and brown for 5 minutes on each side. Ladle the meat onto the vegetables. Crack in an egg, season with salt and pepper and cook for 3 minutes. Remove egg onto the vegetable bowl and fry the remaining 3 eggs. Drizzle beef with hot sauce to serve.

Per serving: Cal 320, Net Carbs 4g, Fat 26g, Protein 15g

Polish Beef Tripe

Ingredients for 6 servings

1 ½ lb beef tripe	2 tsp marjoram
4 cups buttermilk	3 tbsp butter
Salt and black pepper to taste	2 large onions, sliced
1 parsnip, chopped	3 tomatoes, diced

Directions and Total Time: approx. 30 min + cooling time

Put tripe in a bowl and cover with buttermilk. Refrigerate for 3 hours. Remove from buttermilk and season with salt and pepper. Heat 2 tablespoons of butter in a skillet and brown the tripe on both sides for 6 minutes in total; set aside. Add the remaining oil and sauté onions for 3 minutes. Include tomatoes and parsnip, and cook for 15 minutes. Put the tripe in the sauce and cook for 3 minutes.

Per serving: Cal 342, Net Carbs 1g, Fat 27g, Protein 22g

Smoked Paprika Grilled Ribs

Ingredients for 4 servings

4 tbsp sugar-free BBQ sauce + extra for serving	
2 tbsp erythritol	3 tsp smoked paprika
Salt and black pepper to taste	1 tsp garlic powder
1 tbsp olive oil	1 lb beef spare ribs

Directions and Total Time: approx. 35 minutes

Mix erythritol, salt, pepper, oil, smoked paprika, and garlic powder. Brush on the meaty sides of the ribs and wrap in foil. Sit for 30 minutes to marinate.

Preheat oven to 400 F, place wrapped ribs on a baking sheet, and cook for 40 minutes. Remove ribs and aluminium foil, brush with BBQ sauce, and brown under the broiler for 10 minutes on both sides. Slice and serve with extra BBQ sauce and lettuce tomato salad.

Per serving: Cal 395; Net Carbs 3g; Fat 33g; Protein 21g

Beef Broccoli Curry

Ingredients for 6 servings

1 head broccoli, cut into florets	
1 tbsp olive oil	1 tsp garam masala
1 ½ lb ground beef	1 (7 oz) can whole tomatoes
1 tbsp ginger-garlic paste	Salt and chili pepper to taste

Directions and Total Time: approx. 30 minutes

Heat oil in a saucepan, add beef, ginger-garlic paste and season with garam masala. Cook for 5 minutes. Stir in tomatoes and broccoli, season with salt and chili pepper, and cook for 6 minutes. Add ¼ cup of water and bring to a boil for 10 minutes or until the water has reduced by half. Adjust taste with salt. Spoon into serving bowls and serve.

Per serving: Cal 374, Net Carbs 2g, Fat 33g, Protein 22g

Shitake Butter Steak

Ingredients for 4 servings

2 cups shitake mushrooms, sliced	
4 ribeye steaks	2 tsp olive oil
2 tbsp butter	Salt and black pepper to taste

Directions and Total Time: approx. 25 minutes

Heat olive oil in a pan over medium heat. Rub the steaks with salt and pepper and cook for 4 minutes per side. Set aside. Melt butter in the pan and cook the shitakes for 4 minutes. Pour the butter and mushrooms over the steak.

Per serving: Cal 370; Net Carbs 3g; Fat 31g; Protein 33g

Gruyere Beef Burgers with Sweet Onion

Ingredients for 4 servings

4 zero carb hamburger buns, halved	
1 medium white onion, sliced	1 lb ground beef
3 tbsp olive oil	Salt and black pepper to taste
2 tbsp balsamic vinegar	4 slices Gruyere cheese
2 tsp erythritol	Mayonnaise to serve

Directions and Total Time: approx. 35 minutes

Heat 2 tbsp of olive oil in a skillet and add onion. Sauté for 15 minutes until golden brown and add erythritol, balsamic vinegar, and salt. Cook for 3 more minutes; set aside.Make 4 patties out of the ground beef and season with salt and pepper. Then, heat the remaining olive oil in a skillet and cook the patties for 4 minutes on each side. Place a Gruyere slice on each patty and top with the caramelized onions. Put the patties with cheese and onions into two halves of the buns. Serve with mayonnaise.

Per serving: Cal 487; Net Carbs 7.8g; Fat 32g; Protein 38g

PORK

Pancetta & Egg Plate with Cherry Tomatoes

Ingredients for 4 servings

5 oz pancetta, chopped
2 tbsp olive oil
8 eggs
1 tbsp butter, softened
¼ cup cherry tomatoes, halved
2 tbsp chopped oregano

Directions and Total Time: approx. 30 minutes

Pour pancetta in a skillet and fry until crispy, 7 minutes; set aside. Heat half of olive oil in the skillet and crack 4 eggs in. Cook until the whites set, but the yolk are still runny, 1 minute. Spoon two eggs next to pancetta in two plates and fry the remaining eggs with the remaining oil; plate as well. Melt butter in the skillet, fry tomatoes until brown around the edges, 8 minutes. Remove to the same plates. Season to taste, garnish with oregano and serve.

Per serving: Cal 278; Net Carbs 0.5g; Fat 23g; Protein 20g

Chorizo in Cabbage Sauce with Pine Nuts

Ingredients for 4 servings

25 oz green canon cabbage, shredded
6 tbsp butter
25 oz chorizo sausages
1 ¼ cups coconut cream
½ cup fresh sage, chopped
½ lemon, zested
2 tbsp toasted pine nuts

Directions and Total Time: approx. 30 minutes

Melt 2 tbsp of butter in a skillet and fry chorizo until lightly brown on the outside, 10 minutes. Remove to a plate. Melt the remaining butter and sauté cabbage, occasionally stirring until golden brown, 4 minutes. Mix in coconut cream and simmer until the cream reduces. Season with sage, salt, pepper, and lemon zest. Divide the chorizo into four plates, spoon the cabbage to the side of the chorizo, and sprinkle the pine nuts on the cabbage. Serve warm.

Per serving: Cal 914; Net Carbs 16.9g; Fat 76g; Protein 38g

Hawaiian Pork Loco Moco

Ingredients for 4 servings

1 ½ lb ground pork
1/3 cup flaxseed meal
½ tsp nutmeg powder
1 tsp onion powder
5 large egg
2 tbsp heavy cream
3 tbsp coconut oil
1 tbsp salted butter
1 shallot, finely chopped
1 cup sliced oyster mushrooms
1 cup vegetable stock
1 tsp Worcestershire sauce
1 tsp tamari sauce
½ tsp xanthan gum
2 tbsp olive oil
4 large eggs

Directions and Total Time: approx. 40 minutes

In a bowl, combine pork, flaxseed meal, nutmeg and onion powders, salt, and pepper. In another bowl, whisk 1 egg with heavy cream and mix into the pork mixture. The batter will be sticky. Mold 8 patties from the mixture and set aside. Heat coconut oil in a skillet.

Fry the patties on both sides until no longer pink, 16 minutes; set aside. Melt the butter in the same skillet and cook shallot and mushrooms until softened, 7 minutes. In a bowl, mix stock, Worcestershire and tamari sauces, salt, and pepper. Pour the mixture over the mushrooms and cook for 3 minutes. Stir in xanthan gum, and allow thickening, 1 minute. Heat half of olive oil in a skillet, crack in an egg, and fry sunshine style, 1 minute. Plate and fry the remaining eggs using the remaining olive oil. Serve pork with mushroom gravy and top with fried eggs.

Per serving: Cal 655; Net Carbs 2.2g; Fat 46g; Protein 55g

Pork Sausage Omelet with Mushrooms

Ingredients for 2 servings

¼ cup sliced cremini mushrooms
2 tbsp olive oil
2 oz pork sausage, crumbled
1 small white onion, chopped
2 tbsp butter
6 eggs
2 oz shredded cheddar cheese

Directions and Total Time: approx. 30 minutes

Heat olive oil in a pan, add in pork sausage, and fry for 10 minutes; set aside. In the same pan sauté the onion and mushrooms, 8 minutes; set aside. Melt the butter over low heat. Meanwhile, crack the eggs into a bowl and beat with some salt and black pepper until smooth and frothy. Pour the eggs into the pan, swirl to spread around and omelet begins to firm, top with pork, mushroom-onion mixture, and cheese. Using a spatula, carefully remove the egg around the edges of the pan and flip over the stuffing, for 2 minutes. Serve warm for breakfast or brunch.

Per serving: Cal 534; Net Carbs 2.7g; Fat 43g; Protein 29g

British Pork Pie with Broccoli Topping

Ingredients for 4 servings

1 head broccoli, cut into florets
½ cup crème fraîche
1 whole egg
½ celery, finely chopped
3 oz butter, melted
5 oz shredded Swiss cheese
2 tbsp butter, cold
2 lb ground pork
2 tbsp tamari sauce
2 tbsp Worcestershire sauce
½ tbsp hot sauce
1 tsp onion powder

Directions and Total Time: approx. 55 minutes

Preheat oven to 400 F. Bring a pot of salted water to boil and cook broccoli for 3-5 minutes. Drain and transfer to a food processor; grind until rice-like. Pour the broccoli into a bowl. Add crème fraiche, egg, celery, butter, half of Swiss cheese, salt, and pepper. Mix until evenly combined. Melt cold butter in a pot, add and cook the pork until brown, 10 minutes. Mix in tamari, hot and Worcestershire sauces, onion powder, salt, and pepper; cook for 3 minutes. Spread the mixture in a greased baking dish and cover with broccoli mixture. Sprinkle with the remaining cheese and bake for 20 minutes. Serve with leafy greens.

Per serving: Cal 701; Net Carbs 3.3g; Fat 49g; Protein 60g

Hot Tex-Mex Pork Casserole

Ingredients for 4 servings

2 tbsp butter	½ cup crushed tomatoes
1 ½ lb ground pork	½ cup shredded Monterey Jack
3 tbsp Tex-Mex seasoning	1 scallion, chopped to garnish
2 tbsp chopped jalapeños	1 cup sour cream, for serving

Directions and Total Time: approx. 40 minutes

Preheat oven to 330 F and grease a baking dish with cooking spray. Melt butter in a skillet and cook the pork until brown, 8 minutes. Stir in Tex-Mex seasoning, jalapeños, and tomatoes; simmer for 5 minutes and season to taste. Transfer the mixture to the dish and use a spoon to level at the bottom of the dish. Sprinkle the cheese on top and bake for 20 until the cheese melts is golden brown. Serve, garnished with scallions and sour cream.

Per serving: Cal 431; Net Carbs 7.8g; Fat 24g; Protein 43g

Thyme Pork Roast with Brussels Sprouts

Ingredients for 4 servings

2 lb pork roast	2 garlic cloves, minced
Salt and black pepper to taste	1 ½ oz fresh ginger, grated
2 tsp dried thyme	1 tbsp coconut oil
1 bay leaf	1 tbsp smoked paprika
5 black peppercorns	½ lb Brussel sprouts, halved
2 ½ cups beef broth	1 ½ cups coconut cream

Directions and Total Time: approx. 2 hours

Preheat oven to 360 F. Place the meat in a deep baking dish and season with salt, pepper, thyme, bay leaf, and peppercorns. Pour the broth over and cover with aluminum foil. Bake for 90 minutes. Remove the foil, and carefully lift the pork onto a cutting board. Pour the juices into a bowl and reserve. In a bowl, combine garlic, ginger, coconut oil, and paprika. Rub the mixture onto meat and return the meat to the dish. Roast for 10 minutes or until golden brown. Remove, slice thinly, and set aside. Meanwhile, strain the juices through a colander into a pot and bring to boil until reduced to 1 ½ cups. Pour in Brussel sprouts and cook for 8 minutes or until softened. Stir in coconut cream, and simmer for 15 minutes. Serve creamy Brussel sprouts with pork roast.

Per serving: Cal 691; Net Carbs 9.6g; Fat 45g; Protein 59g

Cheesy Pork Quiche

Ingredients for 4 servings

1 ¼ cups almond flour	1 yellow onion, chopped
1 tbsp psyllium husk powder	1 tsp dried thyme
4 tbsp chia seeds	Salt and black pepper to taste
2 tbsp melted butter	1 cup coconut cream
6 egg	¼ cup shredded Swiss cheese
1 tbsp butter	
½ lb smoked pork shoulder	

Directions and Total Time: approx. 70 minutes

Preheat oven to 350 F, grease a springform pan with cooking spray, and line with parchment paper; set aside. To a food processor, add almond flour, psyllium husk, chia seeds, ½ tsp of salt, butter, and 1 egg. Mix until a firm dough forms. Oil your hands and spread the dough at the bottom of the springform pan. Refrigerate while you make the filling. Melt butter in a skillet, and cook the pork and onion until the meat browns, 10-12 minutes. Stir in thyme, salt, and pepper; cook further for 2 minutes. Remove the piecrust from the fridge and spoon pork and onion onto the crust. In a bowl, whisk coconut cream, half of Swiss cheese, and the remaining 5 eggs. Pour the mixture over the meat filling and top with the remaining Swiss cheese. Bake until the cheese melts and a toothpick inserted into the quiche comes out clean, 45 minutes. Remove the pan, release the lock, and take off the ring. Slice and serve.

Per serving: Cal 498; Net Carbs 4.6g; Fat 42g; Protein 24g

Parmesan & Pimiento Pork Meatballs

Ingredients for 4 servings

¼ cup chopped pimientos	1 tbsp Dijon mustard
1/3 cup mayonnaise	4 oz grated Parmesan cheese
3 tbsp softened cream cheese	1 ½ lb ground pork
1 tsp paprika powder	1 large egg
1 pinch cayenne pepper	2 tbsp olive oil, for frying

Directions and Total Time: approx. 30 minutes

In a bowl, mix pimientos, mayo, cream cheese, paprika, cayenne, mustard, Parmesan, pork, salt, pepper, and egg. Mix with hands, and form large meatballs. Heat olive oil in a non-stick skillet and fry the meatballs in batches on both sides until brown, 10 minutes in total. Transfer to a plate and serve on a bed of leafy green salad.

Per serving: Cal 485; Net Carbs 6.8g; Fat 30g; Protein 47g

Pork Bake with Cottage Cheese & Olives

Ingredients for 4 servings

½ cup cottage cheese, crumbled	
2 tbsp avocado oil	2 garlic cloves, minced
1 ½ lb ground pork	½ cup marinara sauce
¼ cup sliced Kalamata olives	1 ¼ cups heavy cream

Directions and Total Time: approx. 40 minutes

Preheat oven to 400 F and grease a casserole dish with cooking spray. Heat avocado oil in a deep skillet, add the pork, and cook until brown, 10 minutes. Stir frequently and break any lumps that form. Spread the pork at the bottom of the casserole dish. Scatter olives, cottage cheese, and garlic on top. In a bowl, mix marinara sauce and heavy cream, and pour all over the meat. Bake until the top is bubbly and lightly brown, 20-25 minutes. Serve warm.

Per serving: Cal 451; Net Carbs 1.5g; Fat 30g; Protein 40g

Buttered Pork Chops with Lemon Asparagus

Ingredients for 4 servings

7 tbsp butter
4 pork chops
Salt and black pepper to taste
4 tbsp butter, softened

2 garlic cloves, minced
1 lb asparagus, trimmed
1 tbsp dried cilantro
1 small lemon, juice

Directions and Total Time: approx. 30 minutes

Melt 3 tbsp of butter in a skillet over medium heat. Season pork with salt and pepper and fry on both sides until brown, 10 minutes in total; set aside. Melt the remaining butter in a skillet, and sauté garlic until fragrant, 1 minute. Add in asparagus, and cook until slightly softened with some crunch, 4 minutes. Add cilantro and lemon juice, toss to coat well. Serve the asparagus with the pork chops.

Per serving: Cal 538; Net Carbs 1.2g; Fat 38g; Protein 42g

Tasty Pork Chops with Cauliflower Steaks

Ingredients for 4 servings

2 heads cauliflower, cut into 4 steaks
4 pork chops
1 tbsp mesquite seasoning
2 tbsp butter

2 tbsp olive oil
½ cup Parmesan cheese

Directions and Total Time: approx. 30 minutes

Season pork with mesquite flavoring, salt, and pepper. Melt butter in a skillet and fry pork on both sides for 10 minutes; set aside. Heat olive oil in a grill pan and cook cauli steaks on all sides for 4 minutes. Sprinkle with Parmesan to melt. Serve the steaks with pork chops.

Per serving: Cal 429; Net Carbs 3.9g; Fat 23g; Protein 45g

Zucchini & Tomato Pork Omelet

Ingredients for 4 servings

3 zucchinis, halved lengthwise
4 tbsp olive oil
1 garlic clove, crushed
1 small plum tomato, diced
2 tbsp chopped scallions
1 tsp dried basil

1 tsp cumin powder
1 tsp smoked paprika
1 lb ground pork
3 large eggs, beaten
3 tsp crushed pork rinds
1/3 cup chopped cilantro

Directions and Total Time: approx. 50 minutes

Preheat a grill to medium, place the zucchinis on top, drizzle with 1 tbsp of olive oil and broil until brown, 5 minutes; set aside. Heat 1 tbsp of olive oil in a skillet and sauté garlic, tomato, and scallions, 8 minutes. Mix in basil, cumin, paprika, and salt. Add the pork and cook until brown, 10 minutes; set aside. Spread the pork mixture onto the grilled zucchini slices; flatten the mixture. In the same skillet, heat the remaining oil over medium and carefully place in the loaded zucchinis. Divide the eggs onto the zucchinis, cover the pan and cook until set, 3 minutes. Sprinkle pork rinds and cilantro on top, and serve.

Per serving: Cal 332; Net Carbs 1.1g; Fat 22g; Protein 30g

Italian Pork with Capers

Ingredients for 4 servings

1 ½ lb thin cut pork chops, boneless
½ lemon, juiced + 1 lemon, sliced
Salt and black pepper to taste
1 tbsp avocado oil
3 tbsp butter

2 tbsp capers
1 cup beef broth
2 tbsp chopped parsley

Directions and Total Time: approx. 30 minutes

Heat avocado oil in a skillet and cook pork chops on both sides until brown, 14 minutes. Transfer to a plate, cover to keep warm. Melt butter in the pan and cook capers until hot and sizzling; keep stirring to avoid burning, 3 minutes.

Pour in broth and lemon juice, use a spatula to scrape any bits stuck at the bottom, and boil until the sauce reduces by half. Add back the pork, arrange lemon slices on top, and sprinkle with 1 tbsp parsley. Simmer for 3 minutes. Serve garnished with parsley and with creamy mashed cauliflower.

Per serving: Cal 341; Net Carbs 0.8g; Fat 18g; Protein 40g

Avocado & Green Bean Pork Sauté

Ingredients for 4 servings

4 tbsp avocado oil
4 pork shoulder chops
2 tbsp avocado oil
1 ½ cups green beans

2 large avocados, chopped
Salt and black pepper to taste
6 green onions, chopped
1 tbsp chopped parsley

Directions and Total Time: approx. 30 minutes

Heat oil in a skillet, season pork with salt and pepper, and fry in the oil until brown, 12 minutes; set aside. To the same skillet, sauté green beans until sweating and slightly softened, 10 minutes. Mix in avocados and half of green onions for 2 minutes. Dish into plates, garnish with the remaining onions and parsley, and serve with pork chops.

Per serving: Cal 557; Net Carbs 1.9g; Fat 36g; Protein 43g

Savory Pork Tacos

Ingredients for 4 servings

2 tbsp olive oil
½ cup sliced yellow onion
2 lb pork shoulder
4 tbsp ras el hanout seasoning
Salt to taste

3 ½ cups beef broth
5 tbsp psyllium husk powder
1 ¼ cups almond flour
2 eggs, cracked into a bowl
2 tbsp butter, for frying

Directions and Total Time: approx. 7 hours

In a pot, heat olive oil and sauté onion for 3 minutes or until softened. Season pork shoulder with ras el hanout, salt, and place in the onion. Sear on each side for 3 minutes and pour the broth on top. Cover the lid, reduce heat to low, and cook for 4 to 5 hours or until the pork softens. Shred the pork with two forks. Cook further over low heat for 1 hour; set aside. In a bowl, combine psyllium husk powder, almond flour, and 1 tsp of salt. Mix in eggs until a thick dough forms and add 1 cup of water.

Separate the dough into 8 pieces. Lay a parchment paper on a flat surface, grease with cooking spray, and put a dough piece on top. Cover with another parchment paper and, using a rolling pin, flatten the dough into a circle. Repeat the same process for the remaining dough balls. Melt a quarter of the butter in a skillet over and fry the flattened dough one after another on both sides until light brown, 40 minutes in total. Transfer the keto tortillas to plates, spoon shredded meat and serve.

Per serving: Cal 520; Net Carbs 3.8g; Fat 30g; Protein 50g

Yummy Spareribs in Béarnaise Sauce

Ingredients for 4 servings

3 tbsp butter, melted	½ tsp onion powder
4 egg yolks, beaten	Salt and black pepper to taste
2 tbsp chopped tarragon	4 tbsp butter
2 tsp white wine vinegar	2 lb spareribs, divided into 16

Directions and Total Time: approx. 30 minutes

In a bowl, whisk butter gradually into the egg yolks until evenly mixed. In another bowl, combine tarragon, white wine vinegar, and onion powder. Mix into the egg mixture and season with salt and black pepper; set aside. Melt the butter in a skillet over medium heat. Season the spareribs on both sides with salt and pepper. Cook in the butter on both sides until brown with a crust, 12 minutes. Divide the spareribs between plates and serve with béarnaise sauce to the side, along with some braised asparagus.

Per serving: Cal 878; Net Carbs 1g; Fat 78g; Protein 41g

Pork & Pecan in Camembert Bake

Ingredients for 4 servings

9 oz whole Camembert cheese	
½ lb boneless pork chops, cut	2 oz pecans
into small cubes	1 garlic clove, minced
3 tbsp olive oil	1 tbsp chopped parsley

Directions and Total Time: approx. 30 minutes

Preheat the oven to 400 F. While the cheese is in its box, using a knife, score around the top and side of about a ¼-inch and take off the top layer of the skin. Place the cheese on a baking tray and melt in the oven for 10 minutes. Meanwhile, heat olive oil in a skillet, season the pork with salt and black pepper, and fry until brown on all sides, 12 minutes. Transfer to a bowl and add pecans, garlic, and parsley. Spoon the mixture onto the cheese and bake for 10 minutes until the cheese softens and nuts toast.

Per serving: Cal 452; Net Carbs 0.2g; Fat 38g; Protein 27g

Cheddar Pork Burrito Bowl

Ingredients for 4 servings

1 tbsp butter	½ cup beef broth
1 lb ground pork	4 tbsp taco seasoning
Salt and black pepper to taste	1 avocado, cubed
½ cup sharp cheddar, shredded	¼ cup tomatoes, diced
½ cup sour cream	1 green onion, sliced
¼ cup sliced black olives	1 tbsp fresh cilantro, chopped

Directions and Total Time: approx. 30 minutes

Melt butter in a skillet over medium heat. Cook the pork until brown while breaking any lumps, 10 minutes. Mix in broth, taco seasoning, salt, and pepper; cook until most of the liquid evaporates, 5 minutes. Mix in half of cheddar cheese to melt. Spoon into a bowl and top with olives, avocado, tomatoes, green onion, and cilantro to serve.

Per serving: Cal 386; Net Carbs 8.8g; Fat 23g; Protein 30g

Parmesan Pork Stuffed Mushrooms

Ingredients for 4 servings

12 medium portabella mushrooms, stalks removed	
2 tbsp butter	3 tbsp chives, finely chopped
½ lb ground pork	7 oz cream cheese
1 tsp paprika	¼ cup shredded Parmesan

Directions and Total Time: approx. 30 minutes

Preheat oven to 400 F and grease a baking sheet with cooking spray. Melt butter in a skillet, add the pork, season with salt, pepper, and paprika. Stir-fry until brown, 10 minutes. Mix in two-thirds of chives and cream cheese until evenly combined. Place mushrooms on the baking sheet and spoon the mixture into the mushrooms. Top with the Parmesan and bake until mushrooms turn golden and the cheese melts, 10 minutes. Remove to plates, garnish with the remaining chives, and serve immediately.

Per serving: Cal 299; Net Carbs 2.2g; Fat 23g; Protein 19g

Florentine-Style Pizza with Bacon

Ingredients for 2 servings

1 cup shredded provolone cheese	
1 (7 oz) can sliced mushrooms, drained	
10 eggs	2 cups chopped kale, wilted
1 tsp Italian seasoning	½ cup grated mozzarella
6 bacon slices	4 eggs
2/3 cup tomato sauce	Olive oil for drizzling

Directions and Total Time: approx. 45 minutes

Preheat oven to 400 F and line a pizza-baking pan with parchment paper. Crack 6 eggs into a bowl; whisk in provolone cheese, and Italian seasoning. Spread the mixture on a pizza-baking pan and bake until golden, 15 minutes. Remove from oven and let cool for 2 minutes. Increase temperature to 450 F. Fry bacon in a skillet until brown and crispy, 5 minutes. Transfer to a plate. Spread tomato sauce on the crust, top with kale, mozzarella, and mushrooms. Bake in the oven for 8 minutes. Crack the remaining 4 eggs on top, cover with bacon, and continue baking until the eggs set, 2-3 minutes. Serve warm.

Per serving: Cal 1093; Net Carbs 6.1g; Fat 77g; Protein 69g

Cheesy Mushrooms & Bacon Lettuce Rolls

Ingredients for 4 servings

½ cup sliced cremini mushrooms
1 iceberg lettuce, leaves separated
8 bacon slices, chopped   1 ½ lb ground pork
2 tbsp olive oil   1 cup shredded cheddar

Directions and Total Time: approx. 30 minutes

In a skillet, cook bacon until brown and crispy. Transfer onto a paper-towel-lined plate. Heat the 1 tbsp of olive oil in the skillet and sauté the mushrooms. Season with salt and pepper; cook for 5 minutes or until softened. Heat the remaining oil and cook the pork until brown, 10 minutes, while breaking the lumps that form. Divide the pork between lettuce leaves, sprinkle with cheddar cheese, top with bacon and mushrooms. Wrap and serve with mayo.

Per serving: Cal 630; Net Carbs 0.5g; Fat 45g; Protein 52g

Saucy Thai Pork Medallions

Ingredients for 4 servings

1 ½ pork tenderloin, sliced into ½ -inch medallions
6 tbsp butter   1 celery, chopped
1 canon cabbage, shredded   1 tbsp red curry powder
Salt and black pepper to taste 1 ¼ cups coconut cream

Directions and Total Time: approx. 45 minutes

Melt 2 tbsp of butter in a skillet, and sauté cabbage until soft and slightly golden; set aside. Melt 2 tbsp of butter in the skillet, season the pork with salt and pepper, and fry until brown on the outside and cooked within 10 minutes; set aside. Add the remaining butter to the skillet and sauté celery until softened. Mix in curry, heat for 30 seconds, and stir in coconut cream. Simmer for 10 minutes. Put the meat into heat. Serve with buttered cabbage.

Per serving: Cal 626; Net Carbs 3.9g; Fat 48g; Protein 43g

Barbecue Baked Pork Chops

Ingredients for 4 servings

½ cup grated flaxseed meal   1 tbsp dried parsley
1 tsp dried thyme   1/2 tsp onion powder
1 tsp paprika   1/8 tsp basil
Salt and black pepper to taste 4 pork chops
¼ tsp chili powder   1 tbsp melted butter
1 ½ tsp garlic powder   ½ cup BBQ sauce

Directions and Total Time: approx. 70 minutes

Preheat oven to 400 F. In a bowl, mix flaxseed meal, thyme, paprika, salt, pepper, chili, garlic powder, parsley, onion powder, and basil. Rub the pork chops with the mixture. Melt butter in a skillet and sear pork on both sides, 8 minutes. Transfer to a greased baking sheet, baste with BBQ sauce and bake for 50 minutes. Allow resting for 10 minutes, slice, and serve with buttered parsnips.

Per serving: Cal 385; Net Carbs 1.6g; Fat 19g; Protein 44g

Dijon Pork Loin Roast

Ingredients for 6 servings

3 lb boneless pork loin roast 1 tbsp Dijon mustard
5 cloves garlic, minced   1 tsp dried basil
Salt and black pepper to taste 2 tsp garlic powder

Directions and Total Time: approx. 30 minutes

Preheat oven to 400 F and place the pork in a baking dish. In a bowl, mix minced garlic, salt, pepper, mustard, basil, and garlic powder. Rub the mixture onto pork. Drizzle with olive oil and bake for 15 minutes or until cooked within and brown outside. Transfer onto a flat surface, and let cool for 5 minutes. Serve sliced with steamed greens.

Per serving: Cal 311; Net Carbs 2g; Fat 9g; Protein 51g

Tender Pork Chops with Basil & Beet Greens

Ingredients for 4 servings

2 cups chopped beetroot greens
2 tbsp balsamic vinegar   1 tbsp olive oil
2 tsp freshly pureed garlic   4 pork chops
2 tbsp freshly chopped basil   2 tbsp butter
4 thyme sprigs

Directions and Total Time: approx. 30 minutes

Preheat oven to 400 F. In a saucepan, add vinegar, salt, pepper, garlic, and basil. Cook over low heat until the mixture is syrupy. Heat olive oil in a skillet and sear pork on both sides for 8 minutes. Brush the vinegar glaze on the pork, add thyme, and bake for 8 minutes. Melt butter in another skillet and sauté beetroot greens for 5 minutes. Serve pork with beetroot greens.

Per serving: Cal 391; Net Carbs 0.8g; Fat 16g; Protein 40g

Ground Pork & Scrambled Eggs with Cabbage

Ingredients for 4 servings

2 tbsp sesame oil   1 habanero pepper, chopped
2 large eggs   1 green cabbage, shredded
2 tbsp minced garlic   5 scallions, chopped
½ tsp ginger puree   3 tbsp coconut aminos
1 medium white onion, diced   1 tbsp white vinegar
1 lb ground pork   2 tbsp sesame seeds

Directions and Total Time: approx. 30 minutes

Heat 1 tbsp of sesame oil in a skillet over and scramble the eggs until set, 1 minute; set aside. Heat 1 tbsp sesame oil in the same skillet and sauté garlic, ginger, and onion until soft and fragrant, 4 minutes. Add ground pork and habanero pepper and season with salt, pepper. Cook for 10 minutes. Mix in cabbage, scallions, aminos, and vinegar and cook until the cabbage is tender. Stir in the eggs. Serve garnished with sesame seeds, and some low carb tortillas.

Per serving: Cal 295; Net Carbs 3.6g; Fat 16g; Protein 29g

Sweet Pork Chops with Brie Cheese

Ingredients for 4 servings

3 tbsp olive oil	Salt and black pepper to taste
2 large red onions, sliced	4 pork chops
2 tbsp balsamic vinegar	4 slices brie cheese
1 tsp maple (sugar-free) syrup	2 tbsp chopped mint leaves

Directions and Total Time: approx. 45 minutes

Heat 1 tbsp olive oil in a skillet until smoky. Reduce to low and sauté onions until brown. Pour in vinegar, maple syrup, and salt. Cook with frequent stirring to prevent burning until the onions caramelize, 15 minutes; set aside. Heat the remaining olive oil in the same skillet, season the pork with salt and black pepper, and cook for 12 minutes. Put a brie slice on each meat and top with the caramelized onions; let the cheese to melt for 2 minutes. Spoon the meat with the topping onto plates and garnish with mint.

Per serving: Cal 457; Net Carbs 3.1g; Fat 25g; Protein 46g

Sesame Pork Meatballs

Ingredients for 4 servings

1 lb ground pork	1 tsp red chili flakes
2 scallions, chopped	2 tbsp tamari sauce
1 zucchini, grated	2 tbsp sesame oil
4 garlic cloves, minced	3 tbsp coconut oil, for frying
1 tsp freshly pureed ginger	

Directions and Total Time: approx. 30 minutes

In a bowl, combine pork, scallions, zucchini, garlic, ginger, chili flakes, tamari sauce, and sesame oil. With hands, form 1-inch oval shapes and place on a plate. Heat coconut oil in a skillet over medium heat and brown the balls for 12 minutes. Transfer to a paper towel-lined plate to drain and serve with creamy spinach puree.

Per serving: Cal 296; Net Carbs 1.5g; Fat 22g; Protein 24g

Hot Pork Stir-Fry with Walnuts

Ingredients for 4 servings

1 ½ lb pork tenderloin, cut into strips

2 tbsp coconut oil	1 tbsp freshly grated ginger
Salt and black pepper to taste	3 garlic cloves, minced
1 green bell pepper, diced	1 tsp sesame oil
1 small red onion, diced	1 habanero pepper, minced
1/3 cup walnuts	2 tbsp tamari sauce

Directions and Total Time: approx. 30 minutes

Heat coconut oil in a wok, season pork with salt and pepper, and cook until no longer pink, 10 minutes. Shift to one side of the wok and add bell pepper, onion, walnuts, ginger, garlic, sesame oil, and habanero pepper. Sauté until fragrant and onion softened, 5 minutes. Mix and season with tamari sauce. Stir-fry until well combined and cook for 1 minute. Serve with cauliflower rice.

Per serving: Cal 325; Net Carbs 2.8g; Fat 16g; Protein 38g

Lemony Greek Pork Tenderloin

Ingredients for 4 servings

¼ cup olive oil	2 tbsp red wine vinegar
2 lemon, juiced	1 ½ lb pork tenderloin
2 tbsp Greek seasoning	2 tbsp lard

Directions and Total Time: approx. 2 hours

Preheat oven to 425 F. In a bowl, combine olive oil, lemon juice, Greek seasoning, vinegar, salt, and pepper. Place the pork on a clean flat surface, cut a few incisions, and brush the marinade all over. Cover in plastic wrap and refrigerate for 1 hour. Melt lard in a skillet, remove and unwrap the pork, and sear until brown on the outside. Place in a greased baking dish, brush with any reserved marinade, and bake for 45 minutes. Serve.

Per serving: Cal 383; Net Carbs 2.5g; Fat 24g; Protein 36g

Flavorful Chipotle-Coffee Pork Chops

Ingredients for 4 servings

1 tbsp finely ground coffee	½ tsp cumin powder
½ tsp chipotle powder	1 ½ tsp swerve brown sugar
½ tsp garlic powder	4 bone-in pork chops
½ tsp cinnamon powder	2 tbsp lard

Directions and Total Time: approx. 20 minutes

In a bowl, mix coffee, chipotle, garlic, cinnamon, cumin, salt, pepper, and swerve. Rub spices all over the pork. Cover with plastic wraps and refrigerate overnight. Preheat oven to 350 F. Melt lard in a skillet and sear pork on both sides for 3 minutes. Transfer the skillet to the oven and bake for 10 minutes. Remove to a cutting board, let cool, slice, and serve with buttered snap peas.

Per serving: Cal 291; Net Carbs 0.5g; Fat 13g; Protein 39g

Pork Belly with Creamy Coconut Kale

Ingredients for 4 servings

2 lb pork belly, chopped	¼ cup ginger thinly sliced
Salt and black pepper to taste	4 long red chilies, halved
1 tbsp coconut oil	1 cup coconut milk
1 white onion, chopped	1 cup coconut cream
6 cloves garlic, minced	2 cups chopped kale

Directions and Total Time: approx. 40 minutes

Season pork belly with salt and pepper and refrigerate for 30 minutes. Pour 2 cups water in a pot, add in pork and bring to a boil for 15 minutes. Drain and transfer to a skillet. Fry for 15 minutes until the skin browns and crackles. Turn a few times to prevent from burning. Spoon onto a plate and discard the fat. Heat coconut oil in the same skillet and sauté onion, garlic, ginger, and chilies for 5 minutes. Pour in coconut milk and coconut cream and cook for 1 minute. Add kale and cook until wilted, stirring occasionally. Stir in the pork. Cook for 2 minutes. Serve.

Per serving: Cal 608; Net Carbs 6.7g; Fat 36g; Protein 57g

Pork Medallions with & Morels

Ingredients for 4 servings4

1 ½ lb pork tenderloin, cut into 8 medallions
2 tbsp olive oil   ½ cup red wine
16 fresh morels, rinsed   ¾ cup beef broth
4 large green onions, chopped   2 tbsp unsalted butter

Directions and Total Time: approx. 25 minutes

Heat olive oil in a pot, season the pork medallions with salt and pepper, and sear until brown, 5 minutes; set aside. Add morels and green onions and cook until softened, 2 minutes. Mix in red wine and broth. Place the pork in the sauce to simmer for 5 minutes. Swirl in butter, adjust the taste, and serve hot with creamy mashed turnips.

Per serving: Cal 328; Net Carbs 1.2g; Fat 15g; Protein 39g

Mozzarella Baked Pork

Ingredients for 4 servings

4 boneless pork chops   1 large egg, beaten
Salt and black pepper to taste   1 cup tomato sauce
1 cup golden flaxseed meal   1 cup shredded mozzarella

Directions and Total Time: approx. 30 minutes

Preheat oven to 400 F and grease a baking sheet. Season the pork with salt and pepper, and add flaxseed meal to a plate. Coat the meat in the egg, then in flaxseed, and place on the baking sheet. Pour tomato sauce over and sprinkle with mozzarella. Bake for 15 minutes or until the cheese melts and pork cooks through. Serve hot with salad.

Per serving: Cal 592; Net Carbs 2.7g; Fat 25g; Protein 62g

Juicy Pork Chops with Parmesan

Ingredients for 4 servings

1 lb pork tenderloin, cut into ½-inch medallions
2 cups fresh raspberries   2/3 cup grated Parmesan
¼ cup water   Salt and black pepper to taste
1 tsp chicken bouillon granules   6 tbsp butter, divided
½ cup almond flour   1 tsp minced garlic
2 large eggs, lightly beaten   Sliced fresh raspberries

Directions and Total Time: approx. 30 minutes

To a blender, add raspberries, water, and chicken granules; process until smooth and set aside. In two separate bowls, pour almond flour and Parmesan cheese. Season the meat with salt and pepper. Coat in the flour, then in the eggs, and then in the cheese. Melt 2 tbsp of butter in a skillet and fry the pork for 3 minutes per side or until the cheese melts and the meat cooks within. Transfer to a plate, cover to keep warm. In the same skillet, melt the remaining butter and sauté garlic for 1 minute. Stir in raspberry mixture and cook for 3 minutes. Dish the pork and spoon sauce on top. Garnish with raspberries and serve with baby spinach.

Per serving: Cal 488; Net Carbs 6.1g; Fat 23g; Protein 34g

Mushroom Pork Meatballs with Parsnips

Ingredients for 4 servings

1 cup cremini mushrooms, chopped
1 ½ lb ground pork   2 tbsp olive oil
2 garlic cloves, minced   2 cups tomato sauce
2 small red onions, chopped   6 fresh basil leaves to garnish
1 tsp dried basil   1 lb parsnips, chopped
Salt and black pepper to taste   1 cup water
1 cup grated Parmesan   2 tbsp butter
½ almond milk   ½ cup coconut cream

Directions and Total Time: approx. 60 minutes

Preheat oven to 350 F and line a baking tray with parchment paper. In a bowl, add pork, half of garlic, half of onion, mushrooms, basil, salt, and pepper; mix with hands until evenly combined. Mold bite-size balls out of the mixture. Pour ½ cup Parmesan and almond milk each in 2 separate bowls. Dip each ball in the milk and then in the cheese. Place on the tray and bake for 20 minutes.

Heat olive oil in a saucepan and sauté the remaining onion and garlic; sauté until fragrant and soft. Pour in tomato sauce and cook for 20 minutes. Add the meatballs, spoon some sauce to cover, and simmer for 7 minutes. In a pot, add parsnips, 1 cup water, and salt. Bring to a boil for 10 minutes until the parsnips soften. Drain and pour into a bowl. Add butter, salt, and pepper; mash into a puree using a mash. Stir in coconut cream and remaining Parmesan until combined. Spoon mashed parsnip into bowls, top with meatballs and sauce, and garnish with basil leaves.

Per serving: Cal 642; Net Carbs 21.1g; Fat 32g; Protein 50g

Smoked Paprika-Coconut Tenderloin

Ingredients for 4 servings

1 lb pork tenderloin, cubed   1 tsp almond flour
4 tsp smoked paprika   1 tbsp butter
Salt and black pepper to taste   3/4 cup coconut cream

Directions and Total Time: approx. 30 minutes

Pat dry the pork pieces with a paper towel and season with paprika, salt, pepper, and sprinkle with almond flour. Melt butter in a skillet and sauté the pork until lightly browned, 5 minutes. Stir in cream; let boil. Cook until the sauce slightly thickens, 7 minutes. Serve over a bed of cauli rice.

Per serving: Cal 310; Net Carbs 2.5g; Fat 21g; Protein 26g

Mushroom & Pork Casserole

Ingredients for 4 servings

1 cup portobello mushrooms, chopped
1 cup ricotta, crumbled   4 green onions, chopped
1 cup Italian cheese blend   15 oz canned tomatoes
4 carrots, thinly sliced   4 tbsp pork rinds, crushed
Salt and black pepper to taste   ¼ cup chopped parsley
1 clove garlic, minced   3 tbsp olive oil
1 ¼ pounds ground pork   ⅓ cup water

Directions and Total Time: approx. 38 minutes

Mix parsley, ricotta cheese, and Italian cheese blend in a bowl; set aside. Heat olive oil in a skillet and cook pork for 3 minutes. Add garlic, half of the green onions, mushrooms, and 2 tbsp of pork rinds. Continue cooking for 3 minutes. Stir in tomatoes and water and cook for 3 minutes. Sprinkle a baking dish with 2 tbsp of pork rinds, top with half of the carrots and a season of salt, 2/3 of the pork mixture, and the cheese mixture. Repeat the layering process a second time to exhaust the ingredients. Cover the baking dish with foil and bake for 20 minutes at 370 F. Remove the foil and brown the top of the casserole with the broiler side of the oven for 2 minutes.

Per serving: Cal 672; Net Carbs 7.9g; Fat 56g; Protein 34.8g

Tangy Lemon Pork Steaks with Mushrooms

Ingredients for 4 servings

8 oz white button mushrooms, chopped
4 large, bone-in pork steaks | 1 cup beef stock
2 tsp lemon pepper seasoning | 6 garlic cloves, minced
3 tbsp olive oil | 2 tbsp chopped parsley
3 tbsp butter | 1 lemon, thinly sliced

Directions and Total Time: approx. 30 minutes

Pat the pork dry with a paper towel and season with salt and lemon pepper. Heat 2 tbsp each of olive oil and butter in a skillet over medium heat and cook the meat until brown, 10 minutes; set aside. Add the remaining oil and butter to the skillet, pour in half of the stock to deglaze the bottom of the pan, add garlic and mushrooms, and cook until softened, 5 minutes. Return the pork, add lemon slices, and cook until the liquid reduces by two-thirds. Garnish with parsley, and serve with steamed green beans.

Per serving: Cal 505; Net Carbs 3.2g; Fat 32g; Protein 46g

Celery Braised Pork Shanks in Wine Sauce

Ingredients for 4 servings

3 tbsp olive oil | 1 ½ cups crushed tomatoes
3 lb pork shanks | ½ cup red wine
3 celery stalks, chopped | ¼ tsp red chili flakes
5 garlic cloves, minced | ¼ cup chopped parsley

Directions and Total Time: approx. 2 hours 30 minutes

Preheat oven to 300 F. Heat olive oil in a Dutch oven and brown pork on all sides for 4 minutes; set aside. Add celery and garlic and sauté for 3 minutes. Return the pork and top with tomatoes, red wine, and chili flakes. Cover the lid and put the pot in the oven. Cook for 2 hours, turning the meat every 30 minutes. In the last 15 minutes, open the lid and increase the temperature to 450 F. Take out the pot, stir in parsley, and serve the meat with sauce on a bed of creamy mashed cauliflower.

Per serving: Cal 520; Net Carbs 1.4g; Fat 20g; Protein 75g

Tuscan Pork Tenderloin with Cauli Rice

Ingredients for 4 servings

1 cup loosely packed fresh baby spinach
2 tbsp olive oil | 2 cups cauliflower rice
1 ½ lb pork tenderloin, cubed | ½ cup water
Salt and black pepper to taste | 1 cup grape tomatoes, halved
½ tsp cumin powder | 3/4 cup crumbled feta cheese

Directions and Total Time: approx. 30 minutes

Heat olive oil in a skillet, season the pork with salt, pepper, and cumin, and sear on both sides for 5 minutes until brown. Stir in cauli rice and pour in water. Cook for 5 minutes or until cauliflower softens. Mix in spinach to wilt, 1 minute, and add the tomatoes. Spoon the dish into bowls, sprinkle with feta cheese, and serve with hot sauce.

Per serving: Cal 377; Net Carbs 1.9g; Fat 17g; Protein 43g

Indian Pork Masala

Ingredients for 4 servings

1 ½ lb pork shoulder, cut into bite-size pieces
2 tbsp ghee | 2 tbsp Greek yogurt
1 tbsp freshly grated ginger | ½ tsp chili powder
2 tbsp freshly pureed garlic | 2 tbsp garam masala
6 medium red onions, sliced | 1 bunch cilantro, chopped
1 cup crushed tomatoes | 2 green chilies, sliced

Directions and Total Time: approx. 30 minutes

Bring a pot of water to a boil to blanch meat for 3 minutes; drain and set aside. Melt ghee in a skillet and sauté ginger, garlic, and onions until caramelized, 5 minutes. Mix in tomatoes, yogurt, and pork. Season with chili, garam masala, salt, and pepper. Stir and cook for 10 minutes. Stir in cilantro and green chilies. Serve masala with cauli rice.

Per serving: Cal 302; Net Carbs 2.2g; Fat 16g; Protein 33g

Cheesy Sausages in Creamy Onion Sauce

Ingredients for 4 servings

2 tsp almond flour | 8 oz cream cheese, softened
1 (16 oz) pork sausages | 3 tbsp freshly chopped chives
6 tbsp golden flaxseed meal | 3 tsp freshly pureed onion
1 egg, beaten | 3 tbsp chicken broth
1 tbsp olive oil | 2 tbsp almond milk

Directions and Total Time: approx. 30 minutes

In a plate, mix flour with salt and pepper, and pour flaxseed meal to a plate. Prick the sausages with a fork all around, roll in the flour, in the egg, and then in the flaxseed meal. Heat olive oil in a skillet and fry sausages until brown, 15 minutes. Transfer to a plate and keep warm. In a saucepan, combine cream cheese, chives, onion, broth, and milk. Cook and stir over medium heat until smooth and evenly mixed, 5 minutes. Plate the sausages and spoon the sauce on top. Serve immediately with steamed broccoli.

Per serving: Cal 461; Net Carbs 0.5g; Fat 32g; Protein 34g

Savory Jalapeño Pork Meatballs

Ingredients for 4 servings

3 green onions, chopped	Salt and black pepper to taste
1 tbsp garlic powder	3 tbsp butter melted + 2 tbsp
1 pound ground pork	4 ounces cream cheese
1 jalapeño pepper, chopped	1 tsp turmeric
1 tsp dried oregano	¼ tsp xylitol
2 tsp parsley	½ tsp baking powder
½ tsp Italian seasoning	1 ½ cups flax meal
2 tsp cumin	½ cup almond flour

Directions and Total Time: approx. 45 minutes

Preheat oven to 350 F. In a food processor, add green onions, garlic powder, jalapeño pepper, and ½ cup water; blend well. Set a pan, warm in 2 tbsp of butter and cook ground pork for 3 minutes. Stir in onion mixture, and cook for 2 minutes. Stir in parsley, cloves, salt, cumin, ½ teaspoon turmeric, oregano, Italian seasoning, and pepper, and cook for 3 minutes. In a bowl, combine the remaining turmeric with almond flour, xylitol, flax meal, and baking powder. In a separate bowl, combine 3 tbsp melted butter with cream cheese. Combine the 2 mixtures to obtain a dough. Form balls from this mixture, set on a parchment paper, and roll each into a circle. Split the pork mixture on one-half of the dough circles, cover with the other half, seal edges, and lay on a lined sheet. Bake for 25 minutes.

Per serving: Cal 598; Net Carbs 5.3g; Fat 45.8g; Protein 35g

Greek-Style Pork Packets with Halloumi

Ingredients for 4 servings

1 lb turnips, cubed	4 boneless pork chops
½ cup salsa verde	Salt and black pepper to taste
2 tsp chili powder	3 tbsp olive oil
1 tsp cumin powder	4 slices halloumi cheese, cubed

Directions and Total Time: approx. 30 minutes

Preheat the grill to 400 F. Cut out four 18x12-inch sheets of heavy-duty aluminum foil. Grease the sheets with cooking spray. In a bowl, combine turnips, salsa verde, chili, and cumin. Season with salt and pepper. Place a pork chop on each foil sheet, spoon the turnip mixture on the meat, divide olive oil on top, and then halloumi cheese. Wrap the foil and place on the grill grate and cook for 10 minutes. Turn the foil packs over and cook further for 8 minutes. Remove the packs onto plates, and serve.

Per serving: Cal 501; Net Carbs 2.1g; Fat 27g; Protein 52g

Pork & Bacon Parcels

Ingredients for 4 servings

4 bacon strips	1 onion, chopped
2 tbsp fresh parsley, chopped	1 tbsp garlic powder
4 pork loin chops, boneless	2 tomatoes, chopped
⅓ cup cottage cheese	⅓ cup chicken stock
1 tbsp olive oil	Salt and black pepper, to taste

Directions and Total Time: approx. 40 minutes

Lay a bacon strip on top of each pork chop, then divide the parsley and cottage cheese on top. Roll each pork piece and secure with toothpicks. Set a pan over medium heat and warm oil, cook the pork parcels until browned, and remove to a plate. Add in the onion, and cook for 5 minutes. Pour in the chicken stock and garlic powder, and cook for 3 minutes. Get rid of the toothpicks from the rolls and return them to the pan. Stir in black pepper, salt, parsley, and tomatoes, bring to a boil, set heat to medium-low, and cook for 25 minutes while covered. Serve.

Per serving: Cal 433; Net Carbs 6.8g; Fat 23g; Protein 44.6g

Hot Pork Chops with Satay Sauce

Ingredients for 4 servings

2 lb boneless pork loin chops, cut into 2-inch pieces	
Salt and black pepper to taste	½ tsp onion powder
1 medium white onion, sliced	½ tsp hot sauce
1/3 cup peanut butter	1 cup chicken broth, divided
¼ cup tamari sauce	3 tbsp xanthan gum
½ tsp garlic powder	1 tbsp chopped peanuts

Directions and Total Time: approx. 80 minutes

Season pork with salt and pepper; put into a pot and add onion. In a bowl, combine peanut butter, tamari sauce, garlic and onion powders, hot sauce, and two-thirds of the chicken broth. Pour the mixture over the meat. Bring to a boil over high heat, reduce the heat, and simmer for 1 hour or until the meat becomes tender. In a bowl, combine the remaining broth and xanthan gum. Stir the mixture into the meat and simmer until the sauce thickens, 2 minutes. Spoon onto a plate, garnish with peanuts and serve.

Per serving: Cal 455; Net Carbs 6.7g; Fat 17g; Protein 61g

Turnip Pork Pie

Ingredients for 8 servings

1 cup turnip mash	1 onion, chopped
2 pounds ground pork	1 tbsp sage
½ cup water	2 tbsp butter

Crust:

2 oz butter	2 cups almond flour
1 egg	¼ tsp xanthan gum
2 oz cheddar, shredded	A pinch of salt

Directions and Total Time: approx. 50 minutes

Stir all crust ingredients in a bowl. Make 2 balls out of the mixture and refrigerate for 10 minutes. In a pan, warm 2 tbsp of butter and sauté onion and ground pork for 8 minutes. Let cool for a few minutes and add in turnip mash and sage. Mix with hands. Roll out the pie crusts and place one at the bottom of a greased pie pan. Spread filling over the crust and top with the other coat. Bake in the oven for 30 minutes at 350 F. Serve.

Per serving: Cal 477; Net Carbs 1.7g; Fat 36.1g; Protein 33g

Sweet Pork Chops with Hoisin Sauce

Ingredients for 4 servings

4 oz hoisin sauce, sugar-free | 1 tbsp xylitol
1 ¼ pounds pork chops | ½ tsp ginger powder
Salt and black pepper to taste | 2 tsp smoked paprika

Directions and Total Time: approx. 2 hours 20 minutes

In a bowl, mix pepper, xylitol, ginger, and paprika; rub pork chops with the mixture. Cover with plastic wraps and refrigerate for 2 hours. Preheat grill. Grill the meat for 2 minutes per side. Reduce the heat and brush with the hoisin sauce, cover, and grill for 5 minutes. Turn the meat and brush again with hoisin sauce. Cook for 5 minutes.

Per serving: Cal 352; Net Carbs 2.5g; Fat 22.9g; Protein 37g

Basil Pork Meatballs in Tomato Sauce

Ingredients for 6 servings

1 pound ground pork | 2 eggs, beaten
2 green onions, chopped | 1 cup asiago cheese, shredded
1 tbsp olive oil | Salt and black pepper to taste
1 cup pork rinds, crushed | 1 can (29-ounce) tomato sauce
3 cloves garlic, minced | 1 cup pecorino cheese, grated
½ cup buttermilk | Chopped basil to garnish

Directions and Total Time: approx. 45 minutes

Preheat oven to 370 F. Mix buttermilk, ground pork, garlic, asiago cheese, eggs, salt, pepper, and pork rinds in a bowl, until combined. Shape pork mixture into balls and place into a greased baking pan. Bake for 20 minutes. Remove and pour in tomato sauce and sprinkle with Pecorino cheese. Cover the pan with foil and put it back in the oven for 10 minutes. Remove the foil and cooking for 5 more minutes. Garnish with basil and serve.

Per serving: Cal 623; Net Carbs 4.6g; Fat 51.8g; Protein 53g

Canadian Pork Pie

Ingredients for 8 servings

1 cup cooked and mashed cauliflower
1 egg | 2 pounds ground pork
¼ cup butter | ⅓ cup pureed onion
2 cups almond flour | ¾ tsp allspice
¼ tsp xanthan gum | 1 tbsp ground sage
¼ cup shredded mozzarella | 2 tbsp butter

Directions and Total Time: approx. 1 hour 40 minutes

Preheat oven to 350 F. Whisk egg, butter, almond flour, mozzarella cheese, and salt in a bowl. Make 2 balls out of the mixture and refrigerate for 10 minutes. Melt butter in a pan and cook ground pork, salt, onion, and allspice for 5-6 minutes. Remove to a bowl and mix in cauliflower and sage. Roll out the pie balls and place one at the bottom of a greased pie pan. Spread the pork mixture over the crust. Top with the other coat. Bake for 50 minutes then serve.

Per serving: Cal 485; Net Carbs 4g; Fat 41g; Protein 29g

Quick Pork Lo Mein

Ingredients for 4 servings

4 boneless pork chops, cut into ¼-inch strips
1 cup green beans, halved | 1 yellow bell pepper, sliced
1 cup shredded mozzarella | 1 garlic clove, minced
1 egg yolk | 4 green onions, chopped
1-inch ginger knob, grated | 1 tsp toasted sesame seeds
3 tbsp sesame oil | 3 tbsp coconut aminos
Salt and black pepper to taste | 2 tsp sugar-free maple syrup
1 red bell pepper, sliced | 1 tsp fresh ginger paste

Directions and Total Time: approx. 25 min + chilling time

Microwave mozzarella cheese for 2 minutes. Let cool for 1 minute and mix in the egg yolk until well-combined. Lay a parchment paper on a flat surface, pour the cheese mixture on top and cover with another parchment paper. Flatten the dough into 1/8-inch thickness. Take off the parchment paper and cut the dough into thin spaghetti strands. Place in a bowl and refrigerate overnight. Bring 2 cups water to a boil in saucepan and add in pasta. Cook for 1 minute and drain; set aside. Heat sesame oil in a skillet, season pork with salt and pepper, and sear on both sides for 5 minutes. Transfer to a plate. In the same skillet, mix in bell peppers, green beans and cook for 3 minutes. Stir in garlic, ginger, and green onions and cook for 1 minute. Add pork and pasta to the skillet and toss well. In a bowl, toss coconut aminos, remaining sesame oil, maple syrup, and ginger paste. Pour the mixture over the pork mixture; cook for 1 minute. Garnish with sesame seeds to serve.

Per serving: Cal 338; Fats 12g; Net Carbs 4.6g; Protein 43g

Tasty Sambal Pork Noodles

Ingredients for 4 servings

2 (8 oz) packs Miracle noodles, garlic, and herb
1 tbsp olive oil | 2 fresh basil leaves, chopped
1 lb ground pork | 2 tbsp sambal oelek
4 garlic cloves, minced | 2 tbsp plain vinegar
1-inch ginger, grated | 2 tbsp coconut aminos
1 tsp liquid stevia | Salt to taste
1 tbsp tomato paste | 1 tbsp unsalted butter

Directions and Total Time: approx. 60 minutes

Bring 2 cups water to a boil Strain the Miracle noodles and rinse well under hot running water. Allow proper draining and pour them into the boiling water. Cook for 3 minutes and strain again. Place a dry skillet and stir-fry the shirataki noodles until visibly dry, 1-2 minutes. Season with salt and set aside. Heat olive oil in a pot and cook for 5 minutes. Stir in garlic, ginger, and stevia and cook for 1 minute. Add in tomato paste and mix in sambal oelek, vinegar, 1 cup water, aminos, and salt. Continue cooking over low heat for 30 minutes. Add in shirataki, butter; mix well into the sauce. Garnish with basil and serve.

Per serving: Cal 505; Fats 30g; Net Carbs 8.2g; Protein 34g

Pasta & Cheese Pulled Pork

Ingredients for 4 servings

1 cup shredded mozzarella cheese1
lb pork shoulders, divided into 3 pieces
1 egg yolk   2 garlic cloves, minced
2 tbsp olive oil   1 cup grated Monterey Jack
Salt and black pepper to taste   4 oz cream cheese, softened
1 tsp dried thyme   1 cup heavy cream
1 cup chicken broth   ½ tsp white pepper
2 tbsp butter   ½ tsp nutmeg powder
2 medium shallots, minced   2 tbsp chopped parsley

Directions and Total Time: approx. 100 min + chilling time

Microwave mozzarella cheese for 2 minutes. Take out the bowl and allow cooling for 1 minute. Mix in egg yolk until well-combined. Lay a parchment paper on a flat surface, pour the cheese mixture on top and cover with another parchment paper. Flatten the dough into 1/8-inch thickness. Take off the parchment paper and cut the dough into small cubes of the size of macaroni. Place in a bowl and refrigerate overnight. Bring 2 cups water to a boil and add in keto macaroni. Cook for 1 minute and drain; set aside. Heat olive oil in a pot, season pork with salt, pepper, and thyme and sear on both sides until brown. Pour in broth, cover, and cook over low heat for 1 hour or until softened. Remove to a plate and shred into small strands. Set aside. Preheat oven to 380 F. Melt butter in a skillet and sauté shallots and garlic for 3 minutes. Pour in 1 cup water to deglaze the pot and stir in half of Monterey Jack and cream cheeses for 4 minutes. Mix in heavy cream and season with salt, pepper, white pepper, and nutmeg powder. Mix in pasta and pork. Pour mixture into a baking dish and cover with remaining Monterey Jack cheese. Bake for 20 minutes. Garnish with parsley and serve.

Per serving: Cal 603; Fats 43g; Net Carbs 4.5g; Protein 46g

Baked Tenderloin with Lime Chimichurri

Ingredients for 4 servings

1 lime, juiced   ¼ cup olive oil
¼ cup chopped mint leaves   4 lb pork tenderloin
¼ cup rosemary, chopped   Salt and black pepper to taste
2 cloves garlic, minced   Olive oil for rubbing

Directions and Total Time: approx. 1 hour 10 minutes

In a bowl, mix mint, rosemary, garlic, lime juice, olive oil, and salt, and combine well; set aside. Preheat charcoal grill to 450 F creating a direct heat area and indirect heat area. Rub the pork with olive oil, season with salt and pepper. Place the meat over direct heat and sear for 3 minutes on each side; then move to the indirect heat area. Close the lid and cook for 25 minutes on one side, then open, flip, and grill closed for 20 minutes. Remove from the grill and let sit for 5 minutes before slicing. Spoon lemon chimichurri over the pork and serve.

Per serving: Cal 388, Net Carbs 2.1g, Fat 18g, Protein 28g

Green Bean Creamy Pork with Fettuccine

Ingredients for 4 servings

4 pork loin medallions, cut into thin strips
1 cup shredded mozzarella   ½ cup green beans, chopped
1 cup shaved Parmesan cheese   1 lemon, zested and juiced
1 egg yolk   ¼ cup chicken broth
1 tbsp olive oil   1 cup crème fraiche
Salt and black pepper to taste   6 basil leaves, chopped

Directions and Total Time: approx. 40 min + chilling time

Microwave mozzarella cheese for 2 minutes. Allow cooling for 1 minute. Mix in egg yolk until well-combined. Lay a parchment paper on a flat surface, pour the cheese mixture on top and cover with another parchment paper. Flatten the dough into 1/8-inch thickness. Take off the parchment paper and cut the dough into thick fettuccine strands. Place in a bowl and refrigerate overnight. Bring 2 cups water to a boil in saucepan and add the fettuccine. Cook for 1 minute and drain; set aside. Heat olive oil in a skillet, season the pork with salt and pepper, and cook for 10 minutes. Mix in green beans and cook for 5 minutes. Stir in lemon zest, lemon juice, and chicken broth. Cook for 5 more minutes. Add crème fraiche, fettuccine, and basil and cook for 1 minute. Top with Parmesan cheese.

Per serving: Cal 586; Fats 32.3g; Net Carbs 9g; Protein 59g

Cauliflower Pork Goulash

Ingredients for 4 servings

2 tbsp butter   14 ounces canned tomatoes
1 cup mushrooms, sliced   1 garlic clove, minced
1 ½ pounds ground pork   1 tbsp smoked paprika
Salt and black pepper, to taste   2 tbsp parsley, chopped
2 cups cauliflower florets   1 tbsp tomato puree
1 onion, chopped   1 ½ cups water

Directions and Total Time: approx. 30 minutes

Melt butter in a pan over medium heat, stir in pork, and brown for 5 minutes. Place in mushrooms, garlic, and onion, and cook for 4 minutes. Stir in paprika, water, tomatoes, tomato paste, and cauliflower, bring to a simmer and cook for 20 minutes. Add in pepper, salt and parsley.

Per serving: Cal 533; Net Carbs 7g; Fat 41.8g; Protein 35.5g

Basil Prosciutto Pizza

Ingredients for 4 servings

4 prosciutto slices, cut into thirds
2 cups grated mozzarella cheese
2 tbsp cream cheese, softened   ⅓ cup tomato sauce
½ cup almond flour   ⅓ cup sliced mozzarella
1 egg, beaten   6 fresh basil leaves, to serve

Directions and Total Time: approx. 45 minutes

Preheat oven to 390 F and line a pizza pan with parchment paper. Microwave mozzarella cheese and 2 tbsp of cream cheese for 1 minute. Mix in almond meal and egg.

Spread the mixture on the pizza pan and bake for 15 minutes; set aside. Spread the tomato sauce on the crust. Arrange the mozzarella slices on the sauce and then the prosciutto. Bake again for 15 minutes or until the cheese melts. Remove and top with the basil. Slice and serve.

Per serving: Cal 160; Net Carbs 0.5g; Fats 6.2g; Protein 22g

Bell Pepper Noodles with Pork Avocado

Ingredients for 4 servings

2 lb red and yellow bell peppers, spiralized
2 tbsp butter   1 tsp garlic powder
1 lb ground pork   2 avocados, pitted, mashed
Salt and black pepper to taste 2 tbsp chopped pecans

Directions and Total Time: approx. 15 minutes

Melt butter in a skillet and cook the pork until brown, 5 minutes. Season with salt and pepper. Stir in bell peppers, garlic powder and cook until the peppers are slightly tender, 2 minutes. Mix in mashed avocados and cook for 1 minute. Garnish with the pecans and serve warm.

Per serving: Cal 704; Fats 49g; Net Carbs 9.3g; Protein 35g

Caribbean Jerk Pork

Ingredients for 4 servings

1 ½ pounds pork roast   2 tbsp soy sauce, sugar-free
1 tbsp olive oil   ½ cup vegetable stock
¼ cup jerk seasoning

Directions and Total Time: approx. 4 hours 20 minutes

Preheat oven to 350 F and rub the pork with olive oil and jerk seasoning. Heat olive oil in a pan over medium heat and sear the meat well on all sides, about 4-5 minutes. Put the pork in a baking dish, add in the vegetable stock and soy sauce, cover with aluminium foil and bake for 45 minutes, turning once halfway. Then, remove the foil and continue cooking until completely cooked through. Serve.

Per serving: Cal 407; Net Carbs 5.6g; Fat 20g; Protein 46g

Parmesan Pork with Green Pasta

Ingredients for 4 servings

4 boneless pork chops   1 cup grated Parmesan cheese
Salt and black pepper to taste   1 tbsp butter
½ cup basil pesto   4 large turnips, spiralized

Directions and Total Time: approx. 1 hour 30 minutes

Preheat oven to 350 F. Season pork with salt and pepper and place on a greased baking sheet. Spread pesto on the pork and bake for 45 minutes. Pull out the baking sheet and divide half of Parmesan cheese on top of the pork. Cook further for 5 minutes; set aside. Melt butter in a skillet and sauté the turnips for 7 minutes. Stir in the remaining Parmesan and serve in plates, topped with the pork.

Per serving: Cal 532; Fats 28g; Net Carbs 4.9g; Protein 54g

Grilled BBQ Pork Chops

Ingredients for 4 servings

4 pork loin chops, boneless   ½ tsp ginger powder
½ cup sugar-free BBQ sauce   ½ tsp garlic powder
1 tbsp erythritol   2 tsp smoked paprika

Directions and Total Time: approx. 1 hour 50 minutes

In a bowl, mix black pepper, erythritol, ginger powder, ½ tsp garlic powder, and smoked paprika, and rub pork chops on all sides with the mixture. Cover the pork chops with plastic wraps and place in the refrigerator for 90 minutes. Preheat grill. Unwrap the meat, place on the grill grate, and cook for 2 minutes per side. Reduce the heat and brush with BBQ sauce; grill for 5 minutes. Flip and brush again with BBQ sauce. Cook for 5 minutes. Serve.

Per serving: Cal 363, Net Carbs 0g, Fat 26.6g, Protein 34.1g

Pecorino Romano Kohlrabi with Sausage

Ingredients for 4 servings

1 cup grated Pecorino Romano cheese
2 tbsp olive oil   6 garlic cloves, minced
1 cup sliced pork sausage   1 cup cherry tomatoes, halved
4 bacon slices, chopped   7 fresh basil leaves
4 large kohlrabi, spiralized   1 tbsp pine nuts for topping

Directions and Total Time: approx. 15 minutes

Heat olive oil in a skillet and cook sausage and bacon until brown, 5 minutes. Transfer to a plate. Stir in kohlrabi and garlic and cook until tender, 5-7 minutes. Add in cherry tomatoes, salt, and pepper and cook for 2 minutes. Mix in the sausage, bacon, basil, and Pecorino Romano cheese. Garnish with pine nuts and serve warm.

Per serving: Cal 229; Fats 20.2g; Net Carbs 2.4g; Protein 8g

Chorizo Smoky Pizza

Ingredients for 4 servings

2 cups shredded mozzarella   1 tbsp olive oil
1 cup sliced smoked mozzarella   1 cups sliced chorizo
2 tbsp cream cheese, softened   ¼ cup marinara sauce
¾ cup almond flour   1 jalapeño pepper, sliced
2 tbsp almond meal   ¼ red onion, thinly sliced

Directions and Total Time: approx. 45 minutes

Preheat oven to 390 F and line a pizza pan with parchment paper. Microwave the mozzarella and cream cheeses for 30 seconds. Remove, and mix in almond flour and almond meal. Spread the mixture on the pizza pan and bake for 10 minutes or until crusty. Heat olive oil and cook chorizo until brown, 5 minutes. Spread marinara sauce on the crust, top with smoked mozzarella cheese, chorizo, jalapeño pepper, and onion. Bake until the cheese melts, 15 minutes. Remove, slice and serve warm.

Per serving: Cal 302; Net Carbs 1.4g; Fats 17g; Protein 31g

Monterey Jack & Sausage-Pepper Pizza

Ingredients for 4 servings

1 ½ lb Italian pork sausages, crumbled
½ cup grated Monterey Jack cheese
1 cup chopped bell peppers   2 eggs
4 cups grated mozzarella   1 tbsp olive oil
¼ cup grated Parmesan   1 onion, thinly sliced
2 tbsp cream cheese, softened   2 garlic cloves, minced
¼ cup coconut flour   1 cup baby spinach
1 cup almond flour   ½ cup sugar-free pizza sauce

Directions and Total Time: approx. 45 minutes

Preheat oven to 390 F and line a pizza pan with parchment paper. Microwave 2 cups of mozzarella cheese and 2 tbsp of the cream cheese for 1 minute. Mix in sausages, coconut flour, almond flour, Parmesan cheese, and eggs. Spread the mixture on the pizza pan and bake for 15 minutes; set aside.

Heat olive oil in a skillet and sauté onion, garlic, and bell peppers for 5 minutes. Stir in spinach and allow wilting for 3 minutes. Spread the pizza sauce on the crust and top with the bell pepper mixture. Scatter mozzarella and Monterey Jack cheeses on top. Bake for 5 minutes.

Per serving: Cal 460; Net Carbs 3g; Fats 25.6g; Protein 47g

Maple Pork with Spaghetti Squash

Ingredients for 4 servings

3 lb spaghetti squashes, halved and deseeded
2 tbsp minced lemongrass   3 tbsp peanut oil
3 tbsp fresh ginger paste   1 tbsp olive oil
2 tbsp sugar-free maple syrup   Salt and black pepper to taste
2 tbsp coconut aminos   1 lb baby spinach
1 tbsp fish sauce   ½ cup coconut milk
4 boneless pork chops   ¼ cup peanut butter

Directions and Total Time: approx. 1 hour + marinating

In a bowl, mix lemongrass, 2 tbsp of the ginger paste, maple syrup, aminos, and fish sauce. Place the pork in the liquid and coat well. Marinate for 45 minutes. Heat 2 tbsp of peanut oil in a skillet, remove pork from the marinade and sear on both sides for 10-15 minutes. Transfer to a plate and cover with foil. Preheat oven to 380 F. Place the spaghetti squashes on a baking sheet, brush with olive oil and season with salt and pepper. Bake for 45 minutes. Remove the squash and shred with two forks into spaghetti-like strands. Keep warm. Heat the remaining peanut oil in the same skillet and sauté the remaining ginger paste. Add in spinach and cook for 2 minutes; set aside. In a bowl, whisk coconut milk with peanut butter until well combined. Divide the pork into four bowls, add the spaghetti squash to the side, then the spinach and drizzle the peanut sauce on top. Serve immediately.

Per serving: Cal 694; Fats 34g; Net Carbs 7.6g; Protein 53g

Spicy Grilled Pork Spareribs

Ingredients for 4 servings

4 tbsp sugar-free BBQ sauce   3 tsp cayenne powder
+ extra for serving   1 tsp garlic powder
2 tbsp erythritol   1 lb pork spareribs
1 tbsp olive oil

Directions and Total Time: approx. 2 hours

Mix erythritol, salt, pepper, oil, cayenne, and garlic. Brush on the meaty sides of the ribs and wrap in foil. Sit for 30 minutes to marinate. Preheat oven to 400 F, place wrapped ribs on a baking sheet, and cook for 40 minutes. Remove foil, brush with BBQ sauce, and brown under the broiler for 10 minutes on both sides. Slice and serve.

Per serving: Cal 395, Net Carbs 3g, Fat 33g, Protein 21g

Asian-Style Pork and Celeriac Noodles

Ingredients for 4 servings

3 tbsp sugar-free maple syrup   2 tbsp butter
3 tbsp coconut aminos   4 large celeriac, spiralized
1 tbsp fresh ginger paste   1 tbsp sesame oil
¼ tsp Chinese five spice   24 oz bok choy, chopped
Salt and black pepper to taste 2 green onions, chopped
1 lb pork tenderloin, cubed   2 tbsp sesame seeds

Directions and Total Time: approx. 1 hour 20 minutes

Preheat oven to 400 F and line a baking sheet with foil. In a bowl, mix maple syrup, coconut aminos, ginger paste, Chinese five-spice powder, salt, and pepper. Spoon 3 tablespoons of the mixture into a bowl and reserve for topping. Mix pork cubes into the remaining marinade and marinate for 25 minutes. Melt butter in a skillet and sauté celeriac for 7 minutes; set aside. Remove the pork from the marinade onto the baking sheet and bake for 40 minutes. Heat sesame oil in a skillet and sauté bok choy and celeriac pasta for 3 minutes. Transfer to serving bowls and top with pork. Garnish with green onions and sesame seeds. Drizzle with the reserved marinade and serve.

Per serving: Cal 409; Fats 17.8g; Net Carbs 3g; Protein 44g

Pulled Pork Tenderloin with Avocado

Ingredients for 8 servings

4 pounds pork tenderloin   ¼ cup jerk seasoning
1 tbsp avocado oil   6 avocado, sliced
½ cup chicken stock   Salt and black pepper to taste

Directions and Total Time: approx. 2 hours

Rub the pork shoulder with jerk seasoning, and set in a greased baking dish. Pour in the stock, and cook for 1 hour 30 minutes in your oven at 350 F covered with aluminium foil. Discard the foil and cook for another 20 minutes. Leave to rest for 10-15 minutes, and shred it with 2 forks. Serve topped with avocado slices.

Per serving: Cal 567, Net Carbs 4.1g, Fat 42.6g, Protein 42g

Broccoli Tips with Lemon Pork Chops

Ingredients for 6 servings

1 lb fresh broccoli tips, halved
3 tbsp lemon juice   6 pork loin chops
3 cloves garlic, pureed   1 tbsp butter
1 tbsp olive oil   2 tbsp white wine

Directions and Total Time: approx. 30 minutes

Preheat broiler to 400 F and mix the lemon juice, garlic, salt, pepper, and oil in a bowl. Brush the pork with the mixture, place in a baking sheet, and cook for 6 minutes on each side until browned. Share into 6 plates. Melt butter in a small wok or pan and cook broccoli tips for 5 minutes until tender. Drizzle with white wine, sprinkle with salt and pepper and cook for another 5 minutes. Ladle broccoli to the side of the chops and serve with hot sauce.

Per serving: Cal 549, Net Carbs 2g, Fat 48g, Protein 26g

Jerk Pork Pot Roast

Ingredients for 8 servings

4-pound pork roast   ¼ cup Jerk spice blend
1 tbsp olive oil   ½ cup beef stock

Directions and Total Time: approx. 4 hours 20 minutes

Rub the pork with olive oil and the spice blend. Heat a dutch oven over medium heat and sear the meat well on all sides. Add the beef broth. Cover the pot, reduce the heat, and let cook for 4 hours.

Per serving: Cal 282; Net Carbs 0g; Fat 24g; Protein 23g

Swiss Pork Patties with Salad

Ingredients for 4 servings

1 lb ground pork   2 firm tomatoes, sliced
3 tbsp olive oil   ¼ red onion, sliced
2 hearts romaine lettuce, torn 3 oz Swiss cheese, shredded

Directions and Total Time: approx. 30 minutes

Season pork with salt and pepper, mix, and shape several medium-sized patties. Heat 2 tbsp oil in a skillet and fry the patties on both sides for 10 minutes. Transfer to a wire rack to drain oil. When cooled, cut into quarters. Mix lettuce, tomatoes, and onion in a bowl, season with oil, salt and pepper. Toss and add the patties on top. Microwave the cheese for 90 seconds, drizzle it over the salad.

Per serving: Cal 310, Net Carbs 2g, Fat 23g, Protein 22g

Maple Scallion Pork Bites

Ingredients for 4 servings

½ cup + 1 tbsp red wine   1 tbsp sesame oil
1 tbsp + 1/3 cup tamari sauce 1 tsp freshly pureed garlic
1 pork tenderloin, cubed   ½ tsp freshly grated ginger
½ cup sugar-free maple syrup   1 scallion, finely chopped
½ cup sesame seeds

Directions and Total Time: approx. 50 minutes

Preheat oven to 350 F. In a zipper bag, combine ½ cup of red wine with 1 tbsp of tamari sauce. Add in pork cubes, seal the bag, and marinate the meat in the fridge overnight. Remove from the fridge and drain. Pour maple syrup and sesame seeds into two separate bowls; roll the pork in maple syrup and then in the sesame seeds. Place on a greased baking sheet and bake for 35 minutes. In a bowl, mix the remaining wine, tamari sauce, sesame oil, garlic, and ginger. Pour the sauce into a bowl. Transfer pork to a platter and garnish with scallions. Serve with sauce.

Per serving: Cal 352; Net Carbs 6.4g; Fat 18g; Protein 39g

Pork Medallions with Pancetta

Ingredients for 4 servings

1 lb pork loin, cut into medallions
2 onions, chopped   ½ cup vegetable stock
6 pancetta slices, chopped   Salt and black pepper, to taste

Directions and Total Time: approx. 55 minutes

Set a pan over medium heat, and cook the pancetta until crispy; remove to a plate. Add onions and stir-fry for 5 minutes; set aside to the same plate as pancetta. Add pork medallions to the pan, season with pepper and salt, brown for 3 minutes on each side, turn, reduce heat, and cook for 7 minutes. Stir in the stock, and cook for 2 minutes. Return the pancetta and onions and cook for 1 minute.

Per serving: Cal 325, Net Carbs 6g, Fat 18g, Protein 36g

Golden Pork Chops with Mushrooms

Ingredients for 6 servings

2 (14-oz) cans Mushroom soup
1 onion, chopped   ½ cup sliced mushrooms
6 pork chops   Salt and black pepper to taste

Directions and Total Time: approx. 1 hour 15 minutes

Preheat the oven to 375 F. Season the pork chops with salt and pepper, and place them in a baking dish. Combine the soup, mushrooms, and onions in a bowl. Pour this mixture over the pork chops. Bake for 45 minutes.

Per serving: Cal 403; Net Carbs 8g; Fat 32.6g; Protein 19g

Cumin Pork Chops

Ingredients for 4 servings

4 pork chops   1 tsp chili powder
¾ cup cumin powder   Salt and black pepper to taste

Directions and Total Time: approx. 25 minutes

In a bowl, combine the cumin with black pepper, salt, and chili. Place in the pork chops and rub them well. Heat a grill over medium temperature, add in the pork chops, cook for 5 minutes, flip, and cook for 5 minutes.

Per serving: Cal 349; Net Carbs 4g; Fat 18.6g; Protein 42g

SEAFOOD

Tasty Shrimp in Creamy Butter Sauce

Ingredients for 2 servings

½ oz grated Parmesan cheese	2 tbsp curry leaves
1 egg, beaten in a bowl	2 tbsp butter
¼ tsp curry powder	½ onion, diced
2 tsp almond flour	½ cup heavy cream
12 shrimp, shelled	½ ounce cheddar cheese
3 tbsp coconut oil	Salt and black pepper to taste

Directions and Total Time: approx. 30 minutes

Combine Parmesan, curry powder, and almond flour in a bowl. Melt the coconut oil in a skillet over medium heat. Dip the shrimp in the egg first, and then coat with the dry mixture. Fry until golden and crispy. In another skillet, melt the butter. Add onion and cook for 3 minutes. Add in curry leaves and cook for 30 seconds. Stir in heavy cream and cheddar cheese and cook until thickened. Add the shrimp and coat well. Adjust the seasoning, and serve.

Per serving: Cal 560; Net Carbs 4.3g; Fat 56g; Protein 18g

Cheesy Baked Trout with Zucchini

Ingredients for 4 servings

4 deboned trout fillets	1 cup Greek yogurt
2 zucchinis, sliced	¼ cup cheddar cheese, grated
1 tbsp butter, melted	Grated Parmesan for topping

Directions and Total Time: approx. 40 minutes

Preheat oven to 390 F and brush the fish and zucchini slices with melted butter. Season with salt and black pepper and spread in a greased baking dish. Mix the Greek yogurt with cheddar cheese in a bowl. Pour and smear the mixture on the fish, and sprinkle with Parmesan cheese. Bake for 30 minutes until golden brown on top.

Per serving: Cal 362; Net Carbs 5.8g; Fat 23g; Protein 25.6g

Chimichurri Shrimp

Ingredients for 4 servings

1 pound shrimp, deveined	Juice of 1 lime
2 tbsp olive oil	Salt and black pepper to taste

Chimichurri sauce:

¼ cup olive oil	¼ cup red wine vinegar
2 garlic cloves	2 cups parsley
¼ cup red onion, chopped	¼ tsp red pepper flakes

Directions and Total Time: approx. 45 minutes

Place all chimichurri ingredients in the blender. Process until smooth. Combine shrimp, olive oil, and lime juice in a bowl and marinate in the fridge for 30 minutes. Preheat grill to medium heat. Add shrimp and cook for 2 minutes per side. Serve drizzled with the sauce.

Per serving: Cal 283; Net Carbs 3.5g; Fat 20g; Protein 16g

Baked Salmon with Pistachio Crust

Ingredients for 4 servings

4 salmon fillets	2 tsp lemon zest
¼ cup mayonnaise	1 tbsp olive oil
½ cup ground pistachios	A pinch of pepper
1 chopped shallot	1 cup heavy cream

Directions and Total Time: approx. 35 minutes

Preheat oven to 375 F. Brush salmon with mayo and season with salt and pepper. Coat with pistachios. Place in a lined baking dish and bake for 15 minutes. Heat the olive oil in a saucepan and sauté shallot for 3 minutes. Stir in heavy cream and lemon zest. Bring to a boil and cook until thickened. Serve salmon with the sauce.

Per serving: Cal 563; Net Carbs 6g; Fat 47g; Protein 34g

Curried Homemade Shrimp

Ingredients for 4 servings

2 tbsp Parmesan, grated	2 tbsp curry leaves
1 egg, beaten	2 tbsp butter
½ tsp curry powder	1 onion, chopped
2 tsp coconut flour	½ cup coconut cream
1 pound shrimp, shelled	2 tbsp mozzarella, shredded
3 tbsp coconut oil	

Directions and Total Time: approx. 25 minutes

In a bowl, combine all dry ingredients for the batter. Melt coconut oil in a skillet over medium heat. Dip the shrimp in the egg first, and then coat with the dry mixture. Fry until golden and crispy. In another skillet, melt butter, and sauté onion for 3 minutes. Add curry leaves, cook for 30 seconds and stir in coconut cream and mozzarella cheese until thickened. Add the shrimp to coat thoroughly. Serve.

Per serving: Cal 422; Net Carbs 4.8g; Fat 32.2g; Protein 29g

Speedy Fish Tacos

Ingredients for 4 servings

1 tbsp olive oil	1 tsp smoked paprika
1 red chili pepper, minced	4 low carb tortillas
1 tsp coriander seeds	Salt and black pepper to taste
4 cod fillets, roughly chopped	1 lemon, juiced

Directions and Total Time: approx. 20 minutes

Season the fish with salt, pepper, and paprika. Heat olive oil in a skillet over medium heat. Add cod and chili pepper and stir-fry for 6 minutes. Pour in lemon juice and cook for another 2 minutes. Divide the fish between the tortillas.

Per serving: Cal 447; Net Carbs 4.3g; Fat 21g; Protein 24.3g

Asian-Style Steamed Mussels

Ingredients for 6 servings

5 tbsp sesame oil	3 lb mussels, cleaned
1 onion, chopped	2 garlic cloves, minced

12 oz coconut milk
16 oz white wine
1 lime, juiced

2 tsp red curry powder
2 tbsp cilantro, chopped

Directions and Total Time: approx. 25 minutes

Warm the sesame oil in a saucepan over medium heat and cook onion and garlic cloves for 3 minutes. Pour in wine, coconut milk, and curry powder and cook for 5 minutes. Add mussels, turn off the heat, cover the saucepan, and steam the mussels until the shells open up, 5 minutes. Discard any closed mussels. Top with cilantro and serve.

Per serving: Cal 323; Net Carbs 5.4g; Fat 16g; Protein 28.2g

Easy Coconut Cocktail Crab Balls

Ingredients for 4 servings

1 lime, juiced
2 tbsp coconut oil
8 oz lump crab meat

2 tsp wasabi sauce
1 egg, beaten
1 tbsp coconut flour

Directions and Total Time: approx. 15 minutes

Mix together the crab meat, wasabi sauce, lime juice, and egg in a bowl. Season with salt and black pepper. Make balls out of the mixture. Fry in melted coconut oil over medium heat for 5-6 minutes in total; serve.

Per serving: Cal 277; Net Carbs 5.1g; Fat 11g; Protein 24.2g

Party Smoked Salmon Balls

Ingredients for 6 servings

12 oz sliced smoked salmon, finely chopped
1 parsnip, cooked and mashed 3 eggs, beaten
Salt and chili pepper to taste 2 tbsp pesto sauce
4 tbsp olive oil 1 tbsp pork rinds, crushed

Directions and Total Time: approx. 30 minutes

In a bowl, add the salmon, eggs, pesto sauce, pork rinds, salt, and chili pepper. With your hands, mix and make 6 compact balls. Heat olive oil in a skillet over medium heat and fry the balls for 3 minutes on each side until golden brown. Remove to a wire rack to cool.

Per serving: Cal 254; Net Carbs 4.3g; Fat 18g; Protein 17g

Tuna Stuffed Avocado

Ingredients for 4 servings

2 avocados, halved and pitted 2 tbsp chives, chopped
4 ounces Colby Jack, grated Salt and black pepper, to taste
2 ounces canned tuna, flaked ½ cup curly endive, chopped

Directions and Total Time: approx. 20 minutes

Set oven to 360 F. Set avocado halves in an ovenproof dish. In a bowl, mix colby jack cheese, chives, pepper, salt, and tuna. Stuff the cheese/tuna mixture in avocado halves. Bake for 15 minutes or until the top is golden brown. Sprinkle with cilantro and serve with curly endive.

Per serving: Cal: 286; Net Carbs 9g; Fat 23.9g; Protein 11g

Mediterranean Tilapia

Ingredients for 4 servings

4 Tilapia fillets
2 garlic cloves, minced
2 tsp oregano
14 ounces diced tomatoes

1 tbsp olive oil
½ red onion, chopped
2 tbsp parsley
¼ cup kalamata olives

Directions and Total Time: approx. 30 minutes

Heat oil in a skillet over medium heat and cook onion for 3 minutes. Add garlic and oregano and cook for 30 seconds. Stir in tomatoes and bring the mixture to a boil. Reduce the heat and simmer for 5 minutes. Add olives and tilapia. Cook for 8 minutes. Serve the fish with tomato sauce!

Per serving: Cal 182; Net Carbs 6g; Fat 15g; Protein 23g

Pomodoro Zoodles with Sardines

Ingredients for 2 servings

½ cup canned chopped tomatoes
4 cups zoodles 1 tbsp capers
2 ounces cubed bacon 1 tbsp parsley
4 oz canned sardines, chopped 1 tsp minced garlic

Directions and Total Time: approx. 10 minutes

Pour some of the sardine oil in a pan. Add garlic and cook for 1 minute. Add the bacon and cook for 2 more minutes. Stir in the tomatoes and let simmer for 5 minutes. Add zoodles and sardines and cook for 3 minutes.

Per serving: Cal 230; Net Carbs 6g; Fat 31g; Protein 20g

Tuna Salad Pickle Boats

Ingredients for 12 servings

18 oz canned and drained tuna
6 large dill pickles ¼ cup sugar-free mayonnaise
¼ tsp garlic powder 1 tsp onion powder

Directions and Total Time: approx. 40 minutes

Mix the mayo, tuna, onion and garlic powders in a bowl. Cut the pickles in half, lengthwise. Top each half with tuna mixture. Place in the fridge for 30 minutes and serve.

Per serving: Cal 118; Net Carbs 1.5g; Fat 10g; Protein 11g

Nutty Sea Bass

Ingredients for 2 servings

2 sea bass fillets
2 tbsp butter

⅓ cup roasted hazelnuts
A pinch of cayenne pepper

Directions and Total Time: approx. 30 minutes

Preheat oven to 420 F. Line a baking dish with waxed paper. Melt butter and brush it over the fillets. In a food processor, combine the remaining ingredients. Coat the fish with the hazelnut mixture. Bake for 15 minutes.

Per serving: Cal 467; Net Carbs 2.8g; Fat 31g; Protein 40g

Blackened Fish Tacos with Slaw

Ingredients for 4 servings

2 tbsp olive oil	½ cup red cabbage, shredded
1 tsp chili powder	1 tbsp lemon juice
2 tilapia fillets	1 tsp apple cider vinegar
1 tsp paprika	1 tbsp olive oil
4 zero carb tortillas	Salt and black pepper to taste

Directions and Total Time: approx. 20 minutes

Season tilapia with chili powder, paprika, salt, and pepper. Heat half of olive oil in a skillet over medium heat. Add tilapia and cook until blackened, about 6 minutes. Cut into strips. Divide tilapia between the tortillas. Combine cabbage, lemon juice, vinegar, and remaining olive oil in a bowl; toss to combine. Add to the tortillas and serve.

Per serving: Cal 260; Net Carbs 3.5g; Fat 20g; Protein 13.8g

Crab Cakes

Ingredients for 8 servings

2 tbsp coconut oil	2 tsp Dijon mustard
1 tbsp lemon juice	1 egg, beaten
1 cup lump crab meat	1 ½ tbsp coconut flour
2 tbsp parsley	Salt and black pepper to taste

Directions and Total Time: approx. 15 minutes

Place crab meat in a bowl. Add the remaining ingredients, except for coconut oil. Mix well to combine. Make 8 crab cakes out of the mixture. Melt the oil in a skillet. Add the crab cakes and cook for 2-3 minutes per side.

Per serving: Cal 65; Net Carbs 3.6g; Fat 5g; Protein 5.3g

Saucy Salmon in Tarragon Sauce

Ingredients for 2 servings

2 salmon fillets	2 tbsp butter
1 tbsp duck fat	½ tsp tarragon
Salt and black pepper to taste	¼ cup heavy cream

Directions and Total Time: approx. 20 minutes

Season the salmon with salt and pepper. Melt the duck fat in a pan over medium heat. Add salmon and cook for 4 minutes on both sides; set aside. In the same pan, melt the butter and add the tarragon. Cook for 30 seconds to infuse the flavors. Whisk in heavy cream and cook for 1 minute. Serve salmon topped with the sauce.

Per serving: Cal 468; Net Carbs 1.5g; Fat 40g; Protein 22g

Garlic-Lime Shrimp Pasta

Ingredients for 4 servings

1 lb jumbo shrimp, deveined	1 lime, zested and juiced
2 tbsp butter	3 zucchinis, spiralized
4 garlic cloves, minced	2 tbsp chopped parsley
1 pinch red chili flakes	1 cup grated Parmesan cheese
¼ cup white wine	Salt and black pepper to taste

Directions and Total Time: approx. 20 minutes

Melt butter in a skillet and cook the shrimp for 3-4 minutes. Flip and stir in garlic and red chili flakes. Cook further for 1 minute; set aside. Pour wine and lime juice into the skillet, and cook until reduced by a third. Stir to deglaze the bottom. Mix in zucchinis, lime zest, shrimp, and parsley. Season with salt and pepper, and toss well. Cook for 2 minutes. Top with Parmesan cheese and serve.

Per serving: Cal 255; Net Carbs 9.8g; Fats 8g; Protein 32g

Angel Hair Shirataki with Creamy Shrimp

Ingredients for 4 servings

2 (8 oz) packs angel hair shirataki noodles

1 tbsp olive oil	½ cup dry white wine
1 lb shrimp, deveined	1 ½ cups heavy cream
2 tbsp unsalted butter	½ cup grated Asiago cheese
6 garlic cloves, minced	2 tbsp chopped fresh parsley

Directions and Total Time: approx. 25 minutes

Heat olive oil in a skillet, season the shrimp with salt and pepper, and cook on both sides, 2 minutes; set aside. Melt butter in the skillet and sauté garlic. Stir in wine and cook until reduced by half, scraping the bottom of the pan to deglaze. Stir in heavy cream. Let simmer for 1 minute and stir in Asiago cheese to melt. Return the shrimp to the sauce and sprinkle the parsley on top. Bring 2 cups of water to a boi. Strain shirataki pasta and rinse under hot running water. Allow proper draining and pour the shirataki pasta into the boiling water. Cook for 3 minutes and strain again. Place a dry skillet and stir-fry the pasta until dry, 1-2 minutes. Season with salt and plate. Top with the shrimp sauce and serve.

Per serving: Cal 493; Net Carbs 6.3g; Fats 32g; Protein 33g

Tuna & Zucchini Traybake

Ingredients for 4 servings

1 bunch asparagus, trimmed and cut into 1-inch pieces
1 (15 oz) can tuna in water, drained and flaked

1 tbsp butter	2 cups coconut milk
1 cup green beans, chopped	4 zucchinis, spiralized
2 tbsp arrowroot starch	1 cup grated Parmesan cheese

Directions and Total Time: approx. 40 minutes

Preheat the oven to 380 F. Melt butter in a skillet and sauté green beans and asparagus until softened, about 5 minutes; set aside. In a saucepan, mix in arrowroot starch with coconut milk. Bring to a boil over medium heat with frequent stirring until thickened, 3 minutes. Stir in half of Parmesan cheese until melted. Mix in the green beans, asparagus, zucchinis, and tuna. Season with salt and pepper. Transfer the mixture to a baking dish and cover with the remaining Parmesan cheese. Bake until the cheese is melted and golden, 20 minutes. Serve.

Per serving: Cal 389; Net Carbs 8.1g; Fats 34g; Protein 11g

Garlic & Parsley Shrimp

Ingredients for 6 servings

½ cup ghee, divided
2 lb shrimp, deveined
Salt and black pepper to taste
¼ tsp sweet paprika
1 tbsp minced garlic
3 tbsp water
1 lemon, zested and juiced
2 tbsp chopped parsley

Directions and Total Time: approx. 30 minutes

Melt half of the ghee in a skillet, season the shrimp with salt, pepper, paprika, and add to the ghee. Stir in garlic and cook for 4 minutes on both sides. Remove to a bowl. Put remaining ghee in the skillet; add lemon zest, juice, and water. Add shrimp, parsley, and adjust taste with salt and black pepper. Cook for 2 minutes on low heat. Serve the shrimp, drizzled with sauce and some squash pasta.

Per serving: Cal 258; Net Carbs 2g; Fat 22g; Protein 13g

Haddock in Garlic Butter Sauce

Ingredients for 6 servings

2 tsp olive oil
6 haddock fillets
Salt and black pepper to taste
4 tbsp salted butter
4 cloves garlic, minced
¼ cup lemon juice
3 tbsp white wine
2 tbsp chopped chives

Directions and Total Time: approx. 20 minutes

Heat oil in a skillet and season the haddock with salt and black pepper. Fry the fillets for 4 minutes on one side, flip and cook for 1 minute; set aside. In another skillet, melt butter and sauté garlic for 2 minutes. Add in lemon juice, wine, and chives. Season with salt, pepper, and cook for 3 minutes. Put the fish in the skillet, spoon sauce over, cook for 30 seconds and turn the heat off. Top with sauce and serve with buttered green beans.

Per serving: Cal 264; Net Carbs 2.3g; Fat 17.3g; Protein 20g

Traditional Salmon Panzanella

Ingredients for 4 servings

1 lb skinned salmon, cut into
4 steaks each
1 cucumber, cubed
Salt and black pepper to taste
8 black olives, chopped
1 tbsp capers, rinsed
2 large tomatoes, diced
3 tbsp white wine vinegar
¼ cup thinly sliced red onion
3 tbsp olive oil
2 slices zero carb bread, cubed
¼ cup sliced basil leaves

Directions and Total Time: approx. 25 minutes

Preheat grill to 360 F. In a bowl, mix cucumbers, olives, pepper, capers, tomatoes, wine vinegar, onion, olive oil, bread, and basil leaves. Let sit for the flavors to incorporate.Season the salmon with salt and pepper; grill them on both sides for 8 minutes. Serve the salmon steaks warm on a bed of the veggies salad.

Per serving: Cal 338; Net Carbs 3.1g; Fat 21g; Protein 28.5g

White Wine Salmon Shirataki Fettucine

Ingredients for 4 servings

2 (8 oz) packs shirataki fettuccine
5 tbsp butter
4 salmon fillets, cubed
Salt and black pepper to taste
3 garlic cloves, minced
1 ¼ cups heavy cream
½ cup dry white wine
1 tsp grated lemon zest
1 cup baby spinach

Directions and Total Time: approx. 35 minutes

Boil 2 cups of water in a pot. Strain the shirataki pasta t and rinse well under hot running water. Allow proper draining and pour the shirataki pasta into the boiling water. Cook for 3 minutes and strain again. Place a dry skillet and stir-fry the shirataki pasta until visibly dry, 1-2 minutes; set aside. Melt half of the butter in a skillet; season the salmon with salt and pepper and cook for 8 minutes; set aside. Add the remaining butter to the skillet and stir in garlic. Cook for 30 seconds. Mix in heavy cream, white wine, lemon zest, salt, and pepper. Boil over low heat for 5 minutes. Stir in spinach, let wilt for 2 minutes and stir in shirataki fettuccine and salmon. Serve warm.

Per serving: Cal 795; Net Carbs 9g; Fats 46g; Protein 72g

Creamy Salmon with Lemon

Ingredients for 4 servings

½ cup grated Pecorino Romano cheese
1 cup sour cream
½ tbsp minced dill
½ lemon, zested and juiced
4 salmon steaks

Directions and Total Time: approx. 30 minutes

Preheat oven to 400 F and line a baking sheet with parchment paper; set aside. In a bowl, mix sour cream, dill, lemon zest, juice, salt, and pepper; set aside. Season the fish with salt and pepper, drizzle with lemon juice and arrange in the baking sheet. Spread sour cream mixture on each fish steak and sprinkle with Pecorino Romano cheese. Bake for 15 minutes. Broil the top for 2 minutes until nicely brown. Serve with buttery green beans.

Per serving: Cal 288; Net Carbs 1.2g; Fat 23.4g; Protein 16g

Coconut Crab Cakes

Ingredients for 8 servings

2 tbsp coconut oil
1 tbsp lime juice
1 cup lump crab meat
2 tsp Dijon mustard
1 egg, beaten
1 ½ tbsp coconut flour

Directions and Total Time: approx. 15 minutes

In a bowl, to the crab meat add all ingredients, except for the oil; mix well to combine. Make patties out of the mixture. Melt coconut oil in a skillet over medium heat. Cook the crabmeat patties for about 3-4 minutes per side.

Per serving: Cal 215; Net Carbs 3.6g; Fat 11g; Protein 15g

Spicy Smoked Mackerel Cakes

Ingredients for 6 servings

4 smoked mackerel steaks, bones removed, flaked
1 rutabaga, peeled and diced   3 eggs, beaten
Salt and chili pepper to taste   2 tbsp mayonnaise
3 tbsp olive oil + for rubbing   1 tbsp pork rinds, crushed

Directions and Total Time: approx. 30 minutes

Bring rutabaga to boil in salted water for 8 minutes. Drain, transfer to a mixing bowl, and mash the lumps. Add mackerel, eggs, mayonnaise, pork rinds, salt, and chili pepper. Make 6 compact patties. Heat olive oil in a skillet and fry the patties for 3 minutes on each side. Remove onto a wire rack to cool. Serve cakes with sesame sauce.

Per serving: Cal 324; Net Carbs 2.2g; Fat 27g; Protein 16g

Stuffed Avocado with Yogurt & Crabmeat

Ingredients for 4 servings

3 oz plain yogurt, strained overnight in a cheesecloth
1 tsp olive oil   ¼ cup almonds, chopped
1 cup crabmeat   1 tsp smoked paprika
2 avocados, halved and pitted Salt and black pepper, to taste

Directions and Total Time: approx. 25 minutes

Set oven to 425 F. Grease oil on a baking pan. In a bowl, mix crabmeat, yogurt, salt, and pepper. Fill avocado halves with almonds and crabmeat/cheese mixture and bake for 18 minutes. Decorate with paprika to serve.

Per serving: Cal 264; Net Carbs 11g; Fat 24.4g; Protein 4g

Hazelnut Cod Fillets

Ingredients for 2 servings

2 cod fillets   ¼ cup roasted hazelnuts
2 tbsp ghee   A pinch of cayenne pepper

Directions and Total Time: approx. 30 minutes

Preheat your oven to 425 F. Line a baking dish with waxed paper. Melt the ghee and brush it over the fish. In a food processor, combine the rest of the ingredients. Coat the cod with the hazelnut mixture. Place in the oven and bake for about 15 minutes. Serve.

Per serving: Cal 467; Net Carbs 2.8g; Fat 31g; Protein 40g

Wine Shrimp Scampi Pizza

Ingredients for 4 servings

½ cup almond flour   ½ tsp dried basil
¼ tsp salt   ½ tsp dried parsley
2 tbsp ground psyllium husk ½ lemon, juiced
3 tbsp olive oil   ½ lb shrimp, deveined
2 tbsp butter   2 cups grated cheese blend
2 garlic cloves, minced ½ tsp Italian seasoning
¼ cup white wine   ¼ cup grated Parmesan

Directions and Total Time: approx. 35 minutes

Preheat oven to 390 F and line a baking sheet with parchment paper. In a bowl, mix almond flour, salt, psyllium powder, 1 tbsp of olive oil, and 1 cup of lukewarm water until dough forms. Spread the mixture on the pizza pan and bake for 10 minutes. Heat butter and the remaining olive oil in a skillet. Sauté garlic for 30 seconds. Mix in white wine, reduce by half, and stir in basil, parsley and lemon juice. Stir in shrimp and cook for 3 minutes. Mix in the cheese blend and Italian seasoning. Let the cheese melt, 3 minutes. Spread the shrimp mixture on the crust and top with Parmesan cheese. Bake for 5 minutes or until Parmesan melts. Slice and serve warm.

Per serving: Cal 423; Net Carbs 3.9g; Fats 34g; Protein 23g

Shallot Mussel with Shirataki

Ingredients for 4 servings

2 (8 oz) packs angel hair shirataki
1 lb mussels   2 tsp red chili flakes
1 cup white wine   ½ cup fish stock
4 tbsp olive oil   1 ½ cups heavy cream
3 shallots, finely chopped 2 tbsp chopped fresh parsley
6 garlic cloves, minced Salt and black pepper to taste

Directions and Total Time: approx. 25 minutes

Bring 2 cups of water to a boil in a pot. Strain the shirataki pasta and rinse well under hot running water. Drain and transfer to the boiling water. Cook for 3 minutes and strain again. Place a large dry skillet and stir-fry the shirataki pasta until visibly dry, 1-2 minutes; set aside. Pour mussels and white wine into a pot, cover, and cook for 3-4 minutes. Strain mussels and reserve the cooking liquid. Let cool, discard any closed mussels, and remove the meat out of ¾ of the mussel shells. Set aside with the remaining mussels in the shells. Heat olive oil in a skillet and sauté shallots, garlic, and chili flakes for 3 minutes. Mix in reduced wine and fish stock. Allow boiling and whisk in remaining butter and then the heavy cream. Season with salt, and pepper, and mix in parsley. Pour in shirataki pasta, mussels and toss well in the sauce. Serve.

Per serving: Cal 471; Net Carbs 6.9g; Fats 34g; Protein 18g

Nori Shrimp Rolls

Ingredients for 5 servings

2 cups cooked shrimp   5 hand roll nori sheets
1 tbsp Sriracha sauce   ¼ cup mayonnaise
¼ cucumber, julienned   1 tbsp dill

Directions and Total Time: approx. 10 minutes

Chop the shrimp and combine with mayo, dill, and sriracha sauce in a bowl. Place a single nori sheet on a flat surface and spread about a fifth of the shrimp mixture. Roll the nori sheet as desired. Repeat with the other ingredients.

Per serving: Cal 130; Net Carbs 1g; Fat 10g; Protein 8.7g

Hazelnut-Crusted Salmon

Ingredients for 4 servings

4 salmon fillets	1 chopped shallot
Salt and black pepper to taste	2 tsp lemon zest
¼ cup mayonnaise	1 tbsp olive oil
½ cup chopped hazelnuts	1 cup heavy cream

Directions and Total Time: approx. 35 minutes

Preheat oven to 360 F. Brush the salmon with mayonnaise and coat with hazelnuts. Place in a lined baking dish and bake for 15 minutes. Heat olive oil in a saucepan and sauté shallot for 3 minutes. Stir in lemon zest and heavy cream and bring to a boil; cook until thickened, 5 minutes. Adjust seasoning and drizzle the sauce over the fish to serve.

Per serving: Cal 563; Net Carbs 6g; Fat 47g; Protein 34g

Fish & Cauliflower Parmesan Gratin

Ingredients for 4 servings

1 head cauliflower, cut into florets	
2 cod fillets, cubed	1 cup crème fraiche
3 white fish fillets, cubed	¼ cup grated Parmesan
1 tbsp butter, melted	Grated Parmesan for topping

Directions and Total Time: approx. 40 minutes

Preheat oven to 400 F. Coat fish cubes and broccoli with butter. Spread in a greased baking dish. Mix crème fraiche with Parmesan cheese, pour and smear the cream on the fish, and sprinkle with some more Parmesan cheese. Bake for 25-30 minutes. Let sit for 5 minutes and serve in plates.

Per serving: Cal 354; Net Carbs 4g; Fat 17g; Protein 28g

Broccoli & Fish Gratin

Ingredients for 4 servings

¼ cup grated Pecorino Romano cheese + some more	
2 salmon fillets, cubed	1 tbsp butter, melted
3 white fish, cubed	Salt and black pepper to taste
1 broccoli, cut into florets	1 cup crème fraiche

Directions and Total Time: approx. 45 minutes

Preheat oven to 400 F. Toss the fish cubes and broccoli in butter and season with salt and pepper. Spread in a greased dish. Mix crème fraiche with Pecorino Romano cheese, pour and smear the cream on the fish. Bake for 30 minutes. Serve with lemon-mustard asparagus.

Per serving: Cal 354; Net Carbs 4g; Fat 17g; Protein 28g

Salmon Caesar Salad with Poached Eggs

Ingredients for 4 servings

½ cup chopped smoked salmon
2 tbsp heinz low carb caesar dressing
3 cups water   6 slices pancetta
8 eggs
2 cups torn romaine lettuce

Directions and Total Time: approx. 15 minutes

Boil water in a pot for 5 minutes. Crack each egg into a small bowl and gently slide into the water. Poach for 2-3 minutes, remove, and transfer to a paper towel to dry. Poach the remaining 7 eggs. Put the pancetta in a skillet and fry for 6 minutes, turning once. Allow cooling, and chop into small pieces. Toss the lettuce, smoked salmon, pancetta, and caesar dressing in a salad bowl. Top with two eggs each, and serve immediately.

Per serving: Cal 260; Net Carbs 5g; Fat 21g; Protein 8g

Avocado & Cauliflower Salad with Prawns

Ingredients for 6 servings

1 cauliflower head, florets only	
1 lb medium-sized prawns	3 tbsp chopped dill
¼ cup + 1 tbsp olive oil	¼ cup lemon juice
1 avocado, chopped	2 tbsp lemon zest

Directions and Total Time: approx. 30 minutes

Heat 1 tbsp olive oil in a skillet and cook the prawns for 8-10 minutes. Microwave cauliflower for 5 minutes. Place prawns, cauliflower, and avocado in a large bowl. Whisk together the remaining olive oil, lemon zest, juice, dill, and some salt and pepper, in another bowl. Pour the dressing over, toss to combine and serve immediately.

Per serving: Cal 214; Net Carbs 5g; Fat 17g; Protein 15g

Fish Fritters

Ingredients for 4 servings

1 pound cod fillets, sliced	Salt and black pepper to taste
¼ cup mayonnaise	1 cup Swiss cheese, grated
¼ cup almond flour	1 tbsp chopped dill
2 eggs	3 tbsp olive oil

Directions and Total Time: approx. 40 min + cooling time

Mix the fish, mayo, flour, eggs, salt, pepper, Swiss cheese, and dill, in a bowl. Cover the bowl with plastic wrap and refrigerate for 2 hours. Warm olive oil and fetch 2 tbsp of fish mixture into the skillet, use the back of a spatula to flatten the top. Cook for 4 minutes, flip, and fry for 4 more. Remove onto a wire rack and repeat until the fish batter is over; add more oil if needed.

Per serving: Cal 633; Net Carbs 7g; Fat 46.9g; Protein 39g

VEGAN & VEGETARIAN

Broccoli & Mushrooms with Pasta

Ingredients for 4 servings

1 cup sliced cremini mushrooms
1 cup grated Gruyere cheese
4 large broccoli   2 tbsp almond flour
2 tbsp olive oil   1 ½ cups almond milk
2 garlic cloves, minced   Salt and black pepper to taste
4 scallions, chopped   ¼ cup chopped fresh parsley

Directions and Total Time: approx. 20 minutes

Cut off the florets of the broccoli heads, leaving only the stems. Cut the ends of the stem flatly and evenly. Run the stems through a spiralizer to make the noodles. Heat olive oil in a skillet and sauté the broccoli noodles, mushrooms, garlic, and scallions until softened, 5 minutes. In a bowl, combine almond flour and almond milk, and pour the mixture over the vegetables. Stir and allow thickening for 2-3 minutes. Whisk in half of the Gruyere cheese to melt and adjust the taste with salt and black pepper. Garnish with the remaining Gruyere cheese and parsley, and serve.

Per serving: Cal 221; Net Carbs 1.4g; Fats 15g; Protein 9.3g

Spaghetti Bolognese with Tofu

Ingredients for 4 servings

2 tbsp butter   1 garlic clove, minced
4 large parsnips, spiralized   2 cups sugar-free passata
2 tbsp olive oil   ¼ cup vegetable broth
1 cup crumbled firm tofu   Salt and black pepper to taste
1 white onion, chopped   1 small bunch basil, chopped
2 celery stalks, chopped   1 cup grated Parmesan cheese

Directions and Total Time: approx. 25 minutes

Melt butter in a skillet and sauté parsnips for 5 minutes. Season with salt and set aside. Heat olive oil in a pot and cook tofu for 5 minutes. Stir in onion, garlic, and celery and cook for 5 minutes. Mix in passata and vegetable broth and season with salt and pepper. Cover the pot and cook until the sauce thickens, 8-10 minutes. Stir in basil. Divide the pasta between serving plates and top with the sauce. Sprinkle the Parmesan cheese on top and serve warm.

Per serving: Cal 424; Net Carbs 31g; Fats 20g; Protein 22g

Tofu Meatballs with Cauli Mash

Ingredients for 4 servings

1 cup white button mushrooms, chopped
1 lb tofu, pressed and cubed   2 cups tomato sauce
2 garlic cloves, minced   6 fresh basil leaves to garnish
2 small red onions, chopped   1 lb cauliflower, cut into florets
1 red bell pepper, chopped   Salt and black pepper to taste
½ cup golden flaxseed meal   2 tbsp butter
½ almond milk   ½ cup heavy cream
1 ½ + 1 tbsp olive oil   ¼ cup grated Parmesan

Directions and Total Time: approx. 65 minutes

Preheat oven to 350 F and line a baking tray with parchment paper. In a bowl, add silken tofu, half of garlic, half of onion, mushrooms, salt, and pepper; mix to combine. Mold bite-size balls out of the mixture. Place flaxseed meal and almond milk each in a shallow dish. Dip each ball in almond milk and then in the flaxseed meal. Place on the baking sheet and bake for 10 minutes. Heat 1 ½ tbsp of olive oil in a saucepan and fry in the oil until golden brown on all sides; set aside. Heat the remaining oil in the same saucepan and sauté onion, garlic, and bell pepper for 5 minutes. Pour in tomato sauce and cook for 20 minutes or until stew forms. Add in tofu balls and simmer for 7 minutes. In a pot, add cauliflower, 1 cup of water, and salt. Bring to a boil for 10 minutes. Drain pour into a bowl. Add in butter, salt, and pepper; mash into a puree using a potato mash. Stir in heavy cream and Parmesan until evenly combined. Spoon the cauli mash into bowls, top with tofu balls and sauce, and garnish with basil leaves.

Per serving: Cal 686; Net Carbs 5.6g, Fat 31g, Protein 22g

Chili Vegetables & Pasta Bake

Ingredients for 4 servings

1 cup sliced white button mushrooms
1 cup shredded mozzarella   Salt and black pepper to taste
1 cup chopped bell peppers   ¼ tsp red chili flakes
1 egg yolk   1 cup marinara sauce
1 tbsp olive oil   1 cup grated mozzarella cheese
1 yellow squash, chopped   1 cup grated Parmesan cheese
1 red onion, sliced   ¼ cup chopped fresh basil

Directions and Total Time: approx. 15 min + chilling time

Microwave mozzarella cheese for 2 minutes. Take out the bowl and allow cooling for 1 minute. Mix in egg yolk until well-combined. Lay a parchment paper on a flat surface, pour the cheese mixture on top and cover with another parchment paper. Flatten the dough into 1/8-inch thickness. Take off the parchment paper and cut the dough into penne-size pieces. Place in a bowl and refrigerate overnight. Bring 2 cups of water to a boil and add in penne. Cook for 1 minute and drain; set aside. Heat olive oil in a pan and sauté bell peppers, garlic, squash, onion, and mushrooms. Cook for 5 minutes. Season with salt, pepper, and red chili flakes. Mix in marinara sauce and cook for 5 minutes. Stir in penne and spread the mozzarella and Parmesan cheeses on top. Bake for 15 minutes. Serve.

Per serving: Cal 248; Net Carbs 4.9g; Fats 12g; Protein 27g

White Egg Tex Mex Pizza

Ingredients for 2 servings

4 eggs   2 tbsp chopped green onions
2 tbsp water   ¼ cup Alfredo sauce
1 Jalapeno pepper, diced   ¼ tsp cumin
2 oz Monterey Jack, shredded   2 tbsp olive oil

Directions and Total Time: approx. 17 minutes

Preheat the oven to 350 F. Heat olive oil in a skillet. Whisk the eggs along with water and cumin; pour into the skillet and cook until set. Top with alfredo sauce and jalapeno. Sprinkle green onions and cheese over. Place in the oven and bake for 5 minutes. Serve.

Per serving: Cal 591; Net Carbs 2g; Fat 55g; Protein 22g

Baked Cauliflower with Shirataki

Ingredients for 4 servings

2 (8 oz) packs spinach angel hair shirataki
1 medium head cauliflower, cut into florets
1 cup grated Monterey Jack cheese
1 cup heavy cream   1 tsp smoked paprika
1 tsp dried thyme   ½ tsp red chili flakes

Directions and Total Time: approx. 45 minutes

To make the shirataki angel hair, boil 2 cups of water in a medium pot over medium heat. Strain the shirataki pasta through a colander and rinse very well under hot running water. Allow proper draining and pour the shirataki pasta into the boiling water. Cook for 3 minutes and strain again. Place a dry skillet over medium heat and stir-fry the shirataki pasta until visibly dry, and makes a squeaky sound when stirred, 1 to 2 minutes. Set aside. Preheat oven to 350 F. Bring 4 cups of water to a boil in a large pot and blanch the cauliflower for 4 minutes. Drain through a colander. In a bowl, mix cauliflower, shirataki, heavy cream, half of Monterey Jack cheese, thyme, paprika, salt, and chili flakes until well combined. Transfer the mixture to a greased baking dish and top with the remaining cheese. Bake for 30 minutes until the cheese melts. Serve.

Per serving: Cal 301; Net Carbs 13g; Fats 21g; Protein 12g

Almond-Flour Pizza with Kale & Artichokes

Ingredients for 4 servings

2 ½ cups grated mozzarella   ½ cup almond flour
¼ cup grated Parmesan   ½ cup chopped kale
6 tbsp cream cheese, softened ¼ cup chopped artichokes
1 egg, beaten   1 lemon, juiced
1 tsp Italian seasoning   ½ tsp garlic powder
½ tsp garlic powder   Salt and black pepper to taste

Directions and Total Time: approx. 45 minutes

Preheat the oven to 390 F and line a round pizza pan with parchment paper. Microwave 2 cups of mozzarella and 2 tbsp of cream cheese for 1 minute. Mix in egg, Italian seasoning, garlic powder, and almond flour. Spread the mixture on the pizza pan and bake for 15 minutes; set aside. In a bowl, mix remaining cream cheese, kale, artichokes, lemon juice, garlic powder, Parmesan cheese, remaining mozzarella cheese, salt, and pepper. Spread the mixture on the crust and bake for 15 minutes. Serve sliced.

Per serving: Cal 223; Net Carbs 3.1g; Fats 10g; Protein 24g

Balsamic Veggie-Pasta Mix

Ingredients for 4 servings

1 cup grated Parmigiano-Reggiano cheese
1 cup shredded mozzarella   1 red bell pepper, sliced
1 head broccoli, cut into florets 5 garlic cloves, minced
1 egg yolk   Salt and black pepper to taste
3 tbsp olive oil   1 tsp dried oregano
1 red onion, thinly sliced   3 tbsp balsamic vinegar
1 lb green beans, halved   2 tbsp chopped walnuts

Directions and Total Time: approx. 25 min + chilling time

Microwave mozzarella cheese for 2 minutes. Let cool for 1 minute and mix in egg yolk until well-combined. Lay a parchment paper on a flat surface, pour the cheese mixture on top and cover with another parchment paper. Flatten the dough into 1/8-inch thickness. Take off the parchment paper and cut the dough into mimicked penne-size pieces. Place in a bowl and refrigerate overnight. Bring 2 cups water to a boil and add in keto penne. Cook for 1 minute and drain; set aside. Heat olive oil in a skillet and sauté onion, garlic, green beans, broccoli, and bell pepper for 5 minutes. Season with salt, pepper, and oregano. Mix in balsamic vinegar, cook for 1 minute, and toss in the pasta. Garnish with Parmigiano-Reggiano cheese and walnuts.

Per serving: Cal 326; Net Carbs 7.5g; Fats 21g; Protein 20g

Fried Mac & Cheese

Ingredients for 4 servings

1 cauliflower head, riced   2 tsp turmeric
1 ½ cups shredded cheese   3 eggs
2 tsp paprika   4 tbsp olive oil

Directions and Total Time: approx. 45 minutes

Microwave the cauliflower for 5 minutes. Place it in cheesecloth and squeeze the extra juices out. Remove to a bowl. Stir in the rest of the ingredients. Heat olive oil in a deep pan over medium heat. Add the 'mac and cheese' and fry until golden and crispy. Serve.

Per serving: Cal 160; Net Carbs 2g; Fat 12g; Protein 8.6g

Quick Grilled Cheddar Cheese

Ingredients for 2 servings

4 eggs   3 tbsp almond flour
1 tsp baking powder   2 tbsp psyllium husk powder
3 tbsp butter   4 oz cheddar cheese

Directions and Total Time: approx. 15 minutes

Whisk together all ingredients, except for 1 tbsp butter and cheddar cheese. Microwave for 90 seconds. Flip the "bun" over and cut in half. Place the cheddar on one half of the bun and top with the other. Melt the remaining butter in a skillet. Add the sandwich and grill until the cheese is melted and the bun is crispy.

Per serving: Cal 623; Net Carbs 6.1g; Fat 51g; Protein 25g

Vegan Olive and Avocado Zoodles

Ingredients for 4 servings

¼ cup chopped sun-dried tomatoes
4 zucchini, spiralized
½ cup pesto
2 avocados, sliced

1 cup kalamata olives, chopped
¼ cup chopped basil
2 tbsp olive oil

Directions and Total Time: approx. 15 minutes

Heat 1 tbsp olive oil in a pan over medium heat. Add zoodles, and cook for 4 minutes. Transfer to a plate. Stir in 1 tbsp olive oil, pesto, basil, salt, tomatoes, and olives. Top with avocado slices.

Per serving: Cal 449; Net Carbs 8.4g; Fat 42g; Protein 6g

Enchilada Vegetarian Pasta

Ingredients for 4 servings

1 cup shredded mozzarella
1 cup chopped bell peppers
1 egg yolk
1 tsp olive oil
6 garlic cloves, minced
2 cups enchilada sauce

1 tsp cumin powder
½ tsp smoked paprika
1 tsp chili powder
Salt and black pepper to taste
¾ cup chopped green onions
1 avocado, pitted, sliced

Directions and Total Time: approx. 20 min + chilling time

Microwave mozzarella cheese for 2 minutes. Take out the bowl and allow cooling for 1 minute. Mix in egg yolk until well-combined. Lay a parchment paper on a flat surface, pour the cheese mixture on top and cover with another parchment paper. Flatten the dough into 1/8-inch thickness. Take off the parchment paper and cut the dough into penne-size pieces. Place in a bowl and refrigerate overnight. Bring 2 cups water to a boil in medium saucepan and add the keto penne. Cook for 1 minute and drain; set aside. Heat olive oil in a skillet and sauté garlic for 30 seconds. Mix in enchilada sauce, cumin, paprika, chili powder, bell peppers, salt, and pepper. Cook for 5 minutes. Mix in pasta. Top with green onions and avocado.

Per serving: Cal 151; Net Carbs 3.3g; Fats 8g; Protein 11.9g

Cheesy Roasted Vegetable Spaghetti

Ingredients for 4 servings

2 (8 oz) packs shirataki spaghetti
1 cup chopped mixed bell peppers
½ cup grated Parmesan cheese for topping
1 lb asparagus, chopped
1 cup broccoli florets
1 cup green beans, chopped
3 tbsp olive oil

1 small onion, chopped
2 garlic cloves, minced
1 cup diced tomatoes
½ cup chopped basil

Directions and Total Time: approx. 45 minutes

Boil 2 cups water in a pot. Strain the shirataki pasta and rinse well under hot running water. Allow draining and pour the shirataki pasta into the boiling water. Cook for 3 minutes and strain again. Place a dry skillet and stir-fry the shirataki pasta until visibly dry, 1-2 minutes; set aside.

Preheat oven to 425 F. In a bowl, add asparagus, broccoli, bell peppers, and green beans and toss with half of olive oil, salt, and pepper. Spread the vegetables on a baking sheet and roast for 20 minutes. Heat the remaining olive oil in a skillet and sauté onion and garlic for 3 minutes. Stir in tomatoes for 8 minutes. Mix in shirataki and vegetables. Top with Parmesan cheese and serve.

Per serving: Cal 272; Net Carbs 7.2g; Fats 12g; Protein 12g

One-Skillet Green Pasta

Ingredients for 4 servings

1 cup shredded mozzarella cheese
1 cup grated Pecorino Romano cheese for topping
1 egg yolk
2 garlic cloves, minced
1 lemon, juiced
1 cup baby spinach

½ cup almond milk
1 avocado, pitted and peeled
1 tbsp olive oil
Salt to taste

Directions and Total Time: approx. 15 min + chilling time

Microwave mozzarella cheese for 2 minutes. Take out the bowl and allow cooling for 1 minute. Mix in egg yolk until well-combined. Lay a parchment paper on a flat surface, pour the cheese mixture on top and cover with another parchment paper. Flatten the dough into 1/8-inch thickness. Take off the parchment paper and cut the dough into thick fettuccine strands. Place in a bowl and refrigerate overnight. Bring 2 cups water to a boil in a saucepan and add the fettuccine. Cook for 1 minute and drain; set aside. In a blender, combine garlic, lemon juice, spinach, almond milk, avocado, olive oil, and salt. Process until smooth. Pour fettuccine into a bowl, top with sauce, and mix. Top with Pecorino Romano cheese and serve.

Per serving: Cal 290; Net Carbs 5.3g; Fats 19g; Protein 18g

Tempeh Taco Cups

Ingredients for 4 servings

8 iceberg lettuce leaves
4 zero carb tortilla wraps
2 tsp melted butter
1 tbsp olive oil
1 yellow onion, chopped
½ cup tempeh, crumbled

1 tsp smoked paprika
½ tsp cumin powder
1 red bell pepper, chopped
1 avocado, halved and pitted
1 small lemon, juiced
¼ cup sour cream

Directions and Total Time: approx. 30 minutes

Preheat oven to 400 F. Divide each tortilla wrap into 2, lay on a chopping board, and brush with butter. Line 8 muffin tins with the tortilla and bake for 9 minutes; set aside. Heat olive oil in a skillet and sauté onion for 3 minutes. Crumble tempeh into the pan and cook for 8 minutes. Stir in paprika and cumin and cook for 1 minute. To assemble, fit lettuce leaves into the tortilla cups, share tempeh mixture on top, top with bell pepper, avocado, and drizzle with lemon juice. Add sour cream and serve.

Per serving: Cal 220; Net Carbs 3.8g, Fat 17g, Protein 6.7g

Bell Pepper & Broccoli Spaghetti

Ingredients for 4 servings

1 head broccoli, cut into florets
1 cup sliced mixed bell peppers
2 tbsp olive oil ¼ tsp red pepper flakes
4 zucchinis, spiralized 1 cup chopped kale
4 shallots, finely chopped 2 tbsp balsamic vinegar
Salt and black pepper to taste ½ lemon, juiced
2 garlic cloves, minced 1 cup grated Parmesan cheese

Directions and Total Time: approx. 20 minutes

Heat oil in a skillet and sauté turnips, broccoli, bell peppers, and shallots until softened, 7 minutes. Mix in garlic, and pepper flakes and cook until fragrant, 30 seconds. Stir in kale and zucchinis; cook until tender, 3 minutes. Mix in vinegar and lemon juice and adjust the taste with salt and pepper. Garnish with Parmesan cheese and serve.

Per serving: Cal 199; Net Carbs 5.9g; Fats 13g; Protein 9g

Rich Veggie Pasta Primavera

Ingredients for 4 servings

2 cups cauliflower florets, cut into matchsticks
½ cup grated Pecorino Romano cheese
1 cup shredded mozzarella 4 garlic cloves, minced
½ cup chopped green onions 1 cup grape tomatoes, halved
1 egg yolk 2 tsp dried Italian seasoning
¼ cup olive oil ½ lemon, juiced
1 red bell pepper, sliced 2 tbsp chopped fresh parsley

Directions and Total Time: approx. 25 min + chilling time

Microwave mozzarella cheese for 2 minutes. Take out the bowl and let cool for 1 minute. Mix in egg yolk until well-combined. Lay a parchment paper on a flat surface, pour the cheese mixture on top and cover with another parchment paper. Flatten the dough into 1/8-inch thickness. Take off the parchment paper and cut the dough into penne-size pieces. Place in a bowl and refrigerate overnight. Bring 2 cups water to a boil and add in penne. Cook for 1 minute and drain; set aside. Heat olive oil in a skillet and sauté onion, garlic cauliflower, and bell pepper for 7 minutes. Stir in tomatoes and Italian seasoning and cook for 5 minutes. Mix in lemon juice, penne, salt, and pepper. Top with Pecorino Romano cheese

Per serving: Cal 283; Net Carbs 5.2g; Fats 18g; Protein 15g

Herby Mushroom Pizza

Ingredients for 4 servings

2 medium cremini mushrooms, sliced
2 ½ cups grated mozzarella ½ cup tomato sauce
½ cup grated Parmesan cheese 1 tsp erythritol
2 tbsp cream cheese, softened 1 tsp dried oregano
½ cup almond flour 1 tsp dried basil
1 egg, beaten ½ tsp paprika
1 tsp olive oil Salt and black pepper to taste
1 garlic clove, minced 6 black olives, sliced

Directions and Total Time: approx. 45 minutes

Preheat oven to 390 F. Line a pizza pan with parchment paper. Microwave 2 cups mozzarella cheese and 2 tbsp cream cheese for 1 minute. Mix in almond meal and egg. Spread the mixture on the pizza pan and bake for 5 minutes; set aside. Heat olive oil in a skillet and sauté mushrooms and garlic until softened, 5 minutes. Mix in tomato sauce, erythritol, oregano, basil, paprika, salt, and pepper. Cook for 2 minutes. Spread the sauce on the crust, top with the remaining mozzarella and Parmesan cheeses and olives. Bake for 15 minutes. Slice and serve.

Per serving: Cal 203; Net Carbs 2.6g; Fats 8g; Protein 24.3g

Cheesy Broccoli Nachos with Salsa

Ingredients for 4 servings

2 heads broccoli, chopped 2 eggs, beaten
3 tbsp coconut flour ¼ cup grated Monterey jack
1 tsp smoked paprika 4 plum tomatoes, chopped
½ tsp coriander powder ½ lime, juiced
1 tsp cumin powder 4 sprigs cilantro, chopped
½ tsp garlic powder 1 avocado, chopped

Directions and Total Time: approx. 30 minutes

Preheat oven to 350 F. Pour broccoli in a food processor and blend into a rice-like consistency. Heat a skillet over low heat, pour in broccoli, and fry for 10 minutes. Transfer to a bowl. Line 2 baking sheets with parchment papers. Onto the broccoli, add coconut flour, paprika, coriander, cumin, garlic, and eggs. Mix and form into a ball. Divide into halves, place each half on each baking sheet, and press down into a rough circle. Bake for 10 minutes. Take out of the oven, cut into triangles, and sprinkle with cheese; let cool. In a bowl, combine tomatoes, lime, cilantro, and avocado. Serve nachos with salsa.

Per serving: Cal 208; Net Carbs 4.5g; Fat 12.4g, Protein 7g

Cheesy Bell Pepper Pizza

Ingredients for 2 servings

6 oz mozzarella, grated 4 oz grated cheddar cheese
2 tbsp cream cheese ¼ cup marinara sauce
2 tbsp Parmesan cheese ⅔ bell pepper, sliced
1 tsp oregano 1 tomato, sliced
½ cup almond flour 2 tbsp chopped basil
2 tbsp psyllium husk 6 black olives

Directions and Total Time: approx. 40 minutes

Preheat the oven to 400 F. Combine all crust ingredients in a bowl, except for the mozzarella. Melt mozzarella in a microwave. Stir it into the bowl and mix to combine. Divide the dough in 2. Roll out the crusts in circles and place on a lined baking sheet. Bake for 10 minutes. Top with cheddar, marinara, bell pepper, tomato, and basil. Return to oven and bake for 10 minutes. Serve with olives.

Per serving: Cal 510; Net Carbs 3.7g; Fat 39g; Protein 31g

Thyme and Collard Green Waffles

Ingredients for 4 servings

2 green onions	1 cup mozzarella, grated
1 tbsp olive oil	½ cauliflower head, chopped
2 eggs	1 tsp garlic powder
⅓ cup Parmesan cheese	1 tbsp sesame seeds
1 cup collard greens	2 tsp chopped thyme

Directions and Total Time: approx. 45 minutes

Place the cauliflower in a food processor and process until a rice-like mixture is formed. Add collard greens, spring onions, and thyme. Pulse until smooth. Transfer to a bowl. Stir in the rest of the ingredients and mix to combine. Heat waffle iron and spread the mixture onto the iron, evenly. Cook following the manufacturer's instructions.

Per serving: Cal 283; Net Carbs 3.5g; Fat 20g; Protein 16g

Stuffed Portobello Mushrooms

Ingredients for 2 servings

4 Portobello mushrooms	2 cups lettuce
2 tbsp olive oil	1 cup crumbled blue cheese

Directions and Total Time: approx. 30 minutes

Preheat oven to 350 F. Remove the stems from the mushrooms. Fill the mushrooms with blue cheese and place on a lined baking sheet. Bake for about 20 minutes. Serve with lettuce drizzled with olive oil.

Per serving: Cal 334; Net Carbs 5.5g; Fat 29g; Protein 14g

Spinach-Olive Pizza

Ingredients for 4 servings

1 cup grated mozzarella	1 cup lukewarm water
½ cup almond flour	½ cup tomato sauce
¼ tsp salt	½ cup baby spinach
2 tbsp ground psyllium husk	1 tsp dried oregano
1 tbsp olive oil	3 tbsp sliced black olives

Directions and Total Time: approx. 40 minutes

Preheat oven to 390 F and line a baking sheet with parchment paper. In a bowl, mix almond flour, salt, psyllium powder, olive oil, and water until dough forms. Spread the mixture on the sheet and bake for 10 minutes. Remove the crust and spread the tomato sauce on top. Add spinach, mozzarella cheese, oregano, and olives. Bake for 15 minutes. Take out of the oven, slice and serve warm.

Per serving: Cal 195; Net Carbs 1.8g; Fats 8g; Protein 11g

Fake Mushroom Risotto

Ingredients for 4 servings

2 shallots, diced	4 tbsp butter
3 tbsp olive oil	3 tbsp chopped chives
¼ cup veggie broth	2 pounds mushrooms, sliced
⅓ cup Parmesan cheese	4 ½ cups riced cauliflower

Directions and Total Time: approx. 15 minutes

Heat 2 tbsp oil in a saucepan. Add the mushrooms and cook over medium heat for 3 minutes. Remove and set aside. Heat the remaining oil and cook the shallots for 2 minutes. Stir in the cauliflower and broth, and cook until the liquid is absorbed. Stir in the rest of the ingredients.

Per serving: Cal 264; Net Carbs 8.4g; Fat 18g; Protein 11g

Vegetarian Ketogenic Burgers

Ingredients for 2 servings

1 garlic cloves, minced	2 eggs, fried
2 Portobello mushrooms	2 zero carb buns
1 tbsp coconut oil, melted	2 tbsp mayonnaise
1 tbsp chopped basil	2 lettuce leaves
1 tbsp oregano	Salt to taste

Directions and Total Time: approx. 20 minutes

Combine the melted coconut oil, garlic, herbs, and salt in a bowl. Place the mushrooms in the bowl and coat well. Preheat the grill to medium. Grill the mushrooms about 2 minutes per side. Slice them and grill for 2 minutes per side. Cut the buns in half. Add the lettuce leaves, mushrooms, eggs, and mayo. Top with the other bun.

Per serving: Cal 637; Net Carbs 8.5g; Fat 53g; Protein 23g

Mediterranean Pasta

Ingredients for 4 servings

¼ cup sun-dried tomatoes	¼ cup crumbled feta
5 garlic cloves, minced	¼ cup Parmesan
2 tbsp butter	10 kalamata olives, halved
1 cup spinach	2 tbsp olive oil
2 Large zucchini, spiralized	2 tbsp chopped parsley

Directions and Total Time: approx. 15 minutes

Heat the olive oil in a pan over medium heat. Add zoodles, butter, garlic, and spinach; stir-fry for 5 minutes. Stir in the olives, tomatoes, and parsley. Cook for 2 more minutes. Stir in the cheeses and serve.

Per serving: Cal 231; Net Carbs 6.5g; Fat 21g; Protein 6g

Mint Ice Cream

Ingredients for 4 servings

2 avocados, pitted	2 tbsp erythritol
1 ¼ cups coconut cream	2 tsp chopped mint leaves
½ tsp vanilla extract	

Directions and Total Time: approx. 10 min+ chilling time

Into a blender, spoon avocado pulps, pour in coconut cream, vanilla extract, erythritol, and mint leaves. Process until smooth. Pour the mixture into your ice cream maker and freeze according to the manufacturer's instructions. When ready, remove and scoop the ice cream into bowls.

Per serving: Cal 370; Net Carbs 4g; Fat 38g; Protein 4g

Eggplant & Goat Cheese Pizza

Ingredients for 4 servings

4 tbsp olive oil
2 eggplants, sliced lengthwise
1 cup tomato sauce
2 garlic cloves, minced
1 red onion, sliced
12 oz goat cheese, crumbled
Salt and black pepper to taste
½ tsp cinnamon powder
1 cup mozzarella, shredded
2 tbsp oregano, chopped

Directions and Total Time: approx. 45 minutes

Line a baking sheet with parchment paper. Lay the eggplant slices in a baking dish and drizzle with some olive oil. Bake for 20 minutes at 390 F. Heat the remaining olive oil in a skillet and sauté garlic and onion for 3 minutes. Stir in goat cheese and tomato sauce and season with salt and pepper. Simmer for 10 minutes. Remove eggplant from the oven and spread the cheese sauce on top. Sprinkle with mozzarella cheese and oregano. Bake further for 10 minutes until the cheese melts. Slice to serve.

Per serving: Cal 557; Net Carbs 8.3g; Fat 44g; Protein 33.7g

Charred Asparagus with Creamy Sauce

Ingredients for 4 servings

½ lb asparagus, no hard stalks
Salt and chili pepper to taste
4 tbsp flax seed powder
½ cup coconut cream
1 cup butter, melted
⅓ cup mozzarella, grated
2 tbsp olive oil
Juice of half lemon

Directions and Total Time: approx. 12 minutes

Heat olive oil in a saucepan and roast the asparagus until lightly charred. Season with salt and pepper; set aside. Melt half of butter in a pan until nutty and golden brown. Stir in lemon juice and pour the mixture over the asparagus. In a safe microwave bowl, mix flax seed powder with ½ cup water and let sit for 5 minutes. Microwave flax egg 1-2 minutes, then pour into a blender. Add the remaining butter, mozzarella cheese, coconut cream, salt, and chili pepper. Puree until well combined and smooth. Serve.

Per serving: Cal 442; Net Carbs 5.4g; Fat 45g; Protein 5.9g

Tomato & Mozzarella Caprese Bake

Ingredients for 4 servings

4 tbsp olive oil
4 tomatoes, sliced
1 cup fresh mozzarella, sliced
2 tbsp basil pesto
1 cup mayonnaise
2 oz Parmesan cheese, grated

Directions and Total Time: approx. 25 minutes

In a baking dish, arrange tomatoes and mozzarella slices. In a bowl, mix pesto, mayonnaise, 1 oz of Parmesan cheese, salt, and pepper; mix to combine. Spread this mixture over tomatoes and mozzarella cheese, and top with remaining Parmesan cheese. Bake for 20 minutes at 360 F. Remove, allow cooling slightly, and slice to serve.

Per serving: Cal 420; Net Carbs 4.9g; Fat 36.6g; Protein 17g

Sweet Onion & Goat Cheese Pizza

Ingredients for 4 servings

2 cups grated mozzarella
2 tbsp cream cheese, softened
2 large eggs, beaten
⅓ cup almond flour
1 tsp dried Italian seasoning
2 tbsp butter
2 red onions, thinly sliced
1 cup crumbled goat cheese
1 tbs almond milk
1 cup curly endive, chopped

Directions and Total Time: approx. 35 minutes

Preheat oven to 390 F and line a round pizza pan with parchment paper. Microwave the mozzarella and cream cheeses for 1 minute. Remove and mix in eggs, almond flour, and Italian seasoning. Spread the dough on the pizza pan and bake for 6 minutes. Melt butter in a skillet and stir in onions, salt, and pepper and cook on low heat with frequent stirring until caramelized, 15- 20 minutes. In a bowl, mix goat cheese with almond milk and spread on the crust. Top with the caramelized onions. Bake for 10 minutes. Scatter curly endive on top, slice and serve.

Per serving: Cal 317; Net Carbs 3.1g; Fats 20g; Protein 28g

Vegan BBQ Tofu Kabobs with Green Dip

Ingredients for 4 servings

½ tbsp BBQ sauce
1 lb extra firm tofu, cubed
1 tbsp vegan butter, melted
1 cup canola oil
5 tbsp fresh cilantro, chopped
3 tbsp fresh basil, chopped
2 garlic cloves
Juice of ½ a lime
4 tbsp capers
Salt and black pepper to taste

Directions and Total Time: approx. 20 minutes

In a blender, add cilantro, basil, garlic, lemon juice, capers, 2/3 cup of canola oil, salt and pepper. Process until smooth. Set aside. Thread the tofu cubes on wooden skewers to fit into your grill pan. Season with salt and brush with the BBQ sauce. Brush the grill pan with remaining canola oil and cook the tofu until browned on both sides. Serve.

Per serving: Cal 471; Net Carbs 3.8g; Fat 47g; Protein 11.9g

One-Pot Spicy Brussel Sprouts with Carrots

Ingredients for 4 servings

1 pound Brussels sprouts
¼ cup olive oil
4 green onions, chopped
2 carrots, grated
Salt and black pepper to taste
Hot chili sauce

Directions and Total Time: approx. 15 minutes

Sauté green onions in warm olive oil for 2 minutes. Stir in salt and pepper; transfer to a plate. Trim the Brussel sprouts and cut in halves. Leave the small ones as wholes. Pour the Brussel sprouts with and carrots into the same saucepan and stir-fry until softened but al dente. Season with salt and pepper, stir in onions, and heat for a few seconds. Top with the hot chili sauce. Serve.

Per serving: Cal 198; Net Carbs 6.5g; Fat 14g; Protein 4.9g

Tofu Nuggets with Cilantro Dip

Ingredients for 4 servings

1 lime, ½ juiced and ½ cut into wedges
1 ½ cups olive oil
28 oz tofu, pressed and cubed
1 egg, lightly beaten
1 cup golden flaxseed meal
1 ripe avocado, chopped
½ tbsp chopped cilantro
Salt and black pepper to taste
½ tbsp olive oil

Directions and Total Time: approx. 25 minutes

Heat olive oil in a deep skillet. Coat tofu cubes in the egg and then in the flaxseed meal. Fry until golden brown. Transfer to a plate. Place avocado, cilantro, salt, pepper, and lime juice in a blender; puree until smooth. Spoon into a bowl, add tofu nuggets, and lime wedges to serve.

Per serving: Cal 665; Net Carbs 6.2g, Fat 54g, Protein 32g

Zucchini-Cranberry Cake Squares

Ingredients for 6 servings

1 ¼ cups chopped zucchinis
2 tbsp olive oil
½ cup dried cranberries
1 lemon, zested
3 eggs
1 ½ cups almond flour
½ tsp baking powder
1 tsp cinnamon powder
A pinch of salt

Directions and Total Time: approx. 45 minutes

Preheat oven to 350 F and line a square cake tin with parchment paper. Combine zucchinis, olive oil, cranberries, lemon zest, and eggs in a bowl until evenly combined. Sift flour, baking powder, and cinnamon powder into the mixture and fold with the salt. Pour the mixture into the cake tin and bake for 30 minutes. Remove; allow cooling in the tin for 10 minutes and transfer the cake to a wire rack to cool completely. Cut into squares and serve.

Per serving: Cal 121; Net Carbs 2.5g, Fat 10g, Protein 4g

Egg Cauli Fried Rice with Grilled Cheese

Ingredients for 4 servings

2 cups cauliflower rice, steamed
½ lb halloumi, cut into ¼ to ½ inch slabs
1 tbsp ghee
4 eggs, beaten
1 green bell pepper, chopped
¼ cup green beans, chopped
1 tsp soy sauce
2 tbsp chopped parsley

Directions and Total Time: approx. 10 minutes

Melt ghee in a skillet and pour in the eggs. Swirl the pan to spread the eggs around and cook for 1 minute. Move the scrambled eggs to the side of the skillet, add bell pepper and green beans, and sauté for 3 minutes. Pour in the cauli rice and cook for 2 minutes. Top with soy sauce; combine evenly, and cook for 2 minutes. Dish into plates, garnish with the parsley, and set aside. Preheat a grill pan and grill halloumi cheese on both sides until the cheese lightly browns. Place on the side of the rice and serve warm.

Per serving: Cal 275; Net Carbs 4.5g, Fat 19g, Protein 15g

Strawberry Faux Oats

Ingredients for 2 servings

2 tbsp coconut flour
2 tbsp golden flaxseed meal
2 tbsp chia seeds
2 tbsp heavy cream
½ cup almond milk
3 tbsp sugar-free maple syrup
1 tsp vanilla extract
1 cup strawberries, halved
¼ cup desiccated coconut

Directions and Total Time: approx. 20 minutes

Combine coconut flour, flaxseed meal, and chia seeds in a saucepan. Stir in heavy cream, almond milk, maple syrup, and vanilla extract. Place the pan over medium heat, whisk the ingredients for 10 minutes. Pour the mixture into 2 serving bowls and top with strawberries and desiccated coconut. Drizzle with some more maple syrup and serve.

Per serving: Cal 289; Net Carbs 6g, Fat 18.5g, Protein 5g

Cheese Quesadillas with Fruit Salad

Ingredients for 2 servings

2 large zero carb tortillas
1 cup grated cheddar cheese
2 green onions, chopped
1 cup mixed berries
½ tsp cinnamon powder
½ lemon, juiced
1 cup Greek yogurt
Sugar-free maple syrup to taste

Directions and Total Time: approx. 10 minutes

Divide the tortillas into two, top half each with the cheddar cheese and spring onions, and cover with the halves. Place in a skillet and heat until golden and the cheese melted. Remove onto a plate, allow cooling, and cut into four wedges. Combine berries, cinnamon powder, lemon juice, Greek yogurt, and maple syrup in a bowl. Divide into 2 bowls and serve with the quesadillas.

Per serving: Cal 135; Net Carbs 3g, Fat 13.5g, Protein 3.5g

Mushroom & Broccoli Pizza

Ingredients for 4 servings

½ cup almond flour
¼ tsp salt
2 tbsp ground psyllium husk
2 tbsp olive oil
1 cup sliced fresh mushrooms
1 white onion, thinly sliced
3 cups broccoli florets
4 garlic cloves, minced
½ cup sugar-free pizza sauce
4 tomatoes, sliced
1 ½ cups grated mozzarella
⅓ cup grated Parmesan

Directions and Total Time: approx. 25 minutes

Preheat oven to 390 F and line a baking sheet with parchment paper. In a bowl, mix almond flour, salt, psyllium powder, 1 tbsp of olive oil, and 1 cup of lukewarm water until dough forms. Spread the mixture on the pizza pan and bake for 10 minutes. Heat the remaining olive oil in a skillet and sauté mushrooms, onion, garlic, and broccoli for 5 minutes. Spread the pizza sauce on the crust and top with the broccoli mixture, tomato, and mozzarella and Parmesan cheeses. Bake for 5 minutes. Serve sliced.

Per serving: Cal 180; Net Carbs 3.6g; Fats 9.4g; Protein 17g

Tofu Radish Bowls

Ingredients for 4 servings

¼ cup chopped baby bella mushrooms
2 yellow bell peppers, chopped
1 (14 oz) block tofu, cubed   4 eggs
1 tbsp + 1 tbsp olive oil   1/3 cup tomato salsa
1 ½ cups shredded radishes   A handful chopped parsley
½ cup chopped white onions   1 avocado, and chopped

Directions and Total Time: approx. 35 minutes

Heat 1 tbsp olive oil in a skillet and add the tofu, radishes, onions, mushrooms, and bell peppers. Season with salt and pepper; cook for 10 minutes. Share into 4 bowls. Heat the remaining oil in the skillet, crack an egg into the pan, and cook until the white sets, but the yolk quite runny. Transfer to the top of one tofu-radish hash bowl and make the remaining eggs. Top the bowls with tomato salsa, parsley, and avocado. Serve.

Per serving: Cal 353; Net Carbs 5.9g, Fat 25g, Protein 19g

Mascarpone and Kale Asian Casserole

Ingredients for 4 servings

2 cups tofu, grilled and cubed   1 tbsp plain vinegar
1 cup smoked seitan, chopped   1 ¼ cups cheddar, shredded
1 cup mascarpone cheese   ½ cup kale, chopped
1 tbsp mustard powder   2 tbsp olive oil

Directions and Total Time: approx. 30 minutes

Mix the mascarpone cheese, mustard powder, plain vinegar, kale, and cheddar cheese in a greased baking dish. Top with the tofu, seitan, and season with salt and black pepper. Bake in the oven until the casserole is golden brown on top, for about 15 to 20 minutes, at 400 F. Serve.

Per serving: Cal 612; Net Carbs 9.1g; Fat 51g; Protein 30.5g

Cauliflower Couscous & Halloumi Packets

Ingredients for 4 servings

2 heads cauliflower, chopped   1 red bell pepper, chopped
¼ cup vegetable broth   1 orange bell pepper, chopped
1 lemon, juiced   ¼ cup cubed halloumi
2 tbsp sugar-free maple syrup   Olive oil to drizzle

Directions and Total Time: approx. 25 minutes

Preheat oven to 350 F. Put cauliflower in a food processor and pulse until a coarse consistency is achieved. Pour the couscous and vegetable stock into a pot and cook for 2-3 minutes. Drain and set aside. In a bowl, whisk lemon juice and maple syrup, and set aside. Cut out two 2 x 15 inches parchment papers onto a flat surface spoon the couscous in the middle of each, top with bell peppers, halloumi cheese, and drizzle the dressing on top. Wrap papers into parcels and place on a baking tray; cook for 15 minutes. Remove and carefully open the pouches. Serve warm.

Per serving: Cal 240; Net Carbs 4.7g, Fat 19g, Protein 5.1g

Mushroom White Pizza

Ingredients for 4 servings

2 tbsp flax egg + 6 tbsp water   1 tbsp oregano
½ cup mayonnaise   1 tbsp basil pesto
¾ cup almond flour   2 tbsp olive oil
1 tbsp psyllium husk powder   Salt and black pepper
1 tsp baking soda   ½ cup coconut cream
½ tsp salt   ¾ cup Parmesan, shredded
¼ cup mushrooms, sliced   6 black olives

Directions and Total Time: approx. 35 minutes

Combine the flax seed powder with water and allow sitting to thicken for 5 minutes. Whisk in mayonnaise, almond flour, psyllium husk powder, baking soda, and salt. Allow sitting for 5 minutes. Pour the batter into a greased baking sheet. Bake for 10 minutes at 350 F. In a bowl, mix mushrooms with pesto, olive oil, salt, and pepper. Remove the crust from the oven and spread the coconut cream on top. Add the mushroom mixture and Parmesan cheese. Bake the pizza further until the cheese melts, for 10 minutes. Spread the olives on top and serve.

Per serving: Cal 346; Net Carbs 5.5g; Fat 32.7g; Protein 8g

Garam Masala Traybake

Ingredients for 4 servings

3 tbsp butter   2 tbsp garam masala
3 cups tempeh slices   1 cup mushrooms, sliced
1 turnip, sliced   1 ¼ cups coconut cream
Salt to taste   1 tbsp fresh cilantro, chopped

Directions and Total Time: approx. 30 minutes

Place a skillet and melt butter. Fry tempeh for 4 minutes. Stir half of the garam masala into the tempeh until evenly mixed and turn the heat off. Transfer the tempeh with the spice into a baking dish and set aside. In a bowl, mix the mushrooms, turnip, coconut cream, cilantro, and remaining garam masala. Pour the mixture over tempeh and bake for 20 minutes at 400 F. Garnish with cilantro.

Per serving: Cal 591; Net Carbs 9.4g; Fat 48.4g; Protein 28g

Walnut Chocolate Squares

Ingredients for 6 servings

3½ oz dairy-free dark chocolate   ¼ cup walnut butter
4 tbsp vegan butter   ½ tsp vanilla extract
1 pinch salt   ¼ cup chopped walnuts

Directions and Total Time: approx. 10 minutes

Microwave chocolate and vegan butter for 2 minutes. Remove and mix in salt, walnut butter, and vanilla extract. Grease a small baking sheet with cooking spray and line with parchment paper. Pour in the batter and top with walnuts and chill in the refrigerator. Cut into squares.

Per serving: Cal 125; Net Carbs 3g; Fat 10g; Protein 2g

Cauliflower & Broccoli Gratin with Seitan

Ingredients for 4 servings

4 tbsp avocado oil	1 cup heavy cream
2 shallots, chopped	2 tbsp mustard powder
2 cups broccoli florets	5 oz Pecorino, shredded
1 cup cauliflower florets	4 tbsp rosemary, chopped
2 cups seitan, crumbled	Salt and black pepper to taste

Directions and Total Time: approx. 40 minutes

Heat half of the avocado oil in a pot and add shallots, broccoli, and cauliflower and cook for 6 minutes. Transfer the vegetables to a baking dish. Warm the remaining avocado oil in a skillet and cook the seitan until browned. Mix heavy cream and mustard powder in a bowl. Then, pour the mixture over the vegetables. Scatter seitan and Pecorino cheese on top and sprinkle with rosemary, salt ,and pepper. Bake for 15 minutes at 400 F. Serve.

Per serving: Cal 753; Net Carbs 12g; Fat 37g; Protein 86g

Baked Creamy Brussels Sprouts

Ingredients for 4 servings

3 tbsp ghee	1 ¼ cups crème fraîche
1 cup tempeh, cubed	1 ⅓ cups cheddar, shredded
1 lb Brussels sprouts, halved	¼ cup Gruyère, shredded
5 garlic cloves, minced	Salt and black pepper to taste

Directions and Total Time: approx. 25 minutes

Melt ghee in a large skillet and fry tempeh for 6 minutes; set aside. Pour Brussels sprouts and garlic into the skillet and sauté until nice color forms. Stir in crème fraîche and simmer for 4 minutes. Add tempeh cubes and mix well. Pour the sautéed ingredients into a baking dish, sprinkle with cheddar cheese and Gruyère cheese. Bake for 10 minutes at 400 F or until golden brown on top. Serve.

Per serving: Cal 563; Net Carbs 8.7g; Fat 44g; Protein 25.2g

Mom's Cheesy Pizza

Ingredients for 4 servings

1 cup sliced mozzarella	2 tbsp ground psyllium husk
1 cup grated mozzarella	1 tbsp olive oil
3 tbsp grated Parmesan	½ cup sugar-free pizza sauce
½ cup almond flour	2 tsp Italian seasoning
¼ tsp salt	1 cup lukewarm water

Directions and Total Time: approx. 35 minutes

Preheat oven to 390 F and line a pizza pan with parchment paper. In a bowl, mix almond flour, salt, psyllium powder, olive oil, and water until dough forms. Spread the mixture on the pizza pan and bake for 10 minutes. Remove the crust and spread the pizza sauce on top. Add the sliced mozzarella, grated mozzarella, Parmesan cheese, and Italian seasoning. Bake for 18 minutes. Slice and serve.

Per serving: Cal 193; Net Carbs 3.2g; Fats 10g; Protein 19g

Easy Cheesy Green Pizza

Ingredients for 4 servings

¼ cup canned artichokes, cut into wedges	
2 tbsp flax seed powder + 6 tbsp water	
1 cup broccoli, grated	2 tbsp marinara sauce
1 red bell pepper, sliced	¼ cup mozzarella cheese
1 cup Parmesan, shredded	1 garlic clove, thinly sliced
½ tsp salt	1 tbsp dried oregano

Directions and Total Time: approx. 40 minutes

In a bowl, mix flax seed powder and water and allow thickening for 5 minutes. Add broccoli, ¾ cup of Parmesan cheese, salt, and stir to combine well. Pour the mixture into a baking sheet and spread out with a spatula. Bake for about 20 minutes at 350 F. Remove from the oven and spread the marinara sauce on top, sprinkle with the remaining Parmesan and mozzarella cheeses, artichokes, red bell pepper slices, and garlic. Spread the oregano on top. Bake for 10 minutes at 420 F. Slice to serve.

Per serving: Cal 108; Net Carbs 4.8g; Fat 5.4g; Protein 9.2g

Keto Brownies

Ingredients for 4 servings

2 tbsp flax seed powder	½ cup erythritol
¼ cup cocoa powder	10 tbsp vegan butter
½ cup almond flour	2 oz dairy-free dark chocolate
½ tsp baking powder	½ tsp vanilla extract

Directions and Total Time: approx. 30 min+ chilling time

Preheat oven to 375 F and line a baking sheet with parchment paper. Mix the flax seed powder with 6 tbsp water in a bowl and allow thickening for 5 minutes. In a separate bowl, mix cocoa powder, almond flour, baking powder, and erythritol until no lumps from the erythritol remain. In another bowl, add butter and dark chocolate and microwave both for 30 seconds. Whisk flax egg and vanilla into the chocolate mixture, then pour the mixture into the dry ingredients; mix well. Pour the batter onto the paper-lined sheet and bake for 20 minutes. Let cool completely and refrigerate for 2 hours. Slice into squares.

Per serving: Cal 227; Net Carbs 3g; Fat 19g; Protein 4g

Mixed Berry Yogurt Ice Pops

Ingredients for 6 servings

2/3 cup frozen strawberries & blueberries, thawed	
2/3 cup avocado, halved, pitted	½ cup coconut cream
1 cup dairy-free yogurt	1 tsp vanilla extract

Directions and Total Time: approx. 2 min+ chilling time

Pour avocado pulp, berries, dairy-free yogurt, coconut cream, and vanilla extract. Process until smooth. Pour into ice pop sleeves and freeze for 8 hours. Serve when ready.

Per serving: Cal 80; Net Carbs 4g; Fat 5g; Protein 2g

Speedy Custard Tart

Ingredients for 4 servings

¼ cup butter, cold and crumbled
¼ cup almond flour / ½ cup swerve sugar
3 tbsp coconut flour / 1 tsp vanilla bean paste
½ tsp salt / 2 tbsp coconut flour
3 tbsp erythritol / 1 ¼ cup almond milk
1 ½ tsp vanilla extract / 1 ¼ cup heavy cream
4 whole eggs / 2 tbsp sugar-free maple syrup
2 whole eggs + 3 egg yolks / ¼ cup chopped almonds

Directions and Total Time: approx. 75 minutes

Preheat oven to 350 F and grease a pie pan with cooking spray. In a bowl, mix almond flour, coconut flour, and salt. Add in butter and mix with an electric mixer until crumbly. Add in erythritol and vanilla extract and mix. Pour in the four eggs one after another while mixing until formed into a ball. Dust a clean flat surface with almond flour, unwrap the dough, and roll out the dough into a large rectangle, fit into the pie pan; prick the base of the crust. Bake until golden. Remove after and allow cooling.

In a mixing bowl, whisk the 2 whole eggs, 3 egg yolks, swerve sugar, vanilla bean paste, and coconut flour. Put almond milk, heavy cream, and maple syrup into a pot and bring to a boil. Pour the mixture into the egg mix and whisk while pouring. Run batter through a fine strainer into a bowl and skim off any froth. Remove the parchment paper, and transfer the egg batter into the pie. Bake for 45 minutes. Garnish with almonds, slice, and serve.

Per serving: Cal 459; Net Carbs 1.2g, Fat 40g, Protein 12g

Vegan Cheesecake with Blueberries

Ingredients for 6 servings

2 oz vegan butter / 2 cups dairy-free cream cheese
1 ¼ cups almond flour / ½ cup coconut cream
3 tbsp Swerve sugar / 1 tsp lemon zest
½ tsp vanilla extract / ½ tsp vanilla extract
3 tbsp flax seed powder / 2 oz fresh blueberries

Directions and Total Time: approx. 70 min+ chilling time

Preheat oven to 350 F. Line a springform pan with parchment paper. Melt vegan butter in a skillet until nutty in flavor. Turn the heat off and stir in almond flour, 2 tbsp swerve, and vanilla until a dough forms. Press the mixture into the springform pan and bake for 8 minutes. Mix the flax seed powder with 9 tbsp water and allow sitting for 5 minutes. In a bowl, combine cream cheese, coconut cream, remaining swerve, lemon zest, vanilla extract, and flax egg. Remove the crust from oven and pour the mixture on top. Bake the cake for 15 minutes at 400 F. Reduce the heat 230 F and bake further for 50 minutes. Refrigerate overnight and scatter the blueberries on top.

Per serving: Cal 330; Net Carbs 4g; Fat 31g; Protein 8g

Pistachio Heart Biscuits

Ingredients for 4 servings

1 cup butter, softened / 2 cups almond flour
2/3 cup swerve sugar / ½ cup dark chocolate
1 large egg, beaten / Chopped pistachios
2 tsp pistachio extract

Directions and Total Time: approx. 30 min + cooling time

Add butter and swerve to a bowl; beat until smooth and creamy. Whisk in egg until combined. Mix in pistachio extract and flour until a smooth dough forms. Wrap the dough in plastic wrap and chill for 10 minutes. Preheat oven to 350 F and lightly dust a chopping board with some almond flour. Unwrap the dough and roll out to 2-inch thickness. Cut out as many biscuits as you can get while rerolling the trimming and making more biscuits. Arrange the biscuits on the parchment paper-lined baking sheet and bake for 15 minutes. Transfer to a wire rack to cool completely. In 2 separate bowls, melt chocolate in a microwave while adding some maple syrup for taste. Dip one side of each biscuit in the dark chocolate and then in the white chocolate. Garnish dark chocolate's side with the pistachios and cool on the wire rack.

Per serving: Cal 470; Net Carbs 3.4g, Fat 45g, Protein 6.2g

Lime Avocado Ice Cream

Ingredients for 4 servings

2 large avocados, pitted / 1¾ cups coconut cream
Juice and zest of 3 limes / ¼ tsp vanilla extract
1/3 cup erythritol

Directions and Total Time: approx. 10 minutes

In a blender, combine avocado pulp, lime juice and zest, erythritol, coconut cream, and vanilla extract. Process until smooth. Pour the mixture into an ice cream maker and freeze. When ready, remove and scoop the ice cream into bowls. Serve immediately.

Per serving: Cal 260; Net Carbs 4g; Fat 25g; Protein 4g

Red Berries Fat Bombs

Ingredients for 4 servings

1 cup strawberries / 16 oz cream cheese, softened
1 cup raspberries / 4 tbsp unsalted butter
1 cup cranberries / 2 tbsp sugar-free maple syrup
1 tsp vanilla extract

Directions and Total Time: approx. 20 minutes

Line a muffin tray with liners and set aside. Puree the fruits in a blender with the vanilla. In a saucepan, melt cream cheese and butter together over medium heat until mixed. In a bowl, combine the fruit, cheese mixtures, and maple syrup evenly and fill the muffin tray with the mix. Refrigerate for 40 minutes and serve.

Per serving: Cal 227, Net Carbs 3.1g, Fat 15g, Protein 4g

Cardamom Coconut Fat Bombs

Ingredients for 6 servings

½ cup grated coconut   ½ tsp vanilla extract
3 oz vegan butter, softened   ¼ tsp cinnamon powder
¼ tsp cardamom powder

Directions and Total Time: approx. 5 minutes

Pour grated coconut into a skillet and roast until lightly brown. Set aside to cool. In a bowl, combine butter, half of the coconut, cardamom, vanilla, and cinnamon. Form balls from the mixture and roll each in the remaining coconut. Refrigerate until ready to serve.

Per serving: Cal 85; Net Carbs 1g; Fat 9g; Protein 1g

Chocolate Peppermint Mousse

Ingredients for 4 servings

¼ cup swerve sugar, divided ¾ tsp peppermint extract
4 oz dairy-free cream cheese, ½ tsp vanilla extract
3 tbsp cocoa powder   1/3 cup coconut cream

Directions and Total Time: approx. 10 min+ chilling time

Put 2 tbsp of swerve, cream cheese, and cocoa powder in a blender. Add in peppermint extract, and ¼ cup warm water; process until smooth. In a bowl, whip vanilla extract, coconut cream, and remaining swerve using a whisk. Fetch out 5 tbsp for garnishing. Fold in cocoa mixture until thoroughly combined. Spoon the mousse into cups and refrigerate. Garnish with whipped cream.

Per serving: Cal 170; Net Carbs 2g; Fat 16g; Protein 3g

Raspberries Turmeric Panna Cotta

Ingredients for 6 servings

½ tbsp unflavored powdered vegetarian gelatin
2 cups coconut cream   1 tbsp erythritol
¼ tsp vanilla extract   1 tbsp chopped toasted pecans
1 pinch turmeric powder   12 fresh raspberries

Directions and Total Time: approx. 10 min+ chilling time

Mix gelatin and ½ tsp water and allow sitting to dissolve. Pour coconut cream, vanilla extract, turmeric, and erythritol into a saucepan and bring to a boil, then, simmer for 2 minutes. Turn the heat off. Stir in gelatin. Pour into 6 glasses, cover with a plastic wrap, and refrigerate for 2 hours. Top with pecans and raspberries, and serve.

Per serving: Cal 270; Net Carbs 3g; Fat 27g; Protein 4g

Dark Chocolate Cake

Ingredients for 4 servings

½ cup olive oil   ½ tsp salt
1 cup almond flour   2 tsp cinnamon powder
½ cup dark chocolate, melted ½ cup boiling water
1 cup swerve sugar   3 large eggs
2 tsp vanilla bean paste

Directions and Total Time: approx. 5 minutes

Preheat oven to 350 F and grease a springform pan and line with parchment paper. In a bowl, combine olive oil, almond flour, chocolate, swerve, vanilla bean paste, salt, cinnamon, and boiling water. Crack the eggs one after the other, beating until smooth. Pour batter into the springform pan and bake for 45 minutes. Remove from oven; allow cooling in the pan for 10 minutes; turn over onto a wire rack. Dust with confectioner's sugar, and serve.

Per serving: Cal 417; Net Carbs 1.7g, Fat 41g, Protein 16g

Mint Chocolate Cheesecake

Ingredients for 4 servings

1 cup raw almonds   2 tbsp lime juice
½ cup salted butter, melted 1 ½ cups cream cheese
2 tbsp + ½ cup swerve sugar 1 cup Greek yogurt
1 cup dark chocolate, chopped 1 tbsp mint extract
2 gelatin sheets

Directions and Total Time: approx. 15 minutes

Preheat oven to 350 F. In a blender, process the almonds until finely ground. Add in butter and 2 tbsp of swerve, and mix until combined. Press the crust mixture into the bottom of the cake pan until firm. Bake for 5 minutes. Place in the fridge to chill. In a pot, combine gelatin with lime juice, and a tbsp of water. Let set for 5 minutes and, place the pot over medium heat to dissolve the gelatin. Pour dark chocolate in a bowl and melt in the microwave for 1 minute; set aside. In another bowl, beat cream cheese and remaining swerve sugar using an electric mixer until smooth. Stir in yogurt and gelatin until combined. Fold in melted chocolate and then the mint extract. Remove the pan from the fridge and pour the cream mixture on top. Tap the side gently to release any trapped air bubbles and transfer to the fridge to chip for 3 hours or more. Remove and release the pan's locker, top with more dark chocolate.

Per serving: Cal 235g, Net Carbs 3.8g, Fat 14g, Protein 7g

Dark Chocolate Fudge

Ingredients for 4 servings

1 cup dark chocolate, melted ½ cup melted butter
4 large eggs   1/3 cup coconut flour
1 cup swerve sugar

Directions and Total Time: approx. 30 minutes

Preheat oven to 350 F and line a rectangular baking tray with parchment paper. In a bowl, cream the eggs with swerve sugar until smooth. Add in melted chocolate, butter, and whisk until evenly combined. Carefully fold in the coconut flour to incorporate and pour the mixture into the baking tray. Bake for 20 minutes or until a toothpick inserted comes out clean. Remove from the oven and allow cooling in the tray. Cut into squares and serve.

Per serving: Cal 491; Net Carbs 2.8g, Fat 45g, Protein 13g

Key Lime Truffles

Ingredients for 6 servings

¼ cup cocoa powder mixed with 2 tbsp swerve sugar
1 cup dark chocolate, chopped
2/3 cup heavy cream
2 tsp lime extract

Directions and Total Time: approx. 5 min + cooling time

Heat heavy cream in a pan over low heat until tiny bubbles form around the edges of the pan. Turn the heat off. Pour dark chocolate into the pan, swirl the pan to allow the hot cream to spread over the chocolate, and then gently stir the mixture until smooth. Mix in lime extract and transfer to a bowl. Refrigerate for 4 hours. Line 2 baking trays with parchment papers; set one aside and pour cocoa powder mixture onto the other. Take out the chocolate mixture; form bite-size balls out of the mix and roll all round in the cocoa powder to completely coat. Place the truffles on the baking tray and refrigerate for 30 minutes before serving.

Per serving: Cal 143; Net Carbs 0.6g, Fat 12g, Protein 2.4g

Lemon Sponge Cake with Cream

Ingredients for 4 servings

1 tbsp swerve confectioner's sugar, for dusting
4 large lemons, chopped
¼ cup sugar-free maple syrup
½ cup butter, softened
½ cup erythritol
1 tsp vanilla extract
½ cup almond flour, sifted
3 large eggs, lightly beaten
½ cup heavy cream

Directions and Total Time: approx. 40 minutes

Place the chopped lemons in a saucepan. Add in sugar-free maple syrup and simmer over low heat for 30 minutes. Pour the mixture into a blender and process until smooth. Pour into a jar and set aside. Preheat oven to 350 F, grease two (8-inch) springform pans with cooking spray, and line with parchment paper. In a bowl, cream the butter, erythritol, and vanilla extract with an electric whisk until light and fluffy. Pour in the eggs gradually while beating until fully mixed. Carefully fold in the almond flour and share the mixture into the cake pans. Bake for 30 minutes or until springy when touched and a toothpick inserted comes out clean. Remove and let cool for 5 minutes before turning out onto a wire rack. In a bowl, whip heavy cream until a soft peak forms. Spoon onto the bottom sides of the cake and spread the lemon puree on top. Sandwich both cakes and sift confectioner's sugar on top. Slice and serve.

Per serving: Cal 266; Net Carbs 4.6g; Fat 25g; Protein 6g

Zucchini Cake Slices

Ingredients for 4 servings

1 cup butter, softened
1 cup erythritol
4 eggs
2/3 cup coconut flour
2 tsp baking powder
2/3 cup ground almonds
1 lemon, zested and juiced
1 cup finely grated zucchini
1 cup crème fraiche
1 tbsp chopped walnuts

Directions and Total Time: approx. 30 min + cooling time

Preheat oven to 375 F, grease a springform pan with and line with parchment paper. In a bowl, beat butter and erythritol until creamy and pale. Add eggs one after another while whisking. Sift coconut flour and baking powder into the mixture and stir along with ground almonds, lemon zest, juice, and zucchini. Spoon the mixture into the pan and bake for 40 minutes or until risen and a toothpick inserted into the cake comes out clean. Let cool inside the pan for 10 minutes, and transfer to a wire rack. Spread crème fraiche on top and sprinkle with walnuts to serve.

Per serving: Cal 778; Net Carbs 3.7g, Fat 71g, Protein 32g

Blackberry Lemon Tarte Tatin

Ingredients for 4 servings

¼ cup butter, cold and crumbled
¼ cup almond flour
3 tbsp coconut flour
½ tsp salt
3 tbsp erythritol
1 ½ tsp vanilla extract
4 whole eggs
4 tbsp melted butter
3 tsp swerve brown sugar
1 cup fresh blackberries
1 tsp vanilla extract
1 lemon, juiced
1 cup ricotta cheese
4 fresh basil leaves to garnish
1 egg, lightly beaten

Directions and Total Time: approx. 50 minutes

Preheat oven to 350 F. In a bowl, mix almond and coconut flour, and salt. Add in butter and mix until crumbly. Mix in erythritol and vanilla extract. Pour in the 4 eggs and mix until formed into a ball. Flatten the dough on a clean flat surface, cover in plastic wrap, and refrigerate for 1 hour. Dust a clean flat surface with almond flour, unwrap the dough, and roll out the dough into a circle. In a greased baking pan, mix butter, swerve brown sugar, blackberries, vanilla extract, and lemon juice. Arrange blackberries uniformly across the pan. Lay the pastry over the fruit filling and tuck the sides into the pan. Brush with beaten egg and bake for 40 minutes. Turn the pie onto a plate, crumble ricotta cheese on top, and garnish with basil.

Per serving: Cal 465; Net Carbs 5.8g, Fat 41g, Protein 16g

Avocado Truffles with Chocolate Coating

Ingredients for 6 servings

1 ripe avocado, pitted
½ tsp vanilla extract
½ tsp lemon zest
5 oz dark chocolate
1 tbsp coconut oil
1 tbsp cocoa powder

Directions and Total Time: approx. 5 minutes

Scoop pulp of the avocado into a bowl and mix with vanilla using an immersion blender. Stir in lemon zest and a pinch of salt. Microwave chocolate and coconut oil for 1 minute. Add to the avocado mixture and stir. Allow cooling to firm up a bit. Form balls out of the mix. Roll each ball in the cocoa powder and serve immediately.

Per serving: Cal 70; Net Carbs 2g; Fat 6g; Protein 2g

Strawberry Blackberry Pie

Ingredients for 4 servings

¼ cup butter, cold and crumbled
2 ¼ cup strawberries and blackberries
1 vanilla pod, bean paste extracted
¼ cup almond flour   1 ½ tsp vanilla extract
3 tbsp coconut flour   4 whole eggs
½ tsp salt   1 egg, beaten
3 tbsp + 1 cup erythritol

Directions and Total Time: approx. 30 min + cooling time

Preheat oven to 350 F. In a bowl, mix almond and coconut flours, and salt. Add in butter and mix until crumbly. Stir in 3 tbsp of erythritol and vanilla extract. Pour in the 4 eggs one after another while mixing until formed into a ball. Cover the dough with plastic wrap, and refrigerate for 1 hour. Dust a clean flat surface with almond flour, unwrap the dough, and roll out into a large rectangle to fit into a greased pie pan; prick the base of the crust. Bake until golden. In a bowl, mix berries, remaining erythritol, and vanilla paste. Spoon mixture into the pie and use the pastry strips to create a lattice over the berries. Brush with beaten egg and bake for 30 minutes. Slice and serve.

Per serving: Cal 262; Net Carbs 3g, Fat 21.7g, Protein 9g

Berry Hazelnut Trifle

Ingredients for 4 servings

1 ½ ripe avocados   1 tbsp vanilla extract
¾ cup coconut cream   3 oz fresh strawberries
Zest and juice of ½ a lemon   2 oz toasted hazelnuts

Directions and Total Time: approx. 5 minutes

In a bowl, add avocado pulp, coconut cream, lemon zest and juice, and half of the vanilla extract. Mix with an immersion blender. Put the strawberries and remaining vanilla in another bowl and use a fork to mash the fruits. In a tall glass, alternate layering the cream and strawberry mixtures. Drop a few hazelnuts on each and serve.

Per serving: Cal 360; Net Carbs 7g; Fat 34g; Protein 4g

Coconut Chocolate Fudge

Ingredients for 6 servings

2 cups coconut cream   3 oz dark chocolate, chopped
1 tsp vanilla extract   Swerve sugar for sprinkling
3 oz vegan butter

Directions and Total Time: approx. 20 min+ chilling time

Pour coconut cream and vanilla into a saucepan and bring to a boil over medium heat, then simmer until reduced by half, about 15 minutes. Stir in vegan butter until the batter is smooth. Add in dark chocolate and stir until melted. Pour the mixture into a baking sheet; chill in the fridge. Cut into squares, sprinkle with swerve sugar, and serve.

Per serving: Cal 116; Net Carbs 3g; Fat 11g; Protein 2g

Raspberry & Red Wine Crumble

Ingredients for 6 servings

2 cups raspberries   1 tsp vanilla extract
¼ cup red wine   1 cup salted butter, cubed
1 teaspoon cinnamon   1 ½ cups almond flour
1 ¼ cup erythritol, divided   ¾ cup coconut flour

Directions and Total Time: approx. 55 minutes

Preheat oven 375 F. In a baking dish, add raspberries, red wine, half of erythritol, vanilla extract, and stir. In a bowl, rub butter with almond and coconut flours, and erythritol until it resembles large breadcrumbs. Spoon the mixture to cover the raspberries, place in the oven, and bake for 45 minutes until the top is golden brown. Cool and serve.

Per serving: Cal 318; Net Carbs 4.8g, Fat 31g, Protein 1.5g

Avocado Fries

Ingredients for 2 servings

½ cup olive oil   Salt and black pepper to taste
3 avocados, sliced   1 cup grated Parmesan cheese
1 ½ tbsp almond flour   2 large eggs, beaten in a bowl

Directions and Total Time: approx. 10 minutes

In a bowl, combine flour, salt, pepper, and Parmesan. Toss avocado slices in eggs and then dredge in the Parmesan mixture. Heat olive oil in a deep pan. Fry avocado slices until golden brown, 2 minutes, and transfer to a wire rack.

Per serving: Cal 849; Net Carbs 7.2g; Fat 77g; Protein 21g

Cacao Nut Bites

Ingredients for 4 servings

3 ½ oz dark chocolate   2 tbsp roasted coconut chips
½ cup mixed nuts   1 tbsp sunflower seeds

Directions and Total Time: approx. 5 minutes

Microwave chocolate for 2 minutes. Into 10 small cupcake liners, share the chocolate. Drop in nuts, coconut chips, sunflower seeds and sprinkle with salt. Chill until firm.

Per serving: Cal 72; Net Carbs 3g; Fat 5g; Protein 2g

Cranberry Coconut Parfait

Ingredients for 4 servings

2 cups coconut yogurt   3 mint sprigs, chopped
¼ cup fresh cranberries   2 tbsp hemp seeds
½ lemon, zested   Sugar-free maple syrup to taste

Directions and Total Time: approx. 5 minutes

In serving glasses, add half of coconut yogurt, cranberries, lemon zest, mint, hemp seeds, and drizzle with maple syrup. Repeat a second layer. Serve with maple syrup.

Per serving: Cal 105; Net Carbs 2.9g, Fat 7.8g, Protein 5g

SNACKS & SIDE DISHES

Jalapeño Nacho Wings

Ingredients for 4 servings

2 cups shredded Mexican cheese blend
16 chicken wings, halved
½ cup butter, melted
1 cup golden flaxseed meal

2 tbsp chopped green chilies
1 cup chopped scallions
1 jalapeño pepper, sliced

Directions and Total Time: approx. 45 minutes

Preheat oven to 350 F. Toss chicken with butter, salt, pepper to coat. Spread the flaxseed meal in a wide plate and roll in each chicken wing. Place on a baking sheet and bake for 30-35 minutes or until golden brown and cooked within. Sprinkle with the cheese blend, green chilies, scallions, and jalapeño pepper on top. Serve immediately.

Per serving: Cal 798; Net Carbs 1.5g; Fat 61g; Protein 48g

Easy Bacon & Cheese Balls

Ingredients for 4 servings

7 bacon slices, chopped
6 oz cream cheese
6 oz shredded Gruyere cheese

2 tbsp butter, softened
½ tsp red chili flakes

Directions and Total Time: approx. 30 minutes

Put bacon in a skillet and fry over medium heat until crispy, 5 minutes. Transfer to a plate, crumble after. Pour the bacon grease into a bowl and mix in cream cheese, Gruyere cheese, butter, and red chili flakes. Refrigerate to set for 15 minutes. Remove and mold into walnut-sized balls. Roll in the crumbled bacon. Plate and serve.

Per serving: Cal 538; Net Carbs 0.5g; Fat 50g; Protein 22g

Chili Turnip Fries

Ingredients for 4 servings

6 large parsnips, sliced
3 tbsp ground pork rinds

3 tbsp olive oil
¼ tsp red chili flakes

Directions and Total Time: approx. 50 minutes

Preheat oven to 425 F. Pour parsnips into a bowl and add in pork rinds, salt, and pepper. Toss and divide the parsnips between 2 baking sheets. Drizzle with olive oil and sprinkle with chili flakes. Bake in the oven until crispy, 40 to 45 minutes, tossing halfway. Serve.

Per serving: Cal 260; Net Carbs 22.6g; Fat 11g; Protein 3g

Baked Toast Strips with Prosciutto Butter

Ingredients for 4 servings

4 slices prosciutto, chopped
2 shallots
½ cup butter, softened
1 tbsp fresh basil

1 tsp tomato paste
4 slices zero carb bread
2 tbsp extra-virgin olive oil

Directions and Total Time: approx. 50 minutes

Add prosciutto, 1 tbsp of butter, and shallots to a skillet. Cook with frequent stirring for 5 minutes; let cool. Mix in the remaining butter, basil, and tomato paste. Season with salt and pepper. Spoon into a bowl and chill for 30 minutes to solidify slightly. Brush zero carb bread with olive oil, cut into strips, place on a baking sheet and toast for 3-5 minutes in a preheated at 400 F oven or until brown and crispy. Sprinkle with salt, and serve with prosciutto butter.

Per serving: Cal 315; Net Carbs 8.8g; Fat 28g; Protein 5g

Wrapped Halloumi in Bacon

Ingredients for 4 servings

16 bacon strips
½ lb halloumi cheese, cut into
16 cubes

½ cup swerve brown sugar
½ cup mayonnaise
¼ cup hot sauce

Directions and Total Time: approx. 30 minutes

Lay bacon in a skillet and cook over medium heat on both sides until crisp, 5 minutes; transfer to a plate. Wrap each halloumi cheese with a bacon strip and secure with a toothpick each. Place on a baking sheet. In a bowl, combine brown sugar, mayonnaise, and hot sauce. Pour the mixture all over the bacon-halloumi pieces and bake in the oven at 350 F for 10 minutes. Let cool and serve.

Per serving: Cal 346; Net Carbs 4.6g; Fat 25g; Protein 13g

Sweet Mustard Mini Sausages

Ingredients for 4 servings

1 cup swerve brown sugar
3 tbsp almond flour
2 tsp mustard powder
¼ cup lemon juice

¼ cup white vinegar
1 tsp tamari sauce
2 lb mini smoked sausages

Directions and Total Time: approx. 15 minutes

In a pot, combine swerve, flour, and mustard. Gradually stir in lemon juice, vinegar, and tamari sauce. Bring to a boil over medium heat while stirring until thickened, 2 minutes. Mix in sausages until properly coated. Cook them for 5 minutes. Dish the food into plates and serve.

Per serving: Cal 744; Net Carbs 7.2g; Fat 45g; Protein 24g

Chili Broccoli & Pancetta Roast

Ingredients for 4 servings

1 lb broccoli rabe, halved
6 pancetta slices, chopped

2 tbsp olive oil
¼ tsp red chili flakes

Directions and Total Time: approx. 40 minutes

Preheat oven to 425 F. Scatter broccoli rabe in a baking sheet, top with pancetta, drizzle with olive oil, season to taste, and with sprinkle chili flakes. Roast for 30 minutes.

Per serving: Cal 125; Net Carbs 0.2g; Fat 10g; Protein 7g

Cheesy Bacon & Eggplant Gratin

Ingredients for 4 servings

6 bacon slices, chopped
3 large eggplants, sliced
1 tbsp dried oregano
1/3 cup chopped parsley

Salt and black pepper to taste
½ cup crumbled feta cheese
¾ cup heavy cream
½ cup shredded Parmesan

Directions and Total Time: approx. 50 minutes

Preheat oven to 400 F. Put bacon in a skillet and fry over medium heat until brown and crispy, 6 minutes; transfer to a plate. Arrange half of eggplants in a greased baking sheet, season with oregano, parsley, salt, and pepper. Scatter half of bacon and half of feta cheese on top and repeat the layering process using the remaining ingredients. In a bowl, combine heavy cream with half of Parmesan, and spread on top of the layered ingredients. Sprinkle with the remaining Parmesan. Bake until the cream is bubbly and the gratin golden, 20 minutes. Serve.

Per serving: Cal 433; Net Carbs 1.7g; Fat 29g; Protein 16g

Buttery Radish & Minute Steak Sauté

Ingredients for 4 servings

10 oz minute steak, cut into small pieces
3 tbsp butter
1½ lb radishes, quartered

1 garlic clove, minced
2 tbsp freshly chopped thyme

Directions and Total Time: approx. 30 minutes

Melt in a skillet over, season the meat with salt and pepper, and fry until brown on all sides, 12 minutes; transfer to a plate. Add and sauté radishes, garlic, and thyme until the radishes cook within, 10 minutes. Plate and serve warm.

Per serving: Cal 252; Net Carbs 0.4g; Fat 16g; Protein 21g

Delicious Pancetta Strawberries

Ingredients for 4 servings

2 tbsp swerve confectioner's sugar
1 cup mascarpone cheese
1/8 tsp white pepper

12 fresh strawberries
12 thin slices pancetta

Directions and Total Time: approx. 30 minutes

In a bowl, combine mascarpone, swerve, and white pepper. Coat strawberries in the cheese mixture, wrap each strawberry in a pancetta slice, and place on an ungreased baking sheet. Bake in the oven for 425 F for 15-20 minutes until pancetta browns and is crispy. Serve warm.

Per serving: Cal 171; Net Carbs 1.2g; Fat 11g; Protein 12g

Salami & Cheddar Skewers

Ingredients for 4 servings

¼ cup olive oil
1 tbsp plain vinegar
2 garlic cloves, minced
1 tsp dried Italian herb blend

4 oz hard salami, cubed
¼ cup pitted Kalamata olives
12 oz cheddar cheese, cubed
1 tsp chopped parsley

Directions and Total Time: approx. 4 hours

In a bowl, mix olive oil, vinegar, garlic, and herb blend. Add in salami, olives, and cheddar cheese. Mix until well coated. Cover the bowl with plastic wrap and marinate in the refrigerator for 4 hours. Remove, drain the marinade and skewer one salami cube, one olive, and one cheese cube. Repeat making more skewers with the remaining ingredients. Plate and garnish with the parsley to serve.

Per serving: Cal 585; Net Carbs 1.8g; Fat 52g; Protein 27g

Chives & Green Beans Ham Rolls

Ingredients for 4 servings

8 oz Havarti cheese, cut into 16 strips
16 thin slices deli ham, cut in half lengthwise
1 medium sweet red pepper, cut into 16 strips
1 ½ cups water
16 fresh green beans

2 tbsp salted butter
16 whole chives

Directions and Total Time: approx. 50 minutes

Bring the water to a boil in a skillet over medium heat. Add in green beans, cover, and cook for 3 minutes or until softened; drain. Melt butter in a skillet and sauté green beans for 2 minutes; transfer to a plate. Assemble 1 green bean, 1 strip of red pepper, 1 cheese strip, and wrap with a ham slice. Tie with one chive. Repeat the assembling process with the remaining ingredients and refrigerate.

Per serving: Cal 399; Net Carbs 8.7g; Fat 24g; Protein 35g

Savory Pan-Fried Cauliflower & Bacon

Ingredients for 4 servings

1 large head cauliflower, cut into florets
10 oz bacon, chopped
1 garlic clove, minced

Salt and black pepper to taste
2 tbsp parsley, finely chopped

Directions and Total Time: approx. 15 minutes

Pour cauliflower in salted boiling water over medium heat and cook for 5 minutes or until soft; drain and set aside. In a skillet, fry bacon until brown and crispy. Add cauliflower and garlic. Sauté until the cauli browns slightly. Season with salt and pepper. Garnish with parsley and serve.

Per serving: Cal 243; Net Carbs 3.9g; Fat 21g; Protein 9g

Roasted Ham with Radishes

Ingredients for 4 servings

1 lb radishes, halved
Salt and black pepper to taste

1 tbsp cold butter
3 slices deli ham, chopped

Directions and Total Time: approx. 30 minutes

Preheat oven to 375 F. Arrange the radishes on a greased baking sheet. Season with salt and pepper; divide butter and ham on top. Bake for 25 minutes. Serve.

Per serving: Cal 68; Net Carbs 0.5g; Fat 4g; Protein 4g

Green Bean & Mozzarella Roast with Bacon

Ingredients for 4 servings

2 tbsp olive oil
1 tsp onion powder
1 egg, beaten

15 oz fresh green beans
5 tbsp grated mozzarella
4 bacon slices, chopped

Directions and Total Time: approx. 30 minutes

Preheat oven to 350 F and line a baking sheet with parchment paper. In a bowl, mix olive oil, onion and garlic powders, salt, pepper, and egg. Add in green beans and mozzarella; toss to coat. Pour the mixture onto the baking sheet and bake until the green beans brown slightly and cheese melts, 20 minutes. Fry bacon in a skillet until crispy and brown. Remove green beans and divide between serving plates. Top with bacon and serve.

Per serving: Cal 208; Net Carbs 2.6g; Fat 19g; Protein 6g

Cheddar Bacon & Celeriac Bake

Ingredients for 4 servings

6 bacon slices, chopped
3 tbsp butter
3 garlic cloves, minced
3 tbsp almond flour
2 cups coconut cream

1 cup chicken broth
Salt and black pepper to taste
2 lb celeriac, peeled and sliced
2 cups shredded cheddar
¼ cup chopped scallions

Directions and Total Time: approx. 1 hour 30 minutes

Preheat oven to 400 F. Add bacon to a skillet and fry over medium heat until brown and crispy. Spoon onto a plate. Melt butter in the same skillet and sauté garlic for 1 minute. Mix in almond flour and cook for another minute. Whisk in coconut cream, broth, and season with salt and pepper. Simmer for 5 minutes. Spread a layer of the sauce in a greased casserole dish, arrange a layer celeriac on top, cover with more sauce, top with some bacon and cheddar cheese, and scatter scallions on top. Repeat the layering process until the ingredients are exhausted. Bake for 75 minutes. Let rest and serve.

Per serving: Cal 981; Net Carbs 20.5g; Fat 86g; Protein 28g

Chicken Ham with Mini Bell Peppers

Ingredients for 4 servings

12 mini green bell peppers, halved and deseeded
4 slices chicken ham, chopped
1 tbsp chopped parsley
8 oz cream cheese
½ tbsp hot sauce

2 tbsp melted butter
1 cup shredded Gruyere

Directions and Total Time: approx. 30 minutes

Preheat oven to 400 F. Place peppers in a greased baking dish and set aside. In a bowl, combine chicken ham, parsley, cream cheese, hot sauce, and butter. Spoon the mixture into the peppers and sprinkle Gruyere cheese on top. Bake until the cheese melts, 15 minutes. Serve.

Per serving: Cal 408; Net Carbs 4g; Fat 32g; Protein 19g

Crispy Baked Cheese Asparagus

Ingredients for 4 servings

1 cup grated Pecorino Romano cheese
4 slices Serrano ham, chopped
2 lb asparagus, stalks trimmed
¾ cup coconut cream
3 garlic cloves, minced

1 cup crushed pork rinds
1 cup grated mozzarella
½ tsp sweet paprika

Directions and Total Time: approx. 40 minutes

Preheat oven to 400 F. Arrange asparagus on a greased baking dish and pour coconut cream on top. Scatter the garlic on top, season with salt and pepper, top with pork rinds, serrano ham, and sprinkle with Pecorino cheese, mozzarella, and paprika. Bake until the cheese melts and is golden and asparagus tender, 30 minutes. Serve.

Per serving: Cal 361; Net Carbs 15g; Fat 21g; Protein 32g

Creamy Ham & Parsnip Puree

Ingredients for 4 servings

2 lb parsnips, diced
3 tbsp olive oil, divided
2 tsp garlic powder
¾ cup almond milk

4 tbsp heavy cream
4 tbsp butter
6 slices deli ham, chopped
2 tsp freshly chopped oregano

Directions and Total Time: approx. 45 minutes

Preheat oven to 400 F. Spread parsnips on a greased baking sheet, drizzle with 2 tbsp olive oil, and season with salt and pepper. Cover tightly with aluminum foil and bake until the parsnips are tender, 40 minutes. Remove from the oven, take off the foil, and transfer to a bowl. Add in garlic powder, almond milk, heavy cream, and butter. Using an immersion blender, puree the ingredients until smooth. Fold in the ham and sprinkle with oregano.

Per serving: Cal 477; Net Carbs 20g; Fat 30g; Protein 10g

Chili Baked Zucchini Sticks with Aioli

Ingredients for 4 servings

¼ cup Pecorino Romano cheese, shredded
¼ cup pork rind crumbs
1 tsp sweet paprika
Salt and chili pepper to taste
1 cup mayonnaise

Juice from half lemon
2 garlic cloves, minced
3 fresh eggs
2 zucchinis, cut into strips

Directions and Total Time: approx. 25 minutes

Preheat oven to 425 F and line a baking sheet with foil. In a bowl, mix pork rinds, paprika, Pecorino Romano cheese, salt, and chili pepper. Beat the eggs in another bowl. Coat zucchini strips in egg, then in the cheese mixture, and arrange on the sheet. Grease lightly with cooking spray and bake for 15 minutes. Combine in a bowl mayonnaise, lemon juice, and garlic, and gently stir until everything is well incorporated. Serve the strips with aioli.

Per serving: Cal 180; Net Carbs 2g; Fat 14g; Protein 6g

Cauliflower Rice & Bacon Gratin

Ingredients for 4 servings

1 cup canned artichoke hearts, drained and chopped
6 bacon slices, chopped
2 cups cauliflower rice
3 cups baby spinach, chopped
1 garlic clove, minced
1 tbsp olive oil

Salt and black pepper to taste
¼ cup sour cream
8 oz cream cheese, softened
¼ cup grated Parmesan
1 ½ cups grated mozzarella

Directions and Total Time: approx. 30 minutes

Preheat oven to 350 F. Cook bacon in a skillet over medium heat until brown and crispy, 5 minutes. Spoon onto a plate. In a bowl, mix cauli rice, artichokes, spinach, garlic, olive oil, salt, pepper, sour cream, cream cheese, bacon, and half of Parmesan cheese. Spread the mixture into a baking dish and top with the remaining Parmesan and mozzarella cheeses. Bake 15 minutes. Serve.

Per serving: Cal 500; Net Carbs 5.3g; Fat 37g; Protein 28g

Crunchy Rutabaga Puffs

Ingredients for 4 servings

1 rutabaga, peeled and diced
2 tbsp melted butter

½ oz goat cheese
¼ cup ground pork rinds

Directions and Total Time: approx. 35 minutes

Preheat oven to 400 F and spread rutabaga on a baking sheet. Season with salt, pepper, and drizzle with the butter. Bake until tender, 15 minutes. Transfer to a bowl. Allow cooling and add in goat cheese. Using a fork, mash and mix the ingredients. Pour the pork rinds onto a plate. Mold 1-inch balls out of the rutabaga mixture and roll properly in the rinds while pressing gently to stick. Place in the same baking sheet and bake for 10 minutes until golden.

Per serving: Cal 129; Net Carbs 5.9g; Fat 8g; Protein 3g

Crispy Pancetta & Butternut Squash Roast

Ingredients for 4 servings

2 butternut squash, cubed
1 tsp turmeric powder
½ tsp garlic powder

8 pancetta slices, chopped
2 tbsp olive oil
1 tbsp chopped cilantro,

Directions and Total Time: approx. 30 minutes

Preheat oven to 425 F. In a bowl, add butternut squash, salt, pepper, turmeric, garlic powder, pancetta, and olive oil. Toss until well-coated. Spread the mixture onto a greased baking sheet and roast for 10-15 minutes. Transfer the veggies to a bowl and garnish with cilantro to serve.

Per serving: Cal 148; Net Carbs 6.4g; Fat 10g; Protein 6g

Simple Stuffed Eggs with Mayonnaise

Ingredients for 6 servings

6 eggs
1 tbsp green tabasco

¼ cup mayonnaise
2 tbsp black olives, sliced

Directions and Total Time: approx. 30 minutes

Place eggs in a saucepan and cover with salted water. Boil for 10 minutes. Place the eggs in an ice bath and let cool. Peel and slice in half lengthwise. Scoop out the yolks to a bowl; mash with a fork. Whisk together the tabasco, mayonnaise, mashed yolks, and salt, in a bowl. Spoon this mixture into egg white. Garnish with olive slices to serve.

Per serving: Cal 178; Net Carbs: 5g; Fat: 17g; Protein: 6g

Cheesy Pork Rind Bread

Ingredients for 4 servings

¼ cup grated Pecorino Romano cheese
8 oz cream cheese
2 cups grated mozzarella
1 tbsp baking powder

1 cup crushed pork rinds
3 large eggs
1 tbsp Italian mixed herbs

Directions and Total Time: approx. 30 minutes

Preheat oven to 375 F and line a baking sheet with parchment paper. Microwave cream and mozzarella cheeses for 1 minute or until melted. Whisk in baking powder, pork rinds, eggs, Pecorino cheese, and mixed herbs. Spread the mixture in the baking sheet and bake for 20 minutes until lightly brown. Let cool, slice and serve.

Per serving: Cal 437; Net Carbs 3.2g; Fat 23g; Protein 32g

Savory Lime Fried Artichokes

Ingredients for 4 servings

12 fresh baby artichokes
2 tbsp lime juice

2 tbsp olive oil
Salt to taste

Directions and Total Time: approx. 20 minutes

Slice artichokes vertically into narrow wedges. Drain on paper towels before frying. Heat olive oil in a skillet. Fry the artichokes until browned and crispy. Drain excess oil on paper towels. Sprinkle with salt and lime juice.

Per serving: Cal 35; Net Carbs: 2.9g; Fat: 2.4g; Protein: 2g

Rosemary Cheese Chips with Guacamole

Ingredients for 4 servings

1 tbsp rosemary
1 cup Grana Padano, grated
¼ tsp sweet paprika

¼ tsp garlic powder
2 avocados, pitted and scooped
1 tomato, chopped

Directions and Total Time: approx. 20 minutes

Preheat oven to 350 F and line a baking sheet with parchment paper. Mix Grana Padano cheese, paprika, rosemary, and garlic powder evenly. Spoon 6-8 teaspoons on the baking sheet creating spaces between each mound.; flatten mounds. Bake for 5 minutes, cool, and remove to a plate. To make the guacamole, mash avocado, with a fork in a bowl, add in tomato and continue to mash until mostly smooth. Season with salt. Serve crackers with guacamole.

Per serving: Cal 229; Net Carbs 2g; Fat 20g; Protein 10g

Parmesan Green Bean Crisps

Ingredients for 6 servings

¼ cup Parmesan, shredded	2 eggs
¼ cup pork rind crumbs	1 lb green beans
1 tsp minced garlic	Salt and black pepper to taste

Directions and Total Time: approx. 30 minutes

Preheat oven to 425 F and line two baking sheets with foil. Mix Parmesan cheese, pork rinds, garlic, salt, and pepper in a bowl. Beat the eggs in another bowl. Coat green beans in eggs, then cheese mixture and arrange evenly on the baking sheets. Grease lightly with cooking spray and bake for 15 minutes. Transfer to a wire rack to cool. Serve.

Per serving: Cal 210; Net Carbs 3g; Fat 19g; Protein 5g

Paprika & Dill Deviled Eggs

Ingredients for 4 servings

1 tsp dill, chopped	3 tbsp sriracha sauce
8 large eggs	4 tbsp mayonnaise
3 cups water	¼ tsp sweet paprika

Directions and Total Time: approx. 20 minutes

Bring eggs to boil in salted water, reduce the heat, and simmer for 10 minutes. Transfer to an ice water bath, let cool completely and peel the shells. Slice the eggs in half height wise and empty the yolks into a bowl. Smash with a fork and mix in sriracha sauce, mayonnaise, and half of the paprika until smooth. Spoon filling into a piping bag and fill the egg whites to be slightly above the brim. Garnish with remaining paprika and dill and serve immediately.

Per serving: Cal 195; Net Carbs 1g; Fat 19g; Protein 4g

Cheese & Garlic Crackers

Ingredients for 6 servings

1 ¼ cups Pecorino Romano cheese, grated	
1 ¼ cups coconut flour	¼ cup ghee
Salt and black pepper to taste	¼ tsp sweet paprika
1 tsp garlic powder	½ cup heavy cream

Directions and Total Time: approx. 30 minutes

Preheat oven to 350 F. Mix flour, Pecorino Romano cheese, salt, pepper, garlic and paprika in a bowl. Add in ghee and mix well. Top with heavy cream and mix again until a thick mixture has formed. Cover the dough with plastic wrap. Use a rolling pin to spread out the dough into a light rectangle. Cut into cracker squares and arrange them on a baking sheet. Bake for 20 minutes.

Per serving: Cal 115; Net Carbs 0.7g; Fat 3g; Protein 5g

Cheesy Chicken Wraps

Ingredients for 8 servings

¼ tsp garlic powder	8 raw chicken tenders
8 ounces fontina cheese	8 prosciutto slices

Directions and Total Time: approx. 20 minutes

Pound chicken until half an inch thick. Season with garlic powder. Cut fontina cheese into 8 strips. Place a slice of prosciutto on a flat surface. Place one chicken tender on top. Top with a fontina strip. Roll the chicken and secure with skewers. Grill the wraps for 3 minutes per side.

Per serving: Cal 174; Net Carbs: 0.7g; Fat: 10g; Protein: 17g

Baked Chorizo with Cottage Cheese

Ingredients for 6 servings

7 oz Spanish chorizo, sliced	¼ cup chopped parsley
4 oz cottage cheese, pureed	

Directions and Total Time: approx. 30 minutes

Preheat the oven to 325 F. Line a baking dish with waxed paper. Bake the chorizo for 15 minutes until crispy. Remove from the oven and let cool. Arrange on a serving platter. Top each slice with cottage cheese and parsley.

Per serving: Cal 172; Net Carbs: 0.2g; Fat: 13g; Protein: 5g

Goat Cheese Stuffed Peppers

Ingredients for 8 servings

8 canned roasted piquillo peppers	
3 slices prosciutto, cut into thin slices	
2 tbsp olive oil	3 tbsp chopped parsley
8 ounces goat cheese	½ tsp minced garlic
3 tbsp heavy cream	1 tbsp chopped mint

Directions and Total Time: approx. 15 minutes

Combine goat cheese, heavy cream, parsley, garlic, and mint in a bowl. Place the mixture in a freezer bag, press down and squeeze, and cut off the bottom. Drain and deseed the peppers. Squeeze about 2 tbsp of the filling into each pepper. Wrap a prosciutto slice onto each pepper. Secure with toothpicks. Arrange them on a serving platter. Sprinkle the olive oil and vinegar over.

Per serving: Cal 110; Net Carbs 2.5g; Fat 9g; Protein 6g

Spinach Cheesy Puff Balls

Ingredients for 8 servings

⅓ cup crumbled ricotta	2 tbsp butter, melted
¼ tsp nutmeg	⅓ cup Parmesan cheese
¼ tsp black pepper	2 eggs
3 tbsp heavy cream	8 ounces spinach
1 tsp garlic powder	1 cup almond flour
1 tbsp onion powder	

Directions and Total Time: approx. 30 minutes

Place all ingredients in a food processor. Process until smooth. Place in the freezer for 10 minutes. Make balls out of the mixture and arrange them on a lined baking sheet. Bake at 350 F for about 10-12 minutes.

Per serving: Cal 60; Net Carbs 0.8g; Fat 5g; Protein 8g

Crispy & Cheesy Salami

Ingredients for 6 servings

7 ounces dried salami   ¼ cup chopped parsley
4 ounces cream cheese

Directions and Total Time: approx. 30 minutes

Preheat oven to 325 F. Slice the salami into 30 slices. Line a baking dish with waxed paper. Bake the salami for 15 minutes until crispy. Remove from the oven and let cool. Arrange on a serving platter. Top each slice with cream cheese. Serve with sprinkled with chopped parsley.

Per serving: Cal 27; Net Carbs 0g; Fat 3g; Protein 2g

Butter-Drowned Broccoli

Ingredients for 6 servings

1 broccoli head, florets only   Salt and black pepper to taste
¼ cup butter, melted

Directions and Total Time: approx. 10 minutes

Place the broccoli in a pot filled with salted water and bring to a boil. Cook for about 3 minutes, or until tender. Drain the broccoli and transfer to a plate. Drizzle the butter over and season with some salt and pepper.

Per serving: Cal 114; Net Carbs 5.5g; Fat 7.8g; Protein 4g

Basic Cauliflower Fritters

Ingredients for 4 servings

1 pound grated cauliflower   ½ cup almond flour
½ cup Parmesan cheese   3 eggs
1 chopped onion   ½ tsp lemon juice
½ tsp baking powder   4 tbsp olive oil

Directions and Total Time: approx. 35 minutes

Sprinkle the salt over the cauliflower in a bowl, and let it stand for 10 minutes. Place the other ingredients in the bowl; mix to combine. Place a skillet over medium heat and heat olive oil. Shape fritters out of the cauliflower mixture. Fry for 3 minutes per side. Serve warm or cold.

Per serving: Cal 109; Net Carbs 3g; Fat 8.5g; Protein 4.5g

Fried Artichoke Hearts

Ingredients for 4 servings

12 fresh baby artichokes   3 tbsp olive oil
2 tbsp lemon juice   Salt to taste

Directions and Total Time: approx. 15 minutes

Slice the artichokes vertically into narrow wedges. Drain them on a piece of paper towel before frying. Heat olive oil in a cast-iron skillet over high heat. Fry the artichokes until browned and crispy. Drain excess oil, sprinkle with salt and lemon juice.

Per serving: Cal 35; Net Carbs 2.9g; Fat 2.4g; Protein 2g

Provolone & Prosciutto Chicken Wraps

Ingredients for 8 servings

¼ tsp garlic powder   8 chicken tenders
8 ounces provolone cheese   8 prosciutto slices

Directions and Total Time: approx. 20 minutes

Pound the chicken until half an inch thick. Season with garlic powder. Cut the provolone cheese into 8 strips. Place a slice of prosciutto on a flat surface. Place one chicken tender on top. Top with a provolone strip. Roll the chicken and secure with previously soaked skewers. Grill the wraps for about 3 minutes per side.

Per serving: Cal 174; Net Carbs 0.7g; Fat 10g; Protein 17g

Tuna Topped Pickles

Ingredients for 8 servings

12 oz smoked canned tuna   ⅓ cup sugar-free mayonnaise
6 large dill pickles, halved   1 tbsp onion flakes
¼ tsp garlic powder

Directions and Total Time: approx. 40 minutes

Combine the seasonings, mayonnaise, and tuna in a bowl. Top each pickle half with the tuna mixture. Place in the fridge for 30 minutes before serving.

Per serving: Cal 118; Net Carbs 1.5g; Fat 10g; Protein 11g

Keto Deviled Eggs

Ingredients for 6 servings

6 eggs   ⅓ cup sugar-free mayonnaise
1 tbsp green tabasco   Salt to taste

Directions and Total Time: approx. 30 minutes

Place eggs in a saucepan and cover with salted water. Bring to a boil over medium heat, for 8 minutes. Place in an ice bath to cool. Peel and slice. Whisk tabasco, mayo, and salt, in a bowl. Top every egg with some mayo dressing.

Per serving: Cal 178; Net Carbs 5g; Fat 17g; Protein 6g

Bacon & Pistachio Liverwurst Truffles

Ingredients for 8 servings

8 bacon slices, cooked and chopped
8 ounces liverwurst   1 tsp Dijon mustard
¼ cup chopped pistachios   6 ounces cream cheese

Directions and Total Time: approx. 45 minutes

Combine liverwurst and pistachios in a food processor. Pulse until smooth. Whisk cream cheese and mustard in another bowl. Make 12 balls out of the liverwurst mixture. Make a thin cream cheese layer over. Coat with bacon pieces. Arrange on a plate and refrigerate for 30 minutes.

Per serving: Cal 145; Net Carbs 1.5g; Fat 12g; Protein 7g

Roasted Broccoli & Cauliflower Steaks

Ingredients for 6 servings

1 head broccoli and 1 head cauliflower, sliced
2 tbsp olive oil   1 tsp ground coriander
Salt and chili pepper to taste

Directions and Total Time: approx. 30 minutes

Preheat oven to 400 F and line a baking sheet with foil. Brush the broccoli and cauliflower steaks with olive oil and season with chili pepper, coriander, and salt. Spread on a greased baking sheet in one layer. Roast in the oven for 10 minutes until tender and lightly browned.

Per serving: Cal 62; Net Carbs 1.4g; Fat 4.9g; Protein 2.4g

Gruyere & Ham Waffle Sandwiches

Ingredients for 4 servings

4 slices smoked ham, chopped   ½ tsp baking powder
4 tbsp butter, softened   ½ tsp dried thyme
½ cup Gruyère cheese, grated   4 tomato slices
6 eggs

Directions and Total Time: approx. 20 minutes

In a bowl, mix eggs, baking powder, thyme, butter and salt. Set a waffle iron over medium heat, add in ¼ cup of the batter and cook for 6 minutes until golden. Do the same with the remaining batter until you have 8 thin waffles. Lay a tomato slice on top of one waffle, followed by a ham slice, then top with ¼ of the grated cheese. Cover with another waffle, place the sandwich in the waffle iron and cook until the cheese melts. Do the same with all remaining ingredients. Serve.

Per serving: Cal 276; Net Carbs 3.1g; Fat 22g; Protein 16g

No Bake Cheesy Walnut Balls

Ingredients for 4 servings

1 ½ cups feta cheese, crumbled   1 habanero pepper, chopped
1 cup ground walnuts   ¼ tsp parsley flakes
½ cream cheese   ½ tsp hot paprika
2 tbsp butter, softened

Directions and Total Time: approx. 15 minutes

In a bowl, mix all ingredients, except for the walnuts, to combine. Cover with foil and refrigerate for 30 minutes to firm up. Remove from the fridge and form balls from the mixture. Place the ground walnuts in a plate and roll the balls to coat on all sides. Serve.

Per serving: Cal 398; Net Carbs 5.4g; Fat 37g; Protein 12.4g

Smoked Bacon & Poached Egg Cups

Ingredients for 6 servings

4 oz smoked bacon, sliced   ½ cup mozzarella, shredded
6 eggs   4 tbsp sour cream
2 tbsp chives, chopped   Salt and black pepper, to taste

Directions and Total Time: approx. 20 minutes

Fry bacon slices in a pan over medium heat for 4 minutes on both sides. With the bacon fat, grease 6 ramekins, then line 2 bacon slices on the inside of each cup. Share the sour cream, mozzarella, and crack an egg in each cup. Sprinkle with salt, pepper and chives. Bake for 15 minutes in a preheated oven at 400 F, until the eggs are set. Serve.

Per serving: Cal 149; Net Carbs 2.4g; Fat 16g; Protein 10g

Cauliflower Popcorn with Walnuts & Parsley

Ingredients for 4 servings

1 head cauliflower, broken into florets
1 tbsp olive oil   1 tsp turmeric
1 cup walnuts, halved   1 tsp fresh parsley, chopped
¼ cup Parmesan cheese, grated   1 tsp chili pepper powder
1 tsp garlic, smashed   Salt to taste

Directions and Total Time: approx. 30 minutes

Preheat oven to 390 F. Coat the florets with olive oil, salt, chili pepper powder, garlic, and turmeric. Pour in a baking dish and add in walnuts and parsley. Bake for 25 minutes until crisp. Sprinkle with Parmesan cheese and bake for another 2-3 minutes until the cheese melts. Serve.

Per serving: Cal 211; Net Carbs 5.7g; Fat 18g; Protein 6.4g

No-Bake & Egg Balls

Ingredients for 6 servings

Salt and crushed red pepper flakes, to taste
3 tbsp mayonnaise   8 black olives, chopped
2 eggs, cooked and chopped   1 oz salami, chopped
½ cup butter, softened   2 tbsp flax seeds

Directions and Total Time: approx. 35 minutes

Throw the eggs, olives, flakes, mayonnaise, butter, and salt in a food processor, and blitz until everything is combined. Stir in the chopped salami. Refrigerate for 20 minutes. Make balls from the mixture. Pour the flax seeds on a large plate; roll the balls through to coat. Serve.

Per serving: Cal 233; Net Carbs 1.3g; Fat 23g; Protein 4.4g

Baked Spicy Eggplants

Ingredients for 4 servings

2 large eggplants   1 tsp red chili flakes
2 tbsp butter   4 oz raw ground almonds

Directions and Total Time: approx. 30 minutes

Preheat oven to 400 F. Cut off the head of the eggplants and slice the body into rounds. Arrange on a parchment paper-lined baking sheet. Drop thin slices of butter on each eggplant slice, sprinkle with chili flakes, and bake for 20 minutes. Slide out and sprinkle with almonds. Roast further for 5 minutes. Serve with arugula salad.

Per serving: Cal 230; Net Carbs 4g; Fat 16g; Protein 14g

Mashed Broccoli with Roasted Garlic

Ingredients for 4 servings

1 large head broccoli, cut into florets
½ head garlic
2 tbsp olive oil
4 oz butter
¼ tsp dried thyme
Juice and zest of half a lemon
4 tbsp coconut cream
4 tbsp olive oil

Directions and Total Time: approx. 45 minutes

Preheat oven to 400 F. Wrap garlic in aluminum foil and roast for 30 minutes; set aside. Pour broccoli into a pot and cover with salted water. Bring to a boil over high heat until tender, about 7 minutes. Drain and transfer to a bowl. Add in butter, thyme, lemon juice and zest, coconut cream, and olive oil. Use an immersion blender to puree the ingredients until smooth. Serve drizzled with olive oil.

Per serving: Cal 376; Net Carbs 6g; Fat 33g; Protein 11g

Spicy Pistachio Dip

Ingredients for 4 servings

3 oz toasted pistachios
3 tbsp coconut cream
¼ cup water
Juice of half a lemon
½ tsp smoked paprika
Cayenne pepper to taste
½ tsp salt
½ cup olive oil

Directions and Total Time: approx. 5 minutes

Pour pistachios, cream, water, lemon juice, paprika, cayenne, and salt in a food processor. Puree until smooth. Add in olive oil and puree again. Spoon into bowls, garnish with pistachios, and serve with celery and carrots.

Per serving: Cal 220; Net Carbs 5g; Fat 19g; Protein 6g

Prosciutto Appetizer with Blackberries

Ingredients for 4 servings

4 zero carb bread slices
¾ cup balsamic vinegar
2 tbsp erythritol
1 cup fresh blackberries
1 cup crumbled goat cheese
¼ tsp dry Italian seasoning
1 tbsp almond milk
4 thin prosciutto slices

Directions and Total Time: approx. 25 minutes

Cut the bread into 3 pieces each and arrange on a baking sheet. Place under the broiler and toast for 1-2 minutes on each side or until golden brown; set aside. In a saucepan, add balsamic vinegar and stir in erythritol until dissolved. Boil the mixture over medium heat until reduced by half, 5 minutes. Turn the heat off and carefully stir in the blackberries. Make sure they do not break open. Set aside. In a bowl, add goat cheese, Italian seasoning, and almond milk. Mix until smooth. Brush one side of the toasted bread with the balsamic reduction and top with the cheese mixture. Cut each prosciutto slice into 3 pieces and place on the bread. Top with some of the whole blackberries from the balsamic mixture. Serve immediately.

Per serving: Cal 175; Net Carbs 8.7g; Fat 7g; Protein 18g

Onion Rings & Kale Dip

Ingredients for 4 servings

1 onion, sliced in rings
1 tbsp flax seed meal
1 cup almond flour
½ cup grated Parmesan
1 tsp garlic powder
½ tbsp sweet paprika powder
2 oz chopped kale
2 tbsp olive oil
2 tbsp dried cilantro
1 tbsp dried oregano
Salt and black pepper to taste
1 cup mayonnaise
4 tbsp coconut cream
Juice of ½ lemon

Directions and Total Time: approx. 35 minutes

Preheat oven to 400 F. In a bowl, mix flax seed meal and 3 tbsp water and leave the mixture to thicken and fully absorb for 5 minutes. In another bowl, combine almond flour, Parmesan cheese, garlic powder, paprika, and salt. Line a baking sheet with parchment paper. When the flax egg is ready, dip in the onion rings one after another, and then into the almond flour mixture. Place the rings on the sheet and spray with cooking spray. Bake for 20 minutes. Remove to a bowl. Put kale in a bowl. Add in olive oil, cilantro, oregano, salt, pepper, mayonnaise, coconut cream, and lemon juice; mix well. Let sit for 10 minutes. Serve the dip with the crispy onion rings.

Per serving: Cal 410; Net Carbs 7g; Fat 35g; Protein 14g

Paprika Roasted Nuts

Ingredients for 4 servings

8 oz walnuts and pecans
1 tbsp coconut oil
1 tsp cumin powder
1 tsp paprika powder

Directions and Total Time: approx. 10 minutes

In a bowl, mix walnuts, pecans, salt, coconut oil, cumin powder, and paprika powder until the nuts are well coated. Pour the mixture into a frying pan and toast over medium heat while stirring continually until fragrant and brown.

Per serving: Cal 290; Net Carbs 3g; Fat 27g; Protein 6g

Mediterranean Deviled Eggs

Ingredients for 6 servings

6 large eggs
Ice water bath
1 tsp Dijon mustard
3 tbsp mayonnaise
1 tsp white wine vinegar
2 tbsp crumbled feta cheese
¼ tsp turmeric powder
1 red chili, minced
1 tbsp chopped parsley
Smoked paprika to garnish

Directions and Total Time: approx. 30 minutes

Boil eggs in salted water for 10 minutes. Transfer to an ice water bath. Let cool for 5 minutes, peel and slice in half. Remove the yolks to a bowl and put the whites on a plate. Mash yolks with a fork and mix in mustard, mayonnaise, vinegar, feta, turmeric, and chili until evenly combined. Spoon the mixture into a piping bag and fill into the egg whites. Garnish with parsley and paprika. Serve.

Per serving: Cal 139; Net Carbs 1.2g; Fat 8.2g, Protein 7g

Mushroom Broccoli Faux Risotto

Ingredients for 4 servings

1 cup cremini mushrooms, chopped
4 oz butter
2 garlic cloves, minced
1 red onion, finely chopped
1 head broccoli, grated
1 cup water
¾ cup white wine
Salt and black pepper to taste
1 cup coconut cream
¾ cup grated Parmesan
Freshly chopped thyme

Directions and Total Time: approx. 25 minutes

Place a pot over medium heat and melt butter. Sauté mushrooms until golden, 5 minutes. Add in garlic and onions and cook for 3 minutes until fragrant and soft. Mix in broccoli, water, and half of white wine. Season with salt and pepper and simmer for 10 minutes. Mix in coconut cream and simmer until most of the cream evaporates. Turn heat off and stir in Parmesan and thyme. Serve warm.

Per serving: Cal 520; Net Carbs 12g; Fat 43g; Protein 15g

Spinach Chips with Guacamole Hummus

Ingredients for 4 servings

½ cup baby spinach
1 tbsp olive oil
½ tsp plain vinegar
3 avocados, chopped
½ cup chopped parsley
½ cup butter
¼ cup pumpkin seeds
¼ cup sesame paste
Juice from ½ lemon
1 garlic clove, minced
½ tsp coriander powder
Salt and black pepper to taste

Directions and Total Time: approx. 30 minutes

Preheat oven to 300 F. Put spinach in a bowl and toss with olive oil, plain vinegar, and salt. Arrange on a parchment paper-lined baking sheet and bake until the leaves are crispy but not burned, 15 minutes. Place avocado to a food processor. Add in butter, pumpkin seeds, sesame paste, lemon juice, garlic, coriander, salt, and pepper; puree until smooth. Spoon into a bowl and garnish with parsley. Serve with the spinach chips.

Per serving: Cal 473; Net Carbs 3g; Fat 45g; Protein 8g

Tofu Stuffed Peppers

Ingredients for 4 servings

2 red bell peppers
1 cup grated Parmesan
1 oz tofu, chopped
1 tbsp fresh parsley, chopped
1 cup cream cheese
1 tbsp chili paste, mild
2 tbsp melted butter

Directions and Total Time: approx. 25 minutes

Preheat oven to 400 F. Cut bell peppers into two, lengthwise and remove the core and seeds. In a bowl, mix tofu with parsley, cream cheese, chili paste, and melted butter until smooth. Spoon the cheese mixture into the bell peppers. Arrange peppers on a greased sheet. Sprinkle Parmesan on top and bake for 20 minutes.

Per serving: Cal 412; Net Carbs 5g; Fat 36g; Protein 14g

Soy Chorizo Stuffed Cabbage Rolls

Ingredients for 4 servings

¼ cup coconut oil
1 onion, chopped
3 cloves garlic, minced
1 cup crumbled soy chorizo
1 cup cauliflower rice
1 can tomato sauce
1 tsp dried oregano
1 tsp dried basil
Salt and black pepper to taste
8 full green cabbage leaves

Directions and Total Time: approx. 35 minutes

Heat coconut oil in a saucepan and sauté onion, garlic, and soy chorizo for 5 minutes. Stir in cauli rice, season with salt and pepper, and cook for 4 minutes; set aside. In the saucepan, pour tomato sauce, oregano, and basil. Add ¼ cup water and simmer for 10 minutes. Lay cabbage leaves on a flat surface and spoon chorizo mixture into the middle of each leaf. Roll the leaves to secure the filling. Put the cabbage rolls in tomato sauce; cook for 10 minutes.

Per serving: Cal 285; Net Carbs 7g; Fat 26g; Protein 5g

Cauliflower Chips with Cheese Dip

Ingredients for 6 servings

1 head cauliflower, cut into florets
¾ cup dried cranberries, chopped
½ cup toasted pecans, chopped
1 ½ tbsp almond flour
1 tbsp flax seeds
4 tbsp chia seeds
8 oz cream cheese, softened
2 tbsp sugar-free maple syrup
1 tbsp lemon zest

Directions and Total Time: approx. 35 minutes

Preheat oven to 350 F. Pour cauliflower and 2 cups salted water in a pot and bring to a boil for 5 minutes. Drain and transfer to a food processor; puree until smooth. Pour into a bowl and stir in flour until combined. Mix in flax seeds and 1 tbsp chia seeds. Line a baking sheet with parchment paper and spread in the batter. Cover with a plastic wrap and use a rolling pin to flatten and level the mixture. Take off the plastic wrap and cut chip-size squares on the batter. Bake for 20 minutes. Let cool for 5 minutes and transfer to a serving bowl. In a bowl, mix cream cheese with maple syrup until properly mixed. Add in cranberries, pecans, remaining chia seeds, and lemon juice; mix well. Serve the dip with cauli chips.

Per serving: Cal 252; Net Carbs 6.2g; Fat 23g; Protein 6g

Mozzarella in Prosciutto Blanket

Ingredients for 6 servings

18 mozzarella cheese ciliegine
6 thin prosciutto slices
18 basil leaves

Directions and Total Time: approx. 15 minutes

Cut the prosciutto slices into three strips. Place basil leaves at the end of each strip. Top with mozzarella. Wrap the mozzarella in prosciutto. Secure with toothpicks. Serve.

Per serving: Cal 163; Net Carbs 0.2g; Fat 12g; Protein 13g

Chocolate, Berries & Nut Mix Bars

Ingredients for 4 servings

¼ cup walnuts	½ cup butter, melted
¼ cup cashew nuts	¼ cup dark chocolate chips
¼ cup almonds	¼ cup mixed seeds
¼ cup coconut chips	Salt to taste
1 egg, beaten	1 cup mixed dried berries

Directions and Total Time: approx. 25 minutes

Preheat oven to 350 F and line a baking sheet with parchment paper. In a food processor, pulse nuts until roughly chopped. Place in a bowl; stir in chips, egg, butter, mixed seeds, salt, and berries. Spread the mixture in the sheet and bake for 18 minutes. Let cool and cut into bars.

Per serving: Cal 384; Net Carbs 6.4g; Fat 37.7g; Protein 6g

Chili Avocado-Chimichurri Appetizer

Ingredients for 4 servings

4 zero carb bread slices	3 garlic cloves, minced
¼ cup + 2 tbsp olive oil	½ tsp red chili flakes
2 tbsp red wine vinegar	½ tsp dried oregano
1 lemon, juiced	½ cup chopped fresh parsley
Salt and black pepper to taste	2 avocados, cubed

Directions and Total Time: approx. 15 minutes

Cut bread slices in half, brush both sides with 2 tbsp of the olive oil, and arrange on a baking sheet. Place under the broiler and toast for 1-2 minutes per side.

In a bowl, mix the remaining olive oil, vinegar, lemon juice, salt, pepper, garlic, red chili flakes, oregano, and parsley. Fold in the avocados Spoon the mixture onto the bread and serve.

Per serving: Cal 305; Net Carbs 5.6g; Fat 26g; Protein 9g

Crispy Squash Nacho Chips

Ingredients for 4 servings

1 yellow squash, sliced	1 ½ cups coconut oil
Salt to season	1 tbsp taco seasoning

Directions and Total Time: approx. 25 minutes

Pour coconut oil in a skillet and heat oil over medium heat. Add in squash slices and fry until crispy and golden brown. Remove to a paper towel-lined plate. Sprinkle the slices with taco seasoning and salt and serve.

Per serving: Cal 150; Net Carbs 1g; Fat 14g; Protein 2g

Chocolate Walnut Biscuits

Ingredients for 4 servings

2/3 cup dark chocolate chips	1 tsp vanilla extract
4 oz butter, softened	½ cup almond flour
2 tbsp swerve sugar	½ tsp baking soda
2 tbsp swerve brown sugar	½ cup chopped walnuts
1 egg	

Directions and Total Time: approx. 30 minutes

Preheat oven to 350 F. In a bowl, whisk butter, swerve sugar, and swerve until smooth. Beat in the egg and mix in the vanilla extract. In another bowl, combine almond flour with baking soda and mix into the wet ingredients. Fold in chocolate chips and walnuts. Spoon tablespoons full of the batter onto a greased baking sheet, creating 2-inch spaces in between each spoon, and press down each dough to slightly flatten. Bake for 15 minutes. Transfer to a wire rack to cool completely. Serve.

Per serving: Cal 430; Net Carbs 3.5g; Fat 42g; Protein 6g

Herby Cheesy Nuts

Ingredients for 4 servings

1 egg white	½ cup mixed seeds
4 tsp yeast extract	Salt and black pepper to taste
1 tsp swerve brown sugar	3 tbsp grated Parmesan
1 ½ cups mixed nuts	½ tsp dried mixed herbs

Directions and Total Time: approx. 20 minutes

Preheat oven to 350 F. In a bowl, beat egg white, yeast extract, and swerve. Add in mixed nuts and seeds; combine and spread onto a baking sheet. Bake for 10 minutes. In a bowl, mix salt, pepper, Parmesan, and herbs. Remove the nuts and toss with the cheese mixture. Bake for 5 minutes until sticky and brown. Let cool for 5 minutes and serve.

Per serving: Cal 494; Net Carbs 6g; Fat 48g; Protein 11g

Mixed Seed Crackers

Ingredients for 6 servings

1/3 cup sesame seed flour	1/3 cup chia seeds
1/3 cup pumpkin seeds	1 tbsp psyllium husk powder
1/3 cup sunflower seeds	1 tsp salt
1/3 cup sesame seeds	¼ cup butter, melted

Directions and Total Time: approx. 60 minutes

Preheat oven to 300 F. Combine sesame seed flour with pumpkin, chia and sunflower seeds, psyllium husk powder, and salt. Pour in butter and 1 cup boiling water and mix until a dough forms with a gel-like consistency.

Line a baking sheet with parchment paper and place the dough on the sheet. Cover with another parchment paper and with a rolling pin to flatten into the baking sheet. Remove the parchment paper on top. Bake for 45 minutes. Turn off and allow the crackers to cool and dry in the oven, 10 minutes. Break and serve.

Per serving: Cal 65; Net Carbs 2g; Fat 5g; Protein 3g

Cheddar and Halloumi Sticks

Ingredients for 6 servings

1/3 cup almond flour	½ cup grated cheddar cheese
2 tsp smoked paprika	2 tbsp chopped parsley
1 lb halloumi, cut into strips	½ tsp cayenne powder

Directions and Total Time: approx. 15 minutes

Preheat oven to 350 F. In a bowl, mix flour with paprika and lightly dredge the halloumi cheese in the mixture. Arrange on a greased baking sheet. In a smaller bowl, combine parsley, cheddar cheese, and cayenne.

Sprinkle the mixture on the cheese and lightly grease with cooking spray. Bake for 10 minutes until golden brown. Serve.

Per serving: Cal 886; Net Carbs 6.1g; Fat 77g; Protein 14g

Pesto Mushroom Pinwheels

Ingredients for 4 servings

¼ cup almond flour	1 ½ tsp vanilla extract
3 tbsp coconut flour	1 whole egg, beaten
½ tsp xanthan gum	1 cup mushrooms, chopped
4 tbsp cream cheese, softened	1 cup basil pesto
1/4 teaspoon yogurt	2 cups baby spinach
¼ cup butter, cold	Salt and black pepper to taste
3 whole eggs	1 cup grated cheddar cheese
3 tbsp erythritol	1 egg, beaten for brushing

Directions and Total Time: approx. 40 minutes

In a bowl, mix almond and coconut flours, xanthan gum, and ½ tsp salt. Add in yogurt, cream cheese, and butter; mix until crumbly. Add in erythritol and vanilla extract until mixed. Pour in 3 eggs one after another while mixing until formed into a ball. Flatten the dough on a clean flat surface, cover in plastic wrap, and refrigerate for 1 hour.

Dust a clean flat surface with almond flour, unwrap the dough, and roll out into 15x12 inches. Spread pesto on top with a spatula, leaving a 2-inch border on one end.

In a bowl, combine baby spinach and mushrooms, season with salt and pepper, and spread the mixture over pesto. Sprinkle with cheddar cheese and roll up as tightly as possible from the shorter end. Refrigerate for 10 minutes. Preheat oven to 380 F. Remove the pastry onto a flat surface and use a sharp knife to into 24 slim discs. Arrange on the baking sheet, brush with the remaining egg, and bake for 25 minutes until golden. Let cool for 5 minutes.

Per serving: Cal 535; Net Carbs 4g; Fat 41g; Protein 34.6g

Hemp Seed Zucchini Chips

Ingredients for 4 servings

4 large zucchinis, sliced	2 tbsp hemp seeds
4 tbsp olive oil	2 tbsp poppy seeds
1 tsp smoked paprika	1 tsp red chili flakes

Directions and Total Time: approx. 15 minutes

Preheat oven to 350 F. Drizzle zucchini with olive oil and sprinkle with paprika. Scatter with the hemp seeds, poppy seeds, and chili flakes. Season with salt, pepper, and roast for 20 minutes or until crispy and golden brown. Serve.

Per serving: Cal 173; Net Carbs 1.3g; Fat 18g; Protein 2.2g

All Seeds Flapjacks

Ingredients for 4 servings

4 tbsp dried goji berries, chopped

6 tbsp salted butter	3 tbsp chia seeds
8 tbsp sugar-free maple syrup	3 tbsp hemp seeds
8 tbsp swerve brown sugar	3 tbsp sunflower seeds
3 tbsp sesame seeds	1 tbsp poppy seeds

Directions and Total Time: approx. 30 minutes

Preheat oven to 350 F and line a baking sheet with parchment paper. Place butter, maple syrup, and swerve brown sugar in a saucepan over low heat, stir in swerve brown sugar until dissolved.

Remove and stir all seeds along with goji berries until evenly combined. Spread into the baking sheet and bake for 20 minutes or until golden brown. Slice flapjacks into the 16 strips. Serve.

Per serving: Cal 300; Net Carbs 3g; Fat 28g; Protein 6.8g

Tasty Keto Snickerdoodles

Ingredients for 4 servings

2 cups almond flour	½ cup butter, softened
½ tsp baking soda	2 tbsp erythritol sweetener
¾ cup sweetener	1 tsp cinnamon

Directions and Total Time: approx. 25 minutes

Preheat oven to 350 F. Combine almond flour, baking soda, sweetener, and butter in a bowl. Make 16 balls out of the mixture. Flatten them with your hands.

Combine the cinnamon and erythritol in a bowl. Dip in the cookies and arrange on a lined cookie sheet. Bake for 15 minutes.

Per serving: Cal 131; Net Carbs 1.5g; Fat 13g; Protein 3g

Basil-Chili Mozzarella Bites

Ingredients for 4 servings

1 cup olive oil, for frying	1 large egg, beaten in a bowl
1 cup almond flour	1 cup golden flaxseed meal
½ tsp chili powder	1 cup mozzarella cheese cubes
1 tsp onion powder	¼ cup small tomatoes, halved
1 tsp garlic powder	A handful of basil leaves
1 tsp dried basil leaves	

Directions and Total Time: approx. 10 minutes

In a bowl, combine flour, chili, onion and garlic powders, and basil; set aside. Pour flaxseed meal in a plate. Coat each cheese cube in the flour mixture, then in the egg, and then lightly in the golden flaxseed meal. Heat olive oil in a deep pan. Fry the cheese until golden brown on both sides.

Transfer to a wire rack to drain grease. On each tomato half, place 1 basil leaf, top with a cheese cube, and insert a toothpick at the middle of the sandwich to hold. Serve.

Per serving: Cal 769; Net Carbs 2.4g; Fat 73g; Protein 18g

DESSERTS

Coconut Cake with Raspberries

Ingredients for 8 servings

2 cups fresh raspberries
2 cups flaxseed meal
1 cup almond meal
½ cup melted butter
1 lemon, juiced
1 cup coconut cream
1 cup coconut flakes
1 cup whipping cream

Directions and Total Time: approx. 30 min + chilling time

Preheat oven to 400 F. In a bowl, mix flaxseed meal, almond meal, and butter. Spread the mixture on the bottom of a baking dish. Bake for 20 minutes until the mixture is crusty. Allow cooling. In another bowl, mash 1 ½ cups of the raspberries and mix with the lemon juice. Spread the mixture on the crust. Carefully, spread the coconut cream on top, scatter with the coconut flakes and add the whipped cream all over. Garnish with the remaining raspberries and chill in the refrigerator for at least 2 hours.

Per serving: Cal 413; Net Carbs 5.4g; Fats 41g; Protein 7g

Lemon Panna Cotta

Ingredients for 4 servings

½ cup coconut milk
1 cup heavy cream
¼ cup swerve sugar
5 tbsp sugar-free maple syrup
3 tsp agar agar
¼ cup warm water
3 tbsp water
½ lemon, juiced

Directions and Total Time: approx. 30 min + chilling time

Heat coconut milk and heavy cream in a pot over low heat. Stir in swerve sugar, 3 tbsp maple syrup, and 2 tsp agar agar. Continue cooking for 3 minutes. Divide the mixture between 4 dessert cups and chill in the refrigerator for 5 hours. In a bowl, soak the remaining agar agar with warm water. Allow blooming for 5 minutes. In a small pot, heat 3 tbsp water with lemon juice. Mix in the remaining maple syrup and add agar agar mixture. Whisking while cooking until no lumps form; let cool for 2 minutes. Remove the cups, pour in the mixture and refrigerate for 2 hours. When ready, remove the cups, let sit for 15 minutes, and serve.

Per serving: Cal 208; Net Carbs 2.8g; Fats 18g; Protein 2g

Vanilla & Blackberries Sherbet

Ingredients for 2 servings

¼ tsp vanilla extract
1 packet gelatine
2 tbsp heavy whipping cream
4 tbsp mashed blackberries
2 cups crushed ice
1 cup cold water

Directions and Total Time: approx. 5 minutes

Put the gelatin in boiling water, until dissolved. Place the remaining ingredients in a blender and add in gelatin. Blend until smooth. Serve.

Per serving: Cal 173; Net Carbs 3.7g; Fat 10g; Protein 4g

Strawberry & Ricotta Parfait

Ingredients for 4 servings

2 cups strawberries, chopped
1 cup ricotta cheese
2 tbsp sugar-free maple syrup
2 tbsp balsamic vinegar

Directions and Total Time: approx. 10 minutes

Divide half of the strawberries between 4 small glasses and top with ricotta cheese. Drizzle with maple syrup, balsamic vinegar and finish with the remaining strawberries. Serve.

Per serving: Cal 164; Net Carbs 3.1g; Fats 8.2g; Protein 7g

Speedy Blueberry Sorbet

Ingredients for 4 servings

4 cups frozen blueberries
1 cup swerve sugar
½ lemon, juiced
½ tsp salt

Directions and Total Time: approx. 15 min + chilling time

In a blender, add blueberries, swerve, lemon juice, and salt; process until smooth. Strain through a colander into a bowl. Chill for 3 hours. Pour the chilled juice into an ice cream maker and churn until the mixture resembles ice cream. Spoon into a bowl and chill further for 3 hours.

Per serving: Cal 178; Net Carbs 2.3g; Fats 1g; Protein 0.6g

Creamy Strawberry Mousse

Ingredients for 4 servings

2 cups frozen strawberries
2 tbsp swerve sugar
1 large egg white
2 cups whipped cream

Directions and Total Time: approx. 10 min + chilling time

Pour 1 ½ cups strawberries in a blender and process until smooth. Add swerve and process further. Pour in the egg white and blend until well combined. Pour the mixture into a bowl and use an electric hand mixer to whisk until fluffy. Spoon the mixture into dessert glasses, top with whipped cream and strawberries. Serve chilled.

Per serving: Cal 145; Net Carbs 4.8g; Fats 6.8g; Protein 2g

Berry Clafoutis

Ingredients for 4 servings

4 eggs
2 tsp coconut oil
2 cups berries
1 cup coconut milk
1 cup almond flour
¼ cup sweetener
½ tsp vanilla powder
1 tbsp powdered sweetener

Directions and Total Time: approx. 45 minutes

Preheat oven to 350 F. Place all ingredients except for the oil, berries, and powdered sweetener in a blender; pulse until smooth. Gently fold in the berries. Grease a flan dish with coconut oil. Pour the mixture into the dish; bake for 35 minutes. Sprinkle with powdered sugar and serve.

Per serving: Cal 198; Net Carbs 4.9g; Fat 16g; Protein 15g

Raspberry Coconut Cheesecake

Ingredients for 8 servings

2 egg whites	3 tbsp lemon juice
2 ¼ cups erythritol	6 ounces raspberries
3 cups desiccated coconut	1 cup whipped cream
1 tsp coconut oil	3 tbsp lemon juice
¼ cup melted butter	24 ounces cream cheese

Directions and Total Time: approx. 4 hours 15 minutes

Preheat oven to 350 F. Grease a springform pan with the oil and line with parchment paper. Mix egg whites, ¼ cup of erythritol, coconut, and butter until a crust forms and pour into the pan. Bake for 25 minutes. Let cool. Beat the cream cheese until soft. Add lemon juice and the remaining erythritol. In another bowl, beat the heavy cream with an electric mixer. Fold the whipped cream into the cheese cream mixture; stir in raspberries gently. Spread the filling onto the baked crust. Refrigerate for 4 hours.

Per serving: Cal 215; Net Carbs 3g; Fat 25g; Protein 5g

Peanut Butter & Chocolate Ice Cream Bars

Ingredients for 8 servings

3 ½ tsp THM super sweet blend
¼ cup cocoa butter pieces, chopped
2 cups heavy whipping cream   6 ½ tbsp xylitol
⅔ cup peanut butter, softened   ¾ cup coconut oil
1 ½ cups almond milk   2 oz unsweetened chocolate
1 tbsp vegetable glycerin

Directions and Total Time: approx. 4 hours 20 minutes

Blend heavy cream, xanthan gum, peanut butter, almond milk, vegetable glycerin, and 3 tbsp of xylitol until smooth. Place in an ice cream maker and follow the instructions. Spread the ice cream into a lined pan, and freeze for 4 hours. Combine coconut oil, cocoa butter, chocolate, and remaining xylitol in a microwave-safe bowl and microwave until melted; let cool slightly. Slice the ice cream into bars. Dip into the chocolate mixture.

Per serving: Cal 345 Net Carbs 5 g; Fat 32g; Protein 4g

Lemon-Yogurt Mousse

Ingredients for 4 servings

24 oz plain yogurt, strained overnight in a cheesecloth
2 cups swerve confectioner's sugar
2 lemons, juiced and zested
1 cup whipped cream + extra for garnish

Directions and Total Time: approx. 5 min + cooling time

Whip the plain yogurt in a bowl with a hand mixer until light and fluffy. Mix in the sugar, lemon juice, and salt. Fold in the whipped cream to evenly combine. Spoon the mousse into serving cups and refrigerate for 1 hour. Swirl with extra whipped cream and garnish with lemon zest.

Per serving: Cal 223; Net Carbs 3g; Fat 18g; Protein 12g

Strawberry Chocolate Mousse

Ingredients for 4 servings

1 cup fresh strawberries, sliced	1 cup heavy cream
3 eggs	1 vanilla extract
1 cup dark chocolate chips	1 tbsp swerve

Directions and Total Time: approx. 30 minutes

Melt the chocolate in a microwave-safe bowl in the microwave oven for a minute on high; let cool for 8 minutes. Meanwhile, in a medium-sized bowl, whip the cream until very soft. Add the eggs, vanilla extract, and swerve; whisk to combine. Fold in the cooled chocolate. Divide the mousse between six glasses, top with the strawberry slices and chill in the fridge for 1 hour. Serve.

Per serving: Cal 400; Net Carbs 1.7g; Fat 25g; Protein 8g

Granny Smith Apple Tart

Ingredients for 8 servings

2 cups almond flour	1 cup sweetener
¼ cup + 6 tbsp butter	2 cups sliced Granny Smith
1 ¼ tsp cinnamon	½ tsp lemon juice

Directions and Total Time: approx. 45 minutes

Preheat oven to 375 F. Combine 6 tbsp of butter, almond flour, 1 tsp of cinnamon, and ⅓ cup of sweetener in a bowl. Press this mixture into a greased pan. Bake for 5 minutes. Combine the apples and lemon juice in a bowl and set aside. Arrange on top of the crust. Combine the remaining butter and sweetener, and brush over the apples. Bake for 20 minutes. Press the apples down with a spatula, return to oven, and bake for 10 more minutes. Dust with mixed remaining cinnamon and serve.

Per serving: Cal 302; Net Carbs 6.7g; Fat 26g; Protein 7g

Maple Lemon Cake

Ingredients for 4 servings

4 eggs	2 tsp baking powder
1 cup sour cream	½ cup xylitol
2 lemons, zested and juiced	1 tsp cardamom powder
1 tsp vanilla extract	½ tsp ground ginger
2 cups almond flour	A pinch of salt
2 tbsp coconut flour	¼ cup maple syrup

Directions and Total Time: approx. 30 minutes

Preheat oven to 400 F and grease a cake pan with melted butter. In a bowl, beat eggs, sour cream, lemon juice, and vanilla extract until smooth. In another bowl, whisk almond and coconut flours, baking powder, xylitol, cardamom, ginger, salt, lemon zest, and half of maple syrup. Combine both mixtures until smooth and pour the batter into the pan. Bake for 25 minutes or until a toothpick inserted comes out clean. Transfer to a wire rack, let cool, and drizzle with the remaining maple syrup. Serve sliced.

Per serving: Cal 441; Net Carbs 8.5g; Fat 29g; Protein 33g

Flan with Whipped Cream

Ingredients for 4 servings

⅓ cup erythritol, for caramel | 1 tbsp lemon zest
2 cups almond milk | ½ cup erythritol, for custard
4 eggs | 2 cup heavy whipping cream
1 tablespoon vanilla | Mint leaves, to serve

Directions and Total Time: approx. 10 minutes

Heat erythritol for the caramel in a pan. Add 2-3 tablespoons of water, and bring to a boil. Reduce the heat and cook until the caramel turns golden brown. Carefully divide between 4-6 metal cups. Let them cool. In a bowl, mix eggs, remaining erythritol, lemon zest, and vanilla. Add milk and beat again until combined. Pour the custard into each caramel-lined cup and place them into a baking tin. Pour enough hot water into baking tin to halfway up sides of cups. Bake at 345 F for 45 minutes. Remove the ramekins and refrigerate them for 4 hours. To serve, take a knife and slowly run around the edges to invert onto dishes. Serve with dollops of cream and mint leaves.

Per serving: Cal 169; Net Carbs 1.7g; Fat 10g; Protein 7g

Chocolate Mocha Ice Bombs

Ingredients for 4 servings

½ pound cream cheese | 2 tbsp cocoa powder
4 tbsp powdered sweetener | 1 ounce cocoa butter, melted
2 ounces strong coffee | 2 ½ oz dark chocolate, melted

Directions and Total Time: approx. 2 hours 10 minutes

Combine cream cheese, sweetener, coffee, and cocoa powder in a food processor. Roll 2 tbsp. of the mixture and place on a lined tray. Mix the melted cocoa butter and chocolate, and coat the bombs with it. Freeze for 2 hours.

Per serving: Cal 127; Net Carbs 1.4g; Fat 13g; Protein 2g

Almond & Coconut Bark

Ingredients for 8 servings

½ cup almonds | ¼ tsp salt
½ cup coconut butter | ½ cup coconut flakes
10 drops stevia | 4 ounces dark chocolate

Directions and Total Time: approx. 1 hour 15 minutes

Preheat oven to 350 F. Place almonds in a baking sheet and toast for 5 minutes. Melt together the butter and chocolate. Stir in stevia. Line a cookie sheet with waxed paper and spread the chocolate evenly. Scatter the almonds on top and sprinkle with salt. Refrigerated for 1 hour.

Per serving: Cal 161; Net Carbs 1.9g; Fat 15g; Protein 2g

Coconut Butter Ice Cream

Ingredients for 4 servings

½ cup smooth coconut butter | 3 cups half and half
½ cup swerve | 1 tsp vanilla extract

Directions and Total Time: approx. 50 min + cooling time

Beat coconut butter and swerve in a bowl with a hand mixer until smooth. Gradually whisk in half and half until thoroughly combined. Mix in vanilla. Pour mixture into a loaf pan and freeze for 45 minutes until firmed up. Scoop into glasses when ready to eat and serve.

Per serving: Cal 290; Net Carbs 6g; Fat 23g; Protein 13g

Saffron & Cardamom Coconut Bars

Ingredients for 4 servings

3 ½ ounces ghee | 1 ¾ cups shredded coconut
10 saffron threads | 4 tbsp sweetener
1 ⅓ cups coconut milk | 1 tsp cardamom powder

Directions and Total Time: approx. 3 hours

Combine the coconut with 1 cup of coconut milk. In another bowl, mix the remaining coconut milk with the sweetener and saffron. Let sit for 30 minutes. Heat the ghee in a wok. Add the coconut mixture as well as the saffron mixture, and cook for 5 minutes on low heat, mixing continuously. Stir in cardamom and cook for 5 more minutes. Spread the mixture onto a greased baking pan. Freeze for 2 hours. Cut into bars to serve.

Per serving: Cal 130; Net Carbs 1.4g; Fat 12g; Protein 2g

Saffron Coconut Bars

Ingredients for 4 servings

3 ½ ounces ghee | 1 ¾ cups shredded coconut
10 saffron threads | 4 tbsp stevia
1 ¼ cups coconut milk | 1 tsp cardamom powder

Directions and Total Time: approx. 20 min + cooling time

Combine shredded coconut with 1 cup of coconut milk. In another bowl, mix the remaining coconut milk with stevia and saffron. Let sit for 30 minutes. Heat ghee in a wok. Add coconut mixture as well as the saffron mixture, and cook for 5 minutes, mixing continuously. Stir in cardamom and cook for 5 minutes. Spread the mixture onto a small container and freeze for 2 hours. Cut into bars to serve.

Per serving: Cal 215; Net Carbs: 1.4g; Fat: 22g; Protein: 2g

Mom's Walnut Cookies

Ingredients for 12 servings

1 egg | ½ tsp baking soda
2 cups ground pecans | 1 tbsp ghee
¼ cup sweetener | 20 walnuts halves

Directions and Total Time: approx. 25 minutes

Preheat oven to 350 F. In a bowl, mix all the ingredients, except for walnuts, until combined. Make balls out of the mixture and press them with your thumb onto a lined cookie sheet. Top with walnuts. Bake for 12 minutes.

Per serving: Cal 101; Net Carbs: 0.6g; Fat: 11g; Protein: 2g

Almond Ice Cream

Ingredients for 4 servings

2 cups heavy cream
1 tbsp xylitol
½ cup smooth almond butter
1 tbsp olive oil
1 tbsp vanilla extract

½ tsp salt
2 egg yolks
½ cup almonds, chopped
½ cup swerve sweetener confectioners

Directions and Total Time: approx. 3 hours 40 minutes

Warm heavy cream with almond butter, olive oil, xylitol, and salt in a small pan over low heat without boiling, for 3 minutes. Beat the egg yolks until creamy in color. Stir the eggs into the cream mixture. Refrigerate cream mixture for 30 minutes, and stir in swerve sweetener. Pour mixture into ice cream machine and churn it according to the manufacturer's instructions. Stir in almonds and spoon mixture into loaf pan. Refrigerate for at least for 2 hours.

Per serving: Cal 552; Net Carbs 6.2g; Fat 45.4g; Protein 9g

Dark Chocolate Cheesecake Bites

Ingredients for 6 servings

10 oz unsweetened dark chocolate chips
½ cup half and half
20 oz cream cheese, softened

½ cup swerve
1 tsp vanilla extract

Directions and Total Time: approx. 5 min + cooling time

In a saucepan, melt the chocolate with half and a half on low heat for 1 minute. Turn the heat off. In a bowl, whisk the cream cheese, swerve, and vanilla extract with a hand mixer until smooth. Stir into the chocolate mixture. Spoon into silicone muffin tins and freeze for 4 hours until firm.

Per serving: Cal 241; Net Carbs 3.1g; Fat 22g; Protein 5g

Cardamom Cookies

Ingredients for 4 servings

2 cups almond flour
½ tsp baking soda
¾ cup sweetener

½ cup butter, softened
1 tbsp vanilla extract

Coating:

2 tbsp erythritol sweetener
1 tsp ground cardamom

Directions and Total Time: approx. 25 minutes

Preheat your oven to 350 F. Combine all cookie ingredients in a bowl. Make balls out of the mixture and flatten them with hands. Combine the cardamom and erythritol. Dip the cookies in the cardamom mixture and arrange them on a lined cookie sheet. Cook for 15 minutes until crispy.

Per serving: Cal 131; Net Carbs: 1.5g; Fat: 13g; Protein: 3g

Keto Fat Bombs

Ingredients for 4 servings

½ cup peanut butter
½ cup coconut oil

4 tbsp cocoa powder
½ cup erythritol

Directions and Total Time: approx. 3 min + cooling time

Melt butter and oil in the microwave for 45 seconds, stirring twice until properly melted. Mix in cocoa powder and erythritol until completely combined. Pour into muffin molds and refrigerate for 3 hours to harden.

Per serving: Cal 193; Net Carbs 2g; Fat 18.3g; Protein 4g

Peanut Dark Chocolate Barks

Ingredients for 6 servings

10 oz unsweetened dark chocolate, chopped
¼ cup toasted peanuts, chopped
¼ cup dried cranberries, chopped
½ cup erythritol

Directions and Total Time: approx. 2 hours

Line a baking sheet with parchment paper. Pour chocolate and erythritol in a bowl, and microwave for 25 seconds. Stir in cranberries, peanuts, and salt, reserving a few cranberries and peanuts for garnishing. Pour the mixture on the baking sheet and spread out. Sprinkle with remaining cranberries and peanuts. Refrigerate for 2 hours to set. Break into bite-size pieces to serve.

Per serving: Cal 225; Net Carbs 3g; Fat 21g; Protein 6g

Tasty Hot Chocolate with Peanuts

Ingredients for 4 servings

3 cups almond milk
4 tbsp cocoa powder
2 tbsp swerve

3 tbsp peanut butter
Chopped peanuts to garnish

Directions and Total Time: approx. 10 minutes

In a saucepan, add the almond milk, cocoa powder, and swerve. Stir the mixture until the sugar dissolves. Set the pan over low to heat through for 5 minutes, without boiling. Swirl the mix occasionally. Turn the heat off and stir in the peanut butter to be incorporated. Pour the hot chocolate into mugs and sprinkle with chopped peanuts.

Per serving: Cal 225; Net Carbs 0.8g; Fat 22g; Protein 4.5g

Peanut Butter Almond Cookies

Ingredients for 4 servings

½ cup peanut butter, softened
2 cups almond flour
½ tsp baking soda
1 cup xylitol

A pinch of salt
2 tbsp xylitol
1 tsp ground cardamom pods

Directions and Total Time: approx. 25 minutes

Combine peanut butter, almond flour, baking soda, ¾ cup of xylitol, and salt in a bowl. Form balls out of the mixture and flatten them. Combine cardamom and remaining xylitol. Dip in the biscuits and arrange them on a lined cookie sheet. Cook in the oven for 15-20 minutes at 350 F.

Per serving: Cal 96; Net Carbs 7.4g; Fat 6.1g; Protein 2.4g

Blueberry Tart

Ingredients for 4 servings

4 eggs
2 tsp coconut oil
2 cups blueberries
1 cup coconut milk
1 cup almond flour

¼ cup sweetener
½ tsp vanilla powder
1 tbsp powdered sweetener
A pinch of salt

Directions and Total Time: approx. 45 minutes

Preheat oven to 350 F. Place all ingredients except coconut oil, berries, and powdered sweetener in a blender, and blend until smooth. Gently fold in the berries. Pour the mixture into a greased dish and bake for 35 minutes. Sprinkle with powdered sweetener.

Per serving: Cal 355; Net Carbs 6.9g; Fat 14.5g; Protein 12g

Matcha Fat Bombs

Ingredients for 4 servings

½ cup coconut oil
1 tbsp vanilla extract
½ cup almond butter

4 tbsp matcha powder powder
½ cup xylitol

Directions and Total Time: approx. 3 min + cooling time

Melt butter and coconut oil in a saucepan over low heat, stirring twice until properly melted and mixed. Mix in matcha powder and xylitol until combined. Pour into muffin moulds and refrigerate for 3 hours to harden.

Per serving: Cal 436; Net Carbs 3.1g; Fat 44.6g; Protein 6g

Coffee Balls

Ingredients for 6 servings

1 ½ cups mascarpone cheese
½ cup melted ghee
3 tbsp cocoa powder

¼ cup erythritol
6 tbsp brewed coffee

Directions and Total Time: approx. 3 min + cooling time

Whisk mascarpone, ghee, cocoa powder, erythritol, and coffee with a hand mixer until creamy and fluffy, for 1 minute. Fill in muffin tins and freeze for 3 hours until firm.

Per serving: Cal 145; Net Carbs 2g; Fat 14g; Protein 4g

Mascarpone Ice Bombs

Ingredients for 4 servings

2 tbsp butter, melted
1 cup mascarpone cheese
4 tbsp xylitol

2 tbsp coffee
2 tbsp cocoa powder
2 ½ oz dark chocolate, melted

Directions and Total Time: approx. 2 hours 10 minutes

Blitz mascarpone cheese, xylitol, coffee, and cocoa powder, in a food processor until mixed. Roll 2 tbsp of the mixture and place on a lined tray. Mix melted butter and chocolate, and coat the bombs with it. Freeze for 2 hours.

Per serving: Cal 286; Net Carbs 7.2g; Fat 23.7g; Protein 10g

Chocolate Mug Cakes

Ingredients for 2 servings

2 tbsp ghee
1 ½ tbsp cocoa powder
2-3 tbsp erythritol
1 egg
2 tbsp almond flour

1 tbsp psyllium husk powder
2 tsp coconut flour
½ tsp baking powder
A pinch of salt

Directions and Total Time: approx. 5 minutes

In a bowl, whisk the butter, cocoa powder, and erythritol until a thick mixture forms. Whisk in the egg until smooth and then the almond flour, psyllium husk, coconut flour, baking powder and salt. Pour the mixture into two medium mugs and microwave for 70 to 90 seconds or until set.

Per serving: Cal 92; Net Carbs 1.8g; Fat 12g; Protein 8.2g

Choco-Coffee Cake

Ingredients for 4 servings

3 tbsp golden flaxseed meal, ground
1 tbsp melted butter
1 cup almond flour
2 tbsp coconut flour
1 tsp baking powder
¼ cup cocoa powder
¼ tsp salt

½ tsp espresso powder
1/3-½ cup coconut sugar
¼ tsp xanthan gum
¼ cup organic coconut oil
2 tbsp heavy cream
2 eggs

Directions and Total Time: approx. 30 minutes

Preheat oven to 400 F and grease a springform pan with melted butter. In a bowl, mix almond flour, flaxseed meal, coconut flour, baking powder, cocoa, salt, espresso, coconut sugar, and xanthan gum. In another bowl, whisk coconut oil, heavy cream, and eggs. Combine both mixtures until smooth batter forms. Pour the batter into the pan and bake until a toothpick comes out clean, 20 minutes. Transfer to a wire rack, let cool, slice and serve.

Per serving: Cal 232; Net Carbs 6.3g; Fat 22g; Protein 5.5g

Keto Caramel Cake

Ingredients for 4 servings

½ cup sugar-free caramel sauce + extra for topping
2 ½ cups almond flour
¼ cup coconut flour
¼ cup whey protein powder
1 tbsp baking powder
½ tsp salt

¾ cup erythritol
4 large eggs
1 tsp vanilla extract
¾ cup almond milk

Directions and Total Time: approx. 30 minutes

Preheat oven to 400 F. In a bowl, mix almond and coconut flours, protein and baking powders, and salt. In another bowl, mix erythritol, eggs, vanilla, milk, and caramel sauce. Combine both mixtures until smooth batter forms. Pour batter into a greased pan; bake for 22 minutes. Let cool and top with caramel sauce to serve.

Per serving: Cal 313; Net Carbs 3.4g; Fat 29g; Protein 8.2g

Gingerbread Cheesecake

Ingredients for 6 servings

For the crust:

1 ¾ cups golden flaxseed meal	¼ swerve sugar
6 tbsp melted butter	A pinch of salt

For the filling

8 oz cream cheese, softened	1 tsp pure vanilla extract
¾ cup swerve sugar	2 tsp smooth ginger paste
¼ cup sugar-free maple syrup	1 tsp cinnamon powder
3 large eggs	¼ tsp nutmeg powder
¼ cup sour cream	¼ tsp salt
2 tbsp almond flour	A pinch of cloves powder

Directions and Total Time: approx. 1 hour 45 minutes

Preheat oven to 325 F and grease a cake pan. In a bowl, mix flaxseed meal, butter, swerve, and salt. Pour and fit the mixture into the pan using a spoon. Bake the crust for 15 minutes or until firm. In a bowl, using an electric mixer, beat cream cheese, swerve sugar, and maple syrup until smooth. Whisk in one after the other, the eggs, sour cream, almond flour, vanilla extract, ginger paste, cinnamon, nutmeg, salt, and cloves powder. Pour the mixture onto the crust while shaking to release any bubbles. Cover with foil and bake for 55 minutes until the center of the cake jiggles slightly. Remove the cake, let cool, and release the cake pan. Garnish with ginger powder, slice and serve.

Per serving: Cal 682; Net Carbs 4.3g; Fat 49g; Protein 31g

Coconut Cake

Ingredients for 4 servings

9 tbsp butter, melted and cooled

6 eggs	9 tbsp coconut flour
2 tsp cream cheese, softened	1 ½ tsp baking powder
1 tsp vanilla extract	2 tbsp coconut flakes
2 tbsp coconut c¼eam	½ tsp salt
½ cup swerve sugar	Coconut flakes for garnishing

Directions and Total Time: approx. 30 minutes

Preheat oven to 400 F and grease cake pan with melted butter. In a bowl, beat the eggs and butter until smooth. Whisk in the cream cheese, vanilla, and coconut cream. In another bowl, mix swerve sugar, coconut flour, baking powder, coconut flakes, and salt. Combine both mixtures until smooth and pour the batter into the pan. Bake for 24 minutes or until a toothpick inserted comes out clean. Transfer to a wire rack and top with coconut flakes.

Per serving: Cal 377; Net Carbs 3.8g; Fat 36g; Protein 9g

Vanilla Berry Mug Cakes

Ingredients for 4 servings

1 tbsp butter, melted	1 tsp vanilla extract
2 tbsp cream cheese	¼ tsp baking powder
2 tbsp coconut flour	1 medium egg
1 tbsp xylitol	6 mixed berries, mashed

Directions and Total Time: approx. 5 minutes

In a bowl, whisk butter, cream cheese, flour, xylitol, baking powder, egg, and mashed berries. Pour the mixture into two mugs and microwave for 80 seconds or until set. Let cool for 1 minute and enjoy.

Per serving: Cal 98; Net Carbs 2.4g; Fat 4g; Protein 3.5g

Chocolate Cake with Raspberry Frosting

Ingredients for 6 servings

2 cups blanched almond flour	½ cup butter, softened
1 cup erythritol	1 tsp vanilla extract
½ cup cocoa powder	2 eggs
1 tsp baking powder	1 cup almond milk

For the frosting:

8 oz cream cheese, softened	2 tbsp heavy whipping cream
½ cup butter, softened	1/3 cup powdered erythritol
1 cup fresh raspberries, mashed	1 tsp vanilla extract
3 tbsp cocoa powder	

Directions and Total Time: approx. 40 minutes

Preheat oven to 350 degrees. In a bowl, mix almond flour, erythritol, cocoa, and baking powder until fully combined. Mix in butter and vanilla. Crack open the eggs into the bowl and whisk until completely combined; stir in almond milk. Prepare three 6-inch round cake pans and generously grease with butter. Divide the batter into the 3 cake pans. Place all the pans in the oven and bake for 25 minutes or until the cakes set. Remove them to a wire rack. In a bowl, whip cream cheese, butter, raspberries, cocoa powder, heavy cream, erythritol, and vanilla extract until smooth. To assemble: place the first cake on a flat surface and spread ⅓ of the frosting over top. Place second cake layer, add and smoothen the frosting, and then do the same for the last cake. Slice and serve immediately.

Per serving: Cal 546; Net Carbs 8.4g; Fat 46g; Protein 9g

Chocolate Snowball Cookies

Ingredients for 4 servings

¼ cup swerve confectioner's sugar

1 cup butter, softened	1 tsp vanilla extract
½ cups erythritol, divided	1 cup pecans, finely chopped
2 cups almond flour	½ tsp salt
2 tsp cocoa powder	2 tbsp water

Directions and Total Time: approx. 35 min + chilling time

Preheat oven to 325 F; line a baking sheet with parchment paper. In a bowl and using a hand mixer, cream the butter and erythritol. Fold in almond flour, cocoa powder, vanilla, pecans, salt, and water. Mold 1 tbsp cookie dough from the mixture and place on the sheet. Chill for 1 hour. Transfer to the sheet and bake for 25 minutes or until the cookies look dry and colorless. Remove them from the oven to cool for 10 minutes. Sprinkle with swerve to serve.

Per serving: Cal 584; Net Carbs 3.7g; Fat 61g; Protein 3g

Classic Zucchini Cake

Ingredients for 4 servings

4 egg	¼ tsp baking soda
4 tbsp butter, melted	½ tsp salt
½ tsp vanilla extract	1 ¼ tsp cinnamon
¼ cup sugar-free maple syrup	½ tsp nutmeg
1 ½ cups almond flour	⅛ tsp ground cloves
½ cup swerve sugar	1 cup grated zucchinis
1 ½ tsp baking powder	

Directions and Total Time: approx. 30 minutes

Preheat oven to 400 F and grease a cake pan with melted butter. In a bowl, beat the eggs, butter, maple syrup, and vanilla extract until smooth. In another bowl, mix almond flour, swerve, baking powder, baking soda, salt, cinnamon, and ground cloves. Combine both mixtures until smooth, fold in the zucchinis and pour the batter into the cake pan. Bake for 25 minutes or until a toothpick inserted comes out clean. Transfer to a wire rack, let cool, and drizzle the remaining maple syrup. Slice and serve.

Per serving: Cal 235; Net Carbs 6.3g; Fat 21g; Protein 9g

Heart-Shaped Red Velvet Cakes

Ingredients for 6 servings

½ cup butter	½ cup coconut flour
6 eggs	2 tbsp cocoa powder
1 tsp vanilla extract	2 tbsp baking powder
1 cup Greek yogurt	¼ tsp salt
1 cup swerve sugar	1 tbsp red food coloring
1 cup almond flour	

For the frosting:

1 cup mascarpone cheese	1 tsp vanilla extract
½ cup erythritol	2 tbsp heavy cream

Directions and Total Time: approx. 30 minutes

Preheat oven to 400 F and grease 2 heart-shaped cake pans with butter. In a bowl, beat butter, eggs, vanilla, Greek yogurt, and swerve sugar until smooth. In another bowl, mix the almond and coconut flours, cocoa, salt, baking powder, and red food coloring. Combine both mixtures until smooth and divide the batter between the two cake pans. Bake in the oven for 25 minutes or until a toothpick inserted comes out clean. Meanwhile, in a bowl, using an electric mixer, whisk the mascarpone cheese and erythritol until smooth. Mix in vanilla and heavy cream until well-combined. Transfer to a wire rack, let cool, and spread the frosting on top. Slice and serve.

Per serving: Cal 643; Net Carbs 9.2g; Fat 46g; Protein 37g

Chocolate Crunch Bars

Ingredients for 4 servings

1 ½ cups chocolate chips	¼ cup melted butter
¼ cup almond butter	2 cups mixed seeds
½ cup sugar-free maple syrup	1 cup chopped walnuts

Directions and Total Time: approx. 5 min + chilling time

Line a baking sheet with parchment paper. In a bowl, mix chips, almond butter, maple syrup, butter, seeds, and walnuts. Spread the mixture onto the sheet and refrigerate until firm, at least 1 hour. Cut into bars and enjoy.

Per serving: Cal 713; Net Carbs 7.1g; Fat 75g; Protein 7.9g

Sticky Maple Cinnamon Cake

Ingredients for 4 servings

9 tbsp butter, melted and cooled
½ cup sugar-free maple syrup + extra for topping

6 eggs	¼ cup almond flour
2 tsp cream cheese, softened	1 ½ tsp baking powder
1 tsp vanilla extract	1 tsp cinnamon powder
2 tbsp heavy cream	½ tsp salt

Directions and Total Time: approx. 30 minutes

Preheat oven to 400 F; grease a cake pan with melted butter. In a bowl, beat the eggs, butter, cream cheese, vanilla, heavy cream, and maple syrup until smooth. In another bowl, mix almond flour, baking powder, cinnamon, and salt. Combine both mixtures until smooth and pour the batter into the cake pan. Bake for 25 minutes or until a toothpick inserted comes out clean. Transfer the cake to a wire rack to cool and drizzle with maple syrup.

Per serving: Cal 362; Net Carbs 1.5g; Fat 35g; Protein 8.9g

Almond Square Cookies

Ingredients for 4 servings

2 ¼ cups almond flour	1 cup swerve sugar
1 tsp baking powder	1 large egg
½ tsp salt	¾ tsp almond extract
1 cup butter, softened	

Directions and Total Time: approx. 30 minutes

Preheat oven to 400 F; line a baking sheet with parchment paper. In a bowl, mix almond flour, baking powder, and salt. In another bowl, mix butter, swerve, egg, and almond extract until well smooth. Combine both mixtures until smooth dough forms. Lay a parchment paper on a flat surface, place the dough and cover with another parchment paper. Using a rolling pin, flatten it into ½-inch thickness and cut it into squares. Arrange on the baking sheet with 1-inch intervals and bake in the oven until the edges are set and golden brown, 25 minutes.

Per serving: Cal 426; Net Carbs 0.4g; Fat 46g; Protein 1.4g

White Chocolate Chip Cookies

Ingredients for 4 servings

3 oz unsweetened white chocolate chips

½ cup unsalted butter	1 ½ cups almond flour
¾ cup xylitol	½ tsp baking powder
1 tsp vanilla extract	½ tsp xanthan gum
1 large egg	¼ tsp salt

Directions and Total Time: approx. 25 minutes

Preheat oven to 350 F; line a baking sheet with parchment paper. In a bowl and using an electric mixer, cream the butter and xylitol until light and fluffy. Add vanilla, egg, and beat until smooth. Add almond flour, baking powder, xanthan gum, salt, and whisk the mixture until smooth dough forms. Fold in chocolate chips. Roll the dough into 1 ½-inch balls and arrange on the sheet at 2-inch intervals. Bake for 12 minutes until lightly golden.

Per serving: Cal 163; Net Carbs 0.3g; Fat 16g; Protein 2.6g

Cowboy Cookies

Ingredients for 8 servings

1 cup butter, softened	1 tbsp cinnamon powder
1 cup swerve white sugar	1 tsp salt
1 cup swerve brown sugar	1 cup sugar-free chocolate chips
1 tbsp vanilla extract	1 cup peanut butter chips
2 large eggs	2 cups golden flaxseed meal
2 cups almond flour	1 ½ cups coconut flakes
2 tsp baking powder	2 cups chopped walnuts
1 tsp baking soda	

Directions and Total Time: approx. 30 minutes

Preheat oven to 375 F; line a baking sheet with parchment paper. In a large bowl and using a hand mixer, cream the butter and swerve until light and fluffy. Slowly, beat in the vanilla and eggs until smooth. In a separate bowl, mix almond flour, baking powder, baking soda, cinnamon, and salt. Combine both mixtures and fold in the chocolate chips, peanut butter chips, flaxseed meal, coconut flaxes, and walnuts. Roll the dough into 1 ½-inch balls and arrange on the baking sheet at 2-inch intervals. Bake for 10 to 12 minutes, or until lightly golden.

Per serving: Cal 435; Net Carbs 4.6g; Fat 39g; Protein 16g

Danish Butter Cookies

Ingredients for 4 servings

¾ cup swerve confectioner's sugar

2 cups almond flour	1 tsp vanilla extract
½ cup butter, softened	3 oz dark chocolate
1 large egg	½ oz cocoa butter

Directions and Total Time: approx. 35 minutes

Preheat oven to 350 F; line a baking sheet with parchment paper. In a food processor, mix almond flour, swerve, and ¼ tsp salt. Add butter and process until resembling coarse breadcrumbs. Add eggs, vanilla, and process until smooth. Pour the batter into a piping bag and press mounds of the batter onto the baking sheets with 1-inch intervals. Bake for 10 to 12 minutes. Microwave dark chocolate and cocoa butter for 50 seconds, mixing at every 10-seconds interval. When the cookies are ready, transfer to a rack to cool and swirl the chocolate mixture.

Per serving: Cal 253; Net Carbs 0.4g; Fat 27.4g; Protein 2g

Dark Chocolate Cookies

Ingredients for 4 servings

1 ½ cups almond flour	¾ cup swerve sugar
½ cup cocoa powder	2 eggs
1 tsp baking soda	1 tsp vanilla extract
12 tbsp butter, softened	1 cup dark chocolate chips

Directions and Total Time: approx. 35 minutes

Preheat oven to 350 F; line a baking sheet with parchment paper. In a bowl, mix flour, cocoa powder, 1 tsp salt, and baking soda. In a separate bowl, cream the butter and swerve sugar until light and fluffy. Mix in the eggs, vanilla extract and then combine both mixtures. Fold in the chocolate chips until well distributed. Roll the dough into 1 ½-inch balls and arrange on the sheet at 2-inch intervals. Bake for 22 minutes until lightly golden.

Per serving: Cal 270; Net Carbs 6.7g; Fat 29g; Protein 6.2g

Ginger Cookies

Ingredients for 4 servings

4 tbsp coconut oil	2 tsp ginger powder
2 tbsp sugar-free maple syrup	1 tsp cinnamon powder
1 egg	½ tsp nutmeg powder
2 tbsp water	1 tsp baking soda
2 ½ cups almond flour	¼ tsp salt
1/3 cup swerve sugar	

Directions and Total Time: approx. 25 minutes

Preheat oven to 350 F; line a baking sheet with parchment paper. In a bowl and using an electric mixer, mix coconut oil, maple syrup, egg, and water. In a separate bowl, mix flour, swerve, ginger, cinnamon, nutmeg, baking soda, and salt. Combine both mixtures until smooth. Roll the dough into 1 ½-inch balls and arrange on the sheet at 2-inch intervals. Bake for 15 minutes until lightly golden.

Per serving: Cal 141; Net Carbs 1.5g; Fat 15g; Protein 2g

Cream Cheese Cookies

Ingredients for 4 servings

¼ cup softened butter	2 tsp vanilla extract
2 oz softened cream cheese	¼ tsp salt
1/3 cup xylitol	1 tbsp sour cream
1 large egg	3 cups blanched almond flour

Directions and Total Time: approx. 25 minutes

Preheat oven to 350 F; line a baking sheet with parchment paper. In a bowl and using an electric mixer, whisk butter, cream cheese, and xylitol until fluffy and light in color. Beat in egg, vanilla, salt, and sour cream until smooth. Add flour and mix until smooth batter forms. With a cookie scoop, arrange 1 ½ tbsp of batter onto the sheet at 2-inch intervals. Bake for 15 minutes until lightly golden.

Per serving: Cal 177; Net Carbs 1.3g; Fat 17g; Protein 3g

Easy No-Bake Cookies

Ingredients for 4 servings

¾ cup coconut oil   1 tsp vanilla extract
¾ cup peanut butter   1 ½ cup coconut flakes
¼ cup cocoa powder   2 tbsp hulled hemp seeds
1 cup swerve brown sugar

Directions and Total Time: approx. 30 minutes

Preheat oven to 350 F; line two baking sheets with parchment paper. Add coconut oil and peanut butter to a pot. Melt the mixture over low heat until smoothly combined. Stir in cocoa powder, swerve sugar, and vanilla until smooth. Slightly increase the heat and simmer the mixture with occasional stirring until slowly boiling. Turn the heat off. Mix in coconut flakes and hemp seeds. Set the mixture aside to cool. Spoon the batter into silicone muffin cups and freeze for 15 minutes or until set. Serve.

Per serving: Cal 364; Net Carbs 5.5g; Fat 37g; Protein 5g

Keto Caramel Shortbread Cookies

Ingredients for 8 servings

¼ cup sugar-free caramel sauce
2 cups butter   1 cup chopped dark chocolate
1 ½ cups swerve brown sugar   Sea salt flakes
3 cups almond flour

Directions and Total Time: approx. 30 minutes

Preheat oven to 350 F; line a baking sheet with parchment paper. In a bowl and using an electric mixer, whisk butter, swerve, and caramel sauce. Mix in flour and chocolate until well combined. Using a scoop, arrange 1 ½ tbsp of the batter onto the sheet at 2-inch intervals and sprinkle salt flakes on top. Bake for 15 minutes until lightly golden.

Per serving: Cal 410; Net Carbs 0.6g; Fat 43g; Protein 5g

Pumpkin Cookies

Ingredients for 4 servings

3 eggs   9 tbsp sugar-free maple syrup
3 tbsp butter softened   1 tsp vanilla extract
1 oz cream cheese softened   ¼ tsp salt
½ cup pumpkin puree   ¾ tsp baking powder
2 tsp pumpkin pie spice   8 tbsp coconut flour

Directions and Total Time: approx. 30 minutes

Preheat oven to 370 F; line a baking sheet with parchment paper. In a food processor, add eggs and butter and blend until smooth. Top with cream cheese, pumpkin puree, pie spice, maple syrup, and vanilla. Process until smooth. Pour in salt, baking powder, flour, and combine the mixture until smooth thick batter forms. Using a cookie scoop, arrange 1 ½ tbsp of the batter onto the sheet at 2-inch intervals. Refrigerate the dough for 30 minutes and then bake for 23 minutes or until set and lightly golden.

Per serving: Cal 238; Net Carbs 4.2g; Fat 22g; Protein 9.3g

Lemon Glazed Cookies

Ingredients for 4 servings

For the lemon cookies:

¼ cup cream cheese   1 egg
¼ cup unsalted butter   2 cups almond flour
5 tbsp xylitol   1 lemon, zested and juiced

For the lemon glaze:

¼ cup swerve sugar   1 ½ tbsp lemon juice

Directions and Total Time: approx. 40 min + chilling time

Preheat oven to 375 F; line a baking sheet with parchment paper. In a food processor, beat cream cheese, butter, xylitol, and egg until smooth. Pour in almond flour, lemon zest and lemon juice. Miw well until smooth batter forms. With a scoop, arrange 1 ½ tbsp of the batter onto the sheets at 2-inch intervals. Bake for 30 minutes or until set and lightly golden. Transfer them to a wire rack to cool. In a bowl, whisk swerve, lemon juice, and lemon zest until well combined. Drizzle over the cookies and serve.

Per serving: Cal 145; Net Carbs 4.4g; Fat 13g; Protein 3.2g

Magic Bars

Ingredients for 4 servings

1 ½ cups almond flour   ¾ cup mini chocolate chips
2 tbsp erythritol   ¼ cup chopped almonds
3 tbsp melted coconut oil   2/3 cup coconut flakes
¼ tsp salt   1 ¼ cups coconut cream

Directions and Total Time: approx. 50 minutes

Preheat oven to 350 F; line a baking sheet with parchment paper. In a bowl, mix flour, erythritol, oil, and salt. Spread and press the mixture onto the baking sheet. Scatter chocolate chips, almonds, and coconut flakes on top. Drizzle coconut cream on top. Bake for 33 minutes or until compacted. Let cool for 15 minutes and cut into bars.

Per serving: Cal 436; Net Carbs 7.8g; Fat 44.2g; Protein 4g

Buckeye Fat Bomb Bars

Ingredients for 4 servings

1 ¼ cups peanut butter   1 tsp swerve sugar
½ cup butter, melted   6 oz dark chocolate chips
½ cup almond flour   6 oz heavy cream
1 tsp vanilla extract   1/8 tsp salt

Directions and Total Time: approx. 5 min + chilling time

Line a baking sheet with parchment paper. In a food processor, mix peanut butter, butter, flour, vanilla, and swerve. Spread onto the sheet and refrigerate to firm, 30 minutes. Add the chips, heavy cream and salt to a pot and melt over low heat until bubbles form around the edges. Turn the heat off and let cool for 5 minutes. Whisk until smooth and refrigerate for 1 hour. Cut into bars and serve.

Per serving: Cal 412; Net Carbs 5.5g; Fat 38g; Protein 10g

Samoa Cookie Bars

Ingredients for 4 servings

For the crust:

1 ¼ cups almond flour | ¼ tsp salt
¼ cup erythritol | ¼ cup butter, melted

For the filling and drizzle:

4 oz dark chocolate | 2 tbsp butter

For the coconut caramel topping:

1 ½ cups shredded coconut | ¾ cup heavy whipping cream
3 tbsp butter | ½ tsp vanilla extract
¼ cup swerve brown sugar | ¼ tsp salt

Directions and Total Time: approx. 1 hour 40 minutes

For the crust:

Preheat oven to 325 F; line a baking sheet with parchment paper. In a bowl, mix flour, erythritol, and salt. Stir in melted butter until well-combined. Spread the mixture onto the sheet and bake for 18 minutes until golden brown. Allow complete cooling while you make the filling.

For the filling and drizzle:

In a microwave-safe bowl, melt chocolate and butter for 30 to 40 seconds, mixing the at 10-seconds interval or until fully melted. Spread two-thirds of the mixture over the cooled crust and reserve the rest. Set aside.

For the coconut filling:

Toast shredded coconut in a skillet over medium heat until golden brown; set aside. Add butter and swerve to a pot and melt over low heat until starting to boiling and golden, 3 minutes. Turn the heat off. Whisk in heavy cream, vanilla, and salt until smoothly combined. Pour the mixture all over and refrigerate for 1 hour. Stir in toasted coconut. Spread the mixture over the chocolate-covered crust; let cool completely, and cut into squares. Reheat remaining chocolate mixture and drizzle over the bars.

Per serving: Cal 313; Net Carbs 5.5g; Fat 23g; Protein 3g

Peanut Butter Bars

Ingredients for 8 servings

For the peanut butter filling:

½ cup smooth peanut butter | 5 tbsp almond flour
4 tbsp melted butter | 1 tsp vanilla extract
4 tbsp swerve sugar

For the coating:

2 ½ oz chopped dark chocolate | A handful peanuts, chopped

Directions and Total Time: approx. 5 min + chilling time

Line a baking sheet with parchment paper. In a bowl, mix peanut butter, butter, swerve, flour, and vanilla. Spread the mixture onto the sheet and top with chocolate and peanuts. Refrigerate until firm, for 1 hour. Cut into bars and enjoy.

Per serving: Cal 155; Net Carbs 5.2g; Fat 12g; Protein 4.9g

All Nuts Bars

Ingredients for 12 servings

1 ½ cups dark chocolate chips | ¼ cup coconut oil
1 cup cashew butter | 3 cups mixed nuts, chopped
½ cup sugar-free maple syrup

Directions and Total Time: approx. 5 min + chilling time

Line a baking sheet with parchment paper. In a bowl, mix chips, cashew butter, maple syrup, coconut oil, seeds, and nuts. Spread the mixture onto the sheet and refrigerate until firm, at least 1 hour. Cut into bars and enjoy.

Per serving: Cal 323; Net Carbs 3.9g; Fat 29g; Protein 3g

Chocolate Chip Bar

Ingredients for 4 servings

8 oz cream cheese, softened | 1/3 cup of coconut flour
½ cup butter, softened | ¼ tsp salt
2 cups xylitol | 1 ½ tsp baking powder
5 eggs | ½ tsp xanthan gum
2 tsp vanilla extract | 1 cup dark chocolate chips
1 cup almond flour | 1 cup chopped walnuts

Directions and Total Time: approx. 40 minutes

Preheat oven to 350 F; line a baking sheet with parchment paper. In a food processor, blitz cream cheese, butter, and xylitol. Add eggs, vanilla, and mix until smooth. Pour in the flours, salt, baking powder, and xanthan gum; process until smooth. Fold in the chocolate chips and walnuts. Spread the mixture onto the sheet and bake for 30 to 35 minutes or until set and light golden brown. Remove from the oven, let cool completely, and cut into bars.

Per serving: Cal 443; Net Carbs 4.8g; Fat 36g; Protein 22g

Shortbread Lemon Bar

Ingredients for 4 servings

For the shortbread crust:

2 ½ cups almond flour | ¼ cup melted butter
¼ cup sugar-free maple syrup | 1 large egg
¼ tsp salt | ½ tsp vanilla extract

For the lemon filling:

1/3 cup sugar-free maple syrup | 4 large eggs
¼ cup blanched almond flour | ¾ cup lemon juice

Directions and Total Time: approx. 40 minutes

Preheat oven to 325 F; line a baking sheet with parchment paper. In a bowl, whisk flour, maple syrup, salt, butter, egg, and vanilla extract until smooth. Spread the mixture onto the sheet and bake for 13 minutes. Allow complete cooling. In a bowl, whisk maple syrup, flour, eggs, and lemon juice until smooth. Spread the mixture over the crust and bake further for 18 minutes or until the filling sets. Remove, let chill for 2 hours and slicing to serve.

Per serving: Cal 139; Net Carbs 4.3g; Fat 13g; Protein 2g

Cinnamon Macadamia Bars

Ingredients for 4 servings

1 ½ cups macadamia nuts
½ cup pepitas
1 cup coconut flakes
1 tsp cinnamon powder
½ cup smooth peanut butter
¼ cup coconut oil, solidified
2 tsp vanilla bean paste

Directions and Total Time: approx. 5 min + chilling time

Line a baking sheet with parchment paper. In a bowl, mix macadamia nuts, pepitas, coconut flakes, cinnamon powder, peanut butter, coconut oil, and vanilla bean paste. Spread the mixture onto the sheet and refrigerate until firm, at least 1 hour. Cut into bars and serve.

Per serving: Cal 417; Net Carbs 5g; Fat 37g; Protein 8g

Cranberry Cheesecake Bars

Ingredients for 4 servings

For the crust:

2 tbsp swerve confectioner's sweetener
8 tbsp melted butter   1 ¼ cups almond flour

For the cheesecake layer:

1/3 cup swerve confectioner's sweetener
8 oz cream cheese   2 tsp pure vanilla extract
1 egg yolk

For the cranberry layer:

1 cup unsweetened cranberry sauce

Directions and Total Time: approx. 40 min + chilling time

Preheat oven to 350 F; line a baking sheet with parchment paper. In a bowl, mix butter, flour and sugar. Spread and press the mixture onto the baking sheet and bake for 13 minutes or until golden brown. Whisk cream cheese, egg yolk, swerve sugar, and vanilla in a bowl using an electric hand mixer until smooth. Spread the mixture on the crust when ready. Bake further for 15 minutes or until the filling sets. Remove from the oven, spread cranberry sauce on top and refrigerate for 1 hour. Cut into bars and serve.

Per serving: Cal 497; Net Carbs 2.5g; Fat 5.2g; Protein 5g

Avocado Custard

Ingredients for 4 servings

½ cup water
2 tsp agar agar powder
3 soft avocados
½ cup heavy cream
½ lime, juiced
Salt and black pepper to taste

Directions and Total Time: approx. 10 min + chilling time

Pour ¼ cup of water in a bowl and sprinkle agar agar powder on top; set aside to dissolve. Core, peel avocados and add the flesh to a food processor. Top with heavy cream, lime juice, salt, and pepper. Process until smooth and pour in agar agar liquid. Blend further until smooth. Divide the mixture between 4 ramekins and chill overnight.

Per serving: Cal 299; Net Carbs 7.9g; Fat 27g; Protein 3g

Minty Coconut Bars

Ingredients for 4 servings

3 cups shredded coconut flakes
1 cup melted coconut oil
1 tsp mint extract
¼ cup sugar-free maple syrup

Directions and Total Time: approx. 5 min + chilling time

Line loaf pan with parchment paper and set aside. In a bowl, mix coconut flakes, coconut oil, mint, and maple syrup until a thick batter forms. Pour the mixture into the loaf pan and press to fit. Refrigerate for 2 hours or until hardened. Remove from the fridge, cut into bars and serve.

Per serving: Cal 366; Net Carbs 4.3g; Fat 36g; Protein 2g

Keto Snickerdoodle Muffins

Ingredients for 4 servings

For the muffin batter:

2 ½ cups almond flour
½ cup swerve sugar
2 tsp baking powder
1 tsp cinnamon powder
3 large eggs
1/3 cup butter, melted
1/3 cup almond milk
½ cup sour cream
1 tsp vanilla extract

For the topping:

1 tbsp swerve confectioner's sugar
¼ tsp cinnamon powder

Directions and Total Time: approx. 35 minutes

Preheat oven to 350 F; line a 12-cup muffin pan with paper liners. In a bowl, mix almond flour, swerve, baking powder, and cinnamon. In bowl, whisk eggs, butter, milk, sour cream, and vanilla extract. Combine both mixture and fill into the muffin cups, two-thirds way up. For the topping, mix swerve sugar and cinnamon in a bowl and sprinkle the batter. Bake the muffins for 25 minutes or until dark golden brown on top and a toothpick inserted into the muffins comes out clean. Let cool and serve.

Per serving: Cal 221; Net Carbs 3.3g; Fat 17.6g; Protein 7g

Almond Biscuits

Ingredients for 4 servings

¾ cup grated Pecorino Romano cheese
2 ½ cups almond flour
2 tsp baking powder
2 eggs beaten
3 tbsp almond butter
1 tsp vanilla extract
A handful almonds, chopped

Directions and Total Time: approx. 30 minutes

Preheat oven to 350 F; line a baking sheet with parchment paper. In a bowl, mix flour, baking powder, and eggs until smooth. Whisk in almond butter, cheese, and vanilla until well combined. Fold in the almonds until well distributed. Mold 12 balls out of the mixture and arrange on the baking sheet at 2-inch intervals. Bake for 25 minutes or until golden brown. Remove, let cool and serve immediately.

Per serving: Cal 196; Net Carbs 3.1g; Fat 16g; Protein 8.4g

Pillowy Chocolate Donuts

Ingredients for 4 servings

For the donut:

2/3 cup almond flour	3 tbsp xyltol
3 tbsp coconut flour	¼ tsp salt
1 tbsp flaxseed meal	3 eggs lightly beaten
1 tsp arrowroot starch	1 tsp vanilla extract
1/3 cup water	1 tsp baking powder
3 tbsp melted butter	

For the chocolate glaze:

¼ cup swerve sugar	1 tsp vanilla extract
2 tbsp cocoa powder	2 tbsp coconut milk
1 tbsp melted butter	

Directions and Total Time: approx. 25 minutes

Preheat oven to 350 F; lightly grease an 8-cup donut pan with cooking spray; set aside. In a bowl, mix almond and coconut flours, flaxseed meal, and arrowroot starch. One after another, mix smoothly the water, butter, xylitol, salt, eggs, vanilla, and baking powder. Pour the batter into the donut cups and bake for 18 minutes or until set. Remove from the oven, flip the donut onto a wire rack and let cool.

In a bowl, whisk swerve sugar, cocoa powder, butter, vanilla extract, and coconut milk until smooth. Drizzle the chocolate glaze over the donut and serve.

Per serving: Cal 335; Net Carbs 5.4g; Fat 23g; Protein 24g

Pancake Muffins

Ingredients for 4 servings

½ cup coconut flour	2 tbsp butter, melted
½ cup erythritol	1 ½ tsp vanilla extract
1 ½ tsp baking powder	6 eggs

Directions and Total Time: approx. 35 minutes

Preheat oven to 350 F and line a 12-cup muffin pan with paper liners. In a food processor, blend coconut flour, erythritol, baking powder, butter, vanilla extract, and eggs until smooth. Pour the batter into the muffin cups two-thirds way up and bake for 25 minutes or until a toothpick inserted into the muffins comes out clean. Remove t from the oven, let cool and serve immediately.

Per serving: Cal 156; Net Carbs 1.8g; Fat 12g; Protein 8.6g

Strawberry Scones

Ingredients for 4 servings

1 cup blanched almond flour	¼ cup almond milk
¼ cup coconut flour	2 tbsp coconut oil
3 tbsp swerve sugar	1 large egg
½ tsp baking powder	1 tsp vanilla extract
¼ tsp salt	½ cup chopped strawberries

For the glaze:

1 tsp swerve confectioner's sugar	
1 tbsp coconut oil	2 tbsp mashed strawberries

Directions and Total Time: approx. 25 minutes

Preheat oven to 350 F; line a baking sheet with parchment paper. In a bowl, mix almond and coconut flours, swerve, baking powder, and salt. In another bowl, whisk milk, coconut oil, egg, and vanilla. Combine both mixtures and fold in the strawberries. Pour and spread the mixture on the baking sheet. Cut into 8 wedges like a pizza and place the baking sheet in the oven. Bake for 20 minutes or until set and golden brown. Remove and let cool. In a bowl, whisk swerve, oil, and strawberries until smoothly combined. Swirl the glaze over the scones to serve.

Per serving: Cal 121; Net Carbs 2.7g; Fat 11g; Protein 2g

Blueberry-Raspberry Muffins

Ingredients for 4 servings

2/3 cup blueberries and raspberries

2 ½ cups almond flour	1/3 cup melted butter
1/3 cup erythritol	1/3 cup almond milk
1 ½ tsp baking powder	3 large eggs
½ tsp baking soda	1 tsp vanilla extract
½ tsp salt	½ lemon, zested

Directions and Total Time: approx. 35 minutes

Preheat oven to 350 F and line a 12-cup muffin pan with paper liners. In a bowl, mix flour, erythritol, baking powder and soda, and salt. In another bowl, whisk butter, almond milk, eggs, and vanilla extract. Combine the mixtures until smooth. Fold in berries, lemon zest and fill the muffin cups two-thirds way up. Bake for 25 minutes.

Per serving: Cal 197; Net Carbs 1g; Fat 19.2g; Protein 5g

Cake Donuts with Chocolate Glaze

Ingredients for 4 servings

1 cup almond flour	4 tbsp melted butter
¼ cup xyltitol	¼ cup heavy cream
2 tsp baking powder	2 large eggs
¼ tsp salt	½ tsp vanilla extract

For chocolate glaze:

1 ½ cups swerve confectioner's sugar	½ cup water
	1 tsp vanilla extract
¼ cup cocoa powder	A pinch salt

Directions and Total Time: approx. 25 minutes

Preheat oven to 350 F and grease an 8-cup donut pan. In a bowl, mix flour, xylitol, baking powder, and salt. In another bowl, mix butter, heavy cream, eggs, and vanilla extract. Combine both mixtures until smooth. Pour the batter into the donut cups and bake for 15 minutes or until set. Remove, flip the donut onto a wire rack and let cool.

In a bowl, whisk swerve, cocoa, water, vanilla extract, and salt until smooth. Swirl the glaze over the donut to serve.

Per serving: Cal 182; Net Carbs 1g; Fat 16.8g; Protein 3.5g

Maple Cashew Scones

Ingredients for 4 servings

1 ½ cups almond flour
½ cup coconut flour
¼ cup swerve sugar
2 tbsp protein powder
½ tsp salt
1 tbsp baking powder

½ cup heavy cream
1 large egg
2 ½ tbsp cold butter, cubed
3 tsp sugar-free maple syrup
2/3 cup chopped cashew nuts

For the glaze:

½ cups swerve confectioner's sugar
1 tsp sugar-free maple syrup   2 tsp water
1 tbsp heavy cream

Directions and Total Time: approx. 25 minutes

Preheat oven to 350 F; line a baking sheet with parchment paper. In a bowl, mix almond and coconut flours, swerve, protein, salt, and baking powder. In another bowl, mix heavy cream, egg, butter, and maple syrup. Combine both mixtures until smooth. Fold in cashew nuts. Pour and spread the mixture on the sheet. Cut into 8 wedges and bake for 20 minutes or until set and golden brown. Remove from the oven and let cool. In a bowl, whisk the swerve sugar, maple syrup, heavy cream, and water until smooth. Swirl the glaze all over the scones and enjoy.

Per serving: Cal 280; Net Carbs 8.3g; Fat 26g; Protein 6g

Silk Chocolate Pie with Coconut Crust

Ingredients for 4 servings

For the crust:

2 eggs
1 tsp vanilla extract
¼ cup erythritol
¼ tsp salt
2/3 cup coconut flour

1/3 cup almond flour
½ cup cold butter, cubed
5 tbsp cold water
1 tbsp olive oil

For the filling:

2 tsp swerve confectioner's sugar
16 oz cream cheese, softened ½ cup swerve sugar
4 tbsp sour cream   ½ cup cocoa powder
4 tbsp butter   1 cup coconut cream
1 tsp vanilla extract

Directions and Total Time: approx. 90 min + chilling time

For the piecrust:

In a bowl, whisk eggs, olive oil, and vanilla until well combined. In another bowl, mix erythritol, salt, coconut and almond flour. Combine both mixtures into a stand mixer and blend until smooth dough forms. Add butter and mix until breadcrumb-like mixture forms. Add one tbsp of water, mix further until the dough begins to come together. Keep adding water until it sticks well together.

Lightly flour a working surface, turn the dough onto it, knead a few times until formed into a ball, and comes together smoothly. Divide into half and flatten each piece into a disk. Wrap in plastic and refrigerate for 1 hour.

Preheat oven to 375 F and lightly grease a 9-inch pie pan with olive oil. Remove the dough from the fridge, let it stand at room temperature and roll one piece into 12-inch round. Fit this piece into the bottom and walls to the rim of the pie pan while shaping to take the pan's form. Roll out the other dough into an 11-inch round and set aside.

For the filling:

In a bowl, using an electric mixer, whisk cream cheese, sour cream, butter, vanilla, swerve, and cocoa powder until smooth. In a separate bowl, whisk the coconut cream, and swerve sugar. Gently fold the cocoa powder mixture into the cream cheese mix until well combined. Fill the pie dough in the pie pan with the cream-cocoa mixture and make sure to level well. Brush the overhanging pastry with water and attach the top pastry on top of the filling. Press the edges to merge the dough ends and then, trim the overhanging ends to 1-inch. Fold the edge under itself and then, decoratively crimp. Cut 4 slits on the top crust. Bake the pie on the middle rack of the oven for 75 minutes or until the bottom crust is golden and the filling is bubbling. Remove, let rest and serve.

Per serving: Cal 433; Net Carbs 5g; Fat 39g; Protein 7g

Cinnamon Roll Scones

Ingredients for 4 servings

2 cups almond flour
6 tbsp swerve sugar, divided
2 tsp baking powder
½ tsp salt
1 large egg

¼ cup unsalted butter, melted
2 tbsp heavy cream
½ tsp vanilla extract
2 tsp cinnamon powder

For the glaze:

1 tbsp swerve confectioner's sugar
1 oz cream cheese softened   ¼ tsp vanilla extract
1 tbsp heavy cream

Directions and Total Time: approx. 40 minutes

Preheat oven to 350 F; line a baking sheet with parchment paper. In a bowl, mix almond flour, swerve, baking powder, and salt until well mixed. In another bowl, mix egg, butter, heavy cream, vanilla, and cinnamon powder. Combine both mixtures until smooth. Pour and spread the mixture on the sheet. Cut into 8 wedges and bake for 20 minutes until set and golden. Remove from the oven and let cool. In a bowl, whisk cream cheese, heavy cream, swerve sugar, and vanilla. Swirl the glaze over the scones.

Per serving: Cal 156; Net Carbs 1.9g; Fat 15.4g; Protein 3g

Mocha Mousse Cups

Ingredients for 4 servings

8 oz cream cheese, softened
3 tbsp sour cream
2 tbsp butter, softened
1 ½ tsp vanilla extract
1/3 cup erythritol

3 tsp instant coffee powder
¼ cup cocoa powder
2/3 cup heavy whipping cream
1 ½ tsp swerve sugar
½ tsp vanilla extract

Directions and Total Time: approx. 10 minutes

In a bowl using an electric hand mixer, beat cream cheese, sour cream, and butter until smooth. Mix in vanilla, erythritol, coffee, and cocoa powders until incorporated. In a separate bowl, beat whipping cream until soft peaks form. Mix in swerve sugar and vanilla until well combined.

Fold 1/3 of the whipped cream mixture into the cream cheese mixture to lighten. Fold in the remaining mixture until well incorporated. Spoon into dessert cups and serve.

Per serving: Cal 308; Net Carbs 4g; Fat 30g; Protein 5g

Blackberry Scones

Ingredients for 4 servings

1 cup almond flour	1 ½ tsp pure vanilla extract
2 eggs, beaten	1 ½ tsp baking powder
3 tsp erythritol	½ cup blackberries, halves

Directions and Total Time: approx. 30 minutes

Preheat oven to 350 F; line a baking sheet with parchment paper. In a food processor, mix flour, eggs, erythritol, vanilla, and baking powder until smooth. Fold in blackberries. Pour and spread the mixture on the sheet. Cut into 8 wedges like a pizza and bake for 20 minutes or until set and golden brown.

Per serving: Cal 47; Net Carbs 3g; Fat 2.3g; Protein 3g

Pumpkin Scones

Ingredients for 4 servings

1 cup almond flour	¼ cup heavy cream
6 tbsp coconut flour	½ cup pumpkin puree
¼ cup erythritol	2 tbsp coconut oil, melted
½ tsp baking powder	1 large egg
½ tsp arrowroot starch	1 tbsp pumpkin pie spice
¼ tsp salt	1 tsp sugar-free maple syrup

Directions and Total Time: approx. 25 minutes

Preheat oven to 350 F; line a baking sheet with parchment paper. In a bowl, mix almond and coconut flours, erythritol, baking powder, arrowroot starch, and salt. In another bowl, mix heavy cream, pumpkin puree, oil, egg, pumpkin spice, and maple syrup. Combine both mixtures until smooth. Pour and spread the mixture on the baking sheet. Cut into 8 wedges and bake for 20 minutes or until set and golden brown. Remove from oven, cool and serve.

Per serving: Cal 199; Net Carbs 4.6g; Fat 18g; Protein 6.4g

Lemon Curd Tarts

Ingredients for 4 servings

For the crust:

¼ cup swerve confectioner's sugar
1 ½ cups almond flour   1 large egg
½ tsp salt
¼ cup unsalted butter, melted

For the filling:

½ cup swerve confectioner's sugar
4 tbsp salted butter   3 large eggs
½ lemon, zested and juiced

Directions and Total Time: approx. 25 min + chilling time

Preheat oven to 350 F and lightly grease 4 (2x12-inch) mini tart tins with cooking spray. In a food processor, blend flour, swerve, salt, butter, and egg. Divide and spread the dough in the tins and press. Bake for 15 minutes. For the filling, melt butter in a pot over medium heat, take off the heat and quickly mix in swerve, lemon zest, and lemon juice until smooth. Whisk in eggs and return the pot to low heat. Cook with continuous stirring until thick. Pour the filling into the crust, gently tap on a flat surface to release air bubbles and chill in the refrigerator for at least 1 hour.

Per serving: Cal 213; Net Carbs 2g; Fat 20g; Protein 7g

Fresh Berry Tarts

Ingredients for 4 servings

For the crust:

6 tbsp butter, melted	1/3 cup xylitol
2 cups almond flour	1 tsp cinnamon powder

For the filling:

1 cup coconut cream	Swerve confectioner's sugar
2 cups frozen berries	for topping

Directions and Total Time: approx. 20 min + chilling time

Preheat oven to 350 F and lightly grease 4 (2x12-inch) mini tart tins with cooking spray. In a food processor, blend butter, flour, xylitol, and cinnamon. Divide and spread the dough in the tart tins and bake for 15 minutes.

Remove crust from oven and let cool. Divide the coconut cream into the tart crusts and divide the berries on top. Garnish with some swerve sugar and enjoy.

Per serving: Cal 246; Net Carbs 5.5g; Fat 21g; Protein 5g

Peanut Butter Mousse

Ingredients for 4 servings

½ cup heavy cream	¼ cup xylitol
4 oz softened cream cheese	½ tsp vanilla extract
¼ cup smooth peanut butter	

Directions and Total Time: approx. 10 minutes

Whip ½ cup of heavy cream in a bowl using an electric mixer until stiff peaks hole; set aside. In another bowl, beat cream cheese and peanut butter until creamy and smooth. Mix in xylitol and vanilla extract until well combined. Gradually, fold in the cream mixture until well combined. If too thick, fold in 2 tbsp of the reserved heavy cream. Spoon the mousse into dessert glasses and serve.

Per serving: Cal 231; Net Carbs 5g; Fat 21g; Protein 6.2g

Strawberry Cheesecake Tart

Ingredients for 4 servings

For the crust:

6 tbsp butter, melted   1/3 cup xylitol
2 cups almond flour   1 tsp cinnamon powder

For the filling:

¼ cup swerve confectioner's sugar
1 cup softened cream cheese   1 tsp vanilla extract
½ cup heavy cream   1 cup halved strawberries

Directions and Total Time: approx. 25 min + chilling time

Preheat oven to 350 F and grease a round baking pan. In a food processor, blend butter, flour, xylitol, and cinnamon until the dough mixture resembles ball-like shape. Stretch out the dough in the pan covering the sides; with a fork stab the bottom of the crust. Bake for 15 minutes. Remove the crust after cooking and let cool. In a bowl, whisk cheese, heavy cream, swerve, and vanilla extract. Pour the filling into the crust, gently tap on a flat surface to release air bubbles and refrigerate for 1 hour. Remove tart from the fridge, and top with strawberries.

Per serving: Cal 401; Net Carbs 6g; Fat 33g; Protein 5g

Simple Chocolate Tart

Ingredients for 4 servings

For the crust:

1 1/3 cups almond flour   1 ½ tsp cold water
1 ½ tsp coconut flour   3 tbsp cold butter
¼ cup swerve sugar

For the filling:

4 oz heavy cream   1/3 cup erythritol
4 oz dark chocolate chips

Directions and Total Time: approx. 25 min + chilling time

Preheat oven to 350 F. In a food processor, blend almond and coconut flours, swerve, water, and butter until smooth. Spread the dough in a greased round baking pan and bake for 15 minutes; let cool. For the filling, heat heavy cream and chocolate chips in a pot over medium heat until chocolate melts; whisk in erythritol. Pour the filling into the crust, gently tap on a flat surface to release air bubbles and chill for 1 hour. Remove from the fridge, and serve.

Per serving: Cal 177; Net Carbs 1g; Fat 19g; Protein 3g

Rhubarb Tart

Ingredients for 6 servings

For the crust:

6 oz almond flour   3 oz butter, melted
1/3 cup swerve sugar   2 tbsp shredded coconut

For the rhubarb filling:

4 ¼ oz butter, softened   ¾ cups almond flour
½ cup swerve sugar   1 cup almond milk

3 eggs   7 oz rhubarb, spiralized
1 tsp vanilla extract

Directions and Total Time: approx. 70 minutes

Preheat oven to 350 F. In a food processor, blend the flour, swerve, butter, and coconut. Spread the dough in a greased tart tin and bake in the oven for 13 minutes; let cool. For the filling, in a bowl, whisk butter, swerve, flour, almond milk, eggs, and vanilla. Pour the filling into the crust, gently tap on a flat surface to release air bubbles and press rhubarb spirals into the filling. Bake further for 35 minutes until the filling sets. Remove, let cool and serve.

Per serving: Cal 478; Net Carbs 7.2g; Fat 33g; Protein 14g

Mixed Berry Custard Pots

Ingredients for 4 servings

6 egg yolks   1 tsp swerve sugar
½ cup almond milk   1 cup mixed berries, chopped
1 tsp vanilla extract

Directions and Total Time: approx. 15 minutes

In a metal bowl, whisk yolks, milk, vanilla, and swerve until smooth. Bring some water to a boil over medium heat and place the bowl over the water. Whisk the mixture constantly until thickened, 5 minutes or until reached 140 F. Take the bowl off the water and mix in the berries. Divide the custard between 4 dessert cups and enjoy.

Per serving: Cal 176; Net Carbs 6.4g; Fat 14g; Protein 4.9g

Swiss Mascarpone Mousse with Chocolate

Ingredients for 6 servings

For the mascarpone chocolate mousse:

8 oz mascarpone cheese   4 tbsp cocoa powder
8 oz heavy cream   4 tbsp xylitol

For the vanilla mousse:

3.5 oz cream cheese   1 tsp vanilla extract
3.5 oz heavy cream   2 tbsp xylitol

Directions and Total Time: approx. 15 minutes

In a bowl using and electric mixer, beat mascarpone cheese, heavy cream, cocoa, and xylitol until creamy. Do not over mix, however. In another bowl, whisk all vanilla mousse ingredients until smooth and creamy. Gradually fold vanilla mousse mixture into the mascarpone one until well incorporated. Spoon into dessert cups and serve.

Per serving: Cal 412; Net Carbs 5.9g; Fat 32g; Protein 8g

Lemon Curd Mousse with Caramel Nuts

Ingredients for 4 servings

For the mousse:

8 oz cream cheese   ¼ cup swerve sugar
1 cup cold heavy cream   ½ lemon, juiced
1 tsp vanilla extract

For the caramel nuts:

2/3 cup swerve brown sugar   1 cup mixed nuts, chopped
A pinch salt

Directions and Total Time: approx. 10 min + chilling time

In a stand mixer, beat cream cheese and heavy cream until creamy. Add vanilla, swerve, and lemon juice until smooth. Divide the mixture between 4 dessert cups, cover with plastic wrap and refrigerate for at least 2 hours.

For the caramel nuts:

Add swerve sugar to a large skillet and cook over medium heat with frequent stirring until melted and golden brown. Mix in water, salt, and cook further until syrupy and slightly thickened. Turn the heat off and quickly mix in the nuts until well coated in the caramel; let sit for 5 minutes or until golden. Remove the mousse from the fridge and top with the caramel nuts. Serve immediately.

Per serving: Cal 516; Net Carbs 8g; Fat 52.7g; Protein 7.3g

Tasty Strawberry Mousse

Ingredients for 4 servings

12 fresh strawberries, hulled + extra for topping
2 tbsp swerve sugar   1 cup heavy whipping cream
½ cup softened cream cheese

Directions and Total Time: approx. 10 min + chilling time

In a food processor, blend strawberries and swerve until smooth. Add cream cheese and process until smooth. Pour in the heavy cream and blend smoothly too. Divide the mousse into 4 medium glasses and refrigerate for 1 hour. Top with some strawberries when ready to serve.

Per serving: Cal 204; Net Carbs 4.7g; Fat 19.8g; Protein 3g

Blackberry Chocolate Mousse Pots

Ingredients for 4 servings

½ cup swerve confectioner's sugar
2 ½ cups unsweetened dark chocolate, melted
3 cups heavy cream   ½ cup blackberries, chopped
½ tsp vanilla extract   Some blackberries for topping

Directions and Total Time: approx. 10 min + chilling time

In a stand mixer, beat heavy cream and swerve sugar until creamy. Add dark chocolate and vanilla extract, and mix until smoothly combined. Fold in blackberries until well distributed. Divide the mixture between 4 dessert cups, cover with plastic wrap and refrigerate for 2 hours. from fridge, garnish with blackberries and serve immediately.

Per serving: Cal 312; Net Carbs 2.6g; Fat 33g; Protein 1.9g

White Chocolate Mousse

Ingredients for 4 servings

6 oz unsweetened white chocolate, chopped
1 ½ cups cold heavy cream

Directions and Total Time: approx. 10 min + chilling time

Add white chocolate and ½ cup of heavy cream to a microwave-safe bowl. Microwave until melted, frequently stirring, for 60 seconds. Remove from the microwave and let cool at room temperature. Pour the mixture into a stand mixer and whisk with the remaining heavy cream until soft peaks form. Divide the mousse between 4 dessert cups, chill for at least 2 hours and serve.

Per serving: Cal 155; Net Carbs 1.3g; Fat 16.7g; Protein 3g

Lime Mousse with Blackberries

Ingredients for 4 servings

½ cup swerve confectioner's sugar
3 cups heavy cream   ½ tsp vanilla extract
2 ½ cups sour cream   Chopped mint to garnish
3 limes, juiced   12 blackberries for topping

Directions and Total Time: approx. 10 min + chilling time

In a stand mixer, beat heavy cream and swerve sugar until creamy. Add sour cream, lime juice, and vanilla; combine smoothly. Divide between 4 dessert cups, cover with plastic wrap and refrigerate for 2 hours. Remove, garnish with mint leaves, top with 3 blackberries and serve.

Per serving: Cal 491; Net Carbs 8.7g; Fat 43g; Protein 4g

Chocolate Avocado Mousse

Ingredients for 4 servings

1 cup full fat coconut cream   2 tbsp cream of tartar
1 avocado, pitted and peeled   1 cup Greek yogurt
1 heaped tbsp cocoa powder

Directions and Total Time: approx. 10 min + chilling time

In a food processor, add coconut cream, avocado, cocoa powder, cream of tartar, and Greek yogurt. Blend until smooth. Divide the mixture between 4 dessert cups and chill in the refrigerator for at least 2 hours. Serve.

Per serving: Cal 333; Net Carbs 8.2g; Fat 31g; Protein 5.7g

Lemon Custard

Ingredients for 4 servings

1 cup heavy cream   A pinch of cinnamon powder
2/3 cup swerve sugar   6 egg yolks
3 large lemons, juiced   2 tsp vanilla extract

Directions and Total Time: approx. 40 minutes

Heat heavy cream over medium heat and whisk in half of swerve until well combined. Turn off the heat and let warm. In a separate bowl, whisk lemon juice, cinnamon, yolks, and vanilla. Mix the egg mixture into the heavy cream one, turn on the heat and cook 10 minutes, whisking until thickened without boiling the mixture. Remove from heat and pour into 4 ramekins. Chill for 4 hours and serve.

Per serving: Cal 225; Net Carbs 4.1g; Fat 18g; Protein 10g

RECIPE INDEX

Printed in Great Britain
by Amazon